Woodrow Wilson and World War I

Woodrow Wilson and World War I

A Burden Too Great to Bear

Richard Striner

ROWMAN & LITTLEFIELD
Lanham • Boulder • New York • Toronto • Plymouth, UK

Published by Rowman & Littlefield
4501 Forbes Boulevard, Suite 200, Lanham, Maryland 20706
www.rowman.com

10 Thornbury Road, Plymouth PL6 7PP, United Kingdom

British Library Cataloguing in Publication Information Available

Library of Congress Cataloging-in-Publication Data

Striner, Richard, 1950–
Woodrow Wilson and World War I : a burden too great to bear / Richard Striner.
pages cm
Includes index.
ISBN 978-1-4422-2937-2 (cloth : alk. paper) — ISBN 978-1-4422-2938-9 (electronic)
1. Wilson, Woodrow, 1856–1924. 2. United States—Foreign relations—1913–1921. 3. World War, 1914–1918—United States. 4. World War, 1914–1918—Diplomatic history. 5. Political leadership—United States—History—20th century. I. Title.
E768.S895 2014
973.913092—dc23
2013046689

♾™ The paper used in this publication meets the minimum requirements of American National Standard for Information Sciences Permanence of Paper for Printed Library Materials, ANSI/NISO Z39.48-1992.

Printed in the United States of America

To Sara Gabbard

Contents

Preface

For most of his career, Woodrow Wilson was highly controversial. Historians have often disagreed about his contradictory record. Today, as we take a fresh look at the First World War in the years of its centennial, the wartime leadership of Wilson is of great interest.

Woodrow Wilson was perhaps the most tragic of American presidents. Almost everyone agrees that by the end of his life he was a wreck. Many attribute his decline to the stroke that he suffered on October 2, 1919—and the medical conditions (such as arteriosclerosis) that preceded it. But the case can be made that Wilson's tragedy was also grounded in character flaws that were evident long before the stroke took place. The most tragic thing of all is that Wilson at his best had been astute, as his admirers frequently—and correctly—observe. His self-destruction was a grievous thing indeed.

The most distinguished recent biographer of Wilson, historian John Milton Cooper Jr., has demolished the cartoon image of Wilson that many of his fiercest detractors created: the stereotype of Wilson as a colorless prig whose deep emotions would only come to life in his speeches. Thanks to Cooper, a better portrait now exists: contemporary readers can appreciate the Wilson who was mischievous, amorous, and prankish, and alert (at his best) to every nuance, a man of immense sophistication. [1]

But while Cooper was careful to leaven this sympathetic treatment with some searching criticism of Wilson's shortcomings—his bad judgment in picking subordinates, his reluctance to subject these subordinates to ongoing supervision, his disastrous policies in race relations, his unpardonable conduct on the issue of wartime civil liberties—Cooper's overall account of Wilson's wartime leadership depicts him in the years before his stroke as a victim of events that provided him with very few options.

But the case can be made that Wilson threw away significant options as his critical faculties declined and he yielded to folly—and delusion.

Granted, the calamity of World War I was the sort of conundrum that would surely have taken its toll on almost any of the politicians who might have occupied the Oval Office at the time—whether Theodore Roosevelt, William Howard Taft, or Charles Evans Hughes. Any of these men would have had to make agonizing, thankless decisions. But this book will argue that Wilson took a bad hand of cards and proceeded to play it as only the worst of incompetent strategists—or the worst of nonstrategists, at least by the end—could have played it.

Half a century ago, the so-called realist school in the field of foreign relations savaged Wilson as a credulous dreamer who—though often quite effective in domestic politics—was out of his element in global realpolitik. Observers such as Hans Morgenthau saw Wilson as naïve when it came to foreign policy. Wilson scholars at the time, such as John Morton Blum, said much the same thing.[2]

My own interpretation owes much to this "realist" critique. In addition, however, my work in the field of Lincoln scholarship has influenced my view of Wilson. In my book *Father Abraham*, I argued that Lincoln was a consummate moral strategist: an idealist with Machiavellian cunning who excelled at doing simultaneous best-case and worst-case contingency planning as he sought to shape the flow of events. By the standard that was set by Abraham Lincoln, Woodrow Wilson fell pitifully short. The most striking thing to me about his wartime record was his failure to engage in sufficient contingency planning when it came to the politics of war.

What could he and should he have done? One can never write a history of paths not taken, or create a clear projection that reveals the different outcomes—*definite* outcomes—that different kinds of choices would have led to. There were simply too many variables. But one can surely delineate an overall path and then show the different places where contingency planning might have given the best of moral strategists, like Lincoln, a chance to shape events in different ways—perhaps in better ways.

As it was, Wilson gave his own cause a bad name and played into the hands of his enemies. And he never knew the truth about his failure.

Part I

Foreshadowings

Chapter One

1914

Woodrow Wilson's self-destruction as a wartime leader started early: the mistakes that would make him his own worst enemy began—in a discernible and embryonic form—at the beginning of World War I. His intelligence was quickly subsumed in dysfunctional patterns of thinking and feeling that precluded a wide range of options that a better and wiser individual might have pursued. However challenging the patterns of the war would have been for any presidential leader, Wilson sank into a mental condition that rendered him incapable of strategy. However wise his decisions might have seemed at the time to some, he made his first major blunders right away.

THIS DREADFUL EUROPEAN CONFLICT

The speed with which World War I broke out in the summer of 1914 was appalling. So was the unthinkable carnage in the first few months of war: by the end of 1914, German war deaths on the western front stood at 241,000—41,000 in the first battle of Ypres alone—French fatalities had reached 306,000, Belgium had lost 30,000, and the British had lost about the same number.[1]

For years before the shooting started, European power rivalries had led to a series of war scares. In 1899, Tsar Nicholas II had convened a conference at The Hague for the purpose of limiting armaments and establishing an International Court. But the Court lacked real viability. And in the very same year, imperial Germany embarked on a program to increase the size of its fleet to the point that it could take on Britain's Royal Navy. The result was a naval armaments race between the British and the Germans that continued to escalate.

Recurrent crises erupted out of rival imperial ambitions in the third world—two Franco-German showdowns over Morocco, for instance, in 1905 and 1911—and recurrent unrest in the Balkans led to back-to-back wars in 1912 and 1913 that threatened the security of the Austro-Hungarian Empire. In 1906, President Theodore Roosevelt had persuaded the French and the Germans to negotiate their differences over Morocco; the result was the Algeciras Conference in Spain. But the power rivalries continued.

Two rival blocs of alliances spanning the continent—the Central Powers comprising Germany, Austria-Hungary, and, preliminarily, Italy, and the Western or Allied Powers comprising Great Britain, France, and Russia—swung into action after the shocking assassination on June 28, 1914: a Serbian nationalist killed Austria's Franz Ferdinand (nephew of the Emperor Franz Josef and heir to the throne), along with his pregnant wife, in Sarajevo, and Austria demanded accountability from Serbia. What might have been a limited war between Austria-Hungary and Serbia dragged in Russia, Germany, France, and Great Britain by August. But the treaty commitments were not exactly ironclad; as historian John Keegan observes, "It was . . . no treaty that caused Austria to go running to Berlin for guidance and support in the aftermath of the Sarajevo assassination—no treaty in any case applied—but anticipation of the military consequences should she act alone."[2] The alliance between Britain and France (1904) was a mere entente, as opposed to the more binding Franco-Russian alliance of 1894. And the chain reaction was punctuated by peace overtures among the great powers: both the kaiser and the tsar would claim they wanted peace, and they exchanged a series of telegrams in late July for the purpose of containing the crisis.[3]

But as Keegan has pointed out, events were increasingly driven by the automatic war plans devised by the military general staffs.[4] Almost all the great powers had plans that began to develop a nightmarish life of their own in July and August: worst-case thinking led to military plans for preemptive strikes that would rock back an enemy before that enemy could strike. Germany's Schlieffen Plan for a strike into France through Belgium, for instance, had a counterpart in France's own Plan XVII—which was designed by General Joseph Joffre—to strike Germany through Lorraine. But time was of the essence, and excessive caution might lead to preemptive success by an enemy. As Keegan has reflected, the situation

> resembled that which would bind the nuclear superpowers sixty years later. "Use them or lose them" became the imperative of missile strategy; for missiles not used in a crisis might become the debris of an opponent's first strike; an army which did not strike as soon as time permitted might be destroyed in mid-mobilisation; even if it completed its mobilisation but then failed to attack, it would have shown its hand and lost the advantage the war plan had been so painstakingly devised to deliver.[5]

The lead time needed for mobilization led to call-ups of troops in July—as contingent "precautionary" measures—and the mobilization of one great power triggered countermobilizations as a matter of course.

Helmuth von Moltke (the younger), chief of staff in imperial Germany, feared that an Austro-Hungarian war against Serbia might threaten both Germany and Austria if Russia intervened for pan-Slavic reasons. So he telegraphed the Austrian chief of staff, urging preventive mobilization against Russia—as well as Serbia. The Austro-Hungarian emperor, Franz Josef, approved, which caused the tsar to agree to a Russian mobilization.

Both the kaiser and his chancellor, Theobald von Bethmann-Hollweg, had tried to contain the crisis, but on July 31 the Germans (who had not yet mobilized) issued an ultimatum demanding that Russia cancel its mobilization. A German ultimatum was also sent to France, which had obligations under the Franco-Russian convention of 1892 and alliance of 1894.

On August 1, Russia refused to accept the Germans' ultimatum. The result was the launching of preemptive strikes simultaneously: attack as preemptive defense. As Keegan has argued, the kaiser, so far from behaving like a willful aggressor in regard to the Schlieffen Plan, "found he did not understand the machinery he was supposed to control, panicked and let a piece of paper determine events."[6] The issue of German culpability—asserted at the end of the war by the victors and then reasserted by historians such as Fritz Fischer—will always be a contentious proposition, especially in light of Kaiser Wilhelm's erratic personality.[7]

Though none of the leaders of the European powers, with the possible exception of some Serbs—especially the Serbian chief of military intelligence, Dragutin Dimitrijević—appeared to be warmongers at first, the eruption of warlike feeling among certain European population groups was startling. Historian Jacques Barzun has written of the speed with which European intellectuals abandoned critical analysis in 1914 and transformed into "rabid superpatriots." "What is truly astonishing," Barzun continues, "is the unanimity, unheard of on any other subject but the war and the enemy. Looking over the roster of great names in literature, painting, music, philosophy, science, and social science, one cannot think of more than half a dozen or so who did not spout all the catchphrases of abuse and vainglory." The process that historian Roland Stromberg once called "redemption by war" became captivating.[8] As with the opinion leaders, so, too, within the general populations: across Europe, as the war began, enthusiastic dreams of martial glory enraptured many.

The violation of Belgian neutrality—guaranteed by an 1839 treaty—put the Germans in the wrong fundamentally, but the allegation of German atrocities in Belgium was of course more grave. Subsequent investigation would reveal that some of the atrocity stories were true: massacres of civilians, including women and children, at Andenne, Seilles, Tamines, and Dinant, and the destruction of cultural treasures at Louvain. Some of the German troops had been supposedly panicked over rumors of Belgian snipers and guerrillas, and the troops were in an anxious frenzy in any case to keep pace with the rigid timetable of the Schlieffen Plan. But there was no excuse for their brutality, and the reputation of Germany had been blackened.[9] The submarine warfare that the Germans would conduct in the Atlantic would blacken it further.[10]

In the first month of war, the international disaster was extended to global dimensions: European colonies in Africa were embroiled, and Japan joined the Allies—not only due to obligations under an Anglo-Japanese treaty of 1902 but also for the opportunistic purpose of seizing German colonies in the Pacific.

THE WORLD ITSELF SEEMS GONE MAD

Woodrow Wilson had little preparation for leadership in foreign affairs or in war. Beginning in 1913, he had intervened in Mexico to topple the regime of Victoriano Huerta, who had murdered the country's constitutional leader, Francisco Madero. Huerta was toppled in 1914, but the landing of U.S. troops in Veracruz had aroused all the other Mexican factional leaders, especially Venustiano Carranza, who would rapidly assume leadership in Mexico City. Wilson would have diplomatic and military problems with Mexico for the rest of his presidency.

Wilson's liberal idealism in the summer of 1914 was displayed in a Fourth of July oration that he gave at Independence Hall. "My dream," he said, "is that, as the years go on and the world knows more and more of America, it will also drink at these fountains of youth and renewal; that it will also turn to America for those moral inspirations which lie at the basis of freedom . . . and that America will come into the full light of the day when all shall know that her flag is the flag, not only of America, but of humanity."[11]

And so, for the sake of humanity—and of peace—Wilson had given approval to a plan that his adviser, Colonel Edward M. House (the military title was honorific, conferred by the governor of Texas), had proposed about six months earlier. House liked to work behind the scenes in politics, domestic and foreign, and to work on an ever-larger scale to shape events. He, like others, felt the threat of a European war in the months before the war broke out. And he envisioned a partnership between the United States, Britain, and Germany to keep the peace.

In December 1913 he had revealed to a British diplomat that he intended to seek the approval of Wilson for a personal mission of his own that might accomplish this objective.[12] He succeeded in obtaining presidential approval for the "Great Adventure," as he called it. And he departed in the spring of

1914. On June 16, Wilson wished him Godspeed: "You have, I hope and believe, begun a great thing and I rejoice in it with all my heart," Wilson wrote.[13]

Visiting Berlin, Paris, and London in sequence from May through the middle of July, House obtained an interview with Kaiser Wilhelm at Potsdam in early June. House wrote to Wilson, informing him that he had "been as successful as anticipated. . . . I told the Kaiser that you thought an American could compose this situation better than a European. He concurred in this view and seemed pleased that I had undertaken to start the work."[14] But at the very time that House was proceeding to his other destinations, the assassination at Sarajevo and its aftermath were unfolding.

If the nations of Europe were enslaved by the consequences of war plans that were dangerously rigid, the United States was in the opposite condition in 1914: war planning was anathema to many Americans, notwithstanding the efforts of certain leaders, such as Theodore Roosevelt, to promote it. American traditions called for no large armies in peacetime, and after every major war the United States had demobilized as rapidly as possible.

The Democratic Party of Woodrow Wilson was gripped by an antiwar fervor at the time. Liberal thinking since the 1890s viewed war as a scheme by which the vested interests would protect their position: business interests used war as a distraction—a red herring—to redirect the passions for economic justice into needless crusades against hapless scapegoats abroad. This was a gross oversimplification; many businessmen had been notably unenthusiastic when the war with Spain had been declared back in 1898—a fact that had disgusted such Republican promoters of the war as Theodore Roosevelt. Yet the Populists of the 1890s, along with the supporters of William Jennings Bryan's insurgent Democratic candidacy in 1896, found it hard to forget how the grassroots protest movements of the decade faded when the war with Spain began under William McKinley; they also remembered how Bryan had tried in the next presidential election (his 1900 rematch with McKinley) to protest the imperialistic policy through which the United States had simply taken Spain's place as the imperial overlord of the Philippines.

William Jennings Bryan was one of the foremost champions of anti-imperialism and peace in the United States. He had been the Democratic nominee for the presidency three times: in 1896, in 1900, and in 1908. In 1913, Woodrow Wilson appointed Bryan secretary of state.

Republican progressives often joined their Democratic counterparts in resistance to war: Senator Robert La Follette of Wisconsin was one of their leaders. Other Republicans, however, carried on in the tradition of Theodore Roosevelt, who glorified war, pushed preparedness as assistant secretary of the navy, practiced what he preached by resigning his civilian post and seeking combat in Cuba with his "Rough Riders" during the Spanish-

American War, and then, as president, crusaded as hard as he could to make America a mighty global power.

Roosevelt was an apostate Republican in 1914; he had broken with the party to run against his own handpicked successor, William Howard Taft, in 1912, thus throwing the election to the Democrats and Woodrow Wilson. Most rank-and-file Republicans were not yet ready to forgive him in 1914. He had sought solace by embarking the previous year on an expedition up an uncharted South American river—and the trip almost killed him. Upon his return, he was bitter, frustrated, and in many ways prematurely old. He was a man spoiling for a fight. And he came to detest Woodrow Wilson.

These divisions of opinion and attitude among the politicians were equaled or exceeded by divisions between, and within, large blocs of the American electorate. Many Americans—including Wilson—were Anglophiles by reflex; the shared traditions of language, literature, and politics that linked the United States and Great Britain were a matter of inspiration to such people. But there was also a significant countertendency within American political culture to "twist the lion's tale," and to view the machinations of perfidious Albion, America's ancestral enemy in two wars, with suspicion. Even Wilson, who, as a professor of politics and government, had praised the British parliamentary system as in some ways superior to American institutions, found himself at times exasperated by the highhandedness of British policy during World War I.

In 1914, however, Wilson harbored extremely bitter thoughts about the Germans, if the diary of Colonel House is to be believed. On August 30, House recorded that Wilson "felt deeply about the destruction of Louvain, and I found him as unsympathetic with the German attitude as is the balance of America. He goes even further than I in his condemnation of Germany's part in this war, and almost allows his feeling to include the German people as a whole rather than the leaders alone." [15]

But others were sympathetic toward the Germans, and hostile toward the British. Americans of Irish extraction were frequently inclined to detest Great Britain in the 1910s, since the centuries-old struggle for Irish independence was approaching its penultimate (and very bloody) phase. Such people would often regard their enemy's enemy as being, perforce, their own friend. And Americans of German background were often (though by no means always) loyal to the Fatherland.

In short, Americans were spectacularly divided in their sympathies when war broke out. Many, such as Theodore Roosevelt and Henry Cabot Lodge, would conclude right away that the Germans were barbarians—latter-day Huns. Some Americans, such as Charles William Eliot, the former president of Harvard, were ardently pro-British. Others, however, blamed Britain for the war; a proponent of this point of view was Rear Admiral French E. Chadwick, who sent a series of anti-British missives to Wilson on August 23,

September 12, and December 16, 1914. Germany had its impassioned defenders, such as Professor John W. Burgess of Columbia University and Walter Rauschenbusch, one of the leaders of America's "Social Gospel" movement. His article "Be Fair to Germany" was printed in religious periodicals such as *Congregationalist* and *Lutheran Church Work* in autumn 1914.

It was therefore an ill-considered act when Woodrow Wilson declared, on August 18, that Americans should react to "these times that are to try men's souls" by being neutral in more than just the sense that was derived from international law; the president called upon Americans in lines that would soon become famous to be "neutral in fact as well as in name . . . impartial in thought as well as in action."[16]

Surely that was impossible. But Wilson was not in a clear state of mind at the moment; he was stricken since the death of his beloved wife, Ellen Axson Wilson, a few weeks earlier. He was hardly in the best condition to approach the early issues of war through critical analysis.

It was, of course, salutary for the president to warn against the irrationality that had spread with such horrifying speed in Europe. In a press conference on August 3, he observed that "the European world is in a highly excited state of mind, but the excitement ought not to spread to the United States."[17] That was a useful thing to say at the time.

Yet to call upon Americans to be, somehow, "impartial in thought" when "excitement" was becoming unavoidable and troubling thoughts might arise as a matter of course—that was surely an unwise action. Perhaps a man who was grieving as bitterly as Wilson might confuse his own emotional challenge with his country's foreign policy needs; in his message of August 18, he proclaimed that America "should show herself in this time of peculiar trial a nation fit beyond others to exhibit the fine poise of undisturbed judgment, the dignity of self-control, the efficiency of dispassionate action" that could be "truly serviceable for the peace of the world." The latter phrase gave away his larger purpose: he was recommending "dispassionate" action, since he hoped to end the war through mediation.

This nobility of purpose was undoubtedly a form of therapy—and Wilson acknowledged as much. On the day before he issued his "appeal to the American people," he wrote to Colonel House as follows: "The absolute imperative character of the duties I have to perform has been my salvation and I am at last able to speak with some degree of composure about the unspeakable loss that I have suffered."[18] A few days later, he confided to House that he avoided some emotions by deflecting them into noble work: "The matters I have to consider are imperative. They compel my attention and my great safety lies in having my attention absolutely fixed elsewhere than upon myself."[19] To his friend Mary Hulbert, he wrote that he found "a sort of grim pleasure, and stern compulsion to keep sane and self-possessed amid the general wreck and distemper," since "the world itself seems gone mad."[20] He would maintain "fine poise" by transmuting his passion into service. And he would do it through the work that he and House had begun: the work of mediation for peace.

But the chance for mediation was a flickering hope, and a better presidential strategist would surely have turned his attention to developing contingency plans—alternative plans—in the event that mediation should fail. Impartiality in thought might fail to be a practical option.

And Americans might have been far better off if they had heard that truth from the beginning.

It would, in short, have been wiser for Wilson to say that this war might produce some vociferous *debates* that would call upon Americans to use their very highest powers of deliberation to determine what the national interest of the United States might require.

At this time, people were quickly taking sides—including Colonel House. On August 22, after flattering Wilson by telling him that his "Address on Neutrality is one of the finest things you have ever done and it has met with universal approbation," House went on to muse that "Germany's success will ultimately mean trouble for us. We will have to abandon the path which you are blazing as a standard for future generations, with permanent peace as its goal and a new international ethical code as its guiding star, and build up a military machine of vast proportions."[21]

The British ambassador to the United States, Cecil Spring-Rice, informed the British foreign minister, Lord Edward Grey—in a letter marked "Private & Secret"—that Wilson had adopted House's point of view a week later: "The President sent you the warmest greeting and expresses his most sincere sympathy. He said: 'Everything that I love most in the world is at stake' and later 'If they succeed, we shall be forced to take such measures of defence here as would be fatal to our form of government and American ideals'. . . . Officially, he would do all that he could to maintain absolute neutrality, and would bear in mind that a dispute between our two nations would be the crowning calamity."[22]

It appears, in short, as if Wilson was becoming quite confused about the chance of achieving "impartiality in thought"—and at times he appeared to believe that he could actually pull this off—and a countertendency to let his deepest passions flow unimpeded where they might.

IT CAN, AT LEAST, DO NO HARM

Notwithstanding the appearance of habits that would cripple his presidency later—his tendency to dally with dreamy ideals like the notion of perfect "impartiality" in thought—Wilson showed some prescience and clarity as war was unleashed in late summer. On July 31, he summoned congressional leaders to the White House and warned that the outbreak of war might lead to disruptions of maritime commerce; he urged legislation to expand the size of the U.S. Merchant Marine.[23] He asked Congress to appropriate funds on August 3 to help Americans stranded in Belgium and elsewhere; the American ambassador to Great Britain, Walter Hines Page, tapped a businessman, Herbert Hoover, to organize the effort, and Hoover performed supremely well. His actions led to the establishment of a Committee for the Relief of Belgium—to send food relief to the Belgian population—that would constitute Hoover's apprenticeship in public service.

On the day of his wife's funeral, Wilson told his brother-in-law Stockton Axson that he was "afraid something will happen on the high seas that will make it impossible for us to keep out of the war."[24] A month later, he told Colonel House that the situation might begin to parallel the War of 1812, and that, like his predecessor James Madison, he might find himself leading a nation caught in the middle of a European war that made commerce impossible.[25] Indeed, on August 20, the British cabinet had issued Orders in Council that created a blockade of the Central Powers.

For this reason, Wilson's thoughts turned over and over again to his pet scenario: perhaps he could end the war himself by acting as a mediator. Some of the impetus for this idea carried over from the "Great Adventure" of House. On August 3, Wilson commiserated with House about the "sorrow that must have come to you out of this dreadful European conflict in view of what we had hoped the European world was going to turn to, but we must face the situation with the confidence that Providence has deeper plans than we could possibly have laid ourselves."[26] House replied by praising Wilson's efforts to date. "The more terrible the war becomes," House wrote, "the greater credit it will be that you saw the trend of events long before it was seen by other statesmen of the world" and "had done all that was humanly possible to avert it."[27] Wilson answered the very next day: "Letter of the third received. . . . do you think I could and should act now and if so how."[28]

House advised caution, but Wilson acted quickly, telling House on August 5 that "events moved so fast yesterday that I came to the conclusion that if you had known what I knew as soon as I knew it, the advice of your telegram would probably have been different. At any rate, I took the risk and sent messages to the heads of several countries. It can, at least, do no harm."[29]

Wilson's message to the kaiser, the tsar, the Austro-Hungarian emperor, the president of France, and the king of England read as follows: "As official head of one of the powers signatory to the Hague convention, I feel it to be my privilege and my duty under article three of that convention to say to you in a spirit of most earnest friendship that I should welcome an opportunity to act in the interest of the European peace, either now or at any other time that might be thought more suitable, as an occasion to serve you and all concerned in a way that would afford me lasting cause for gratitude and happiness."[30]

House advised Wilson that "nothing further should be done now than to instruct our different ambassadors to inform the respective governments . . . that you stand ready to tender your good offices whenever such an offer is desired."[31] Wilson agreed; he told House that he hoped "you do not disapprove my little attempt at mediation. I have received no replies whatever yet from the governments concerned, but that is no matter. All I wanted to do was to let them know that I was at their service."[32]

But he continued to watch for signs of interest. And others were acting independently to foster the idea. About a month later, on September 5, an American banker named James Speyer dined with the German ambassador to the United States, Johann von Bernstorff, to discuss the subject of mediation, and Bernstorff informed him that the kaiser might be receptive. Speyer relayed this information to Secretary of State Bryan, and the matter was pursued.[33]

On the same day, Colonel House sent a message to the German foreign minister, informing him that Wilson's "offer of mediation is not an empty one, for he would count it a great honor to be able to initiate a movement for peace. . . . If I could serve in any way to be a medium it would be a great source of happiness to me."[34]

But the hope for mediation proved vain, as it would in future months. The impulse among the warring powers to redeem the horrid casualties—to win, so that all the brave men who had been killed would not have died in vain—was too strong. On September 7, Bernstorff wrote to the German foreign office as follows: "Here everyone desires peace, for the United States suffers heavily because of the war. I, therefore, did not reject the offer [of mediation], since I wanted to leave the odium of rejection to our enemies. But I definitely said to Mr. Bryan that there could be no talk of an armistice, since it would be useful exclusively to our enemies."[35] The very next day, the French ambassador, Jean Jules Jusserand, informed his own government that

> Count Bernstorff has confirmed to the Secretary of State that his government would accept an American mediation. . . . This démarche seems to me capable of being interpreted as only a sign of anxiety, and we should be able to gain from it an increase of confidence in the success of our resistance. . . . I did not conceal from Mr. Bryan that the chances of success of the intervention envisaged were infinitesimal, each day adding to the list of German crimes. . . . As at one moment he had made allusion to a return to the status quo, I replied that we would accept it when the Germans, in order to re-establish it, could give us back the lives of our dead ones.[36]

Secretary Bryan urged Wilson to redouble his efforts on September 19, observing that each of the nations at war would like to have the war stop at such a time as to give it the prestige of having the advantage, but war necessarily has in it an element of uncertainty; successes may alternate, as for instance, when the Germans almost reached Paris and then were driven back. . . . The world looks to us to lead the way and I know how deeply you desire to render every possible assistance. . . . It is not likely that either side will win so complete a victory as to be able to dictate terms and if either side does win such a victory, it will probably mean preparation for another war.[37]

This latter observation would prove quite prophetic, and Wilson would be thinking along similar lines by the end of the year. In an interview with Herbert Bruce Brougham, the editor of the *New York Times*, Wilson said on December 14 that he hoped "for a deadlock in Europe," adding that "the chance of a just and equitable peace . . . will be the happiest if no nation gets the decision by arms; and the danger of an unjust peace, one that will be sure to invite further calamities, will be if some one nation or group of nations succeeds in enforcing its will upon the others." He added that "it may be found before long that Germany is not alone responsible for the war . . . and it might be well if there were no exemplary triumph or punishment."[38] Wilson's later doctrine of "peace without victory" owed much to the influence of Bryan.

More than Bryan, however, it was House who enjoyed Wilson's confidence. Serving as the president's personal agent, House tried to arrange a secret meeting of the German and British ambassadors, Bernstorff and Spring-Rice. House flattered Wilson to increase his own discretionary authority. "Now that I am in touch with Bernstorff I hope to persuade him to close his mouth for awhile," House informed the president on September 18. "He promises that no human shall know of these negotiations [*sic*]. The world expects you to play the big part in this tragedy, and so indeed you will, for God has given you the power to see things as they are."[39]

The meeting between the ambassadors did not come off, but House tried to be reassuring—even nonchalant—as he increased his own role in the proceedings: "It is an extraordinarily delicate undertaking and any misstep may be fatal to your final influence. What I would advise, is to let me go along with the negotiations [*sic*] . . . until we find we can go no further in that direction. Then I have something else to suggest to you."[40]

Wilson continued to watch for any opening that fortunes of war might provide. Notwithstanding an early German victory at Tannenberg on the eastern front, the Germans and Austrians were faring very badly at the hands of the Russians in Poland. Consequently, Wilson told House to try a different ploy with the British. "The President thought I should write Sir Edward Grey," wrote House on September 28, "and tell him of the danger of postponing peace negotiations. If Germany and Austria are entirely crushed, neither of us could see any way by which Russia could be restrained."[41]

But the fighting on both the fronts devolved into a grinding stalemate. Trench warfare set in before the end of the year, and on a massive scale. The German trenches in France were made particularly strong so that German troops could be shifted out of France to the East.[42] And Turkey joined the Central Powers in October.

Earlier that month, Spring-Rice had told House that mediation was out of the question for the near future. House wrote to Wilson, informing him that he asked the British ambassador "if he saw light in the direction of peace. He saw none. He expressed himself as very glad that you were doing nothing. In his opinion, it would be a mistake for you to make any move just now for it would probably prejudice the cause later."[43]

But Wilson could not let go of his hope to be a mediator. The emotional power of his wish to give "service" had merged with his deep Presbyterian piety. Wilson's spiritual side was far from narrow-minded—he would, after all, nominate the first Jewish member of the Supreme Court—but it was fundamental. In a letter to his confidante Mary Hulbert in late September, Wilson descanted on the blow that Providence had dealt him: "My loss has made me humble. I know there is nothing *for me* in what I am doing. And I hope that that will make me more serviceable. I have succeeded so far, I believe, only because I have not sought my own pleasure in the work. . . . And now self is killed more pitilessly than ever,—there is nothing but the work for me [original emphasis]."[44]

Here was a Christian conundrum: in resisting pride, the source of all sin, could one avoid an unconscious kind of pride in one's own . . . humility? It appears that Wilson could not avoid this snare; he protested too much about the selflessness of his motives. More and more, as the war progressed, his sense of mission would glorify itself into an aura of oracular sanctity, one that his flatterers worsened as they sought to gain power and influence.

As all of these events were unfolding, economic events were keeping pace. A major American recession had started at the end of the previous year. The threat of a full-scale depression was looming, as Europeans started cashing in American securities when war broke out. This wave of selling caused the worst financial panic on Wall Street since 1907.

A "gold drain" was feared. Some of the securities were redeemable in gold, which served as a reserve for the checking accounts in commercial banks (the Federal Reserve system with its legal tender notes was still in the process of being phased in), and excessive loss of gold to Europe could trigger bank defaults if bank panics started. Wilson had his treasury secretary, William Gibbs McAdoo, issue a round of "emergency currency," per the terms of the 1908 Aldrich-Vreeland Act. It was clear at the time that this was merely a stopgap measure, since the regional banks that had been set up under the Federal Reserve Act of 1913 would become operational by the autumn of 1914, thereby serving as "lenders of last resort." McAdoo also allowed the New York Stock Exchange to shut down temporarily.

Wilson likewise showed due diligence in averting a decline in exports by siding with McAdoo in advocacy of a government-owned-and-operated shipping line. In August, the administration introduced legislation to appropriate $30 million for this purpose, the money to be spent not in new construction but rather in the purchase of existing ships—*German* ships that were stranded in American ports. The British protested that the action would be unneutral, and Republicans—Henry Cabot Lodge in particular—opposed the bill as socialistic. They also complained that the action had definite anti-British overtones. Wilson stood firm, but the bill would be defeated in the spring of 1915.[45]

Simultaneously, a controversy over war loans raged. In early August, the French had asked J.P. Morgan & Co. to facilitate a $100 million loan. Concerns about the fragility and turbulence of the American financial sector played a role in the administration's disapproval. But a far more significant reason was Bryan's belief that such a loan would be "unneutral." On August 15, he declared that "in the judgment of this Government loans by American bankers to any foreign nation which is at war is [*sic*] inconsistent with the true spirit of neutrality."[46]

In September, however, France asked for a smaller loan of $10 million from a different firm, the National City Bank of New York. Jusserand paid a call upon Bryan and convinced him somehow that to *refuse* the loan would be unneutral. Bryan reversed course by mid-October, saving face by agreeing to call foreign loans "commercial credits" instead. On October 23, Wilson told Robert Lansing, who was counselor of the State Department, that he agreed with this policy shift. Historian Arthur S. Link has attributed the policy change to stark realism; if the loan ban "had been faithfully adhered to it would have ended by destroying the only foreign trade in which the United States could then engage on a large scale—trade with its natural customers, Britain and France."[47] Those countries were "natural customers" by dint of the Royal Navy's control of the sea-lanes.

The first naval battle of World War I, which occurred on August 28, 1914—the battle of Heligoland Bight—had been a German defeat. In general, the Germans' attempt to outbuild Britain's Royal Navy had failed, resulting in a 1912 directive from the kaiser that the German fleet in the event of war should restrict itself to cautious attacks on blockading forces and attempt more ambitious attacks if, and only if, circumstances were favorable.[48] Britain's command of the seas, as of 1914, remained intact.

Even so, American exporters tried to fill foreign orders from the Central Powers (and from neutral powers such as Holland) using Rotterdam and certain Scandinavian ports as neutral conduits. In September the British dramatically tightened their blockade of the Central Powers by publishing an expanded list of "contraband" goods that would be subject to seizure by the British. Among these goods were some important American export commodities. Since Secretary Bryan was out of town, Lansing at the State Department drafted a protest note, which Colonel House asked Wilson to soften. Wilson did; he was reportedly disturbed by the tone of Lansing's draft.[49]

The British were quick to conciliate. Lord Grey, the British foreign minister, responded by exempting cotton from the list of embargoed goods; indeed, the British started buying American cotton, not only to keep it out of the enemy's hands but also to soften the economic impact of war on the American South. Most British and American leaders were anxious to avoid a confrontation. Still, the Anglo-American tension over contraband seizures—and ship seizures—continued through the end of the year, and the State Department sent another mild protest note to the British on December 26.[50]

An excerpt from a letter that was sent by Spring-Rice to Wilson in October is representative of the diplomatic give and take between America and Britain in the autumn of 1914:

> I saw Mr. Lansing today and told him that I was without any news as to the seizures of American oil ships. . . . The evidence was convincing that an attack by submarines and Zeppelins was contemplated and supplies of oil were absolutely essential to Germany. The measure taken, even if irregular, as to which I expressed no opinion, was a measure of obvious self-defense and was imperatively demanded by popular opinion. If we are in the wrong, we must of course pay the penalty and see that the United States are not losers by wrongful action. . . . We each wish to defend our rights. But I am sure you will remember that the rights we are defending are our existence.[51]

Page, the American ambassador to Britain, thought Lansing's defense of every jot and tittle of American rights was pedantic and complained to Wilson about it. Wilson's reply to Page is revealing in a number of ways:

> I have been distressed to have to maintain our recent debate with Sir Edward Grey, but it was absolutely necessary that we should discuss the matters that Mr. Lansing presented, because not the least part of the difficulty of this war is going to be the satisfaction of opinion in America and the full performance of our utmost duty as the only powerful neutral. More and more, from day to day, the elements (I mean the several racial elements) of our population seem to grow restless and catch more and more the fever of the contest. We are trying to keep all possible spaces cool, and the only means by which we can do so is to make it demonstrably clear that we are doing everything that it is possible to do to define and defend neutral rights. . . . I mean that if we are to remain neutral and to afford Europe the legitimate assistance possible in such circumstances, the course we have been pursuing is the absolutely necessary course.[52]

These were the priorities, arranged hierarchically in order of presupposition, that would rule out a range of other options for Wilson in the following years. The presuppositions contained in Wilson's message to Page were as follows: (1) the war should be ended through mediation by America; (2) in order for America to mediate the war, the United States must be unimpeachably neutral; (3) public opinion in America must be shaped to rule out the risk of taking sides; (4) America's bona fides as a neutral must be zealously demonstrated if the chance to act as a neutral mediator were to be protected; (5) in order to demonstrate its bona fides as a neutral, America must advertise itself as an exemplary neutral nation; (6) to do so, America must stubbornly but politely make an issue over any breach of neutral rights.

In December, a significant if quiet confrontation occurred between Wilson and Republican partisans who favored taking sides with Britain. Former president Theodore Roosevelt, Senator Henry Cabot Lodge, and Lodge's son-in-law, Representative Augustus Peabody Gardner, had been spreading their belief that the German cause was, to quote Gardner's words, "unholy and . . . a menace to civilization."[53] They started to advocate a major military buildup.

In a letter sent to Wilson on November 23, Gardner proposed an investigation by Congress into the state of national preparedness.[54] Gardner met with Wilson on the day before the president delivered his annual message to Congress. The *New York Times* reported that

> cold water was dashed on the defense agitation by President Wilson today. He came out flatly, in a conversation with Representative Gardner, against the latter's proposal that there should be an investigation by a committee of Congress into the whole question of national military preparedness. After Mr. Gardner left the White House, the President authorized the following formal statement: "The President told Representative Gardner that he was opposed . . . because he thought it was an unwise way of handling a question which might create very unfavorable international impressions."[55]

In Wilson's annual message to Congress—equivalent in those days to the State of the Union Address, but still by tradition delivered at the end of the year—Wilson looked Gardner in the eye and insisted that only minimal increases in American military strength were advisable. He said:

> We must depend in every time of national peril, in the future as well as in the past, not upon a standing army, nor yet upon a reserve army, but upon a citizenry trained and accustomed to arms. It will be right enough, right American policy, based upon our accustomed principles and practices, to provide a system by which every citizen who will volunteer for the training may be made familiar with the use of modern arms. . . . More than this, proposed at this time, permit me to say, would mean merely that we had lost our self-possession, that we had been thrown off our balance by a war with which we

have nothing to do, whose causes cannot touch us, whose very existence affords us opportunities of friendship and disinterested service which should make us ashamed of any thought of hostility or fearful preparation for trouble.[56]

In the opinion of historian John Milton Cooper Jr., Wilson's tactics "succeeded brilliantly. . . . Democrats rallied to his side, and Republicans displayed their disunity."[57] But the political (or partisan) success was overbalanced by Wilson's indulgence of a dangerous delusion—the delusion that America had "nothing to do" with the war, and that the war could not "touch us." It might have been wiser and better for Wilson to have tried to reach out across the party lines, to consult at least with Roosevelt and Lodge, to agree that the war had indeed been "touching" American interests, to seek their views about the contingencies for prudent military mobilization, just in case—as he had privately confided to Stockton Axson—events on the high seas "might make it impossible for us to keep out of the war."

Consultations with Roosevelt and Lodge might have turned them into potentially responsive—or at least minimally civil—"stakeholders"; the ego boost to Roosevelt might have done a great deal to preempt his later attacks upon Wilson (indeed, his experience in long-term military planning might have been extremely useful). Cultivation of these two men—a behind-the-scenes cultivation that might have made them feel that this Democratic president welcomed and respected their views, even though he might disagree in the short run—could have changed the course of history, in many different ways for the better. At the very least, it would have been worth a try.

As it was, Wilson chose to redouble his efforts to end the war through mediation; on December 16, he authorized House to have talks with the British and German ambassadors in Washington and then depart for Europe to conduct negotiations. House recorded in his diary that Wilson "spoke of my going abroad in order to initiate peace conversations. He desires me to take charge of it and to go whenever I think it advisable. . . . I said I would be glad to go at any time and under any conditions."[58] House departed for the second phase of his "Great Adventure" on January 30, 1915.[59]

More than ever, it was House who commanded Wilson's confidence. Earlier in the month of December—if House's diary is to be believed—Wilson "spoke with extreme regret of Mr. Bryan's unsuitability for the office of Secretary of State, but did not know what could be done." House recorded, no doubt with the greatest of pleasure, that "the President said that he, Mr. Bryan, did not know that he, The President, was working for peace wholly through me, and he was afraid to mention this fact to him for fear it would offend him. He said Mr. Bryan might accept it gracefully, but not being certain, he hesitated to tell him. I advised not telling him for the moment."

Wilson's justification, according to House, was his "feeling that I could do more to initiate peace unofficially than anyone could do in an official capacity, for the reason I could talk and be talked to without it being binding upon anyone."[60] For all the genuine merits of this approach—and it did possess some merits—Wilson's habit of keeping the State Department "out of the loop" in regard to the maneuverings of House would have fateful consequences later.

Wilson seemed not to notice the fact that Colonel House could be a shifty adviser. It bears noting that House had recommended a military buildup to Wilson a month before the latter's address to Congress. In a diary entry for November 4, 1914, House recorded the following exchange of thoughts:

> We passed then to the question of a reserve army. He baulked [*sic*] somewhat at first. . . . He did not believe there was any necessity for immediate action, he was afraid it would shock the country. He made the statement that no matter how the great war ended, there would be complete exhaustion, and, even if Germany won, she would not be in a condition to seriously menace our country for many years to come. I combatted this idea, stating that Germany would have a large military force ready to act in furthering the designs which the military party evidently have in mind. He said she would not have the men. I replied that she could not win unless she had two or three million men under arms at the end. He evidently thought the available men would be completely wiped out. I insisted it was time to do a great constructive work for the army and one which would make the country too powerful for any nations to think of attacking us. . . . The President does not seem to fully grasp the importance of such matters.[61]

After Wilson's message to Congress, however, House flattered the president as follows: "You go far enough to satisfy any reasonable man and your reasons for not going further are, I think, conclusive. . . . I have a feeling that when this war is over, the whole world will have a different outlook in regard to militarism, and that public opinion in this country will applaud you for not being carried away by the excitement of the moment."[62]

One other potent war-related issue was evident before the end of the year: Americans were beginning to manufacture and ship war materiel to Europe. In November, this issue was called to Wilson's attention in a letter from Jacob Henry Schiff, who pointed out that "large quantities of ammunition are being purchased in this country by the belligerents in the European war." Schiff suggested that "the furnishing of the weapons with which this terrible slaughter is now going on in Europe" was "immoral and obnoxious to a large majority of our people." He guessed that "this has likely already occurred to you," and he therefore called upon Wilson to "make a public utterance . . . calling upon manufacturers of weapons and ammunition to stop selling their wares to the European belligerents."[63]

It is interesting to note that the president was deeply conflicted, and the nature of his ambivalence regarding this issue reveals that his powers of critical analysis were working, albeit at a low level of energy. A few days later he told Colonel House that Schiff's suggestion was "a foolish one as it would restrict our plants and, in a way, make us less prepared than now."[64] To this extent—though perhaps grudgingly—Wilson was allowing himself to do contingency planning in regard to preparation for war. All the same, when he replied to Schiff, he asserted that the issue was "one of the most perplexing things I have had to decide." "The law standing as it does," he continued, he had no direct power to intervene. He therefore adopted a defeatist stance, observing that "the sales proceed from so many sources, and my lack of power is so evident, that I have felt that I could do nothing else than leave the matter to settle itself."[65]

There were many ways in which Congress might have addressed this matter. An American mobilization—adequately funded—might have channeled the production of armaments and weapons to American military stockpiles. Wilson's inaction—his reluctance to confront this issue—would have major economic and policy repercussions in 1915.

As 1914 drew to a close, Wilson's situation was as follows: he was fixated on the highly problematical scenario of ending the war through mediation. His position on American neutrality was stiff and legalistic when it came to the formalities, but inattentive when it came to the realities of a commerce in arms that would benefit one of the wartime coalitions—the Allied or Western Powers—while hurting the other. His contingency planning for the possibility of American participation in the war was minimal. He had thrown away the chance of bipartisan dealings on the issue of preparedness—an important scenario in light of his own party's aversion to military action—by alienating Republicans who might have been cultivated. He had created the potential for diplomatic confusion by keeping the State Department in the dark in regard to the free-wheeling activities of his agent Colonel House.

Attentive though he was to the dangers of the situation, he was also extremely myopic. And his notion that a single magnificent gesture of his own could end the tragedy would deepen the tragedy year by year until it played the central role in his final agony and failure.

Chapter Two

1915

Wilson was a victim of events throughout 1915. Shoved this way and that, he just continued to cling to international law, which permitted the sale of munitions, which sustained the economy. He sought solace in the hope that he could end the war himself—somehow.

By the end of the year, through the prompting of House, he pursued that idea in a particularly grandiose manner, augmented by the slow recognition of the fact that the United States should build up its military might. But his moves in that direction were belated. His few visible successes were mostly due to luck, and they did little to prepare him and his people for their full immersion in the decade's ordeal.

PROSPECTS FOR PEACE SEEM VERY DIM

In 1915, as the stalemate on the western front hardened, the war intensified. The struggle on the seas continued in January and February. On January 23, the second major naval battle of the war—the Battle of Dogger Bank—resulted in another German defeat. The following month, the Germans attempted to counter the blockade of the Allies by proclaiming their own blockade of the British Isles—a blockade to be enforced by submarine.

The Central Powers began to improve their position on the Eastern front in the spring: in May, German troops commanded by General August von Mackensen broke through in the Gorlice-Tarnow campaign and forced a massive Russian retreat. The Russians were subjected to further pressure as Turkey, which had joined the Central Powers the previous autumn, attacked in the Caucasus. To help relieve this pressure, the British launched their ill-fated Gallipoli campaign in the Dardanelles. This campaign resulted in horrid casualties: by the end of the year, about 265,000 on the Allied side and roughly 300,000 for the Turks.

In partial reaction to the Allied failure in Gallipoli, Bulgaria joined the Central Powers. In the autumn, the Bulgarians, Germans, and Austrians invaded Serbia. To support Serbia, the British and French established a military presence in neutral Greece.

Italy, which had switched sides and joined the Allies in the late spring, created a new stalemate with a series of futile attempts to attack Austria across the Alps. A mountain line almost 375 miles long confronted the Italians, who tried in vain to break through in attacks along the Isonzo River. On the western front, spring and autumn Allied offensives in Artois and Champagne were repulsed with extremely heavy casualties. And the use of poison gas made the struggle particularly hideous.

Almost no one had expected a war of this duration and intensity. Accordingly, both sides were forced to play catchup in logistics. The Allies found themselves short of ammunition; according to Keegan, "By April 1915 . . . the field artillery of the BEF [British Expeditionary Force] was receiving ten rounds of 18-pounder ammunition per gun per day, when ten rounds was easily shot off in a minute of bombardment. Britain managed to increase its production of field-artillery ammunition from 3,000 rounds per month at the outbreak to 225,000 rounds by April 1915, and acquired other stocks by placing purchasing orders in America."[1]

America—the avowedly neutral nation whose economy was rising to the level of a boom by its lopsided trade in armaments with the Allies.

Total war intensified the conflict on the high seas—the war of blockade and counterblockade. According to Keegan, "The British merchant fleet continued to lose between fifty and a hundred ships a month to submarine attack during 1915 but could maintain supply to the home country nonetheless." By contrast, the Central Powers were in trouble: the Allies "sustained a blockade of Germany that denied it all trade with the world beyond Europe and which was extended, by British, French and Italian naval dominance in the Mediterranean, against Austria and Turkey. The 'central position' of the Central Powers, a strategic posture ordained by military theorists to be one of great strength, had been reduced to one of infirmity, perhaps disabling weakness, by the constriction of an all-encircling blockade."[2] And this weakness began to prompt some bold and desperate actions by the Germans.

YOU TRIED TO KEEP THE SCALE FROM TIPPING

By the spring of 1915, the premonition of Wilson regarding the War of 1812 and its similarities to the existing situation came true. Moreover, as James

Madison and the nation he led were ill prepared to confront their predicament, Wilson and his nation were ill prepared.

Because of the choices that Wilson had made in the previous year—acquiescence in the munitions trade and inattentiveness to the issues of preparedness—the task of maintaining neutrality became precarious. Regardless of compliance with international law, the strategic realities of the situation made neutrality in some respects an illusion. As Arthur S. Link observed many years ago, "impartiality was no longer possible for the United States" by 1915: "Any American action against one belligerent was bound to benefit the other; American acquiescence in the maritime measures of one belligerent would injure the other."[3]

The illusory nature of America's technical neutrality—and the impossibility of *any* American action that would not be construed as unneutral by one side or the other—is illustrated in a letter that Secretary of State Bryan sent to Wilson on January 6. Bryan agreed with Wilson's aversion to interference in the munitions traffic, and he, like Wilson, opposed a measure that was introduced in the House by Congressman Richard Bartholdt, a bill that would have banned the exportation of munitions. "Any action," Bryan wrote, "looking to interference with the right of belligerents to buy arms here would be construed as an unneutral act, not only because the effect of such action would be to assist one party at the expense of the other, but also because the *purpose* of the resolution is plainly to assist one party at the expense of the other [original emphasis]."[4]

The Bartholdt resolution would have helped the Central Powers. Opposition to the Bartholdt resolution would help the Allies. To avoid the charge of being unneutral, Wilson and Bryan did nothing, thus maintaining *de jure* neutrality. And yet, to be neutral *de jure*, the president and his secretary of state were helping the Allies *de facto*. And there was no escape from this dilemma.

Only two days later, in a Jackson Day address in Indianapolis, Wilson posed this rhetorical question: "Do you not think it likely that the world will some time turn to America and say: 'You were right, and we were wrong. You kept your heads when we lost ours; you tried to keep the scale from tipping, but we threw the whole weight of arms in one side of the scale. Now, in your self-possession, in your coolness, in your strength, may we not turn to you for counsel and for assistance?'"[5]

At that very moment, the United States was "throwing the whole weight" of its munitions trade into "one side of the scale" as a matter of unavoidable *fact*.

Wilson's treasury secretary William Gibbs McAdoo wrote candidly to Wilson months later in regard to the economic benefits of the war trade:

Great Britain is, and always has been, our best customer. Since the war began, her purchases and those of her allies, France, Russia, and Italy, have enormously increased. . . . The high prices for food products have brought great prosperity to our farmers, while the purchases of war munitions have stimulated industry and have set factories going to full capacity throughout the great manufacturing districts, while the reduction of imports and their actual cessation in some cases, have caused new industries to spring up and others to be enlarged. Great prosperity is coming.[6]

In the course of the year, administration officials would use both logic and sarcasm to defend their neutral—and unneutral—position. When Germany complained about the lopsidedness of America's munitions trade, Robert Lansing drafted a reply that contained the following nonchalant exercise of wit: "I am unable to perceive any justification for [Germany's] unfavorable comments upon this Government's failure to insist upon an equalization of American trade conditions with all belligerent nations which the fortunes of war have made unequal."[7]

The essence of the message was this: Any time the German surface fleet could manage to fight its way out of the North Sea in order to convoy German merchant vessels, the United States would be perfectly willing to sell munitions to Germany as well as Great Britain. In the meantime, let the German navy get off its duff—case closed.

But however reasonable or glib—or both—this stance might have been, it did nothing to mitigate the danger of America's oceanic situation.

Wilson continued to be entranced by the vision of acting as a mediator, and his emissary, Colonel House, was preparing for his next trip to Europe. House had a number of preliminary conferences with diplomats in January— his departure was scheduled for the end of the month—and he took note of the arms trade controversy as follows in a letter to Wilson: "The Germans are a little irritated just now at our sale of munitions to the Allies. . . . They say [the Kaiser] is angry at Americans over the sale of arms, but I do not think he would shut up the Krupps factory if we were at war with Japan."[8]

House told Wilson that he hoped an opportunity for peace might be over the horizon: "Prospects for peace seem very dim, but in about three months from now the plain people in every land are going to be very sick of this business, and then unless one side has some startling success (which all hope for in the Spring) peace will come grudgingly."[9]

Already, some visions of a postwar settlement were making the rounds. Chandler Parsons Anderson, a former counselor in the State Department, told Wilson about some conversations he had recently had with Sir Edward Grey regarding British and French territorial war aims. Anderson expressed the belief that the war would be over by summer.[10] Paul Samuel Reinsch, the American ambassador to China, wrote to Wilson on the terms of a postwar settlement, recommending that "the organization of civilized society be strengthened by providing The Hague Court with an executive supported by the armies and navies of the Allied Powers; that a world-wide government of law be thus instituted."[11]

At the end of the month, the American ambassador to Germany, James W. Gerard, informed Wilson that Americans did not "realize how excited the Germans have become on the question of the selling of munitions of war by America to the Allies." According to Gerard, the German undersecretary of foreign affairs, Arthur Zimmermann, "said that perhaps it was as well to have the whole World against Germany, and that in case of trouble there *were five hundred thousand trained Germans in America who would join with the Irish and start a revolution* [original emphasis]."[12] Wilson forwarded this message to House, who replied that it confirmed the "highly nervous condition of these people, and present troubles are evidently putting them over the border line."[13]

Upon House's departure for Europe, Wilson told him (according to House's diary) that he was "the only one in all the world to whom he could open his entire mind."[14] Wilson wished his representative luck in "a mission fraught with so many great possibilities, and which may, in the kind providence of God, prove the means of opening a way to peace."[15] House departed on January 30—aboard the *Lusitania.*

In February, Wilson confessed to Stockton Axson that he was envisioning a postwar settlement that some might regard as utopian. "No nation shall ever again be permitted to acquire an inch of land by conquest," Axson recalled Wilson saying. Then the president declared that "there must be an association of nations, all bound together for the protection and integrity of each, so that any one nation breaking from the bond will bring upon herself war; that is to say, punishment, automatically."[16]

TOO PROUD TO FIGHT

In January 1915, an American company, the W. L. Greene Commission Company, shipped a cargo of food to Germany aboard the *Wilhelmina*, a privately owned vessel. Since the German Bundesrat had passed a measure making all foodstuffs within the German empire liable to confiscation for military use, the British cabinet decreed that all shipments of food from the United States to Germany were liable to seizure. In response, the Germans exempted all food shipments from neutrals from the Bundesrat's order, but the British seized the *Wilhelmina* anyway on February 11. Meanwhile, in order to retaliate for what the Germans were calling the "food blockade," the German admiralty announced a submarine blockade of the British Isles on February 4.

The following day, Lansing advised Wilson that a "protest in regard to [the German declaration] should only be drawn after careful deliberation," since the "delicate situation" required "extreme care."[17] Lansing drafted a preliminary note of protest. After editing by Wilson, the note declared that a "critical situation" would arise if a German submarine should "cause the death of American citizens." The note further declared that to sink a vessel "without first determining its belligerent nationality and the contraband character of its cargo" would be an act "unprecedented in naval warfare." In such a case, the United States would hold Germany to "strict accountability" and take whatever steps "might be necessary" in order to "safeguard American lives and property and to secure to American citizens the full enjoyment of their rights on the high seas."[18]

This message was sent to the Germans on February 10. Lansing and Wilson would insist upon every right of neutral nations under international law. In the case of the submarine blockade, this meant that the Germans would have to use traditional methods of "visit and search," which would allow any citizens of neutral nations who were traveling aboard a vessel carrying contraband cargo to be rescued before the vessel was seized or destroyed.[19]

The German government issued an announcement explaining the risks (and constraints) that it claimed were unavoidable in this situation:

> Just as England has designated the area between Scotland and Norway as an area of war, so Germany now declares all the waters surrounding Great Britain and Ireland, including the entire English channel, as an area of war, and thus will proceed against the shipping of the enemy. For this purpose, beginning February 18, 1915, it will endeavor to destroy every enemy merchant ship that is found in this area of war, without its always being possible to avert the peril that thus threatens persons and cargoes. Neutrals are therefore warned against further intrusting crews, passengers, and wares to such ships. Their attention is also called to the fact that it is advisable for their ships to avoid entering this area, for even though the German naval forces have instructions to avoid violence to neutral ships, in so far as they are recognizable, in view of the misuse of neutral flags ordered by the British government and the contingencies of naval warfare, their becoming victims of torpedoes directed against enemy ships cannot always be averted.[20]

The options available to the United States in this situation spanned a broad range. At one extreme was the option of armed defiance: to help the British, who were working on a range of antisubmarine tactics, including depth charges, and "Q-ships" (to be discussed later). At the other extreme was the possibility of isolated defiance: to use the force of both persuasion and law to pull Americans out of harm's way.

Consistent with his wish to preserve impeccable neutrality—at least by the standards of international law—Wilson chose a different path, one that was more legalistic than strategic. He would try to contain and minimize the submarine threat, to play for time in the hope that his bid to serve as a mediator might provide a way out of the predicament.

Meanwhile, the most relevant objective of the Germans in regard to the United States was to interdict the shipments of munitions that America was sending to the Allies. As historian John Morton Blum observed, the president's stance "prevented the genuine neutrality that Wilson professedly cultivated, for the Germans could not afford by abandoning the submarine to clear the highway for the Allies' supplies. The use of the submarine, moreover, was bound to give rise to incidents that would test Wilson's definition of strict accountability."[21]

Wilson, through his sequence of choices, was stuck at this point with only one real possibility: to wait upon events. In the short run, he would stay in a reactive posture (with the single exception of House's "Great Adventure"). There was seldom any real examination of a broad range of best-case and worst-case alternatives, excepting the best-case hope for mediation.

Wilson's fixation on the mediation hope was abetted by House and by others: Ambassador Walter Hines Page, for instance, who wrote to Wilson from London on February 10 to the effect that the Germans would seek negotiations "unless these late new stages of bitterness make it possible for the military party in Germany to fight it out to the last man and the last cartridge; and this seems incredible."[22] Gerard, from Berlin, sent Wilson an excited message on February 11 to the effect that a peace opportunity was beckoning: it "would be fatal to hesitate or wait a moment," he wrote.[23] House contradicted this message, averring that "Germany . . . is now almost wholly controlled by the militarists."[24] House later wrote that Gerard "seems to have a touch of the general madness."[25] Wilson needed solid information; what he got too often from his agents were ill-informed hunches and guesswork.

From the first, Wilson's effort to reckon with the submarine challenge was agonizing. At a press conference on February 9, a reporter asked Wilson about the British practice of using neutral flags—not only aboard merchant vessels but also on some passenger liners—for the purpose of deception. The reporter's questions and Wilson's answers illustrate the president's awkward reaction to the situation he confronted:

> Mr. President, is it a common practice for belligerents to use neutral flags, as the *Lusitania* used our flag the other day, for the purposes of deception?
>
> It has been very common, yes, sir.

There is no basis for a protest, then, in that sort of practice?

> I would rather you gentlemen would not quote me on that subject, but I am
> perfectly willing to show you my mind about it, on that understanding. There
> is no rule of international law that prevents it. Of course, it involves manifest
> risks and embarrassments; but there is no basis, so far as I now know, for
> anything like a protest by one government to another. Besides, it wasn't a
> government ship; it was a privately owned ship. My information is that it is
> not an uncommon practice, though I must admit that I didn't know it until
> recently.[26]

All through February and March, Wilson clung to the hope that "cool
self-possession" would see him (and America) through the dangers of submarine warfare. On March 4 he released a statement to the press, declaring
that "the circumstances created by the war put the nation to a special test, a
test of its true character and of its self-control."[27] Shortly afterward, House
left Britain for Berlin, via Paris. He told Wilson that his hope was to "get
directly at the Kaiser," admitting that "the great question is, who really
controls in Germany."[28]

On March 11, the British issued an Order in Council that tightened its
blockade. Wilson drafted a very mild protest.[29] For a while, in light of
Wilson's insistence on neutral rights, the propaganda advantage of this situation shifted to the Central Powers, especially when Germany offered to rescind its submarine blockade if the British would rescind what the Germans
were calling the "food blockade." There was—and still is, among historians—a debate regarding the food situation in Germany as of this relatively
early date. But there is no doubt that the Germans were seeking a relaxation
in the British controls.[30]

When House reached Berlin, he wrote to Wilson in regard to munitions
sales. House was unsympathetic to the Germans, exclaiming that "the bitterness of their resentment towards us for this is almost beyond belief. It seems
that every German soldier that is now being killed or wounded is being killed
or wounded by an American bullet or shell. I never dreamed before of the
extraordinary excellence of our guns and ammunition."[31]

House tried to interest the Germans in the following deal: in return for
German concessions on Belgium, the United States would try to pressure
Great Britain into granting "freedom of the seas"—whatever that meant—in
a postwar settlement.

On March 28, a German submarine sank a British passenger vessel, the
SS *Falaba*. An American citizen named Leon Thrasher was killed. Within
days, Bryan and Lansing were debating what response should be made. On
April 2, Lansing queried Bryan as to whether the United States "should not
hold the German Government responsible for the death of an American
through the act of their naval forces, when that act is in violation of the

established rules of naval warfare?"[32] Bryan was averse to taking action, telling Wilson he was troubled by the question of "whether an American citizen can, by putting his own business above his regard for his country, assume for his own advantage unnecessary risks and thus involve his country in international complications."[33]

Bryan wrote to Wilson again the next day with more vehemence, observing that

> Great Britain has permitted the arming of some of her merchant vessels and we have received a note from the British Ambassador saying that if her vessels are permitted to arm it is because of the action of the German submarines. The German government seems to assume that British merchantmen are armed, and gives that as a reason why her submarines cannot insure the rescue of crew and passengers. . . . If the arming of a merchant vessel so changes its character as to effect the rights of those who travel on it, the risks assumed by an American passenger would necessarily be greatly increased and he might occupy the position of a foreigner who goes into a fortified city, or exposes himself when a battle is on. . . . It would be a sacrifice of the interests of all the people to allow one man . . . to involve the entire nation in difficulty when he had ample warning of the risks which he assumed.[34]

Though Wilson tended to agree with Lansing that a protest was necessary, the president delayed his response and sought to contain the incident. In a speech on April 20 at a meeting of the Associated Press, he declared that "there is something so much greater to do than fight: there is a distinction waiting for this country that no nation has ever yet got. That is the distinction of absolute self-control and self-mastery."[35]

But Wilson's hope for any chance at mediation had been dashed in the short term; after House had left Berlin to return to Paris and London, he had written Wilson on April 11 that

> my visit in Berlin was exceedingly trying and disagreeable in many ways. I met there no one of either high or low degree who did not immediately corner me and begin to discuss our shipment to the Allies of munitions, and sometimes their manner was almost offensive.[36]

On April 22, Wilson tried to talk Bryan into a mild note of protest regarding the death of Thrasher. He suggested they "raise in a very earnest, though of course entirely friendly, way the whole question of the use of submarines against merchant vessels," and "on these grounds, enter a very moderately worded but none the less solemn and emphatic protest against the whole thing. . . . My idea, as you will see, is to put the whole note on very high grounds,—not on the loss of this single man's life, but on the interests of mankind."[37]

Bryan was not impressed; he advised Wilson to seek mediation. Wilson began to back down to the point of avoidance: a week later he wrote that "perhaps it is not necessary to make formal representations in the matter at all."[38]

And then the *Lusitania* was sunk.

The RMS *Lusitania*, sister ship to the *Mauritania*, was one of the most magnificent passenger liners in the British Cunard Line. Her sinking on Friday, May 7, 1915, by the submarine U-20 only eleven miles off the coast of Ireland, resulted in the deaths of 1,198 people, 128 of them Americans. The ship had sunk in only eighteen minutes. This event, like Pearl Harbor and 9/11, would sear itself into the memories of millions, especially since the great liner went down only three years after the *Titanic*.

Alongside the final sailing notice for the *Lusitania* in several newspapers was an advisory notice from the German embassy in Washington, stating that

> travelers intending to embark on the Atlantic voyage are reminded that a state of war exists between Germany and her allies and Great Britain and her allies; that the zone of war includes the waters adjacent to the British Isles; that, in accordance with the formal notice given by the Imperial German Government, vessels flying the flag of Great Britain, or of any of her allies, are liable to destruction in those waters and that travelers sailing in the war zone on ships of Great Britain or her allies do so at their own risk.[39]

Before the *Lusitania* departed from New York, the collector of customs certified that she carried, along with her passengers, cargo including "180 cases of military goods; 1,271 cases of ammunition and . . . 4,200 cases of cartridges."[40]

After the news of the sinking reached America, a reporter from the Associated Press called Theodore Roosevelt on the telephone and asked for his reaction. Colonel Roosevelt, after hearing the details, said, "That's murder," and continued as follows: "This represents not merely piracy, but piracy on a vaster scale of murder than any old-time pirate ever practiced. This is the warfare which destroyed Louvain and Dinant, and hundreds of men, women and children in Belgium. It is warfare against innocents traveling on the ocean, and to our fellow countrywomen, who are among the sufferers. It seems inconceivable that we can refrain from taking action." Roosevelt's words were published in American newspapers the following day.[41]

After Wilson heard the news, he walked out of the White House (evading the Secret Service) and traveled the nocturnal streets of Washington. He stayed alone in his study for much of the weekend, issuing a statement on Saturday to the effect that he was considering the issue of how to respond.

On Monday he exchanged some notes with William Jennings Bryan but did not meet with the cabinet. Indeed, the only person with whom he met that day was a pretty widow named Edith Bolling Galt, with whom he had recently fallen in love.

On Monday evening he departed for Philadelphia to give a scheduled speech to an audience of four thousand newly naturalized citizens. In the course of this speech he extemporized and uttered words he would soon regret. "The example of America," he said, "must be the example, not merely of peace because it will not fight, but of peace because peace is the healing and elevating influence of the world, and strife is not. There is such a thing as a man being too proud to fight."[42]

Wilson knew that he had blundered, and he made the following statement at a press conference the next day: "I was not thinking of our policy in any particular matter yesterday. I was thinking wholly of the people I was addressing." He confessed in a rueful note to Edith that "I do not know just what I said at Philadelphia" because his mind was as much on her as on the *Lusitania* crisis.[43] In a subsequent note he wrote, "I did not know before I got up very clearly what I was going to say, nor remember what I had said when I sat down."[44] He tried to have the statement about being too proud to fight deleted from published versions of the speech a few months later.[45]

Theodore Roosevelt, like many other detractors of Wilson, was livid. To his son Archie, Roosevelt wrote that "the murder of the thousand men, women and children in the *Lusitania* is due, solely, to Wilson's cowardice and weakness."[46]

THESE THINGS WILL MOVE UPON THE WATERS

Woodrow Wilson was not the right person to lead the United States in this crisis. Whether his immediate predecessor, William Howard Taft, if reelected in 1912, might have done significantly better in a second term is a problematical question—unanswerable. So is the question of whether Theodore Roosevelt, had he made different choices in 1912—if he had managed to maintain cool self-possession instead of rashly challenging his own handpicked successor, dividing his party, delivering the election to Wilson, and then languishing in the political wilderness—might have been positioned to run for the presidency again in 1916, thus giving the United States leadership grounded in preparedness and *machtpolitik*.

We will never know.

As it was, Wilson's legalistic and reactive stance became untenable as his hopes to act as a mediator succumbed to the fortunes of war. Two days after the *Lusitania* sinking, House cabled Wilson as follows: "America has come to the parting of the ways, when she must determine whether she stands for civilized or uncivilized warfare. Think we can no longer remain neutral spectators."[47] Two days later House addressed the issue of preparedness: "If, unhappily, it is necessary to go to war I hope you will give the world an exhibition of American efficiency that will be a lesson for a century or more. It is generally believed throughout Europe that we are so unprepared and that it would take so long to put our resources into motion, that our entering would make but little difference. In the event of war we should accelerate the manufacture of munitions to such an extent that we could supply not only ourselves, but the Allies, and so quickly the world would be astounded."[48]

House ended his European mission on June 5, and Wilson's efforts to act as a mediator—including a direct conversation with the German ambassador on May 28—came to an end, at least for the season. It would thus be his task to try to formulate a strategy with little or nothing in the way of preparation except for legalistic thinking and moralistic posturing.

Former President Taft recommended breaking diplomatic relations with Germany.[49] Lansing and Bryan conferred regarding diplomatic alternatives, with Lansing offering options including a demand for an apology, reparations, and punishment of the submarine commander.[50] On May 11, the Navy League—a nonprofit organization that was founded in 1902 with the support of Theodore Roosevelt—called for a special session of Congress that would appropriate $500 million for naval expansion.

Wilson, who had drafted a note demanding a German disavowal of the sinking and reparations, called a cabinet meeting on May 11. Wilson's note—which alleged that he could not believe the German submarine commander was acting in accordance with orders—contended that "submarines cannot be used against merchantmen without an inevitable violation of many sacred principles of justice and humanity," and he expressed the confidence that Germany would "make reparation so far as reparation is possible."[51]

The cabinet meeting was difficult: Bryan accused other cabinet members of being unneutral.[52] On the following day, Bryan sent the president three successive letters proposing not only a protest of the Allied blockade but also a cooling-off period to avert a rush to war.[53] Wilson liked the latter idea, and he agreed to include it in a supplemental message to Germany, with a "tip" to the press expressing "confidence in Administration circles that Germany will respond to this note in a spirit of accommodation."[54]

But Lansing, behind Bryan's back, convinced other cabinet members, including Secretary of War Lindley M. Garrison and Postmaster General Albert Burleson, to talk Wilson out of the idea.[55] The first of several protest notes to Germany in response to the *Lusitania* sinking went out on May 13 with Bryan's grudging endorsement.

As Wilson awaited the German reply, he did his best to maintain his rhetorical theme of self-possession. Admirers, not least of all Edith Bolling Galt, encouraged him. Oswald Garrison Villard wrote to Wilson as follows: "If he who conquers his spirit is greater than he who taketh a city your achievement of self-restraint . . . must surely put you ahead of any of the generals in our history."[56] With encouragement like that, Wilson felt justified in defying such palpable militarists as Theodore Roosevelt.

A symbolic occasion was illustrative of Wilson's state of mind. On May 17, as the president reviewed some vessels of the Atlantic fleet as they lay at anchor off New York City, he attempted to imbue the might of the United States—such as it was—with his own ideals, and one surmises that his talk, with its oracular tone, and occasionally odd syntax, was extemporaneous:

> These quiet ships lying in the river have no suggestion of bluster about them, no intimation of aggression. They are commanded by men thoughtful of the duty of citizens. . . . When a crisis occurs in this country, gentlemen, it is as if you put your hand on the pulse of a dynamo; it is as if the things that you were in connection with were spiritually bred, as if you had nothing to do with them except, if you listen truly, to speak the things that you hear. These things now brood over the river; this spirit now moves with the men who represent the nation in the navy; these things will move upon the waters in the maneuvers— no threat lifted against any man, against any nation.[57]

In light of the Navy League's demand for a naval expansion program, Admiral George Dewey, the hero of Manila Bay in 1898, declared that the United States "should continue the wise policy of increasing the size of our navy [since] adequacy is not reached until the navy is strong enough to meet on equal terms the navy of the strongest possible adversary." In response to this, Wilson issued a tepid reply to the effect that "the country has every reason to wish to go forward in its policy of steadily adding to its strength and equipment."[58] Perhaps this was the moment when Wilson—belatedly— began to reconsider his opposition to preparedness measures.

Wilson, after exchanging a series of messages with House on the subject, was informed on May 25 that the German offer to cease submarine operations if Britain lifted the "food blockade" had been a ruse. House conveyed the following message from Ambassador Gerard in Berlin: "The proposition of permitting the passage of food [in return for] cessation of submarine methods already made and declined. If raw materials are added [matter] can perhaps be arranged. Germany in no need of food."[59]

On May 28, Wilson made an overture to Johann von Bernstorff, the German ambassador, on behalf of a mediated peace.[60] Yet the German reply to the *Lusitania* note, which arrived at the White House on May 31, was not acceptable: the German note attempted to justify the sinking of the ship. So Wilson solicited the views of Bryan and Lansing.

Bryan made another attempt to coax Wilson into getting American travelers out of harm's way: "The German Government pleads as one reason for the attack upon the *Lusitania* that it was carrying 5,400 cases of ammunition. . . . Would it not be advisable to reverse the rule by which passenger ships are permitted to carry ammunition?"[61]

On June 4, Wilson read a draft of a second protest to Germany at a cabinet meeting. Bryan once again accused his colleagues of being unneutral. On the same day, two Democratic leaders in Congress, Senator Thomas S. Martin, chairman of the Senate Appropriations Committee, and Representative Henry (Hal) De La Warr Flood, chairman of the House Foreign Affairs Committee, visited Bryan and declared their opposition to war. Bryan conveyed their sentiments to Wilson, following up with a letter in which he declared that three steps should be taken to prevent war with Germany: a policy of compulsory delay in the case of international disputes, a protest against the British blockade, and a policy of prohibiting passenger ships from carrying ammunition.[62]

Wilson rejected these proposals "with deep misgiving," since he feared that such proposals could not be made "without hopelessly weakening our protest."[63]

And so Bryan resigned.

Wilson considered several candidates to replace Bryan, including Colonel House, Lansing, and Secretary of Agriculture David F. Houston (a friend of House). In an earlier meeting with Houston and Treasury Secretary William Gibbs McAdoo, Wilson had mused that Lansing was unfit as a replacement for Bryan because "he was not a big enough man" and "did not have enough imagination."[64] But after House, who had just returned from Europe, convinced Wilson that "it would be better to have a man with not too many ideas of his own," Wilson decided to appoint Lansing.[65]

In John Milton Cooper's opinion, "this would be one of the worst appointments Wilson would ever make as president," since Lansing could be "furtive and underhanded." According to Cooper, "Wilson's treating him like a clerk for the next four years would understandably breed resentment and aggravate Lansing's inclinations to try to undermine the president."[66]

By the end, Lansing was able to return Wilson's cold insult—the assertion that Lansing "did not have enough imagination"—with a devastating counterassertion: that Wilson had too much imagination of the wrong kind, imagination that could override evidence and common sense: "With him [Wilson] it was a matter of conviction formed without weighing evidence," Lansing wrote in a 1921 reminiscence. "His judgments were always right in his own mind, because he knew that they were right. How did he know that they were right? Why he *knew* it and that was the best reason in the world. No other was necessary."[67]

Cruel and unfair as this was if it were taken as a generalization, it was all too true by the time that Lansing wrote the words.

BEWARE OF HERESIES

As the first anniversary of the outbreak of war approached, the fact could not be avoided, though Wilson's admirers celebrated it—Wilson had done next to nothing to prepare the country to fight. To be sure, his countrymen were deeply divided, and a widespread aversion to war was quite obvious, and understandable. The terrible casualties of this war, and the hideous combat conditions, including the use of poison gas, made it natural for millions to hope that the United States could stay out. And the longer Wilson could prolong his improvisational tactics, the more American lives would be spared. Moreover, Wilson's party was overwhelmingly insistent on peace.

All true, but the fact remained that if every effort of Wilson to avoid war should fail, the weakness of America's army and navy would limit the extent to which America could affect not only the war but also the postwar settlement. In the short run, the country's weakness would make Wilson's bargaining position weak; when he had warned in February that his policy of "strict accountability" would be enforced by "any steps it might be necessary to take to safeguard American lives," the threat rang hollow, as House would acknowledge after the *Lusitania* sinking.

In June, the National Security League—an influential preparedness group that was created in December 1914—held a huge convention in New York attended by public officials, including some governors, from twenty-five states. The theme of the convention was preparedness.

Wilson at last came out of avoidance: on July 21, 1915, he asked Secretary of War Lindley Garrison and Secretary of the Navy Josephus Daniels for preparedness recommendations.[68] A public announcement on the same date marked this policy reversal. The announcement stated, in part, that

> the best minds of the various departments of the Government, both of the Army and of the Navy, are now and have been at work on these important matters for sometime [*sic*]. . . . [The president] is seeking advice from the men in those departments who have been most directly in touch with the new conditions of defense that have been evolved out of modern experience. He not only wishes advice from those who have a knowledge of actual modern conditions of warfare, but he is seeking light from those who are able to understand and comprehend the altered conditions of land and naval warfare.[69]

Time would eventually reveal the inadequacy of this planning. But even the inadequate measures that emerged from this exercise would face significant opposition from figures in Wilson's party, especially William Jennings Bryan. For that reason, bipartisan efforts on Wilson's part might have been helpful from the outset, not least for the dividends that they could have conferred in the electoral politics of 1916. Even at this point, one is tempted to imagine, Wilson might have found some ways to cultivate Theodore

Roosevelt—not to win him over completely, of course, but to soften his indignation and to draw upon his undeniable experience in military planning. As events in 1917 would show, the volatile Roosevelt was willing to let bygones be bygones with Wilson in order to play a major role in the war.

But bipartisan strategy would seldom be significant in Wilson's thinking—except as a rhetorical gesture when he issued calls for unity or else as a tactic of last resort.[70] Here, as elsewhere, the deficiencies in Wilson's performance would guide his Democratic successor Franklin Delano Roosevelt, who sought and received maximum advantage from bipartisan strategy before and during World War II.

An early indication of Wilson's aversion to bipartisanship was his reaction to a temporary training camp set up at the U.S. Army post at Plattsburgh, New York. At this camp, from August 9 to September 13, 1915, 1,200 men—mostly business and professional men who might constitute a supplemental officer corps in the event of a short-term war emergency—received training in drill and field maneuvers. The experiment was largely the work of General Leonard Wood, the former army chief of staff who was also a friend of Theodore Roosevelt.[71]

With the approval of Secretary of War Garrison, Wood (while still chief of staff) had launched the idea of summer training camps for civilians as early as 1913. By 1915, the program was politicized and Wood had been replaced as chief of staff. In a letter to Edith Bolling Galt, Wilson wrote that "I shall have an interesting tale to tell you about Plattsburg [sic] (a Wood-Roosevelt affair in which we spiked their guns). . . . I ought not to go because a speech on preparedness would be expected of me which Wood and his like would try to use to show that (in another sense) they had 'taken me into camp.'"[72]

Though the action of Wilson on preparedness was belated—"behind the curve," as we might say—it was probably a sign of Wilson's fear that his short-term luck might be running out in the summer of 1915.

On June 6, the German government had quietly ordered submarine commanders to spare large passenger liners.[73] On July 8, the Germans responded to the second *Lusitania* note; while the response was still unsatisfactory, its tone was more conciliatory. Nonetheless, Wilson's third *Lusitania* note of July 21 told the Germans that continued submarine warfare resulting in American deaths would be regarded as an "unfriendly act"—that is to say, an act that bordered on war.[74]

A crisis with Britain came and went in midsummer as cotton growers in the South began to fear that the British might not continue to support the price of the staple. Wilson warned the British, who secretly bought enough Southern cotton to keep the price high, notwithstanding the cutoff of American cotton to the German market by the British blockade.[75]

On August 19, a German submarine sank the White Star liner SS *Arabic*, with the loss of two American lives.[76] Wilson told Edith that the sinking might mean "something very serious for this dear country we love."[77] When she quoted him some pacifistic lines from an Albany newspaper editorial, he wrote to her as follows:

> You came very near being corrupted there, young lady, by *Bryanism*! The opinions you quote from an Albany paper about the loss of American lives on the *Arabic* are rank Bryanism. . . . Beware of heresies! It may very well be that this Bryan and Albany doctrine is the more reasonable and practical one, my precious Sweetheart, but it is not the doctrine of international law, and we must base our claims of right on the undoubted practice of nations,—for which Germany is showing such crass and brutal contempt. The road is hard to travel, but it lies plain before us [original emphasis].[78]

But the road was not "plain" for Wilson, whose sense of desperation was clear as he requested the views of House on August 21: "I greatly need your advice what to *do* in view of the sinking of the *Arabic*, if it turns out to be the simple case it seems. I know that Lansing will be as desirous as I am to learn what you are thinking. Two things are plain to me: 1. The people of this country count on me to keep them out of the war. 2. It would be a calamity to the world at large if we should be drawn actively into the conflict and so deprived of all disinterested influence over the settlement [original emphasis]."[79]

Wilson's friend and secretary Joseph Patrick Tumulty recommended severing diplomatic relations with Germany.[80] And House came very close to concurring:

> Our people do not want war, but even less do they want you to recede from the position you have taken. . . . Further notes would disappoint our own people and would cause something of derision abroad. In view of what has been said, and in view of what has been done, it is clearly up to this Government to act. The question is, when and how? To send Bernstorff home and to recall Gerard would be the first act of war, for we would be without means of communication with one another and it would not be long before some act was committed that would force the issue. If you do not send Bernstorff home and if you do not recall Gerard, then Congress should be called to meet the emergency and assume the responsibility. This would be a dangerous move because there is no telling what Congress would do in the circumstances. . . . It is an unhappy position, but it might as well be faced.[81]

Wilson was soon to be saved by a stroke of good luck: the position of the Germans began to soften. Bernstorff gave a hint of this change in a letter to House, in which he confided, "I know now that we will certainly make concessions [but] before I can do anything in this matter, I must be able to give my people at home some proof that President Wilson wishes to give us a square deal."[82] On August 24, Bernstorff sent a telegram to Lansing stating that "in case Americans should actually have lost their life this would naturally be contrary to the intention of the German Government who would deeply regret this fact."[83]

Meanwhile, Lansing's thoughts were turning to the possible long-term advantages of entering the war on the side of the Allies. On August 24 he warned the president that "we are losing the friendship of both parties." The United States would "have little influence upon either in . . . moulding [*sic*] the terms of peace." For that reason, Lansing was inclined to disengage with the Germans and support the Allies instead:

> Now, on the assumption that we sever diplomatic intercourse with the German Government, which responds by a declaration of war, the consequences internationally would seem to be the complete restoration of friendship and confidence with the Allies and the necessary recognition of the United States as a party to the peace negotiations. We would be in a position to influence the Allies, if they should be victorious, to be lenient in their demands and to regain a part of the good will of Germany by being a generous enemy. If, on the other hand, Germany should triumph, we would be included in any settlement made, and Germany would be deprived of the free hand she would otherwise have in dealing with us after she had overcome her European adversaries.[84]

However far-fetched the latter part of this scenario was—or was not—this exercise in contingency thinking depended, like all such thinking, on the efficacy of an American mobilization.

On August 25, the German chancellor, Bethmann-Hollweg, declared that if the submarine commander exceeded his instructions, then Germany would give the United States full satisfaction.[85] The next day, August 26, in a conference at Pless Castle, the kaiser supported his chancellor.[86] Wilson wrote to Edith that day to the effect that "the German authorities are *very* anxious to effect an amicable settlement with us [original emphasis]."[87]

Sensing the advantage, Lansing pressed Bernstorff, telling him that "to advance any excuse of mistake by the submarine commander would be absurd and would irritate rather than relieve the situation."[88] Bernstorff worked up a cable to be sent to Berlin, and both Lansing and Wilson revised the draft of this message.

The Germans were obviously backing down for reasons of their own. House suggested that "it is now time to show a disposition to meet Germany half way. It may be their intention to create differences between America and England, and probably is, nevertheless if I were you," he told Wilson, "I would adopt a distinctly more cordial tone towards them."[89]

Wilson agreed that "it certainly does look as if a way were opened out of our difficulties, so far as Germany is concerned." But he went on: "That only makes more perplexing our question as to how to deal with England, for apparently we have no choice now but to demand that she respect our rights a good deal better than she has been doing." He continued: "Bernstorff is now demanding of us, in a note from his government, that we insist on Germany's getting our cotton 'for the use of her civilian population.' Germany has at last come to her senses and is playing intelligent politics. She is seeking to put us, and is likely to succeed in putting us, into a position where we shall have to play to some extent the role of catspaw for her in opening trade to her."[90]

Is it fanciful to behold in this statement something strange: that Wilson's previous mood of desperation in regard to being "caught in the middle" now seemed to be yielding to a mood of almost mischievous amusement?

On September 1, Bernstorff made the so-called *Arabic* pledge: that "liners will not be sunk by our submarines without warning and without safety of the lives of noncombatants, provided that the liners do not try to escape or offer resistance."[91] The submarine threat began to recede. House congratulated Wilson regarding the "great diplomatic triumph in your negociations [*sic*] with Germany. . . . There will be nothing in history to compare with it."[92]

Wilson had by no means abandoned his hope to act as a mediator. In late June, when House mentioned the possibility of a third mission to Europe, Wilson replied, "That is a matter for you to determine. I want you to go whenever you consider the time propitious."[93] But Wilson revealed some very interesting thoughts about House to his sweetheart, Edith.

Edith was naturally intoxicated by her new romantic situation. She began to play unwholesome games: like House, she used flattery to influence Wilson for the purpose of reveling in the thrill of making history. She began to see House as a competitor. And she began to experiment with the following sorts of tactics in a letter to Wilson in August:

> I hope if Col. House comes to Washington . . . I will see him. I know I am wrong but I can't help feeling he is not a very *strong* character. I suppose it is in comparison to you, for really every other man seems like a dwarf when I put them by you in my thoughts. I know what a comfort and staff Col. House is to you Precious One and that your judgment about him is correct, but he does look like a weak vessel. . . . This is perfectly unnecessary for me to tell this but it is such fun to shock you and you are so sweet in your judgments of people and I am so radical. Never mind I always acknowledge my mistakes and take a secret joy in finding you right and stronger than I am in every way [original emphasis].[94]

Wilson sent her this revealing reply:

> About [House] . . . you are no doubt partly right. You have too keen an insight and too discerning a judgment to be wholly wrong, even in a snap judgment of a man you do not know! House *has* a strong character,—if to be disinterested and unafraid and incorruptible is to be strong. He has a noble and lovely

character, too, for he is capable of utter self-forgetfulness and loyalty and devotion. And he is wise. . . . But you are right in thinking that intellectually he is not a great man. His mind is not of the first class. He is a counselor, not a statesman. And he has the faults of his qualities. His very devotion to me, his ardent desire that I should play the part in the field of international politics that he has desired and foreseen for me, makes him take sometimes the short and personal view when he ought to be taking the big and impersonal one— thinking, not of my reputation for the day, but of what is fundamentally and eternally right. [95]

The paradox of Christian ethics had returned, unbeknownst to Wilson: the conundrum of becoming too proud of one's own humility. In the guise of humility—as he praised the "self-forgetfulness" of House while dismissing his excessive "devotion" to Wilson's own career (the "personal view")— Wilson seemed to be telling Edith (and himself) that *he*, as opposed to all lesser men like House, could think only of the things that are "fundamentally and eternally right." He was preening himself on his power to transcend the ego.

Wilson's notion that he had the power to rid himself of egotism was— ironically—a form of unconscious conceit. It was egotism rendered more pernicious by the fact that it was turned upside-down. Wilson seemed to be oblivious to this.

Writing Edith again the next day, he confided that "I see very few people, you know, and there is no one about me just now who really interests me out of business hours." [96] Wilson was becoming more solitary. He seemed to be increasingly swayed by the thought that only one great American could measure his steps by the categorical imperative of Kant, only one great statesman could heed the great standards that are true for every place and every time—regardless of the messy details of the present.

Only one.

THE PRESIDENT'S PURPOSE IS TO INTERVENE

In the aftermath of the *Arabic* pledge, congratulations poured into the White House.

Here are some examples:

- Navy Secretary Josephus Daniels: "I must tell you of my happiness in the complete vindication of your policy with reference to Germany. . . . It makes me happy to be associated with you in these epoch-making times." [97]
- Herbert Hoover: "I should like to convey to you on behalf of myself and all my colleagues in this Commission the sincere gratitude which we feel

to you over the success of the German negotiations. We are certain, from intimate contact in Germany, that this has only been accomplished with the extraordinary appeal which you formulated to justice and humanitarian sentiment in Germany as well as the firmness you displayed, and that in any less able hands this situation would have drifted us into the appalling result of war."[98]

- Oswald Garrison Villard: "I could not refrain from telegraphing you yesterday to express to you even slightly my deep feeling of gratitude as an individual citizen, and more than that, my profound satisfaction as friend, that my certain faith, beginning with the *Lusitania* episode, that you would find a way out in peace, was justified. And now I am praying with all my heart that you will set your face against any surrender to the advocates of militarism. . . . I trust that you will deem it wise . . . to postpone any recommendations as to preparation for war until the war in Europe is over."[99]

The last of these congratulations was fraught with menace, for Wilson's policy reversal on preparedness was irrevocable, and a brawl within the Democratic Party was imminent. Moreover, notwithstanding the *Arabic* pledge, there were still significant tensions in German-American relations.

As to preparedness, Daniels and Garrison referred the directives of Wilson to, respectively, the General Board of the Navy (an advisory body established in 1900) and the Army War College. The recommendations that emerged by October were, in the aggregate, impressive. The navy recommended a long-term buildup consisting of a shipbuilding program designed to produce, by 1925, ten battleships, six battle cruisers, ten cruisers, fifty destroyers, and one hundred submarines. The goal was to equal the size of the Royal Navy, and the cost was $500 million—precisely the amount that was demanded by the Navy League. The army recommendation included, in addition to significant increases in the regular army, the scrapping of the National Guard and its replacement by a four-hundred-thousand-man "continental army."[100]

As to relations with Germany, the *Arabic* pledge was a definite relief, and yet Lansing and Wilson were seeking not only a promise in regard to the future behavior of Germany but also *reparations*, for both the *Arabic* sinking and the *Lusitania* sinking. Furthermore, tremendous bad feelings had been caused by the discovery of a German "propaganda machine" in the United States. German privy counselor Heinrich Albert lost a briefcase containing secret documents in regard to German propaganda in New York City, and the briefcase fell into the hands of the U.S. Secret Service. Wilson released the documents to the New York *World*; the articles, which ran from August 15 to August 23, caused widespread outrage.[101]

In July, Lansing was informed by American agents that a German espionage and provocation network, headed by Franz Rintelen von Kleist, was active in America. Among its projects were the development of schemes to interfere with American munitions exports to Britain and to worsen the tense relationship between the United States and Mexico to the point of war. [102] On August 4, Wilson wrote that America was "honeycombed with German intrigue and infested with German spies." [103] At the end of the month, he told Edith that "there might be an armed uprising of German sympathizers," though he admitted that the fear was "very slightly founded." [104]

These fears would later erupt into the massive wartime campaigns against the civil liberties of German Americans. At the end of the year, Lansing demanded the recall of Franz von Papen and Karl Boy-Ed, respectively German military and naval attaches, on charges of espionage.

It was against this background that Lansing continued to pursue the submarine issue in relation to the *Arabic* and *Lusitania* sinkings. In the case of the *Arabic*, the Germans tried to claim that the ship had been menacing the submarine; Lansing feared that this response might require a severing of diplomatic relations. [105] Wilson wrote that the German position was "ominous of the worst." [106] By September 22, with the Germans still averse to an open disavowal, Wilson told House that "he had never been sure that we ought not to take part in the conflict and if it seemed evident that Germany and her militaristic ideas were to win, the obligation upon us was greater than ever." [107] By September 26, the Germans were willing to submit the case to arbitration and accept the principle of indemnity. At last, on October 5, Bernstorff delivered a letter that disavowed the sinking and agreed to reparations. [108] But the case of the *Lusitania* had not been resolved. [109]

As the *Lusitania* case dragged out, Lansing—reverting to his earlier mood of even-handed legalism—opened up a new front with the *British* in the controversies over submarine warfare. On September 12, he had written to Wilson recommending a new policy regarding British deck guns:

> We have for several days held at Norfolk a British merchant vessel "Waimana" because she had on board a mounted 4.7 gun, endeavoring to have the British Admiralty direct its removal before the vessel left our port. We are now advised that the British Admiralty declines to remove the gun and asserts, correctly, that the vessel has complied with our declaration of September 19, 1914, as to armed merchant vessels. Up to the present time the British Admiralty as a result of an informal understanding have kept guns off British merchant vessels entering American ports. . . . Meanwhile submarine warfare has developed as a practical method of interrupting merchant vessels. At the time we issued the declaration . . . this use of the submarine as a commerce destroyer was unknown. . . . I feel in my own mind that these changed conditions require a new declaration because an armament, which under previous condi-

tions, was clearly defensive, may now be employed for offensive operations against so small and unarmored a craft as a submarine.[110]

Lansing's new position on the use of deck guns would have consequences in 1916. Wilson took Lansing's arguments seriously: on October 4, he wrote to House that "it is hardly fair to ask Submarine commanders to give warning by summons if, when they approach as near as they must for that purpose they are to be fired upon. . . . It is a question of many sides and is giving Lansing and me some perplexed moments."[111]

Simultaneously, Wilson's love life was coming to a crisis. In the 1910s, it was unconventional to marry again so soon after the death of a spouse. But Wilson and Edith were desperate. To make matters more nerve-wracking, a rumor was circulating to the effect that some letters that Wilson had foolishly sent years earlier to Mary Hulbert, with whom he apparently had an affair—or with whom he came close to having an affair—were about to be leaked. Wilson wrote an agonized confession, then visited Edith and revealed his old indiscretion.[112]

Edith was forgiving, Wilson was jubilant, and then, as they prepared to announce their engagement (it was announced on October 6), their exultation could not be restrained. By several accounts, Wilson's amorous euphoria was such that he literally danced as he walked and sang aloud the words to the hit song "Oh, You Beautiful Doll."[113]

Two days after the engagement was announced, House met with Wilson in New York and proposed an audacious plan. His proposal to Wilson was recounted in his diary this way:

> I outlined very briefly a plan which has occurred to me and which seems of much value. I thought we had lost our opportunity to break with Germany, and it looked as if she had a better chance than ever of winning, and if she did win, our turn would come next, and we were not only unprepared but there would be no one to help us stand the first shock. Therefore, we should do something decisive now—something that would either end the war in a way to abolish militarism or that would bring us in with the Allies to help them do it. My suggestion is to ask the Allies, unofficially, to let me know whether or not it would be agreeable to them to have us demand that hostilities cease. . . . If the Allies understood our purpose, we could be as severe in our language concerning them as we were with the Central Powers[;] the Allies, after some hesitation, could accept our offer or demand, and if the Central Powers accepted, we would then have accomplished a master stroke in diplomacy. If the Central Powers refused to acquiesce, we could then push our insistence to a point where diplomatic relations would first be broken off, and later the whole force of our Government, and perhaps the force of every neutral, might be brought against them. The President was startled by this plan. He seemed to acquiesce by silence.[114]

What House was proposing was a secret arrangement with the Allies, whereby Wilson would demand an end to the war on the basis of a visionary peace. If both sides accepted, then Wilson would have ended the war. If the Allies accepted, they would know—through a secret understanding—that refusal by the Central Powers would unleash "the whole force" of America.

Surely House was aware that he was bringing this idea to Wilson at a moment when he floated in erotic euphoria. Wilson liked the idea—very much.

This would lead to the final phase of House's "Great Adventure" and the short-lived House-Grey agreement. In actuality, much of the scheme had been suggested to House beforehand by Grey on September 22.[115] The essentials, indeed, had been sketched by Grey even earlier than that, in July.[116]

Together, Wilson and House worked up a draft of a letter that House would send to Grey. This scenario—it was almost a theatrical script—required House to pretend for the record, with the knowledge of Grey, that Wilson knew nothing of the plan. But it was actually part of the plan to brief Wilson in advance and then proceed with the president's knowledge. It was all a maneuver to create the public illusion of spontaneity. Only careful review of the multiple deceptions can reveal the scheme in its totality.

After Wilson had been briefed, House wrote the following pseudospontaneous message to Grey:

> It has occurred to me that the time may soon come when this Government should intervene between the belligerents and demand that peace parlays begin upon the broad basis of the elimination of militarism and navalism. I would not want to suggest this to the President until I knew in advance that it would meet the approval of the Allies. This approval, of course, would have to be confidential and known only to me. . . . What I want you to know is that whenever you consider the time is propitious for this intervention I will propose it to the President. He may then desire me to go to Europe. . . . It is in my mind that after conferring with your Government, I should proceed to Berlin and tell them that the President's purpose is to intervene and stop this destructive war, provided the weight of the United States thrown on the side that accepted our proposal could do it. I would not let Berlin know of course of any understanding had with the Allies. . . . If the Central Powers were still obdurate, it would *probably* be necessary for us to join the Allies and force the issue.[117]

Wilson approved this draft on October 18, and House sent it to Grey. On November 9, Grey replied, requesting a clarification of the passage on "elimination of militarism and navalism" and asking whether it related to the "fourth paragraph of letter to you of September 22nd."[118] This maneuver appears to have been part of the prearranged script: by back-referencing a letter of his own, Grey positioned House to reply in the affirmative, as House proceeded to do. Paragraph 4 of Grey's September 22 letter had stated, in part:

> To me, the great object of securing the elimination of militarism and navalism is to get security for the future against aggressive war. How much are the United States prepared to do in this direction? Would the President propose that there should be a League of Nations binding themselves to side against any Power which broke a Treaty . . . or which refused, in case of dispute, to adopt some other method of settlement than that of war?[119]

In the course of these maneuvers, House flattered Wilson, as usual: "This is the part I think you are destined to play in this world tragedy, and it is the noblest part that has ever come to a son of man. This country will follow you along such a path, no matter what the cost may be."[120]

But the House-Grey scheme bogged down because of changes in British politics. In mid-November, House received a letter from Grey that was dated November 11. Grey appears to have been changing the script—or changing its use—as his political base began to weaken, for the tone of his letter was discouraging. He wrote, in part, that

> if I were to approach the Allies, or even the Cabinet, about the elimination of militarism and navalism, they would ask what was meant by it; and I should have to put some definite proposal before them. That is why I cabled to ask exactly what you meant. I do not see how they could commit themselves in advance to any proposition without knowing exactly what it was, and know that the United States of America were prepared to intervene and make it good if they accepted it. The position at present is this: France and Russia and this country have made up their minds to a winter campaign. . . . I see two possibilities: One is that the President should let it be known that he is prepared to mediate, and that, if either side desires it, he will state the conditions on which he will do so. The other is that he should wait until he gets an intimation from one side or the other that mediation would be acceptable. . . . I wish you were here, so that I could talk things over; but the situation at the moment and the feelings here and among the Allies, and in Germany so far as I know, do not justify me in urging you to come on the ground that your presence would have any practical result at the moment.[121]

House transmitted this letter to Wilson on November 25.[122] A few days later they conferred, and Wilson urged House to go ahead with his trip to Europe. Mere letters, Wilson said, were not important; indeed, "he would very much prefer not putting our thoughts and intentions into writing. He would rather have them conveyed by word of mouth."[123]

By the end of the year, House was given his commission to embark; on December 24, Wilson authorized him to go to London and Berlin to discuss new peace negotiations with the object of future guarantees of world peace to be based on "(a) military and naval disarmament and (b) a league of nations to secure each nation against aggression and maintain the absolute freedom of the seas. If either party to the present war will let us say to the other that they are willing to discuss peace on such terms, it will clearly be our duty to use our utmost moral force to oblige the other to parley, and I do not see how they could stand in the opinion of the world if they refused."[124]

THE YOUTH AND FIRST CONSCIOUSNESS OF OUR POWER

On November 4, Wilson introduced his preparedness proposals in a speech at the Manhattan Club in New York. He presented the idea of the "continental army" as a supplementation of—rather than a replacement for—the National Guard, and he minimized the impact of its activities: "It [the proposal] calls for the training within the next three years of a force of 400,000 citizen soldiers to be raised in annual contingents of 133,000, who would be asked to enlist for three years. . . . During their three years of enlistment [they] would not be organized as a standing force but would be expected merely to undergo intensive training for a very brief period of each year."

Surely Wilson knew that even this proposal would elicit resistance from many antiwar Democrats. With his naval proposals he decided to be more bold—and frank—in his rhetoric, observing that "part of our problem is the problem of what I may call the mobilization of the resources of the nation at the proper time if it should ever be necessary to mobilize them for national defense." But he did not address the fact that the shipbuilding program was designed to be extended over years, without a short-term plan for fast tracking. Indeed, he did not spell out the full scope of this shipbuilding program at all in his Manhattan Club speech.

Here again, he sought to calm down the Bryanites as follows: "No thoughtful man feels any panic haste in this matter. The country is not threatened from any quarter. She stands in friendly relations with all the world." Only at the end did Wilson hint that the forces he intended to create might be used in bold ways, at least for leverage:

> Here is the nation God has builded by our hands. What shall we do with it? . . .
> We are yet only in the youth and first consciousness of our power. The day of our country's life is still but in its fresh morning. Let us lift our eyes to the great tracts of life yet to be conquered in the interests of a righteous peace. Come, let us renew our allegiance to America, conserve her strength in its purity, make her chief among those who serve mankind, self-reverenced, self-commanded, mistress of all forces of quiet counsel, strong above all others in good will and the might of invincible justice and right.[125]

Progressive Democrats of the pacifist persuasion were not won over; they began to see Wilson as a dupe of the militarists. Their antipathy was worsened by the foolish decision of Wilson's treasury secretary, William Gibbs McAdoo, to finance the military buildup by taxes that would hit the lower and middle classes harder than the rich.[126]

In his annual message to Congress, Wilson specified more of the details of his military buildup. The duration of the shipbuilding program had been speeded up with a target completion date of 1921 instead of 1925.[127] In the course of this message, he devoted a significant and vehement section to the issue of disloyalty and espionage. Some excerpts:

> I am sorry to say that the gravest threats against our national peace and safety have been uttered within our own borders. There are citizens of the United States, I blush to admit, born under other flags but welcomed under our generous naturalization laws . . . who have poured the poison of disloyalty into the very arteries of our national life, who have sought to bring the authority and good name of our Government into contempt, to destroy our industries wherever they thought it effective for their vindictive purposes to strike at them, and to debase our politics to the uses of foreign intrigue. . . . A little while ago such a thing would have seemed incredible. Because it was incredible we made no preparation for it. . . . But the ugly and incredible thing has actually come about and we are without adequate federal laws to deal with it. I urge you to enact such laws at the earliest possible moment. . . . Such creatures of passion, disloyalty, and anarchy must be crushed out.[128]

This outburst was aimed at American citizens of German background, and not primarily at the German nationals who were serving as agents of the German government. Whatever prompted this excess from someone who sought to exemplify cool self-possession—perhaps months of pent-up frustration and tension that were seeking a convenient outlet—it foreshadowed the later hysteria that would cause such gross violations of American civil liberties from 1917 through 1919. Wilson was beginning to reveal his worst, his most petulant, his most hypocritical side.

Furthermore, his indignation at espionage (as opposed to sabotage) was ill advised, since his own grasp of international power realities would have been better if the United States had had an adequate capability for intelligence gathering. (The existing Office of Naval Intelligence and Army Military Intelligence Division had both shrunk due to budget cuts since the Spanish-American War, and the State Department did not begin to do effective intelligence gathering until 1916.)

As the coming presidential election year dawned, Wilson faced a bitter fight within his party to create sufficient military force to make his efforts to intervene in the international politics of World War I effective. And even if he won the preparedness fight, his proposals were behind the flow of events: proposals that could only evolve into a well-trained, well-supplied fighting force after years of development.

There were times when this occurred to Wilson: he mused to House on December 15 that since it "would take too long for us to get into a state of preparedness" it would be a "useless sacrifice on our part to go in."[129]

But Wilson was in one respect a happy man: on December 18, he married Edith. And so, with this worshipful woman at his side, he prepared to seek a second term in office.

Chapter Three

1916

Wilson's troubles continued to accumulate in 1916 as he sought—and won—reelection. In the year before the United States entered the war, his long effort to act as a mediator succumbed to his own mistakes and the worsening events of the war itself. And though he won his fight on preparedness by the time that Congress adjourned, the task of planning an effective mobilization eluded him—as the events of 1917 would show.

And to his amazement, his standing presumption that America might have to join the Allies if his efforts to act as a mediator failed was reversed in a way that he had never foreseen: as Anglo-American relations worsened, a hitherto unthinkable scenario unfolded—a scenario in which the United States would actually support the Central Powers. By the end of the year, his relations with the British were bitter and his dealings with Germany were cordial. But the Germans were in many ways "using him."

He was being set up by the flow of events for a cataclysmic plunge into war.

HELL WILL BREAK LOOSE IN EUROPE

In 1916, the long stalemate on the western front continued. But the carnage increased to a monstrous degree as each side attempted, unsuccessfully, to break the deadlock.

In February, the Germans launched a massive attack against the French fortress of Verdun. This attack was planned by General Erich von Falkenhayn, who succeeded Moltke as chief of staff. Falkenhayn proposed to the kaiser a decisive stroke called Operation Judgment (Gericht), in which Germany would force an enormous battle of attrition in a narrow corner of the western front. The French commander was Philippe Pétain, and the French resistance gave Falkenhayn the battle of attrition he wanted. But the Germans were unable to prevail. By June, each side had lost about two hundred thousand men. The fighting continued through the end of the year, and the results cost Falkenhayn his command; he was replaced in August by Paul von Hindenburg.

In July, the new British commander, General Douglas Haig, launched a massive attack of his own: the battle of the Somme. After a weeklong bombardment of the German lines (with over a million shells), a huge Anglo-French attack was launched, but the German lines could not be broken. Haig, who was also oblivious (or at least hardened) to casualties, kept up the assault, as his troops got caught in barbed wire and were mowed down by machine-gun fire. Keegan has argued that Haig had few decent alternatives; the broadening and deepening of fronts put the action far beyond the view of commanders, and the absence of radio made it hard to coordinate waves of attack, to direct the artillery fire where the troops needed it, or even to understand what the troops were encountering in "real time." Telephonic communications were inadequate, since lines were frequently cut.[1]

By the end of July, the British and French had lost over 200,000 men; the Germans had lost 160,000. The battle continued into autumn, when the British introduced a new weapon: the army tank. But the Allies could still not prevail against the German lines. By November, each side had lost approximately six hundred thousand men. As Keegan remarks, "The holocaust of the Somme was subsumed for the French in that of Verdun. To the British, it was and would remain their greatest military tragedy of the twentieth century, indeed of their national military history. . . . The Somme marked the end of an age of vital optimism in British life."[2]

On May 31, the largest naval battle of the war—indeed the largest naval battle in all recorded history up to that time—took place as massive numbers of British and German warships engaged one another in the North Sea: the Battle of Jutland. As Keegan has written, "No sea had ever seen such a large concentration of ships or of ships so large, so fast and so heavily armored. . . . The spectacle they presented never left the memory of those who took part. . . . So large was the number of ships hurrying forward that the more distant formations blurred into the horizon or were lost to sight in the play of cloud and rain squall."[3] The British losses of ships and men were much greater than those of the Germans, but the British retained their control of the North Sea.

Elsewhere, the war was more fluid. In Mesopotamia the Turks defeated an Anglo-Indian force in April at Kut al-Amara, but the British recovered their position by the end of the year. The fighting on the Italian front intensified. Though Italian troops were unable to mount a successful invasion of Austria, the campaign drew enough Austrian troops away from the eastern front to facilitate a Russian success: under General Alexei Brusilov, the

Russians mounted an overwhelming attack against Austrian positions in the summer. Based upon this Russian success, Romania joined the Allies in August, but Bulgarian, Turkish, Austrian, and German forces defeated the Romanians.

As winter approached, the new German high command—generals Paul von Hindenburg and his operations chief, Erich Ludendorff—were leaning toward the fateful decision that they reached in the first week of 1917: to hold the line on the western front, push for absolute victory over Russia, and resume unrestricted submarine warfare.

The prospects for mediation were nil: Woodrow Wilson had been living in a dream world. As historian David Stevenson has written, "Each winter new strategic assessments were undertaken, and each summer new peace feelers were rejected; and as the casualty tolls mounted . . . it became harder to liquidate the conflict without commensurate gains to show for the sacrifice. As a contemporary caricaturist pointed out, the opposing leaders found themselves like so many Macbeths, 'in blood stept in so far that should I wade no more, returning were as tedious as go o'er.'"[4]

A GREAT OPPORTUNITY IS YOURS, MY FRIEND

In the first two months of 1916, Woodrow Wilson committed what Arthur S. Link called "one of the most maladroit blunders in American diplomatic history," one that revealed "the immaturity and inherent confusion of the President's policies."[5]

The blunder resulted from Wilson's failure to coordinate three simultaneous actions: (1) the latest consultations of Colonel House in Europe; (2) the ongoing negotiations with Germany on *Lusitania* reparations; and (3) new negotiations with Britain and Germany on the deck gun issue. Because of Wilson's inattention, the work of Lansing and House collided, embarrassing everyone, causing damage to America's credibility, and triggering a furor in Congress when Wilson was struggling to secure passage of his preparedness legislation.

House arrived in London on January 6. He met with Grey and Arthur Balfour, at that time head of the admiralty, discussing the outlines of the scenario that he and Grey had been working on. House asked Wilson for instructions as to "what to say in London and what to say in Berlin and how far I shall go."[6] House would go far—very far, as events turned out—because Wilson answered him as follows: "You ask me for instructions as to what attitude and tone you are to take at the several capitals. I feel that you do not need any."[7]

House sent Wilson a cautionary message from London, telling him that the thoughts of Grey and Balfour "run parallel with ours but I doubt their colleagues."[8] Then House met with David Lloyd George, who "agreed that the war could only be ended by your [Wilson's] intervention." Lloyd George advised that "intervention should not come until around the 1st of September [because] it will be apparent by then that no decisive victory can be had by either side."[9]

After spending two weeks in London, House traveled to Berlin, where, from January 26 to January 29, he advocated negotiations. But the chancellor, Bethmann-Hollweg, insisted on indemnities and control of Belgium and Poland. House wrote that he was "most unreasonable."[10] On February 2, House went to Paris, from where he predicted to Wilson—correctly—that "Hell will break loose in Europe this spring and summer as never before."[11]

Meanwhile, Lansing was active. On January 2, he sent Wilson a memorandum on the subject of deck guns, timely since a British ship that the Germans had recently sunk (SS *Persia*) had carried such a gun. Lansing recommended "a new statement setting forth the new conditions" of submarine warfare, specifically stating "the unreasonableness of requiring a submarine to run the danger of being almost certainly destroyed by giving warning to a vessel carrying an armament, and that, therefore, merchant vessels should refrain from mounting guns large enough to sink a submarine."[12] Lansing followed up with some text for the "new statement"—text that would serve as the announcement of a policy change—telling Wilson that "I think that I appreciate the German point of view" in this matter.[13] The statement proposed that "a merchant vessel . . . carrying an armament should be treated by a belligerent or neutral as an armed ship of the enemy."[14]

It bears noting that the antisubmarine tactics of the British involved the use of "Q-ships" by 1916. These were decoy ships designed to lure submarines to the surface. The ships were designed to look like easy targets, in the hope that the submarine commander would surface his craft and try to sink them with the submarine's own deck gun instead of wasting a torpedo from his limited supply. But the Q-ships carried guns of their own—hidden guns—that would blow the sub out of the water.[15]

On January 17, Lansing sent Wilson the draft of a letter to be sent to the British proposing a *modus vivendi* whereby a "reasonable and reciprocally just" arrangement would be imposed, to wit: "Submarines should be caused to adhere strictly to the rules of international law" and "merchant vessels of belligerent nationality should be prohibited and prevented from carrying any armament whatever."[16] Wilson told Lansing that "this draft has my entire approval" and directed him to send it.[17] Lansing sent it the very next day, just as House was preparing to travel from London to Berlin.

When Lansing's letter arrived in London, the effects were explosive. In a cable to Washington, Sir Edward Grey wrote that "I cannot adequately express the disappointment and dismay with which such an attitude on the part of the United States will be viewed here."[18]

Simultaneously, Lansing had been working on the issue of *Lusitania* reparations, but he had no success in eliciting a German admission of guilt. So Wilson and Lansing moved closer to a diplomatic rupture with Germany.[19] On January 24—just after his *modus vivendi* bombshell exploded in London—Lansing wrote to Wilson as follows:

> I received late Saturday night a letter from Count Bernstorff enclosing two drafts of memoranda on the *Lusitania* case. . . . Neither of the drafts seems to be at all satisfactory. There is no acknowledgement of the illegality of the sinking of the *Lusitania* and no admission of liability for the indemnity offered. . . . I am disposed to tell [Bernstorff] very frankly that further conversations will be useless. . . . Of course if we take this step and Germany fails to comply with our demands it will mean that we will have to send Bernstorff home or announce that we will do so unless full satisfaction is given within a definite time.[20]

It bears noting that as all of these events unfolded—House's departure from London, Lansing's transmission of the *modus vivendi* to London (unbeknownst to House), and Lansing's subsequent recommendation that relations with Germany might have to be severed—the president was getting ready for a hastily scheduled multi-city speaking tour on behalf of his preparedness program.

Wilson seemed to have very little aptitude for coordinating these efforts. It bears noting that House had sent Wilson a recommendation to avoid unnecessary friction with the British or the Germans in the short term.[21] Wilson took this advice (after making the mistake of letting Lansing send the *modus vivendi*) when he told the secretary of state to play for time on January 24.[22] But except for the venture of House, the legalistic posture of the president on international issues had been reducing his foreign policy to something very much like theater—to an ongoing series of *demonstrations* that his policies and postures were *correct* and the "right thing to do"—instead of *leverage* designed to be used in an overall strategic pattern.

Luckily for Wilson, the Germans were about to back down, as they had done the previous year. On February 4 Lansing forwarded a new memorandum that the Germans had sent, a memorandum that "comes so near to meeting our demands that I wish to study it with care to see if it cannot be considered acceptable." The memorandum stated that the German government "expresses profound regret that citizens of the United States suffered by the sinking of the *Lusitania* and assuming liability therefor offers to make reparation."[23]

Wilson agreed that this was sufficient. So the long diplomatic sparring match in regard to *Lusitania* reparations seemed to be over.

But it was not. And the deck gun controversy with Britain was just getting started.

Meanwhile, House had been meeting with the French premier, Aristide Briand, and the foreign minister, Jules Cambon, from February 2 through 8. According to Cambon, House stated that "inevitably America will enter the war, *before the end of the year*, and will align herself on the side of the Allies. However, for that to happen, it would be necessary for an incident to occur that would cause all the American people to rally behind the President." Cambon expressed "astonishment" as he listened to this rosy scenario, and he asked House to repeat the statement. "I had him repeat it," Cambon wrote, "and, after having noted it in English, I had him read it. He said to me, 'Exactly.'"[24]

House reported to Wilson the following agreement with the French: "In the event the Allies had some notable victories during the spring and summer, you would intervene, and in the event that the tide of war went against them, or remained stationary you would intervene." In other words—unless House had inadvertently omitted the crucial word *not* in the clause pertaining to the prospect of Allied victories—House seemed to be promising an intervention by Wilson regardless of circumstances. In closing, House told the president—characteristically—that "a great opportunity is yours, my friend, the greatest perhaps that has ever come to any man."[25]

It bears noting that Cambon recalled the conversation with House differently; according to Cambon, House stated that "if the Allies should have a little success, this spring or summer, the United States would intervene in favor of peace, but if they have a setback, the United States will intervene militarily and take part in the war against Germany."[26] If Cambon's account is correct, then House had promised something that no one—neither he nor Wilson nor anybody else—could have promised in February 1916: a declaration of war by Congress.

Back in London on February 9, House met with Grey and revisited the proposal on which the two of them had been working. Then, on February 14, House met with the entire British cabinet during a dinner at the home of Lord Reading. Throughout this round of meetings with the British, House had been bombarded with complaints about the implications of the *modus vivendi* proposal that Lansing had sent. That same day, House cabled Lansing and told him it was urgently necessary to table the proposal.[27]

House would soon get his way.

There were other good reasons for tabling the *modus vivendi*. On January 26, Lansing had made the mistake of sharing its contents with the Austrian chargé, Baron Erich Zwiedinek, on the condition that the information would remain confidential. Zwiedinek pounced at once: He told Lansing that the Germans and Austrians were thinking of resuming unrestricted submarine warfare against *armed* ships, and then he asked whether Lansing believed that such a course of action was advisable if the British refused to remove their deck guns. Lansing impulsively replied in the affirmative, and Zwiedi-nek shared this information with Berlin. [28]

And so on February 10, the Germans announced the resumption of unre-stricted submarine warfare on *armed* merchant vessels of the enemy. In light of this news, Wilson instructed Lansing to tell the Germans that the *Lusitania* deal was in jeopardy; the new German announcement, wrote Wilson, "inevi-tably throws doubt upon the whole future, and makes it necessary that we should think the situation out afresh." [29]

On the same day Wilson wrote House an almost pitiful plea on behalf of the *modus vivendi*: "Germany is seeking to find an excuse to throw off all restraints in under-sea warfare," he wrote. "If she is permitted to assume that English steamers are armed she will have found that excuse. If the English will disarm their merchant ships she will be without that excuse and the English will have made a capital stroke against her. We are amazed the English do not see this opportunity to gain a great advantage without losing anything." [30]

Wilson's letter fell on deaf ears. House had written him already that "there is great feeling against disarming merchantmen and I am glad you are holding this in abeyance." [31] House appeared to be taking it for granted that his cables would dissuade the president and Lansing from pursuing the *modus vivendi*. He was right. On February 15, Lansing told some newspaper reporters that, despite the new German policy, the administration would not insist on the disarming of merchantmen and would not warn Americans to refrain from traveling on such ships. [32]

As Link has summarized the situation, "It was no mere coincidence that the British leaders consented to the possibility of Wilson's mediation on the same day the President abandoned the ill-fated *modus vivendi*." [33]

But the British were understandably cautious. The members of the cabinet insisted on exploring many best-case and worst-case contingencies. Prime Minister Herbert Asquith asked House what Wilson would do if the Allies insisted on terms that the president considered unjust in the course of a peace conference. House replied that Wilson would probably withdraw from the conference and leave the participants to their own devices. [34]

On February 17, House and Grey drafted the document that came to be known as the "House-Grey agreement." Grey initialed the memorandum, which was written by him in the first person, on February 22, and House sailed for the United States bearing the document on February 25 and pre-sented it to Wilson on March 6. Grey was pointedly (and properly) circum-spect at the conclusion. Some excerpts:

> Colonel House told me that President Wilson was ready, on hearing from
> France and England that the moment was opportune, to propose that a confer-
> ence should be summoned to put an end to the war. Should the Allies accept

this proposal and should Germany refuse it, the United States would probably enter the war against Germany. . . . Colonel House expressed an opinion decidedly favourable to the restoration of Belgium, the transfer of Alsace and Lorraine to France, and the acquisition by Russia of an outlet to the sea. . . . I said I felt the statement, coming from the President of the United States, to be a matter of such importance that I must inform the Prime Minister and my Colleagues; but that I could say nothing until it had received their consideration. The British Government could, under no circumstances, accept or make any proposal except in consultation and agreement with the Allies.[35]

Within six months, this document—which House and Wilson considered so momentous—would become little more than a historical footnote, a worthless piece of paper.

I DO NOT DOUBT THAT I WILL CONTINUE TO SUCCEED

As House and Grey drafted their text, the fiasco of the *modus vivendi* led to more complications with the Germans. Their decision to claim, in effect, that they had gotten Lansing's verbal permission to turn their submarines loose against armed vessels ruined the *Lusitania* settlement. Lansing made this clear to Bernstorff on February 17.

Even worse, Lansing's remarks to the press, abandoning the *modus vivendi* while rejecting the idea that Americans should be warned against traveling on armed belligerent ships, caused an ugly revolt in Congress.

Opponents of Wilson's preparedness program smelled a rat. They took the missteps of Wilson and Lansing as a dastardly maneuver to sneak the United States into the war. So on February 21, Senate majority leader John Kern, along with Senate Foreign Relations Committee chairman William J. Stone and House Foreign Affairs Committee chairman Hal Flood, visited the White House. They asked Wilson what would happen if a German submarine sank an armed merchantman with American passengers. Wilson reiterated his standing position to hold the Germans to strict accountability. At that point, according to some accounts, Stone hammered on the president's desk and shouted, "Mr. President, would you draw a shutter over my eyes and my intellect? You have no right to ask me to follow such a course."[36] Two days later, Democratic members of the House Foreign Affairs Committee demanded action on a resolution introduced by Texas representative Atkins Jefferson McLemore to make it federal policy to warn American citizens against traveling on belligerent ships. On February 25, Senator Thomas P. Gore of Oklahoma introduced a comparable resolution in the Senate.

Wilson felt that he had to strike back hard. In an answer to a follow-up letter from Stone, he insisted that "I shall do everything in my power to keep the United States out of war. . . . I do not doubt that I will continue to succeed." He averred that the recent German announcement was "so manifestly inconsistent with explicit assurances recently given us by those powers . . . that I must believe that explanations will presently ensue which will put a different aspect upon it." Nonetheless, he insisted, "I cannot consent to any abridgement of the rights of American citizens in any respect. . . . Once accept a single abatement of right and many other humiliations would certainly follow, and the whole fine fabric of international law might crumble under our hands piece by piece."[37]

On February 25, at 9:00 a.m. (this would later be called the "sunrise conference"), Speaker of the House Champ Clark, House Majority Leader Claude Kitchin, and Chairman Hal Flood visited Wilson and told him that the McLemore resolution would pass two-to-one in the House if a vote were allowed to occur.[38]

With the assistance of Postmaster General Albert Burleson, Wilson used party discipline to force recalcitrant Democrats into line. William Jennings Bryan fought back hard against the administration. The showdowns came in the first week of March, when the Senate voted to table the Gore resolution on March 3 and the House voted down the McLemore resolution on March 7.

The next few weeks were dominated by events pertaining to Mexico, with which Wilson had been embroiled—for reasons too lengthy to summarize here—since 1914. Specifically, Pancho Villa conducted his across-the-border raid on Columbus, New Mexico.

And then, on March 24, the French channel steamer *Sussex* was attacked by a German submarine.

For a long time, a heated policy struggle had raged in Berlin regarding submarine tactics, with Chancellor Bethmann-Hollweg pleading for caution and the high command pushing for maximum use of submarines.[39] American policymakers, due to the limitations of American intelligence gathering, had little power to discern which way the crosscurrents in Berlin were flowing, except for the gossip that Ambassador Gerard passed along and occasional radio interceptions of German messages.[40] By contrast, a British intelligence operation (code-named "Room 40") had been routinely intercepting American diplomatic cables for months.[41] (One can only imagine what Wilson would have said if he had known about this when he condemned German espionage with such indignant passion in December 1915.)

As Wilson agonized over how to respond to the *Sussex* sinking, the members of his inner circle on foreign policy—Lansing, House, and his wife—urged him to be harsh. Lansing on March 27 wrote that "we can no longer temporize in the matter of submarine warfare. . . . The time for writing notes discussing the subject has passed." Lansing recommended severing relations with Germany unless the Germans paid an indemnity and agreed that submarine warfare "will cease."[42] On April 6 he discarded the idea of an indemnity; in a draft message for the purpose of severing relations, Lansing wrote that "no apology, no disavowal, no admission of wrongdoing, no punishment of a guilty officer, and no payment of indemnity will satisfy the Government of the United States."[43] House also urged severing relations, while hoping that Wilson might still be able to initiate a peace conference under such conditions.[44]

On April 10 Wilson drafted a protest note that merely *threatened* to sever relations unless Germany abandoned the methods of submarine warfare that jeopardized American lives.[45] House and Mrs. Wilson made suggestions for revising the note, and Wilson agreed to delete a sentence that would have given the Germans a chance to reply.[46] Lansing poured out his disappointment that the president was issuing a threat instead of breaking off relations until such time as the Germans did what the United States demanded.[47]

Wilson sent the redrafted *Sussex* note to Germany on April 18.[48] On the following day, he delivered an address to a joint session of Congress reiterating much of the rhetoric contained within the note. "What this Government foresaw must happen has happened," he intoned. "Tragedy has followed tragedy on the seas in such fashion . . . as to make it grossly evident that warfare of such a sort, if warfare it be, cannot be carried on without the most palpable violation of the dictates alike of right and of humanity." He went on: "I have deemed it my duty, therefore, to say . . . that unless the Imperial German Government should now immediately declare and effect an abandonment of its present methods of warfare against passenger and freight carrying vessels this Government can have no choice but to sever diplomatic relations with the Government of the German Empire."[49]

Wilson again got lucky: German naval authorities decided to support Bethmann-Hollweg and recommended that Germany should accede to Wilson's ultimatum. Their reasoning was strategic: resumption of unrestricted submarine warfare would be better deferred until a time when that decision would work to the maximum advantage of Germany.[50]

On May 4, Germany issued what would soon become known as the "*Sussex* pledge": a pledge to forswear further unrestricted submarine attacks, so long as the British were required to make comparable concessions. In other words, the Germans left themselves flexibility in the long run while performing a tactical retreat in the short run. The note declared, in part, that

> The German Government . . . notifies the United States that the German naval forces have received the following orders: In accordance with the general principles of visit and search and destruction of merchant vessels recognized by international law, such vessels . . . shall not be sunk without warning and without saving human lives, unless these ships attempt to escape or offer resistance. But neutrals cannot expect that Germany, forced to fight for her existence, shall, for the sake of neutral interest, restrict the use of an effective weapon if her enemy is permitted to continue to apply at will methods of warfare violating the rules of international law. . . . Accordingly the German

Government is confident that . . . the United States will now demand and insist that the British Government shall forthwith observe the rules of international law universally recognized before the war. . . . Should the steps taken by the Government of the United States not attain the object it desires . . . the German Government would then be facing a new situation, in which it must reserve itself complete liberty of decision.[51]

Wilson chose to disregard this caveat in his response, which he sent on May 8. He wrote that

the Government of the United States notifies the Imperial Government that it cannot for a moment entertain, much less discuss, a suggestion that respect by German naval authorities for the rights of citizens of the United States upon the high seas should in any way or in the slightest degree be made contingent upon the conduct of any other Government. . . . Responsibility in such matters is single, not joint; absolute, not relative.[52]

Absolute, not relative. Wilson once again seemed to be slipping into his old oracular mode—the very mode in which he had written to Edith in the previous year about the principles that are "fundamentally and eternally right." Perhaps buoyed by a sense of destiny ("I do not doubt that I will continue to succeed"), a mood that House and other flatterers had worsened, the Christian moralist was hammering down all the pride-based calculations that distracted individuals and nations from the principles that rose above strategic interests. If this conclusion seems to be fanciful, consider a series of statements that Wilson had been making during roughly the same period in which he responded to the *Sussex* pledge.

On April 13, at a Jefferson Day address to a Democratic Party organization—the Common Counsel Club—Wilson posed as a figure who transcended egotism, party politics, national self-interest, or any other selfish consideration. Some excerpts:

Frankly, gentlemen, I am not interested in personal ambitions. May I not admit, even in this company, that I am not enthusiastic over mere party success? I like to see men, generations strong, take fire of great progressive ideas and, banding themselves together like a body of thoughtful brothers, put their shoulders together and lift some part of the great load that has depressed humanity. . . . Gentlemen, are you ready for the test? God forbid that we should ever become directly or indirectly embroiled in quarrels not of our own choosing and that do not affect what we feel responsible to defend. But if we should ever be drawn in, are you ready to go in only where the interests of America are coincident with the interests of mankind and to draw out the moment the interest centers in America and is narrowed from the wide circle of humanity?[53]

Wilson seemed to be saying that America should *not* defend its own national interest unless it were "coincident" with the interests of all mankind. Such a proposition would go down hard among people such as Theodore Roosevelt and Henry Cabot Lodge.

On April 17, in an address to the Daughters of the American Revolution, Wilson preached that "America will have forgotten her traditions whenever, upon any occasion, she fights merely for herself under such circumstances as will show that she has forgotten to fight for all mankind."[54]

These speeches were a warm-up for the message that Wilson would deliver on May 27 to the first annual dinner of the League to Enforce Peace. That organization—founded on June 17, 1915—was a pressure group that was seeking to shape the postwar policies of the United States. The LEP, as it was popularly known, was dedicated to "enforcing peace" through judicial arbitration, backed up by international force if necessary. Former president William Howard Taft was the president of LEP in 1916.

Wilson found himself, awkwardly, seated on the dais very close to Henry Cabot Lodge at the LEP dinner. His remarks would be potent with the themes that would clash with Lodge's nationalism in 1919. At the heart of the matter was Wilson's disavowal of national interest in favor of the interests of "the world" and the principles that ought to govern it. Wilson professed that "the principle of public right must henceforth take precedence over the individual interests of particular nations." In words that he would utter again within a year, he claimed that Americans "have nothing material of any kind to ask for ourselves."

This speech was an occasion for Wilson to adumbrate themes he later included within his Fourteen Points. "We believe in these fundamental things," he stated: "First, that every people has a right to choose the sovereignty under which they shall live. . . . Second, that the small states of the world have a right to enjoy the same respect for their sovereignty . . . that great and powerful nations expect and insist upon. And, third, that the world has a right to be free from every disturbance of its peace that has its origin in aggression."

Wilson set forth some other goals that would figure in his imminent crusades. "It is plain," he avowed, "that this war could have come only as it did, suddenly and out of secret counsels, without warning to the world, without discussion, and without any of the deliberate movements of counsel with which it would seem natural to approach so stupendous a contest." Here, in embryonic form, was Wilson's vision of "open covenants, openly arrived at." Later in the speech he advocated "a universal association of nations to maintain the inviolate security of the highway of the seas for the common and unhindered use of all the nations of the world, and to prevent any war begun either contrary to treaty covenants or without warning and full submission of the causes to the opinion of the world."[55]

Here, conflated, were the themes of a league of nations—so widely discussed by so many people at the time and the subject of discourse between Edward House and Sir Edward Grey—the principle of "freedom of the seas" that House had tried (in vain) to dangle in front of the Germans as enticement to negotiate peace, and, again, the principles of open covenants, open deliberation, and civilized conduct consistent with the vision of Tennyson, the vision of a radiant future in which

> the war-drum throbb'd no longer, and the battleflags
> Were furl'd
> In the Parliament of man, the Federation of the World. [56]

I DO NOT KNOW WHAT A SINGLE DAY MAY BRING FORTH

The campaign on behalf of his preparedness program was good for Wilson: it brought out the man's better qualities. The task of advocating *power* to be used in confronting a dangerous world summoned themes of practicality, prudence, wisdom—common sense in the president's mind. When preparedness occupied his thinking, it began to serve as a counterforce against cant, self-righteous naïveté, and mysticism.

The opposition to preparedness within his own party was fierce, and the participation of William Jennings Bryan made it worse. One of Wilson's leading opponents in Congress was the new House majority leader, Claude Kitchin of North Carolina. A pivotal figure was Representative James Hay of Virginia, who chaired the House Military Affairs Committee. To bolster his position, Wilson turned at last to bipartisan strategy; he reached out to the House and Senate minority leaders, respectively James R. Mann of Illinois and Jacob H. Gallinger of New Hampshire.

As 1916 dawned, the bill to expand the size of the navy seemed destined to succeed. But the army bill was mired in controversy centered on the four-hundred-thousand-man "continental army" proposed by Secretary of War Garrison. The National Guard lobby resisted the idea. Democratic pacifists decried it as a militaristic "standing army." Garrison insisted that only a *national* "reserve" would be acceptable. His attitude in testimony before the committee was domineering; it alienated Chairman Hay.

Hay developed a compromise plan to expand the national guard to the size of Garrison's proposed reserve force while giving the president authority to "federalize" it. Garrison refused to consider this. In a series of letters to Wilson, he wrote that "there can be no honest or worthy solution which does not result in national forces under the exclusive control and authority of the national government."[57]

As this controversy brewed in January, Wilson's secretary, Joseph Tumulty, sent him a memorandum urging him to take his case to the public in a speaking tour. "I cannot impress upon you too forcibly the importance of an appeal to the country at this time on the question of preparedness," he wrote. "The great bulk of the people are looking for leadership. . . . Now is the time when impressions are being made and the impression abroad in the country is that we are drifting and that there was an utter lack of leadership."[58]

Surely this stung, but it also appealed to Wilson's forté: rhetoric. And the rhetoric that Wilson would create for this campaign would reveal his most becoming side.

In his first address, to the Railway Business Association in New York on January 27, he displayed a realism that was starkly at odds with his perennial susceptibility to utopian dreams. "We live in a world which we did not make," he observed, "which we cannot alter, which we cannot think into a different condition from that which actually exists."[59]

A world which we *cannot alter*: this statement is impossible to reconcile with the words that Wilson spoke just a few months later, when he conjured with a number of visions of earthly perfection. In April, for example, on Jefferson Day, he preached that Americans should fight *only* for altruistic reasons. When he addressed the League to Enforce Peace, he observed that the war had erupted "without discussion, and without any of the deliberate movements of counsel with which it would seem natural to approach so stupendous a contest." It almost sounded as though this *naïf* were astonished that European leaders had *dared* to go to war without a parliamentary debate—astonished to encounter such things as secret plans and preemptive strikes—and convinced that a world of open covenants and universal candor could be crafted through a moral transformation that could *really happen*. The problem of reconciling innocence of this magnitude with the shrewdness that Wilson could display on other occasions is nothing less than the problem of explaining the . . . *mystery* of Wilson's mind.

A caveat: There was nothing unreasonable in the hope for a postwar order to prevent another catastrophic war. That was what the Congress of Vienna had achieved in the nineteenth century. And that was what sober men such as William Howard Taft and Henry Cabot Lodge were discussing. But for men such as these it was a matter of adjusting the balance of power; with Wilson it was often a perfectionist fantasy with overtones of a millennial nature.

As John Morton Blum once reflected, Wilson "had to live in a world made up in part of illusions. In the case of so able a man as Wilson, this led to tragedy." Blum went so far as to say that Wilson's "optimistic rationalism" did not "satisfy the data of his senses. This was not a matter of dishonesty. He had never much relied on data. But he fixed his own security in the doctrines he promulgated. He could not afford to modify these doctrines for fear of losing hold of his personality."[60]

There are elements of truth in this assessment, but it goes too far, underestimating the tragedy of Wilson by ignoring the degree to which he recognized—intermittently, to be sure—the danger that his mental proclivities presented and tried (insufficiently) to struggle against them. An account of his preparedness work will reveal this, for the speeches that he gave were often excellent.

It is time to hear Wilson as he sounded on the stump, and the extracts to follow will be generous, for good reason. His preparedness speeches of 1916 are essential reading for an understanding of the deep complexity, the stunning contradictions, of the Wilson tragedy.

In the realistic mode that he displayed on January 27, he came close to poking fun at himself (in a serious way) when he observed that

> perhaps when you learned, as I dare say you did learn beforehand, that I was expecting to address you on the subject of preparedness, you recalled the address which I made to Congress something more than a year ago, in which I said that this question of military preparedness was not a pressing question. But more than a year has gone by since then, and I would be ashamed if I had not learned something in fourteen months. The minute I stop changing my mind as President, with the change of all the circumstances in the world, I will be a back number. . . . I have come to have a wholesome respect for the facts. I have had to yield to them sometimes before I saw them coming, and that has led me to keep a weather eye open in order that I may see them coming. [61]

Wilson went on to suggest an intelligent proposal for manpower training, as follows:

> We ought to have in this country a great system of industrial and vocational education under federal guidance and with federal aid, in which a very large percentage of the youth of this country will be given training in the skillful use and application of the principles of science in manufacturing and business . . . as will make these same men . . . immediately serviceable for national defense. [62]

Wilson added observations that bespoke an understanding of lead time:

> But, gentlemen, you cannot create such a system overnight. . . . It has got to be built up, and I hope it will be built up, by slow and effective stages. And there is something to be done in the meantime. We must see to it that a sufficient body of citizens is given the kind of training which will make them efficient now for call into the field in case of necessity. . . . I am not a partisan of any one plan. I have had too much experience to think that it is right to say that the plan that I propose is the only plan that will work, because I have a shrewd suspicion that there may be other plans which will work. But what I am for, and what every American ought to insist upon, is a body of at least half a million trained citizens who will serve under conditions of danger as an immediately available national reserve. [63]

Wilson was trying to make up for lost time with these speeches, and, given the less than auspicious circumstances—some of which he came close to admitting were his own fault—this was a decent beginning.

And it was interesting, too, how these speeches could emphasize *irrationality*, not only in the obvious sense of all the wartime hatred but also in some senses that were far more revealing. Perhaps, as he admitted some mistakes (tacitly) and acknowledged the fact that one must think strategically, Wilson was secretly revealing to himself that his oracular side could steer him wrong.

In the first of these speeches, cited above, he acknowledged he had changed his mind about preparedness due to his encounter with some new "facts." But in another speech that he delivered on the same day, he poked fun at himself in almost slapstick terms and then he talked about his turbulent feelings—about those *inward* facts that could also affect one's judgment. This speech was delivered to the Motion Picture Board of Trade:

> I have sometimes been very much chagrined in seeing myself in a motion picture. I have wondered if I really was that kind of a "guy." The extraordinary rapidity with which I walked, for example, the instantaneous and apparently automatic nature of my motion, the way in which I produce uncommon grimaces, and altogether the extraordinary exhibition I make of myself sends me to bed very unhappy. . . . And I often think to myself that, although all the world is a stage and men and women but actors upon it, after all, the external appearances of things are very superficial, indeed. . . . While we unconsciously display a great deal of human nature in our visible actions, there are some very deep waters which no picture can sound. . . . I have a lot of emotions that do not show on the surface. . . . All these volcanic forces, all these things that are going on inside of me, have to be concealed under a most grave and reverend exterior. [64]

Two days later in Pittsburgh, Wilson spoke to two thousand people at the Soldiers Memorial Hall—as another five thousand waited outside (he made an "overflow" address to them later). "The world is on fire," Wilson told them. "There is tinder everywhere. The sparks are liable to drop anywhere, and somewhere there may be material which we cannot prevent from bursting into flame. . . . America can't afford to be weak." [65]

To the overflow crowd, he observed that with a population of one hundred million, the United States, with "time enough," could "assert any amount of force we please to assert. But when the world is on fire, how much time do you want to take to be ready? . . . When the sky is full of floating sparks from a great conflagration, are you going to sit down and say it will be time enough, when the fire begins, to do something about it?" [66]

In Cleveland, still on the very same day—and it has to be observed that Wilson's power to create new oratory, hour after hour, was almost inexhaustible—he worked the crowd over this way:

> The characteristic desire of America is, not that she should have a great body of men whose chief business it is to fight, but a great body of men who know how to fight and are ready to fight when anything that is dear to the nation is threatened. . . . Let me tell you, very solemnly, you cannot afford to postpone this thing. I do not know what a single day may bring forth. . . . I know that we are daily treading amidst the most intricate dangers. [67]

On January 31, he varied his themes in the course of a speech in Chicago, reiterating some and introducing others. Regarding the navy, for example, he admitted

> that we have followed plans piecemeal, a little bit at a time, now in this direction, now in that direction; that we have never had a plan thought out to cover a number of years in advance. . . . The plans that are being proposed to the present Congress . . . are plans to remedy this piecemeal treatment of the navy and bring it to its highest point of efficiency by steady plans. [68]

On war itself, he grew bolder in embracing its heroism—almost bold enough to meet the standards of Theodore Roosevelt, with a touch of Rooseveltian whimsy:

> Have you looked at the most valued souvenir of families in America? Have you never seen a rusty sword treasured from the days of the Revolution or from the days of the Civil War? Have you never seen an old-fashioned musket hung up in some conspicuous place of honor? Did you ever see a spade hung up, or a pick hung up, or a yardstick hung up, or a ledger hung up? Did you ever see in such a place of honor any symbol of the ordinary occupations of peace? Why? Because America loves war and honors it more than she honors peace? Certainly not! But because America honors utter self-sacrifice more than she honors anything else. [69]

And, again, he admitted he had learned:

> It is not a happy circumstance to have these tense moments of national necessity arise, and yet I, for my part, am not sorry that this necessity has arisen. It has awakened me, myself, I frankly confess to you, to many things and many conditions, which a year ago I did not realize. . . . I am glad that I know better than I knew then exactly the sort of world we are living in. [70]

In Des Moines, on February 1, before a crowd of eight thousand, he acknowledged that the geographical target of this tour was the Midwest, the heart of isolationist convictions. He used the tone of self-possession to soothe the feelings of the audience:

> Someone who does not know our fellow citizens quite as well as he ought to know them told me there was a certain degree of indifference and lethargy in the Middle West with regard to the defense of our nation. I said, "I do not believe it, but I am going out to see." And I have seen. I have seen what I expected to see—great bodies of serious men, great bodies of earnest women, coming together to show their profound interest in the objects of this visit of mine. [71]

He went on slowly—step by delicate step—delivering his message:

> No voice has ever come to any public man more audibly, more unmistakably, than the voice of this great people has come to me, bearing this impressive lesson: "We are counting on you to keep this country out of war." And I call you to witness, my fellow countrymen, that I have spent every thought and energy that has been vouchsafed to me in order to keep this country out of war. [72]

Still, there were limits to what a sane man could do: "There is a price which is too great to pay for peace, and that price can be put in one word. One cannot pay the price of self-respect." Wilson did his best to link the subtleties of international law to the reflex of national pride:

> What is America expected to do? She is expected to keep law alive while the rest of the world burns. You know that there is no international tribunal, my fellow citizens. I pray God that, if this contest is to have no other result, it will at least have the result of creating . . . some sort of joint guarantee of peace on the part of the great nations of the world. But it has not yet done that, and the only thing, therefore, that keeps America out of danger is that, to some degree, the understandings, the ancient and honorable understandings, of nations with regard to their relations to one another are to some extent still observed and followed. And whenever there is a departure from them, the United States is called upon to intervene—to speak its voice of protest, to speak its voice of insistence. Do you want it to be only a voice of insistence? Do you want the situation to be such that all that the President of the United States can do is to write messages, to utter words of protest? . . . Do you wish to have all the world say that the flag of the United States, which we love, can be stained with impunity? Why, to ask the question is to answer it. [73]

Then he got down to business:

> War has been transformed almost within the memory of men. The mere mustering of volunteers is not war. Mere bodies of men are not an army, and we have neither the men nor the equipment for the men if they should be called out. It would take time to make an army of them—perhaps a fatal length of

time—and it would take a long time to provide them with the absolute neces-sities of warfare. America is not going to sacrifice her youth after that fashion. It is going to prepare for war by preparing citizens who know what war means and how war can be conducted. [74]

In Topeka the next day—after suffering a frosty introduction by the state's Republican governor, Arthur Capper—Wilson was slightly more dar-ing, even challenging:

> I was told, before I came here, and I read in one of your papers this morning, that Kansas was not in sympathy with any policy of preparation for national defense. I do not believe a word of it. I long ago learned to distinguish between editorial opinion and popular opinion. Moreover, having been addicted to books, I happened to have read the history of Kansas. And, if there is any place in the world fuller of fight than Kansas, I would like to hear of it—any other place fuller of fight on the right lines. Kansas is not looking for trouble, but Kansas has made trouble for everybody that interfered with her liberties or her rights. . . . If Kansas is opposed, or has been opposed, to the policy of prepara-tion for national defense, it has been only because somebody has misrepresent-ed that policy. [75]

Could even Theodore Roosevelt have done much better in a speech along these lines?

To an overflow crowd at a Topeka high school later that day, Wilson poured it out again:

> I have been bred, and a good many Kansans have been bred, in a pretty stern school of religion, and there are some religions that have been worth fighting for. There are some political religions that are worth fighting for, and I would not care to hold any conviction that I was not ready to fight for if that convic-tion were too rudely challenged. [76]

On the same day, in Kansas City, Wilson spoke to a crowd of fifteen thousand—at the Kansas City Convention Hall—and he asked these direct questions:

> When I, as your spokesman and representative, utter a judgment with regard to the rights of the United States in its relations to other nations, what is the sanction? What is the compulsion? What lies back of that? You will say, "The force and majesty of the United States." Yes, the force and majesty of the United States. But is it ready to express itself? [77]

He imputed noble feelings to the crowds that came to see him, and then contrasted those feelings, with a mischievous guile, to those of hucksters who edited newspapers:

I have seen editorials written in more than one part of the United States sneering at the number of notes that were being written from the State Department to foreign governments, and asking, "Why does not the government act?" And, in those same papers, I have seen editorials against the preparation to do anything effective if those notes are not regarded. Is that the temper of the United States? It may be the temper of some editorial offices, but it is not the temper of the people of the United States. I came out upon this errand from Washington, and see what happened. Before I started, everybody knew what errand I was bound on. I expected to meet quiet audiences and explain to them the issues of the day, and what did I meet? At every stop of the train, multitudes of my fellow citizens crowded out, not to see the President of the United States merely—he is not much to look at—but to declare their ardent belief in the majesty of the government which he stands for. [78]

Wilson shared some accurate observations about the price that was paid in the Spanish-American War for America's demobilized condition:

Do you remember the experiences of the Spanish-American War? That was not much of a war, was it? . . . [But] you sent thousands of men to their death because they were ignorant. They did not get any further than the camps in Florida. They did not get on the water even, much less get to Cuba, and they died in the camps like flies, of all sorts of camp diseases, of all sorts of diseases that come from the ignorance of medical science and camp sanitation. Splendid boys, boys fit, with a little training, to make an invincible army, but sent to their death by miserable disease, the soil of which was ignorance, helpless ignorance. . . . Do you want to repeat that? [79]

In his final speech in St. Louis on the same day—this time before a crowd of twelve thousand—Wilson again used editors (along with the much-maligned culture of out-of-touch "Washington") as foils to elicit the support of his audience:

I came out into the Middle West to find something, and I found it. I was told in Washington that the Middle West had a different feeling from the portions of the country that lie upon either coast, and that it was indifferent to the question of preparation for national defense. I knew enough of the Middle West of this great continent to know that the men who said that did not know what they were talking about. . . . The judgment of America is not based upon sentiment; it is based upon facts. And I want to say to you that nothing has encouraged me more, upon this trip that I have been making, than the consciousness that America is awake to the facts. (Applause.) I do not want to say anything disrespectful about any newspaper, but it is astonishing how little some newspaper editors know. (Long applause.) And I would like from some of them a candid expression of the impression they have got from what has happened since I left Washington. They probably will give it their own interpretation, but they will not (and this ought to comfort them if they are moral men), they will not deceive anybody. Because, from the time I left Washington until now,

I have had this feeling: The country is up. There is not a man who is not awake.[80]

These speeches showed Wilson at his best—smart, adroit, resourceful, practical, funny, and inspiring, by turns—as he sought to change feelings in the heartland. After this whirlwind tour (it had lasted little more than a week), the president returned to confront congressional politics.

Shortly after he returned, the confrontation between Secretary of War Garrison and Chairman Hay of the House Military Affairs Committee was resolved: Garrison resigned. To replace him as secretary of war, Wilson tapped Newton D. Baker, mayor of Cleveland, Ohio.

Though Wilson's tour had been exciting, it did not result in a change of isolationist opinion that registered in Washington. "I see no real change in the attitude of the Members since the President's Western tour," wrote Claude Kitchin to Bryan on February 9.[81] Wilson abandoned Garrison's "continental army" and settled for Hay's proposal to expand the national guard. Working with Hay did the trick, and the defeat of the McLemore resolution changed the tone of House deliberations.

On March 23, the House, by the overwhelming vote of 402–2, approved a substantial expansion of the regular army—from 100,000 to 140,000—and gave the War Department ultimate control of the national guard. The army bill was helped in the Senate by the *Sussex* crisis. On April 18, the Senate resurrected the continental army (at the size of 261,000 men), increased the size of the regular army to 250,000, and, as a gesture to opponents of "war profiteering," established a government-owned nitrate factory.

In May, Wilson mediated between the Senate and House. The resulting army bill, hammered out on May 13, scrapped the continental army but increased the size of the national guard to 440,000 men and 17,000 officers, a goal to be achieved in five years. The size of the regular army was increased from 100,000 men and 5,029 officers to 208,338 men and 11,327 officers. The nitrate plant was retained.

The National Security League condemned this plan as inadequate and urged a presidential veto. Roosevelt's criticism was scathing. Though the legislation certainly represented a major accomplishment for Wilson and a first step toward adequate military force, the arguments of the above-mentioned critics would be largely borne out in 1917.

On April 7, Newton Baker, the new secretary of war, wrote Wilson in regard to mobilization. He informed Wilson that Howard Earle Coffin, vice president of the Hudson Motor Car Company and chairman of the Naval Consulting Board's Committee on Industrial Preparedness, was making an inventory of industrial resources for wartime purposes. Baker then advised Wilson that the body of this work is extensive, but [it] begins to lose value at once with the constant change of our industrial condition. All of this work ought, therefore, to be brought to some national agency which could coordinate it, prevent duplication, and provide for the continuation. To this end a certain amount of new national machinery is necessary. The minimum would seem to be the creation of a council of national strength. [82]

Baker and navy secretary Josephus Daniels had collaborated on this memo. Wilson supported their recommendation, and Congress provided for the creation of a Council of National Defense. Wilson established it in August, and then added a nonpartisan advisory commission in October. [83]

The navy bill would be dramatically changed by the Senate in the summer, with the ship construction program speeded up from five years to three and with construction of four battleships in the first year alone. The Battle of Jutland was cited by many as a clinching demonstration of the "dreadnought's" power. After the Senate had acted on July 21, the anti-preparedness leaders in the House were thrown into consternation. Wilson put pressure on Lemuel P. Padgett, chairman of the House Naval Affairs Committee. On August 15, the House adopted most of the key provisions of the Senate bill. "The United States today becomes the most militaristic naval nation on earth," thundered Claude Kitchin. [84]

Kitchin and his allies gained a measure of revenge by defeating the administration's revenue bill and replacing it with a measure that taxed the rich harder to pay for the military buildup. The revenue bill of 1916 would pay for all of the preparedness measures. [85]

Thus, between May and September, Wilson and Congress created the most substantial increase of military power that congressional politics would sustain. Less than a year remained before the United States declared war.

WE ARE SAVING OURSELVES FOR SOMETHING GREATER THAT IS TO COME

Germany did not present a serious problem for Wilson for the rest of the year. But relations with the British began to get surprisingly ugly.

It began with the Irish rebellion of April 24, which the British repressed with such brutality that even some of the staunchest friends of Britain in the United States were appalled. The execution of the men who led the "Easter Rising" followed. The case of Sir Roger Casement attracted special attention. The pope appealed to the British to spare Casement's life, and the U.S. Senate passed a resolution pleading for the same thing. Nonetheless, the British executed him with the others. Americans of Irish background, an important Democratic Party constituency of long standing, were outraged.

All the while, House kept up his efforts to revive the House-Grey agreement. After the *Sussex* pledge, with Wilson's approval, House sent the following message to Grey on May 7:

> There is an increasingly insistent demand here for the President to take some action towards bringing the war to a close. Germany will foster this sentiment and if she ceases her submarine warfare and England continues the blockade, one can foresee a change of feeling towards Germany. Will it not be said that the Allies are fighting more for the purpose of punishing Germany than for any good results that may come from any further loss of blood and treasure?[86]

Four days later, House tried to persuade Grey that "this is the psychological moment to strike for those things which the President and you have so near at heart. Delay is dangerous and may defeat our ends."[87] House seemed to be forgetting that Grey, Lloyd George, and other British leaders had advised him that autumn would be the best time for initiating mediation attempts.

Grey replied quickly, telling House that mediation efforts would be "premature," and that the "suggestion of summoning a peace conference without any indication of a basis on which peace might be made would be construed as instigated by Germany to secure peace on terms unfavourable to the Allies."[88] Wilson's response to this was stern. He told House that

> the situation has altered altogether since you had your conferences in London and Paris. The at least temporary removal of the acute German question has concentrated attention here on the altogether indefensible course Great Britain is pursuing with regard to trade to and from neutral ports and her quite intolerable interception of mails on the high seas carried by neutral ships. Recently there has been added the great shock opinion in this country has received from the course of the British Government towards some of the Irish rebels.

Wilson concluded that

> we are plainly face to face with this alternative, therefore. The United States must either make a decided move for peace (upon some basis that promises to be permanent) or, if she postpones that, must insist to the limit upon her rights of trade . . . with the same firmness that she has used against Germany. And the choice must be made immediately.[89]

House conveyed that message to Grey on May 19: "America has reached the crossroads, and if we cannot soon inaugurate some sort of peace discussion there will come a demand from our people in which all neutrals will probably join, that we assert our undeniable rights against the Allies with the same insistence we have used towards the Central Powers."[90]

Perhaps Wilson felt the imperative to act "immediately" because of politics; the party conventions were barely a month away. No doubt the tension of facing a national plebiscite on his leadership was at work in Wilson's mind. But there were other emotions at work. Wilson's speech to the League to Enforce Peace would be given just a few weeks after he wrote to House regarding the need for "immediate" choice. Wilson had come to view this speech as supremely important. He told House it "may be the most important I shall ever be called upon to make."[91] In the course of a visit to Charlotte, North Carolina, on May 20, Wilson spoke once again in his oracular state of mind:

> What you see taking place on the other side of the water is the tremendous—I had about said final—process by which a contest of elements may, in God's Providence, be turned into a coordination and cooperation of elements. For it is an interesting circumstance that the processes of the war stand still. These hot things that are in contact with each other do not make very much progress against each other. When you cannot overcome, you must take counsel.[92]

If Wilson's reading of "Providence" was accurate—if the great contending forces of destruction were being held at bay—perhaps this was the moment for a world-historical figure to intervene. Perhaps the current state of war was something of a sign.

Wilson's contradictory moods could interpenetrate each other. Though religious fervor was just below the surface—waiting to erupt—he could still maintain his outward pattern of "cool" behavior, thus fooling some observers into discounting the impulsiveness that often lurked just below. After a conversation with Wilson that had taken place a few weeks earlier, the admiring journalist Ray Stannard Baker had written, "I have never talked with any public man who has such a complete control over his whole intellectual equipment as he. . . . Wilson himself inspires people with confidence. He is *safe*."[93]

As usual, House abetted these developments in ways that preserved his pet project. In a letter to Wilson on May 21, he shared the following thoughts that he knew would receive a good reception since they spoke to Wilson's visionary impulse: "One Reason this war has come, one reason why other wars will come is because nations are secretive as to their intentions towards one another and do not in advance outline their thoughts and purposes."[94]

Things continued to worsen for the Wilson mediation scenario. On May 22, Frank Polk, who was serving as councilor at the State Department (Lansing was intermittently disabled by diabetes and out of commission), sent Wilson a message from the French ambassador, who "spoke of rumors in the press of your taking some steps toward bringing about peace. . . . He said he sincerely hoped that nothing would be said at present. . . . France could not consider peace until it could be assured that it was a real peace and not a breathing spell for Germany."[95]

Walter Hines Page wrote to House along the same lines from London. He said that "peace talk doesn't go over here now, and the less we indulge in it, the better. . . . They [the British] get more and more on edge as the strain becomes severer."[96]

As the horror of the Battle of the Somme took shape, the British tightened their blockade of Germany as much as they possibly could. Grey, that champion of Anglo-American harmony, began to lose influence, and Anglo-American relations took a turn for the worse. Grey candidly confessed to House that the Somme offensive made it useless to discuss any peace mediation until the results of the fighting were clear. House relayed this information to Wilson: "They should know by September 1st whether it is to be a success or failure. Then would be the time to press some proposal on them."[97]

But Anglo-American tensions kept increasing too fast for that to happen. For months, the British had been intercepting American mail, and Lansing had complained to Wilson about it.[98] In addition, Lansing brought to Wilson's attention the news that an Economic Conference of the Allied Powers, held in Paris from June 14 to June 17, had adopted resolutions to continue economic warfare against Germany even after Germany had been defeated— "to prevent as far as possible the rebuilding of their industries and commerce after the war."[99]

Then, on July 19, the British published a "blacklist" of 87 American firms (and 350 Latin American firms) with whom no further commerce would be tolerated. These were firms that attempted to do business with the Central Powers. "I am, I must admit, about at the end of my patience with Great Britain and the Allies," Wilson wrote to House on July 23. "This blacklist business is the last straw. . . . I am seriously considering asking Congress to authorize me to prohibit loans and restrict exportations to the Allies."[100]

Wilson instructed Polk to draft a protest note, which was sent on July 26.[101] But the British did not reply. So in the following months, Wilson persuaded Congress to empower him to strike back by refusing clearance to any vessel that refused to carry the freight of firms that were listed on the blacklist, to deny the use of port facilities to ships of any nation that discriminated against American firms, and to use armed force to back up these policies.[102]

By August, the House-Grey agreement was dead. Grey presented the reasons to House. All were political, and some concerned American credibility:

> The continual reports that public opinion in the United States is determined at all costs to keep out of the war, makes people ask whether even with a League

of Nations the United States could be depended upon to uphold treaties and agreements by force. If feeling in the United States is one of congratulation that they did not intervene to prevent the violation of Belgium or to avenge the loss of life on the "Lusitania," can they ever be expected to intervene? [103]

Then there was the matter of the Irish rebellion:

> We are not favourably impressed by the action of the Senate in having passed a resolution about the Irish prisoners, though they have taken no notice of outrages in Belgium and massacres of Armenians. These latter were outrageous and unprovoked, whereas the only unprovoked thing in recent Irish affairs was the rising itself, which for a few days was a formidable danger. [104]

Grey's letter was replete with signs of bitterness, disappointment at his own loss of influence, and demoralization. "There is nothing more that I can do at the moment," he concluded. He was right: Balfour would soon take over as foreign minister, and Lloyd George would take over as prime minister by the end of the year.

In the meantime, the Democratic and Republican conventions were held in June. The Republicans nominated Charles Evans Hughes, a moderate. He was serving at the time on the Supreme Court, and he stepped down to accept the nomination. Prior to that, he had served as governor of New York.

The Republican rift of 1912 had not yet fully healed. Wilson and the Democrats deliberately courted the progressives who had bolted the Republican Party in 1912 to support Theodore Roosevelt. Domestic reform was a major theme in the politics of 1916, though Roosevelt was silent for the moment on the issue for reasons of his own. The Republicans would naturally criticize the Democrats' performance on foreign policy issues, and Hughes—with a sidelong glance at the bellicosity of Roosevelt—contended that he would have handled the Germans much better than Wilson had done, though without really specifying how. At times he made bids for the German American vote. In truth, Hughes ran a lackluster campaign; Roosevelt privately derided him as "the bearded lady." Other detractors called him the "animated feather duster."

Notwithstanding Wilson's preparedness program—and the significant internal Democratic resistance to it—the orators at the Democratic Convention, which was held in St. Louis on June 14, strove for unity. They boasted endlessly that the president had kept the country out of war; indeed, the platform itself contained language that "commended to the American people the splendid diplomatic victories of our President, who has . . . kept us out of war." Former New York governor Martin Glynn, who delivered the keynote address at the convention, did a recitation of the times in American history when cool heads had prevailed. Then he chanted out the following refrain: "We didn't go to war!"

Wilson was nominated for a second term by acclamation. And, at his behest, text was added to the platform calling for American participation in a league of nations. [105]

On the same day as the Democratic Convention, June 14—"Flag Day," a new national holiday that Wilson himself had established—Wilson was elsewhere: he led a huge preparedness parade along Pennsylvania Avenue in Washington and gave a speech at the Washington Monument. He wore a "natty" outfit that had been carefully selected by Edith—white flannel trousers, white shoes, blue blazer, straw boater hat—and he carried a large American flag.

It was still customary in those days for the nominee to make an acceptance speech later, when a delegation of party leaders called upon him to inform him of his nomination. Wilson rented a beach estate called "Shadow Lawn" at Long Branch, New Jersey—it was also customary in those days for the well-to-do to flee humid Washington in the summer—and there, on September 2, he met the delegation and delivered his acceptance speech. Though he barnstormed the country in the fall, he also made "front porch" addresses at Shadow Lawn that were reminiscent of McKinley's 1896 campaign. Bryan, who decided to patch up his differences with Wilson, not least to conserve his own future influence, campaigned hard on behalf of the Democratic ticket, especially in the Midwest and West. Naturally, peace was the gist of Bryan's theme—and Wilson's as well.

On September 30, at Shadow Lawn, Wilson showed no hesitation in using the theme as follows:

> Am I not right that we must draw the conclusion that, if the Republican party is put into power at the next election, our foreign policy will be radically changed? I cannot draw any other inference. All our present foreign policy is wrong, they say, and if it is wrong, and they are men of conscience, they must change it. And if they are going to change it, in what direction are they going to change it? There is only one choice as against peace, and that is war. [106]

In another speech on October 21, Wilson said, "I am not expecting this country to get into the war. I know that the way in which we have preserved peace is objected to, and that certain gentlemen say they would have taken some other way that would inevitably have resulted in war. But I am not expecting this country to get into the war, partly because I am not expecting these gentlemen to have a chance to make a mess of it." [107]

In Indianapolis he touched on postwar objectives, stating that "when the great present war is over, it will be the duty of America to join with the other nations of the world in some kind of league for the maintenance of peace." [108]
At Shadow Lawn, on October 14, he was more expansive:

What Europe is beginning to realize is that we are saving ourselves for something greater that is to come. We are saving ourselves in order that we may unite in that final league of nations in which it shall be understood that there is no neutrality where any nation is doing wrong, in that final league of nations which must, in the providence of God, come into the world, where nation shall be leagued with nation in order to show all mankind that no man may lead any nation into acts of aggression without having all the other nations of the world leagued against it. [109]

More and more, he blamed secret covenants for the war. In Cincinnati, on October 26, he asked

Have you ever heard what started the present war? If you have, I wish you would publish it, because nobody else has. So far as I can gather, nothing in particular started it, but everything in general. There had been growing up in Europe a mutual suspicion, an interchange of conjectures about what this government and that government was going to do, an interlacing of alliances and understandings, a complex web of intrigue and spying. [110]

At another address the same day, he announced that

America has pledged itself to this principle—that it will not be governed in secret, that it will not be led by purposes which are not avowed, that it will not follow policies which are not exposed to it for its approval and adoption. . . . When war comes, it comes on a colossal scale. We have seen that, in this instance, it has come because of suspicion and intrigue, on the working of secret influences confined to small circles of men in which nations as nations had no part at all. . . . The nations of the world must . . . covenant with one another that no nation shall go to war upon any pretext which it is not willing to submit to the opinion of mankind. [111]

Again, he showed the religious component of his vision, this time more explicitly than ever: "We do not love peace in order that we may enjoy it privately. . . . But we do love peace because we think the human race ought to have it. . . . We know that the destiny of mankind is moving along that path which that lonely figure of the Prince of Peace once tried to point out and which he once trod himself with bleeding feet. We are disciples of righteousness, and we want peace because we know righteousness can breathe no other air." [112]

Through it all, Wilson started to think of himself in Lincolnesque terms. On September 4, he presided over a ceremony in Hodgenville, Kentucky, in which he accepted on behalf of the American people the cabin where Lincoln had been born. In his remarks, he reflected on Lincoln's persona, as he understood it: "It was a very lonely spirit that looked out from underneath those shaggy brows and comprehended men without fully communing with them, as if, in spite of all its genial efforts at comradeship, it dwelt apart, saw its visions of duty where no man looked on. . . . This strange child of the cabin kept company with invisible things."[113] There is no doubt at all that Wilson identified with this persona—that he was speaking as much about himself as he was speaking of Lincoln. A month later, he was interviewed by Ida Tarbell, the muckraking journalist and early biographer of Lincoln. She asked him whether he would have been able "to say the other day at the dedication of the Lincoln cabin what you did of Lincoln's isolation, his loneliness, if it had not been for your own deep experience of the last two years." Wilson answered that, indeed, just as Lincoln "could make no associate in his great crisis . . . I felt this profoundly in the acute stage of our trouble with Germany. . . . The awful and overwhelming thought was that the country trusted me. . . . I feared to be overwhelmed by a storm of feeling."[114]

On November 7, Woodrow Wilson was reelected. He got 277 electoral votes compared to 254 for Hughes. The popular margin, however, was wider: 9,129,606 to 8,538,221.

LEST A VIOLENCE BE DONE CIVILIZATION ITSELF

In early autumn, Bethmann-Hollweg, the German chancellor, made overtures to Wilson.

As the Germans prepared for new strategic decisions, the chancellor was curious to see whether Wilson's desire to be a mediator might serve German interests. All had been quiet since the *Sussex* pledge; though the submarines continued to sink British merchantmen, they had generally left passenger vessels alone. The unresolved state of the *Lusitania* case was, for reasons of expediency, ignored by Lansing and Wilson, notwithstanding some occasional Republican attempts to make an issue of it. [115]

On September 25, Ambassador Gerard wrote Lansing as follows: "I can state on best authority that if the President will make offer of good offices in general terms . . . Germany will accept in general terms immediately and state readiness to send delegates to proposed peace conference."[116] At the request of Bethmann-Hollweg, Gerard left for Washington to convey in person the Germans' new interest in peace negotiations.

Four days after Gerard wrote to Lansing, the British began to look worse than ever by Wilsonian standards: Lloyd George declared that the British would ignore American attempts at mediation; they intended to keep fighting until "Prussian military despotism is broken beyond repair."[117]

Ambassador Bernstorff met with Wilson around October 10 and had a friendly talk. Eight days later, he sent House a copy of a memorandum to be given to Gerard before the ambassador met with Wilson. In his diary, House wrote that the memorandum was "clearly a threat to resume submarine warfare in the event the President does not immediately intervene in the European war."[118] The memorandum stated that "the constellation of war has taken such a form that the German Government foresees the time at which it will be forced to regain the freedom of action that it has reserved to itself in the note of May 4th last."[119]

Gerard met with Wilson on October 24, and he confirmed that Bethmann-Hollweg was under pressure to abandon the *Sussex* pledge. And the chancellor believed that only a successful peace bid by Wilson could prevent this development.[120] On November 6, the British liner *Arabia* was torpedoed, in an apparent violation of the *Sussex* pledge. German pressure on Wilson was increasing.

House tried to put the German peace overture in the worst light. He told Wilson that "I find indisputable evidence that Germany is not yet willing to peace terms that this country could recommend to the Allies. They sneer at such proposals as a league to enforce peace. . . . The only way that I see for an early end to the war is for the Allies to agree to the proposal which you made through me."

House was willing to say almost anything to revivify his cherished scenario. He even tried the far-fetched argument that Lloyd George "gave the interview of not long ago under the impression that it would help you in holding Germany off concerning mediation until after the election."[121]

But none of this reasoning had any effect upon Wilson, who was ready to *force* events before they placed him in another dilemma. In the aftermath of the election, he was no longer patient with the British. The Germans, however, were willing to behave if Wilson did the very thing that he had wanted to do from the beginning: mediate the war. He told House on November 14 that he would definitely "write a note to the belligerents demanding that the war cease." Wilson said that "unless we do this now, we must inevitably drift into war with Germany upon the submarine issue." House replied that "the Allies would consider it an unfriendly act if done at a time when they are beginning to be successful after two years of war."[122] The men discussed sending House to Europe again, but without reaching any decision.

The next morning they met again for what, according to House's diary, was an astonishing impromptu session that he would never forget. It began, more or less, with discussion of a new German outrage: the deportation of about three hundred thousand Belgians for forced labor in the Reich. Wilson had just received news of this from Lansing, and he conferred with the secretary of state, in House's presence, by telephone. To House's frustration, Wilson was not inclined to protest:

> The President's viewpoint was that it was ridiculous for us to protest about the deportation of Belgians, when we did not protest over the violation of their territory. I disagreed with him. . . . I thought it was one of the most brutal and indefensible acts Germany has yet committed. The tearing away of fathers,

brothers and young girls from their families to become practically slaves, is something I thought we might well protest against." [123]

Wilson remained dubious.

Then Wilson reiterated his determination to intervene for peace. House contended that under the existing conditions "a proposal of peace would be accepted by Germany and refused by the Allies, and that Germany would then feel that she could begin an unrestricted u-boat warfare." And the American people might well go along with this: "Germany, having consented to peace parleys, would be thought more or less justified in employing submarine warfare." [124] Wilson was apparently unfazed.

So House confronted him directly with a worst-case possibility: if America were to "drift into a sympathetic alliance" with Germany, "England and France might, under provocation, declare war on us." House probably thought that the freakishness of this scenario—its simple shock value— would prompt the president to back down and be reasonable. But to House's dismay, the effect was precisely the reverse. It was House who was shocked. He found himself horrified by Wilson's state of mind as the two men discussed this hitherto unthinkable scenario as follows:

> He [Wilson] thought they would not dare resort to this and if they did, they could do this country no serious hurt. I disagreed with him again. I thought Great Britain might conceivably destroy our fleet and land troops from Japan in sufficient numbers to hold certain parts of the United States. He replied that they might get a good distance but would have to stop somewhere, to which I agreed. [125]

Wilson concluded that "if the Allies wanted war with us, we would not shrink from it." [126]

House excused himself, and then hurried over to the State Department, where he informed Polk and Lansing of Wilson's state of mind. They all agreed that "it would be stupendous folly to wage war against the Allies." In light of the president's volatile mood, the men decided to "drift for awhile until we could get our bearings." [127] House had never expected this sort of thing to happen.

Wilson started working on his diplomatic note. In the meantime, the president suggested to House that he write to Edward Grey and tell him that Americans "were growing more and more impatient with the intolerable conditions of neutrality, their feeling as hot against Great Britain as it was at first against Germany and likely to grow hotter still against an indefinite continuation of the war." [128]

By November 26, Wilson's peace note was ready. In composing it, he wrote some commentary (in an unpublished memorandum) on the sheer futility of the war. He saw the possibility of recurrent war if either side were to prevail: "In the language of the street, the victorious nation, as the man, gets 'cocky' again, places another chip on its shoulder and becomes unendurable as a neighbor." Would this war be different due to its sickening conditions of battle?

> Never before have the losses and the slaughter been so great with as little gain in military advantage. Both sides have grown weary of the apparently hopeless task of bringing the conflict to an end by the force of arms; inevitably they are being forced to the realization that it can only be brought about by the attrition of human suffering, in which the victor suffers hardly less than the vanquished. . . . The mechanical game of slaughter today has not the same fascination as the zest of intimate combat of former days; and trench warfare and poisonous gases are elements which detract alike from the excitement and tolerance of modern conflict. [129]

In light of these conditions, Wilson wrote, it would be best to "make of this mightiest of conflicts an object lesson for the future by bringing it to a close with the objects of each group of belligerents still unaccomplished and all the magnificent sacrifices on both sides gone for naught." [130]

Wilson's draft began with an avowal that "both my heart and my reason tell me that the time has come to take counsel lest a violence be done civilization itself which cannot be atoned for or repaired." He complained that the neutral nations had been placed in an intolerable situation. Then he set forth a larger complaint: "The objects which would, if attained, satisfy the one group of belligerents or the other have never been definitely avowed. The world can still only conjecture what definitive results, what actual exchange of guarantees, what political readjustments or changes, what stage or degree of military success even, would bring it to an end."

This was not exactly true: House's consultations had revealed the "definitive results" that would have been demanded at various stages of the conflict. But as rhetoric, the contention of Wilson worked effectively to renew the complaints of hapless neutrals: "If any other nation now neutral should be drawn in, it would know only that it was drawn in by some force it could not resist, because it had been hurt and saw no remedy but to risk still greater . . . injury, in order to make the weight in one scale or the other decisive."

Then, to be *diplomatic*, Wilson credited both sides with . . . sincerity. Taking their propaganda at its face value, he concluded that all wanted peace: "They have declared their desire for peace, but for a peace that will last, a peace based, not upon the uncertain balance of powerful alliances offset against one another, but upon guarantees in which the whole civilized world would join." This generalization was at odds with the bellicose demands on both sides for territorial concessions. But Wilson would not be deterred by recalcitrant facts. "We are ready to join in a league of nations," he proclaimed. Americans "are ready when the right moment comes to cooperate to bring it about. But how are they to know when that moment comes unless they be apprised by what test the nations now at war will judge the time of settlement and definition to have come?"

Therefore, Wilson wrote, "I deem myself to be clearly within my right as the representative of a great neutral nation" in urging "that some means be immediately taken . . . to define the terms upon which a settlement of the issues of the war may be expected."[131]

On November 26, Wilson asked House for his reactions to the note; House complained that some of the language might cause the Allies to feel that "he did not understand their viewpoint." House demurred when Wilson asked him to deliver it to the British.[132]

Wilson delayed sending the note. But he maintained his tilt toward the Germans. And he decided to respond to some new British escalations of economic war—he decided to retaliate.

The British had not reconsidered their blacklist. On the contrary, they had instituted an additional form of coercion: the "bunkering agreement." In return for the privilege of buying British coal at various ports of call, neutral shippers had to accept regulation by the British admiralty. Wilson now threatened to strike at Allied war finance. The British were using up the securities that they could furnish as collateral for additional war loans. When J.P. Morgan & Co. recommended accepting unsecured bills from the British and the French, Wilson and the Federal Reserve resisted. Wilson met with W. P. G. Harding of the Federal Reserve on November 25, and an agreement was reached to discourage American bankers from doing business with the Allies along the lines that the House of Morgan had suggested.[133]

In December 1916, the outward solidarity of the administration on foreign policy issues was crumbling. Lansing was partial to the Allies. He fretted in his diary about the possibilities "if Germany listens to the President and the Allies decline to do so."[134] Moreover, Lansing had doubts about the League of Nations idea. "I do not believe that it is wise," he had written to Wilson, "to limit our independence of action, a sovereign right, to the will of other powers beyond this hemisphere. In any representative international body clothed with authority to require of the nations to employ their armies and navies to coerce one of their number, we would be in the minority."[135]

When David Lloyd George became the new prime minister, House suggested to Wilson that he (House) should send a congratulatory cable and remind the new prime minister of what he had said months earlier about the prospect of Wilson ending the war. Wilson disapproved, and he seized the opportunity to discourage House from any further attempts to reweave the disintegrated fragments of the House-Grey accord: "The time is near at hand for *something*! But that something is not mediation such as we were proposing when you were last on the other side of the water. . . . We cannot go back to those old plans. We must shape new ones."[136]

Meanwhile, Lansing attempted to convince Wilson that "a crisis has come in the submarine matter" because of some recent incidents at sea.[137] But Wilson could not be maneuvered into his old position. So Lansing tried some other tactics; in offering comments on Wilson's peace note, he asked the following questions: "Unless the answers of both parties are made in the right spirit, will there be any other course than to declare in favor of the one most acceptable . . . ? But suppose that the unacceptable answer comes from the belligerents whom we could least afford to see defeated on account of our national interests and on account of the future domination of the principles of liberty and democracy in the world—then what?"[138]

Then, suddenly, the German chancellor took action in early December. He could no longer wait for the American president to take the initiative; he was under pressure from the military chiefs and the kaiser. In a speech to the Reichstag, Bethmann-Hollweg announced that Germany was ready to discuss peace with the Allied Powers immediately. A translation of this speech was published in the *New York Times* on December 13. The chancellor presented the peace offer to Joseph Grew, chargé at the American embassy in Berlin (Gerard had not yet returned from America), with the request that it be forwarded to the governments of the Allied Powers.[139]

Lansing and Wilson began writing answers to the new German offer.[140] House recorded in his diary that Wilson "seemed depressed because the Germans had launched their bolt today asking for a peace conference." Wilson hated to be preempted—or, to be blunt about the matter, upstaged. House seemed to take the matter in stride. Perhaps because his own preferred plan was in limbo, he consoled himself that he was off the hook and no longer responsible for changing the course of history. "My desire for peace is so much keener than my wish to bring it about personally," he told himself, "that I feel a certain elation not felt for a long while."

In any case, House went on to write some scathing observations about Wilson:

> I am convinced that the President's place in history is dependent to a large degree upon luck. If we should get into a serious war and it should turn out disastrously he would be one of the most discredited Presidents we have had. He has had nearly three years in which to get the United States into a reasonable state of preparedness and we have done nothing. Neither the Army nor the Navy are in condition to meet an enemy of the class of Roumania [*sic*] or Bulgaria, provided they could reach us. . . . We have no air service, nor men to exploit it, and so it is down the list. A combination of Great Britain and Japan could put us out of business just as rapidly as they could march through the country. . . . If Great Britain and Japan wished to combine against us they could pretend to be conveying Japanese troops through Canada to France, and in this way we could not know just what they were doing or how many men were in Canada. . . . I dislike to record this criticism of the President because

he is one of the great men of the world today, but he sadly lacks administrative ability.[141]

Unfair as this criticism was in obvious ways—it understated the obstacles that Wilson had faced and it ignored the degree to which House had been complicit in a number of Wilson's miscalculations—there was surely truth in this assessment. Only a few more months of peace remained for the United States. The ink on the preparedness acts was barely dry. If Wilson had had the strategic foresight to join with Theodore Roosevelt in autumn 1914— before the *Lusitania* sinking—perhaps a strong and bipartisan preparedness crusade might have given the United States substantive military power by December 1916.

Wilson came out of his depression soon enough to express the hope that the German offer would succeed. "We are just now . . . holding our breath for fear the overtures of the Central Powers with regard to peace will be met with a rebuff instead of an acceptance," he wrote.[142] In fact, the tsar had already rejected the Germans' overture (on December 15). On December 19, Lloyd George declared himself unwilling to negotiate with Germany unless the Germans would state their war aims first.[143]

As to that, Wilson finally sent his own peace note, which was altered due to revisions suggested by Lansing and House.[144] The note, which was sent on December 18, was written with references to Wilson in the third person. It stated that the president was "somewhat embarrassed" to offer his appeal "at this particular time because it may now seem to have been prompted by the recent overtures of the Central Powers. It is in fact in no way connected with them in its origin." The note stated that

> the President suggests that an early occasion be sought to call out from all the nations now at war such an avowal of their respective views as to the terms upon which the war might be concluded. . . . He is indifferent as to the means taken to accomplish this. He would be happy to serve or even take the initiative in its accomplishment . . . but he has no desire to determine the method or the instrumentality.[145]

At this point, Lansing—afraid of a breach with the Allies—went to work behind the president's back. He met with the British and the French ambassadors, counseled them regarding war aims, and expressed his own skepticism about a league of nations. He met with the press on December 21 and stated that the peace note was sent because "we are drawing nearer the verge of war ourselves, and therefore we are entitled to know exactly what each belligerent seeks. . . . Of course the difficulties that face the President were that it might be construed as a movement toward peace and in aid of the German overtures. He specifically denies that that was the fact in the document itself."[146]

In the opinion of John Milton Cooper, this was a "dastardly act of duplicity aimed at destroying Wilson's peace initiative. . . . Wilson should have fired him on the spot."[147] Wilson later revealed that he had considered asking Lansing for his resignation.[148] Instead, he told Lansing to issue a new statement claiming that his previous statement had been "radically misinterpreted."[149] Lansing grudgingly did so.

On December 26, the Germans answered Wilson's peace note. Arthur Zimmermann, the new German foreign minister, handed Gerard the reply in Berlin, and then Gerard sent it to Lansing. The Germans did not declare their war aims. But they did declare that the best way to peace was through direct conversations among the belligerents. In other words, Wilson would not be asked to participate in any peace talks.[150]

The results of Wilson's peace diplomacy appeared, at this point, to be nil. Bethmann-Hollweg could no longer restrain the German high command. And on December 30, the Allied governments unanimously rejected the peace offer of the Germans.[151] They declined to state their war aims. And not a single one of the American grievances against the British had been resolved.

Perhaps Wilson could sense that his time was running out: there was no more room for maneuvers in the final days of 1916. Events would soon show the American people and their reelected leader where the course of history was taking them.

A photographic portrait of Woodrow Wilson taken on November 5, 1912, at the Pach Brothers studio in New York. *Credit*: Library of Congress.

Woodrow Wilson, photographed circa 1913. *Credit*: Library of Congress.

Wilson on the stump during his "preparedness" speaking tour, January 1916.
Credit: Library of Congress.

Woodrow Wilson (far right) and others inspecting a military vehicle on the White House lawn. *Credit*: Library of Congress.

Colonel Edward M. House. *Credit*: Library of Congress.

Robert Lansing, photographed in 1915. *Credit*: Library of Congress.

David Lloyd George, photographed circa 1915. *Credit*: Library of Congress.

Georges Clemenceau, photographed on November 26, 1917. *Credit*: Library of Congress.

Senator Henry Cabot Lodge, circa 1916. *Credit*: Library of Congress.

Woodrow Wilson and his presidential successor, Warren G. Harding, riding to the latter's inauguration on March 4, 1921. *Credit*: Library of Congress.

Part II

Nemesis

Chapter Four

1917

Because of previous events and his previous decisions, Wilson found himself in a lamentable position as America entered the war. The belatedness of his preparedness measures prevented him from putting troops in the field for a long time, and this weakened his bargaining position with the Allies. Even worse, he neglected to use the leverage that *was* at his disposal to compel an agreement with the British and the French on war aims, an agreement that might have precluded the sort of peace that was eventually forced at Versailles.

Perhaps in compensation for these frustrations, Wilson was complicit in a crackdown (both orchestrated and spontaneous) on freedom of expression—one of the worst suppressions of civil liberties in the history of the United States—that was grotesquely at odds with his rhetoric about making the world safe for democracy. Wartime repression under Wilson went far beyond anything justifiable for reasons of national security.

Meanwhile, the confusion of Wilson's wartime mobilization caused a political crisis that led to accusations of presidential incompetence—incompetence approaching such scandalous dimensions that drastic measures were discussed at both ends of Pennsylvania Avenue as 1917 drew to a close.

DEATH AND RUIN

The price to be paid for the millions of casualties—and the enormous stress upon civilian populations—was a series of political and military breakdowns in 1917.

Another Allied offensive on the western front led only to additional failure. In early April, a British attack at Arras was driven back by the Germans; fighting resumed later on and continued into May, with no other result than

130,000 British casualties and a comparable number for the Germans. The French, under new command—General Joseph Joffre had been promoted out of command and replaced by Robert Nivelle—attacked in April at Chemin des Dames. Nivelle had some new ideas about artillery tactics that he hoped would lead to "rupture" of the German lines. It didn't work, and the French casualties were high. Nivelle was replaced by Philippe Pétain.

And then, a development that some observers and historians have termed "mutiny" appeared in the ranks of the French army. The revolt, as to some extent it was, fell short of an actual mutiny; it consisted of increasing non-compliance with orders, together with hints that the troops were unwilling to attack any longer in light of the suicidal odds. Though some of the "muti-neers" were punished, Pétain resolved to delay any further attacks—with the exceptions of some limited offensives in Flanders in July, at Verdun in August, and upon the Aisne in October—until the mood of the troops had settled down. Over a million French men had died since 1914. And this, in Keegan's view, had "deadened the French will to fight. Defend the homeland the soldiers of France would; attack they would not. Their mood would not change for nearly a year."[1]

For reasons of their own, the Germans pulled back a little on the western front—they gave up some ground in order to shorten supply lines and tighten their fortifications—into a new and more formidable position, the "Hindenburg Line." The Germans were preparing to turn their full force in other directions, principally toward Russia. The German mood was better than the French, since the Germans were successfully occupying foreign territory. But there was one exception: the food situation on the home front was turning grim.

In Russia, the process of breakdown that happened in France went further: the breakdown was total, since it merged with the Russian Revolution. In the "February Revolution," protests in Petrograd over food shortages led to repression, but the Petrograd garrison refused to assist the police. Then the troops supported the insurgents. "Soviets," spontaneous committees of civic leaders, sprang up, and the swift-moving sequence of events led to agitation in the Russian political class for a new government. Tsar Nicholas abdicated in March.

A provisional revolutionary government formed, and a dynamic leader, Alexander Kerensky, took over as minister of war. In June, he directed General Brusilov to resume the offensive, but events went badly and the German and Austrian counterattacks were effective. In August, a German offensive in the northern sector resulted in the seizure of Riga. The German position continued to improve. Kerensky—prime minister by July—was defeated by a sequence of events in which Russian revolutionary politics became more chaotic. The famous German gambit of assisting Lenin, the exiled Bolshevik leader, in his bid to return from Zurich to Petrograd paid off spectacularly:

the Bolshevik coup in October led to Lenin's offer to the Central Powers of a three-month armistice. Russia was effectively out of the war by the end of the year.

The Central Powers were the winners on the eastern front, and their success was magnified by the defeat of the Italians in the Battle of Caporetto in late October. German troops, augmenting the Austrian forces, made the Italians retreat over eighty miles; by early November, the Germans and Austrians were in striking distance of Venice.

The British commander, General Haig, decided to attack the German position in Flanders, and another battle at Ypres began in July. After a bombardment four times as massive as that unleashed before the Battle of the Somme, British troops, augmented by some elements of the French First Army, moved forward on July 31. Like the Battle of the Somme a year before, this battle at Ypres—actually the third battle to be fought at this locale—became a long and murderous waste. The German positions were among the strongest on the western front. And torrential rains reduced much of the battleground to mud. Keegan describes the fighting at "Passchendaele"—as the British would call this battle in commemoration of a devastated village that was one of their objectives—as a matter of

> constant exposure to enemy view in a landscape swept bare of buildings and vegetation, sodden with rain and in wide areas actually under water, on to which well-aimed shellfire fell almost without pause and was concentrated in lethal torrents whenever an assault was attempted against objectives which, nearby in distance, came to seem unattainably remote as failure succeeded failure.[2]

The fighting continued through November, and the British losses were 170,000 wounded and 20,000 killed. In Keegan's view, there was no excuse this time for the decisions—for the behavior—of Haig: "On the Somme he had sent the flower of British youth to death or mutilation; at Passchendaele he had tipped the survivors into the slough of despond." Haig's attitude "defies explanation."[3]

Another British offensive, late in November, occurred at Cambrai, where three hundred British tanks were massed in an attempt to cut the German lines. But the troops were kept too far behind the tanks, and a German counterattack was successful.

Early in the year, the Germans had resumed unrestricted submarine warfare, the objective being to bring the British to their knees by cutting supplies. Indeed, by April the British had begun to suffer fearful losses. But new British tactics, especially the use of convoys, denied the Germans the decisive victory they hoped for. Even so, as the Germans prepared to shift troops from the eastern theater to France by the spring of the following year, there was reason for the Central Powers to entertain hope of total victory—before the disorganized Americans could muster sufficient strength to shift the odds. Erich Ludendorff believed that the Americans would not be able to put an army in the field until 1919.[4]

I AM SPEAKING FOR THE SILENT MASS
OF MANKIND EVERYWHERE

In the final weeks of 1916, Chancellor Bethmann-Hollweg began to lose control of German policy. On December 22, Admiral Henning von Holtzendorff circulated a memo advocating maximum use of submarine tactics. He prevailed on January 9, at an imperial conference. "Fear of a break" with the United States, he argued, "must not hinder us from using this weapon that promises success." Holtzendorff calculated that if U-boats could sink some six hundred thousand tons of British shipping per month, the war might be won on that basis by the end of 1917.[5] Admiral Eduard von Capelle, the German secretary of state for the navy, went so far as to claim on January 31 that submarines would prove so effective as to nullify America's ability to transport troops to Europe.[6]

The German decision to unleash the submarines overlapped with a last-ditch effort by House and Bernstorff to revivify the German call for negotiations. Evidently alarmed at the course that events were taking, House was willing for the moment to put aside his earlier aversion to taking the German proposal of a peace conference seriously.

The process began on December 27, when Bernstorff called upon House and confessed that he was disappointed with his government's reply to Wilson's peace note (the Germans had, among other things, ignored Wilson's request for a statement of war aims). Bernstorff suggested to House that the war aims of each side might be stated confidentially. House agreed and suggested to Bernstorff that the German government might also state that "the essential object to be accomplished at a peace conference is to agree upon some plan by which such another war can never again be possible," and that "all territorial questions should be subservient to the main one."[7]

On December 29, Bernstorff cabled Zimmermann at the foreign office, and he relayed the ideas that he and House had discussed, imputing all of the ideas to House: "House told me that, in Wilson's view, there will be no peace conference without prior confidential negotiations, because, as things now stand, our enemies would refuse the invitation or accept only conditionally. House accompanied this statement with a request for absolutely confidential negotiations which only he, Wilson, and I were to know about."[8]

House reported these developments to Wilson, who liked the idea of "making the keystone of the settlement arch the future security of the world against wars, and letting territorial adjustments be subordinate to the main purpose."[9] Perhaps this was a way for Wilson to console himself for the fact that his demand for the articulation of specific war aims had failed to elicit any meaningful response from either side.

In any case, this was the inception for the speech that Wilson would give before the Senate on January 22, the speech in which he called for "peace without victory."

On January 3, he and House—while allowing themselves to think aloud about a number of specific territorial war aims—decided that Wilson should enunciate a vision of a postwar settlement that would be "the fairest and the best that the human mind can devise." House told Wilson he should "outline the terms in an address to Congress if he wished to make it impressive."[10]

Wilson started drafting this speech right away. In this happy frame of mind, he allowed himself to believe that his ability to stave off American participation in the war would continue indefinitely. On January 4, he told House that "there will be no war. This country does not intend to become involved in this war. We are the only one of the great White nations that is free from war today, and it would be a crime against civilization for us to go in."[11] This was avoidance—if not denial—by a man whose mind should have been engaged in the strategic questions of war and peace that could not be escaped forever. Instead, he was dallying again with his perennial delusion that beautiful ideals, expressed by beautiful words, would somehow solve all his problems.

Wilson's draft was preliminarily complete by January 11. He and House decided it should take the form of a speech to be delivered to the Senate and cabled beforehand to the capitals of the belligerent nations and published, since, according to House, Wilson was "not so much concerned about reaching the governments as he is about reaching the people."[12]

On January 10, the Allied Powers at last sent a formal reply to Wilson's note. Anglo-French deliberations on the nature of this reply had taken place at 10 Downing Street on December 26 and 28.[13] The reply, which the French did the honors in sending, stated in part that the objectives of the Allies

> will not be made known in detail with all the equitable compensation and indemnities for damages suffered until the hour of negotiations. But the civilized world knows that they imply in all necessity and in the first instance the restoration of Belgium, of Servia [*sic*], and of Montenegro and the indemnities which are due them; the evacuation of the invaded territories of France, of Russia and of Roumania [*sic*] with just reparation; the reorganization of Europe . . . [and] the enfranchisement of the populations subject to the bloody tyranny of the Turks.[14]

The German decision to resume unrestricted submarine warfare was made on January 9—the actual resumption of all-out submarine war would commence on February 1—and this decision was not revealed to Ambassador Bernstorff until January 16. Once he knew, however, the ambassador launched a campaign to get his government to delay taking this step until the prospects for peace negotiations had played out.[15] Bernstorff had already received—and acted on—an encouraging reply from Zimmermann to the proposals that he and House had transmitted.

Zimmermann said that while Germany did not desire Wilson's participation in peace negotiations, Bernstorff should endorse the arbitration of disputes, a league of nations, and other Wilsonian principles. Zimmermann also requested suggestions as to how Germany might resume unrestricted submarine warfare without triggering war with the United States.[16] In all likelihood, Bernstorff suspected the truth: that Zimmermann's message was essentially propagandistic and designed to place the Allies in a bad light as a prelude to Germany's new offensive on the seas.

House, however, had no such knowledge, and on January 15 he wrote to Wilson in a state of near elation that

> in a conference with Bernstorff this morning he authorized me to say to you (1) His Government are willing to submit to *arbitration* as a means of peace; (2) They are willing to enter a league of nations for the enforcement of peace and for the limitations of armaments both on land and sea; (3) They propose that you submit a *program* for a peace conference and they agree to give it their approval. . . . To my mind, this is the most important communication we have had since the war began and gives a real basis for negotiations and for peace [original emphasis].[17]

Several days later, House enthused that the German government "is completely in the hands of the liberals and the war has cut so deeply into the very heart of the nation that their entire attitude seems changed, and today, if we are to believe Bernstorff, they are willing to reverse their former position and take a stand as advanced as any of the democracies. . . . In my opinion, the best interests of the Allies and ourselves would be met by taking Germany at her word and concluding peace as speedily as possible."[18] Wilson told House to elicit greater clarity from Bernstorff regarding the German position.[19]

Bernstorff could not hide the truth much longer, and his next communication to House reiterated the fact that a preliminary conference should involve the *belligerents only*—that is, Wilson would be excluded—and that German agreement with Wilsonian principles applied to the future.[20] House quickly began to retreat (and save face); he told Wilson that "German diplomacy is of the devious kind," and that "it is possible they are manoeuvering [*sic*] for position in regard to the resumption of their unbridled submarine warfare. They would like to put the Allies wholly in the wrong."[21] So House reverted to courting the British and began some conversations with a new acquaintance, Sir William Wiseman, the chief of British intelligence in the United States. The British, through Wiseman, were also beginning to maneuver for position, to put the Germans wholly in the wrong, and to palliate the recent harshness of British policy. And so Wiseman humored House and spoke in a conciliatory manner of Wilsonian ideals.[22]

On the same day, Bernstorff began a more definitive retreat, telling House that "I am afraid the situation in Berlin is getting out of our hands," that "in Berlin they seem to believe, that the answer of our enemies to the President has finished the peace movement for a long time to come," and that "it will be very difficult to get any more peace terms from Berlin."[23]

As these letters were crossing in the mail, Wilson gave his big speech to the Senate on January 22. This speech is a major item in the Wilson canon, and for good reason.

Wilson interpreted recent developments—incorrectly—to mean that "we are that much nearer a definite discussion of peace which shall end the present war." It was therefore "taken for granted," he continued, that "peace must be followed by some definite concert of power which will make it virtually impossible that any such catastrophe should ever overwhelm us again."[24] Wilson told the senators he was addressing them because the Senate must ratify treaties, and American participation in a postwar peace would perforce involve a treaty.

Wilson contended that America's founders had "set up a new nation in the high and honorable hope that it might in all that it was and did show mankind the way to liberty." Americans cannot "withhold that service," he continued, but if the service should involve the cooperation with other nations to "guarantee peace" through a "formal and solemn adherence to a League for Peace," then American leaders should "frankly formulate the conditions" for such a service to humanity.[25]

The war must be ended, he said, but "it will be absolutely necessary that a force be created as a guarantor of the permanency of the settlement so much greater than the force of any nation now engaged or any alliance hitherto formed or projected that no nation . . . could face or withstand it."[26]

Any decent resolution of the war, he asserted, must create "not a balance of power, but a community of power." Any decent peace must be essentially a "peace among equals"—a "peace without victory." In using this formulation (Wilson had borrowed the phrase from the title of an editorial that appeared in *The New Republic* on December 23, 1916), Wilson was perhaps recalling his previous mistake in blurting out the "too proud to fight" formulation, so he sought to offer commentary on his new slogan:

> It is not pleasant to say this. I beg that I may be permitted to put my own interpretation upon it and that it may be understood that no other interpretation was in my thought. I am seeking only to face realities and to face them without soft concealments. Victory would mean peace forced upon the loser, a victor's terms imposed upon the vanquished. It would be accepted in humiliation,

under duress, at an intolerable sacrifice, and it would leave a sting, a resentment, a bitter memory upon which terms of peace would rest, not permanently, but only as upon quicksand.[27]

He included among the great principles for "peace among equals" the proposition of national self-determination—"no right anywhere exists to hand peoples about from sovereignty to sovereignty as if they were property"—and freedom of the seas, as embodied in the proposition that "every great people now struggling toward a full development of its resources and of its powers should be assured a direct outlet to the great highways of the sea." The "cooperation of the navies of the world" could ensure such access. To that end, a limitation of armaments should be established, a limitation "which makes of armies and navies a power for order merely, not an instrument of aggression or of selfish violence."[28]

Wilson ventured to observe that these ideals were nothing less than "the doctrine of President Monroe," which should become "the doctrine of the world": the doctrine that "no nation should seek to extend its policy over any other nation or people, but that every people should be left free to determine its own polity."[29]

He confessed that he would "fain believe that I am speaking for the silent mass of mankind everywhere who have as yet had no place or opportunity to speak their real hearts out concerning the death and ruin they see to have come already upon the persons and the homes they hold most dear."[30]

The reactions to Wilson's speech were extremely mixed. House wrote to Wilson immediately, telling him that Walter Lippmann and Herbert Croly of *The New Republic* had praised the speech, with Croly supposedly declaring that "it was the greatest event in his own life."[31] William Howard Taft applauded the speech, and many anti-interventionists, including Republican senators Robert La Follette and George Norris, along with Democrats such as William Jennings Bryan, praised it. Bryan went so far as to tell Wilson that "the basis of peace which you propose is a new philosophy—that is, new to governments but as old as the Christian religion. . . . Your message is epochmaking and will place you among the Immortals."[32] Isolationist William Borah, however, warned that once the United States had entered "the maelstrom of European politics," it would be "impossible to get out."[33]

Roosevelt, not surprisingly, vilified the speech, sneering that "peace without victory is the natural ideal of the man who is too proud to fight."[34] Henry Cabot Lodge—who had begun to drift away from his previous interest in the League to Enforce Peace—ridiculed Wilson by calling his formulations "collections of double-dealing words under which men can hide and say they mean anything and nothing," adding that "if we have a Monroe doctrine everywhere we may be perfectly certain that it will not exist anywhere."[35]

Wilson scholars have regarded this speech and its message in different ways. John Milton Cooper, for instance, has recently concluded that the vision of Wilson was "not necessarily an impossible dream," though there were doubtless "huge practical and emotional barriers in the way of its realization."[36] Arthur S. Link, however, came to different conclusions in the 1960s when he labeled Wilson's vision a dream of "a postwar order founded upon the principle of Christian love, rather than the precepts of *Realpolitik*," and then asked, rhetorically, whether "the millennium could be conceived during such a war and given birth during a conference of mortal men?"[37]

Within the particular circumstances that Wilson faced, there is reason to point out some wishful thinking—to the point of outright fantasy—in his grand gesture. It is telling that, according to House, Wilson had aimed this speech at "the people" more than "the governments." One can possibly sympathize with Wilson's hope ("I would fain believe") that he was speaking for "the silent mass of mankind everywhere," but surely public opinion was not the same "everywhere," among the great nations or within them. While there was definitely a movement of antiwar feeling in France and in Russia, as events would soon show, there is absolutely no basis for concluding that the public opinion in Britain or in Germany was, however "silent," a consensus for peace without victory in January 1917, though some demonstrations of support in Britain—including a meeting at which Wilson's name was cheered for a full five minutes in response to his speech—caught the eye of Americans who duly reported it to Wilson.[38]

The effort to achieve a nonvindictive peace was a very tall order, a challenge that demanded the utmost skills in political strategy. It might have been achievable if the man in the White House had acted in a timely fashion to generate the power that would blossom into leverage: military power. If the United States had been able to mobilize by 1917 (to put fully trained armies in the field), and if the man in the White House had sensed the likelihood and imminence of war—instead of languishing, as Wilson was doing, in the feeble illusion that "there will be no war"—then a crafty method might have been employed to put pressure on the Allies, pressure of the sort that would precommit them to a nonvindictive peace. It is possible—or at least it is not impossible—to imagine an American leader playing "hard to get" in these circumstances, telling the British and the French that even new and grave German provocations might be insufficient to generate the votes in Congress for a declaration of war. And then the ploy might have worked like this: if, such a president might have declared, he could tell the members of Congress *in truth* that he and the Allied leaders saw eye-to-eye in regard to war aims, then his hand would be strengthened and the troops that the Allies needed so desperately might be furnished. In other words, offer the Allies a simple and perhaps non-negotiable *quid pro quo*: a push for American military action in exchange for Allied cooperation in a nonvindictive peace. No agreement, no dice: a deal of leverage.

Would it have worked? It would certainly have meant a bit of bluff, and yet the Allies might have found themselves reluctant to call such a bluff. Who can say?

In any case, Wilson was not in a position to work in this way, and his *modus operandi* was different when it came to the moral propositions that elicited his deepest passion.

Link once mused that if the Germans had actually been serious about peace and had persisted in the Bethmann-Hollweg policy, "the Allies would probably have consented to a negotiated settlement under Wilson's direction. But if the Allies had refused to mediate on this basis, Wilson would almost certainly have used strong diplomatic pressure to force them to the peace table."[39] As Link pointed out, another method existed for pressuring the Allies: the policy that Wilson and the Federal Reserve had developed in the previous autumn, the policy of discouraging American banks from lending to the Allies with short-term notes as collateral. Link spelled this out in a treatment of the subject that he wrote in the 1970s:

> British gold and other reserves would be utterly exhausted by April 1, 1917; after that date, a [British] Treasury official said, Great Britain and the Allies would be at the mercy of the President of the United States. Wilson probably did not know the precise details. But he did know that he had the power absolutely to coerce the Allies.[40]

Wilson certainly possessed some financial leverage to use for "peace without victory." But it was *words* that he counted on to move the opinions of "the people." Beyond that, one is forced to ask the question: What leverage—what power—what strategy was hidden up his sleeve?

Did he have any strategy?

A TERRIBLE LIKELIHOOD

The preliminary break with Germany was not far away. Just after he delivered his "peace without victory" speech, Wilson told House it was necessary to resolve all the issues with Germany decisively:

> If Germany really wants peace she can get it, and get it soon, *if she will but confide in me and let me have a chance.* . . . It occurs to me that it would be well for you to see Bernstorff again at once (not where your meeting can be noted, as the last one was, but at some place which is not under observation) and tell him that this is the time to accomplish something . . . and that otherwise, with the preparations they are apparently making with regard to unrestrained attacks on merchantmen on the plea that they are armed for offense,

there is a terrible likelihood that the relations between the United States and Germany may come to a breaking point. . . . Feelings, exasperations are neither here nor there. Do they in fact want me to help? [41]

It was, however, the British who began to seem receptive: they abandoned the harshness they had shown in the previous summer and autumn. Link has argued that "the British already knew of the German decision to launch unrestricted submarine warfare, and it is possible this was an important factor in their willingness to talk of peace" in late January 1917. [42] Cooper observes that Lloyd George had come to believe "it was essential to maintain American goodwill." As to "why Lloyd George, who had previously taken a harsh line toward the United States, shifted his ground," Cooper argues that "perhaps the warnings of the British Treasury's brilliant young economist, John Maynard Keynes, who held that the Allied war effort was becoming totally dependent on supplies and credit from America" was a factor, along with Lloyd George's "deep suspicions about the promises of his military leaders to win the war by sacrificing still more thousands of men," which "led him to believe that only American intervention could break the stalemate." [43]

In any case, it was Sir William Wiseman who became the chief spokesman in Washington for the new and friendly British attitude. (The British ambassador, Cecil Spring-Rice, had such a high-strung personality that Americans, especially House, dreaded talking with him.) At first, Wiseman reasserted the earlier British line, telling House on January 25 that "pressing the Allies too hard for peace at this time" would do "the cause of democracy harm," since "every belligerent government is now in the hands of the reactionaries." [44] The next day, however, Wiseman made an about-face; he told House that "the atmosphere had cleared wonderfully since yesterday" and the two men "got down to a discussion of actual peace terms, and the conference which he seemed to now think could be brought about in the event that Germany returns a favourable reply." House told Wilson that Wiseman "is in direct communication with the Foreign Office, and the Ambassador and other members of the Embassy are not aware of it." [45]

Meanwhile, Bernstorff confided to House that "the military have complete control in Germany with von Hindenburg and Ludendorff at the head." [46] Even so, House went through the empty exercise of discussing yet another peace message to Berlin.

On January 31, the Germans announced the resumption of all-out submarine warfare. In a note from Bernstorff to Lansing, the German government predicted the measure would bring "a speedy end of the horrible and useless bloodshed." The Germans announced that "all ships" would be sunk within their blockade zone beginning on February 1. "All navigation, that of neutrals included," would be sunk off the coasts of Britain, France, Italy, and the eastern Mediterranean.[47]

Everything was blamed upon the Allies. In a letter to House sent the same day as the submarine announcement was sent to Lansing, Bernstorff relayed his government's "complete confidence in the President." The letter continued with an empty declaration of Germany's continued willingness to enter into peace negotiations. As to war aims, the German government was "not prepared to publish any peace terms at present, because our enemies have published such terms which aim at the dishonor and destruction of Germany and her allies. . . . However, to show President Wilson our confidence, my Government through me desires to inform him *personally* of the terms under which we would have been prepared to enter into negotiations if our enemies had accepted our offer of December 12th [original emphasis]." The terms included withdrawal from Belgium and occupied French territory with reparations, in exchange for guarantees of Germany's security.[48]

Bernstorff had already tried to talk his government out of these steps; on January 28, he had written to Berlin that

> if submarine warfare is now begun without further ado, the President will take this as a slap in the face and war with the United States cannot be avoided. . . . In my view the end of the war will be unforeseeable, because—despite all that can be said to the contrary—the power and resources of the United States are very great.[49]

In Link's opinion, the German decision was "one of the greatest blunders in history" because the sinkings would be indiscriminate. "Wilson would almost certainly have accepted an all-out submarine campaign against *belligerent* merchantmen, exclusive, perhaps, of unarmed passenger ships," Link theorized, "and such a campaign could have been devastating, perhaps decisive." He continued: "American public opinion was overwhelmingly opposed to war; Congress certainly would not have adopted a war resolution over the issue of the safety of belligerent merchantmen and the right of a few Americans to work on them."[50]

Wilson hesitated to break off relations with Germany, though Lansing (naturally) advocated this course of action on the evening of January 31. According to Lansing, Wilson said that "he was willing to go to any lengths rather than to have the nation actually involved in the conflict." Part of Wilson's reasoning perforce sounds grotesque to our generation: he said "he had been more and more impressed with the idea that 'white civilization' and its domination in the world rested largely on our ability to keep this country intact."[51] Lansing was not the only one to attribute this notion to Wilson; according to agriculture secretary David F. Houston, Wilson opened a cabinet meeting on February 2 by wondering "what effect would the depletion of man power have upon the relations of the white and yellow races" if America entered the war. "Would the yellow races take advantage of it and attempt to subjugate the white races?"[52]

Wilson said a number of things that reflected a mind out of balance as he struggled to react to what Germany was doing. House recorded on February 1 that he found the president "sad and depressed." Wilson said that he felt as if "the world had suddenly reversed itself, that after going from east to west, it had begun to go from west to east and that he could not get his balance."[53] Lansing arrived and the three of them decided it would be best if the United States severed relations with Germany immediately.

Wilson made a short speech to Congress on February 3, reciting the events and announcing the severance of relations. Wilson said he would give the Germans the benefit of the doubt (as if there were any doubt)—he would play for time—by declaring, "I refuse to believe that it is the intention of the German authorities to do in fact what they have warned us they will feel at liberty to do." But he added that if "American ships and American lives should in fact be sacrificed," he would ask Congress for authority "to use any means necessary" to protect American lives and American interests.[54] The Senate passed a resolution approving Wilson's action, with a number of senators stating for the record that they wanted to stay out of war.

So did multitudes of Americans, and huge antiwar rallies were organized. Groups such as the American Union Against Militarism and leaders such as William Jennings Bryan led the campaigns. The most radical antiwar leaders talked of a referendum on war, of a general strike, and similar measures.

Wilson shared the antiwar feeling to a great extent, and so he dragged his feet—he slipped into avoidance—on contingency planning. General Hugh Scott, the army chief of staff, wrote on February 15 that "the President does not want to do anything which will give the Germans an idea that we are getting ready for war, so we are not allowed to ask for any money or to get ready in a serious way."[55]

But in this, as other matters, Wilson was often inconsistent; in a different mood, he had asked Congress in his annual report of December 1916 for the power "to take control of such portions and such rolling stock of the railways of the country as may be required for military use and to operate them for military purposes, with authority to draft into the military service of the United States such train crews and administrative officials as the circumstances require for their safe and efficient use."[56] It bears noting that Wilson already had the authority to run the railroads: he had gotten it in a provision of an army appropriations bill. What he needed was additional authority to draft engineers and train crews.

By the same token, the Army War College was authorized to prepare a conscription bill, and a naval appropriations bill under consideration in the

House provided for faster construction and empowered the president to seize shipyards.[57]

The Germans began to make good on their threat: American ships were attacked. American exporters started keeping their ships at home, and goods began to accumulate in warehouses. At meetings on February 6 and 13, the cabinet discussed the issue of protecting American commerce, with alternatives ranging from the arming of merchant vessels to battleship convoys to accompany them through the war zone. After a cabinet meeting on February 23, Wilson lashed out at several cabinet members, accusing them of "appealing to the spirit of the *Code Duello*."[58]

Wilson was drifting—back and forth—and his vacillations, though to some extent normal, began to reach a level of magnitude that justifies the term *mood swings*. His behavior was erratic, and the man who kept trying to emphasize self-control began to snap at his colleagues and subordinates. He also continued to generate irrational worst-case visions, as when he asserted to Josephus Daniels that war would mean control of the government by business, adding that "neither you nor I will live to see government returned to the people."[59]

This particular notion played a role in Wilson's continuing aversion to bipartisanship. Granted, Republicans such as Roosevelt and Lodge had reacted to the peace without victory speech in a contemptuous manner, and Wilson had taken their ridicule personally. To one correspondent he wrote that while "the country has responded very nobly to what I said, the Republicans in the Senate have responded very ignobly."[60] He had persuaded himself that, notwithstanding the Republican Party's progressive wing, Republicans were mostly champions of the privileged, so he rejected some overtures in February by a number of Republicans—including some conservative Republicans—to put aside other differences and consult with Wilson on the issues of peace and war. He told House he was leery of accepting "the support I am receiving from once hostile quarters. . . . It is the *Junkerthum* trying to creep in under cover of the patriotic feeling of the moment. They will not get in. . . . I know them too well, and will hit them straight between the eyes, if necessary, with plain words." He would not abet the attempts of big business to control the government.[61]

This was epic folly—an enormous mistake—that would cost Wilson dearly in 1919, when he would need every vote that he could get in the Senate to approve the Versailles treaty after the Republicans had taken control of Congress.

Perhaps this is the time for a discussion of Wilson's worsening mental condition. Wilson had been diagnosed with arteriosclerosis as early as 1906. His first wife, Ellen, had lamented the fact that "hardening of the arteries . . . is an awful thing—a dying by inches, and incurable."[62] There is reason to suspect that this condition was impacting Wilson's judgment well before the stroke that he suffered in October 1919. In light of the many strange things that he would say and do in the course of the war, one cannot avoid wondering how much of the tragedy was grounded in pathologies of blood circulation and brain physiology. Of course, the problem in separating medical issues from the judgments that we reach about a person's "character"—the degree to which we are inclined to believe that our conscious self is to a certain extent self-created—is not only a mystery in regard to the workings of the mind but also a mystery of higher metaphysics. To this extent, as we behold the misjudgments of Wilson—the avoidance and fantasy and arrogance—we are torn between anger at this man who was capable of so much better at his best and lamentation in regard to ways in which his condition was perhaps not fully his fault.

On February 24, some sensational news was relayed by the British: the Germans had made overtures to Mexico so as to exploit Wilson's "Mexico problem." The famous "Zimmermann telegram," sent by Foreign Minister Arthur Zimmermann to the German embassy in Mexico, proposed that Mexico should join the Central Powers in the event of war between Germany and the United States. If the Central Powers won, the Mexicans would get back Texas, New Mexico, and Arizona, lost to the Mexicans in 1848. War with Mexico would tie down American troops in the Western Hemisphere.

The British had intercepted the German cable, but to conceal this capacity from the Americans, the British had spies in the German embassy in Mexico City steal a decoded copy, which the British turned over to the American ambassador Walter Hines Page on February 24. Wilson had it on his desk the next day.[63]

The president decided not to make the news public for the moment. But on February 26 he went before Congress requesting new authority. He announced the sinking of two American merchant vessels, commented on the "congestion of our commerce" that resulted from the "unwillingness of our shipowners to risk their vessels at sea," and averred that, in addition to his existing authority as commander in chief, he wished "to feel that the authority and power of Congress are behind me," especially since this lame-duck session of Congress would adjourn very soon.

So Wilson requested Congress to give him authority "to supply our merchant ships with defensive arms, should that become necessary, and with the means of using them." But Wilson went further: he also requested authority "to employ any other instrumentalities or methods that may be necessary and adequate" for protecting American property and lives.[64]

This latter request prompted massive resistance from noninterventionists. The resistance actually increased after Wilson released the Zimmermann telegram to the press on March 1. Naturally a wave of indignation at the Germans swept over the country, but this simply redoubled the determination of noninterventionists to prevent the country from being swept into war. On

March 1, the House overwhelmingly approved the armed ships resolution, but without the broader authority that Wilson requested. When the bill reached the Senate it was filibustered to death on March 4 by a group of senators led by Robert La Follette and George Norris. The atmosphere was so bitter at the time that La Follette brought a loaded pistol with him into the Senate chamber. After an all-night session, the Senate adjourned at noon on March 4—at the very moment when Wilson was sitting down the hall, in the President's Room of the U.S. Capitol, waiting to be sworn in for his second term of office in a private ceremony. Later that day, Wilson issued his soon-to-be-famous rebuke: "A little group of willful men, representing no opinion but their own, have rendered the great Government of the United States helpless and contemptible." [65]

Congress adjourned, but since a great deal of necessary business had not been completed—especially appropriations bills—Wilson would be forced to call the new Congress into special session shortly.

On March 9, after consultations with Lansing and Attorney General Thomas Watt Gregory, Wilson authorized the arming of merchant ships on his own and called Congress into a special session that would begin on April 16. [66] The brief interlude of "armed neutrality" ensued as the work of placing armaments on American merchant vessels began.

But the interlude was short-lived because the submarine campaign of the Germans accelerated, and American public opinion responded. Though vast numbers of Americans remained opposed to participation in the war, interventionism surged after three American vessels, the *City of Memphis*, *Illinois*, and *Vigilancia*, were all sunk by torpedoes on a single day, March 18. Two days later Theodore Roosevelt called for war, and the New York *World* editorialized for a war declaration. A pro-intervention crowd of twelve thousand cheered for war at Madison Square Garden on March 22, and even previously isolationist politicians in the Midwest began to join in. So did a number of dissident socialists.

Appeals on behalf of the British flooded into the White House. Walter Hines Page wrote from London pleading for financial relief for Great Britain. [67] British credit in America would end in April, and the Germans had succeeded in sinking almost six hundred thousand tons of Allied shipping in March—precisely the goal of the German naval high command.

At a cabinet meeting on March 19—the day after the sinking of the three American ships—every member of the Wilson cabinet recommended a declaration of war. [68] Slowly, Wilson took some steps in that direction. He speeded up the convening of the special session of Congress, and he summoned the legislators to "receive a communication on grave matters of national policy" on April 2. He had navy secretary Josephus Daniels begin coordinating naval operations with the British. He sent Rear Admiral William S. Sims and an aide to Great Britain under assumed names and wearing civilian clothes. He also began to call some units of the national guard into federal service.

He was sleep deprived, battered by events. On March 19, he summoned Frank Cobb, the editor of the New York *World*, and made an agonized statement. Cobb recalled later that Wilson said that he "had tried every way he knew to avoid war. . . . So far as he knew he had considered every loophole of escape and as fast as they were discovered Germany deliberately blocked them with some new outrage." Then, according to Cobb, Wilson painted a ghastly picture of the damage to democracy that would result from participation in the war:

> "Once lead this people into war," he said, "and they'll forget there ever was such a thing as tolerance. To fight you must be brutal and ruthless, and the spirit of ruthless brutality will enter into the very fibre of our national life, infecting Congress, the courts, the policeman on the beat, the man in the street." He thought the Constitution would not survive it; that free speech and the right of assembly would go. He said a nation couldn't put its strength into a war and keep its head level; it had never been done. [69]

Some historians have questioned the veracity of Cobb's reporting, but the consensus of opinion, led by Arthur S. Link, has regarded Cobb's account as authentic. [70] If so, this particular Wilsonian outburst is notable in several respects.

First, the historical and cultural generalizations of Wilson were irresponsible, for the level of protection of civil liberties had varied tremendously in the course of America's previous wars.

Second, the defeatism that Wilson expressed in regard to the protection of civil liberties was both unfounded—much would depend upon his very own actions and the standards he would set himself—and perverse, for predictions of this kind by the highest magistrate in the land can become self-fulfilling.

And third, his defeatism was symptomatic of a leader who doubted his ability to lead. Cooper has confirmed that Wilson was not cut out to be a war leader. [71] Indeed, Wilson himself told House on March 27 that "he did not believe he was fitted for the presidency under such conditions." [72]

He had hoped against hope to be a mediator, and in patient but desperate expectation of playing such a role he had drifted and reacted as events unfolded, engaged in avoidance and wishful thinking, his twin objectives being (1) to preserve his ability to extricate himself from tight places and (2) to maintain an immaculate posture as he did so.

He had come to his senses on preparedness, yes, but he had little instinct for shaping events through an architectonic use of force. On the issue of preventing a vindictive peace, this particular stretch of time—March—could have been an almost perfect moment for action. The clock was running out for British credit. Lloyd George, via Wiseman, seemed ready to listen and accommodate.[73] Events erupted, crises multiplied, but surely the cool-headed strategists—those with "self-possession," to use Wilson's phrase—may prevail and even turn the situation to advantage when caught in what seems to be a trap. One thinks of the communication from General Ferdinand Foch in the worst of the fighting on the western front during autumn 1914: "My center is giving way, my right is in retreat, situation excellent. I attack."[74]

But Wilson let the opportunity go.

He tried to master the events of this war and to elevate them all to a world-redemptive opportunity. Yet he lacked the sheer joy of maneuver—the cunning—to *manipulate* force to serve his ends. The best that he could manage in these dreadful weeks of March was to react with reluctance to the flow of events, then come to his terrible decision.

Slowly, he pulled himself together and in solitude composed what almost every Wilson scholar has regarded as his crowning composition: the war message that he gave as a speech before Congress, presented at 8:30 p.m. on April 2, 1917.

As a masterpiece of the oratorical art, it is an object of beauty. As a specimen of Wilson's histrionics, it pulses with danger. But on the surface it suggests no danger at all: the effect of this speech is reassurance, and its tone suggests a sober maturity. It is (or seems to be) a confident summation—strong, lucid, a summons to a work both righteous and majestic, rational and fine, a work for men of courage and intelligence.

He began by vilifying the cruelty of the Germans' new policy of submarine warfare:

> Vessels of every kind, whatever their flag, their character, their cargo, their destination, their errand, have been ruthlessly sent to the bottom without warning and without thought of help or mercy for those on board, the vessels of friendly neutrals along with those of belligerents. Even hospital ships and ships carrying relief to the sorely bereaved and stricken people of Belgium, though the latter were provided with safe conduct through the proscribed areas by the German Government itself and were distinguished by unmistakable marks of identity, have been sunk with the same reckless lack of compassion.[75]

Wilson went on:

> Property can be paid for; the lives of peaceful and innocent people cannot be. The present German submarine warfare against commerce is a warfare against mankind. It is a war against all nations. . . . There has been no discrimination. The challenge is to all mankind. Each nation must decide for itself how it will meet it.[76]

Then Wilson told Congress how to meet it. "Armed neutrality," he declared, "is ineffectual at best; in such circumstances . . . it is worse than ineffectual."

It was time to make the only real choice of honor, the choice to affirm self-respect:

> There is one choice we cannot make, we are incapable of making: we will not choose the path of submission and suffer the most sacred rights of our nation and our people to be ignored or violated. The wrongs against which we now array ourselves are no common wrongs; they cut to the very roots of human life.[77]

At this point applause began: Chief Justice Edward White began and soon the whole House chamber reverberated with approval. Wilson's draftsmanship and timing were perfect for what came next:

> With a profound sense of the solemn and even tragical character of the step I am taking and of the grave responsibilities which it involves, but in unhesitating obedience to what I deem my constitutional duty, I advise that the Congress declare the recent course of the Imperial German Government to be in fact nothing less than war against the government and people of the United States.[78]

Wilson set forth the challenges of mobilization, and he gave the British instant relief: he would initiate "the utmost practical cooperation in counsel and action with the governments now at war with Germany, and, as incident to that, the extension to those governments of the most liberal financial credits."[79] Then he called for national mobilization, for improvement of anti-submarine capabilities, for "immediate addition to the armed forces" of "at least five hundred thousand men," to be drafted according to the "principle of universal liability for service," with authorization for additional increments of "equal force" just as soon as the first draftees could be trained, and for "adequate credits to the Government" (deficit spending via war bonds) that could be "sustained by the present generation by well conceived taxation."[80]

Soon enough he descanted—in characteristically Wilsonian terms—upon the deeper issues of the war. His abhorrence of secrecy and deception propelled his crusade for "open covenants" into a crusade for democracy itself:

> We have no quarrel with the German people. We have no feeling towards them but one of sympathy and friendship. It was not upon their impulse that their government acted in entering this war. It was not with their previous knowledge and approval. It was a war determined upon as wars used to be determined upon in the old, unhappy days when peoples were nowhere consulted by their rulers and wars were provoked and waged in the interests of dynasties or little groups of ambitious men who were accustomed to use their fellow men as pawns and tools. Self-governed nations do not fill their neighbor states with spies or set the course of intrigue to bring about some critical posture of affairs which will give them an opportunity to strike and make conquest. Such

designs can be successfully worked out only under cover and where no one has the right to ask questions. [81]

Here were some issues that reached to the heart of Wilson's troubles as a strategist and pointed the way to the utopianism that infected his doctrines when anyone put them to the test of international politics. The Germans were hardly the only ones to use spies: how else would Wilson have known about the Zimmermann telegram if British intelligence, including British spies in the German embassy in Mexico, had not been used to alert him? As to working "under cover" through private "intrigue," in a manner that did not permit the people to ask any questions, what else was the House-Grey diplomacy but a venture in secret understandings undertaken without the knowledge and approval of the public? What else was the confidentiality of House's maneuverings—two secretaries of state were kept ignorant of its details—except the work of a "little group of men"—namely, Wilson, House, and Grey (who were eventually joined by the British cabinet)?

Can democracy function effectively without the leadership of people who, governed by conscience, good judgment, and law, take some initiatives—take some liberties—in formulating policy?

It was just as well that peace with Germany had proven impossible, Wilson avowed, for "the Prussian autocracy was not and could never be our friend"; in any effort at cooperation with such an autocracy, America would soon get betrayed, for the autocrats would always be "lying in wait to accomplish we know not what." [82] After taking note of the recent abdication of the tsar, Wilson rejoiced that the democratic principle was rising in the world, and he proclaimed that the war itself should become a crusade that would speed the process along:

> The world must be made safe for democracy. Its peace must be planted upon the tested foundations of political liberty. We have no selfish ends to serve. We desire no conquest, no dominion. We seek no indemnities for ourselves, no material compensation for the sacrifices we shall freely make. We are but one of the champions of the rights of mankind. [83]

The world should be safe for democracy, Wilson proclaimed—and democracy could save the world. "A steadfast concert for peace can never be maintained except by a partnership of democratic nations," Wilson proclaimed. "No autocratic government could be trusted to keep faith within it or observe its covenants." [84] Wilson now began to toy with the idea that the League of Nations should be open to democracies only.

Wilson reiterated his friendship with the German people, and he declared that an opportunity existed to prove this here in America—the chance to "prove that friendship in our daily attitude and actions towards the millions of men and women of German birth and native sympathy who live among us." This was an excellent thing for him to say. Alas, he betrayed this pledge through inattention, at least until the very last months of the war.

His closing peroration must rank as a classic in English literature:

> It is a fearful thing to lead this great peaceful people into war, into the most terrible and disastrous of all wars, civilization itself seeming to be in the balance. But the right is more precious than peace, and we shall fight for the things which we have always carried nearest our hearts,—for democracy, for the right of those who submit to authority to have a voice in their own governments, for the rights and liberties of small nations, for a universal dominion of right by such a concert of free peoples as shall bring peace and safety to all nations and make the world itself at last free. To such a task we can dedicate our lives and our fortunes, everything that we are and everything that we have, with the pride of those who know that the day has come when America is privileged to spend her blood and her might for the principles that gave her birth and happiness and the peace which she has treasured. God helping her, she can do no other. [85]

It is one of the curious things about John Milton Cooper's biography of Wilson that he makes the repeated assertion that Wilson "opposed mixing religion and politics." [86] But Wilson's politics were drenched in religion, and his powerful sense of Christian piety would grow until he finally offered to America the League of Nations as a veritable fulfillment of the vision set forth in Isaiah. But even Cooper has noticed the fact that Wilson's war message ends with a statement that paraphrases Luther: "God helping her, she can do no other," which is close to the famous original—*Hier stehe ich. Ich kann nicht anders. Gott helfe mir.* [87]

I HAVE NOT BEEN ABLE TO THINK MYSELF ONTO SAFE GROUND

Wilson's war message was, of course, a catharsis, and the national mood changed accordingly. The war declaration passed easily, in the Senate by a vote of 82 to 6 on April 4 and in the House by a vote of 373 to 50 on April 6.

As with the preparedness fight, the mobilization challenge brought out some of Wilson's better qualities: the task of summoning power sharpened Wilson's intelligence and sense of practicality. The defeatism and avoidance of his mood in February and March started fading; in their place was the release of pent-up tension and energy—and anger. Cooper correctly observes that while "many in Congress and elsewhere appeared to believe that the United States would mostly continue to furnish food, munitions, and money to the Allies [Wilson] meant to wage war with every resource at his command, and he meant to do it his way." The task would include expanding the authorized size of the army "possibly ten times or more," recruiting "more men than the nation had ever put under arms," transporting them to Europe, and mobilizing the entire economy to support the effort.[88] On April 9, Wilson told Carter Glass that "we are mobilizing the nation as well as creating an Army, and that means that we must keep every instrumentality in it at its highest pitch of efficiency and guided by thoughtful intelligence."[89]

As with preparedness, however, Wilson found himself playing catch-up. John Morton Blum once complained that Wilson "had to feel his way toward the creation of agencies sufficiently powerful" to manage the job; "the absence of forehandedness made the task enormous. When the war came, the army lacked data even on the uniforms and shoes it would need; neither military nor civilians had an inventory of resources or a plan for priorities."[90] This statement contains both truth and falsehood: Wilson and Baker had set up the Council of National Defense in the previous year, and an inventory was in fact being compiled. On February 7, Baker sent Wilson a memorandum on war preparations, informing him that

> all Bureaus and Divisions of this Department are preparing estimates of supplies necessary to be bought and arrangements necessary to be made in the event of an order being given to increase the Regular Army and National Guard to war strength, and undertake the training of a large volunteer force.[91]

Furthermore, "We are making immediate purchases in anticipation of pending appropriations for supplies, such as clothing, shoes, foodstuffs, tentage, etc., to the fullest amount possible."[92]

But these efforts were late and insufficient. And this experience would instill a resolution in the officers who had to live through it that if and when another major war should develop, civilian leaders simply had to be made to see the necessity of sufficient lead time for mobilization. George C. Marshall, in particular, would put this experience to use in his tenure as army chief of staff before and during World War II.

Even though Wilson was becoming alert to the practical challenges of mobilization, his stubborn and myopic habits were in full force on other fronts, and they continued to mar his strategic thinking on matters political, domestic, and foreign. He made some fateful blunders that would undermine his chances for achieving the kind of postwar settlement that he wanted. And one of his very worst blunders was his treatment of Theodore Roosevelt.

Granted, Roosevelt projected nothing less than hate toward Wilson, both in public and in private, and Wilson was justified in feeling the resentment that any sane person would experience due to such abuse. But Roosevelt wanted something very keenly—desperately—by the spring of 1917, and he was ready to hold out the olive branch to Wilson in order to get it.

Roosevelt wanted to do what he had done in the Spanish-American War: he wanted to summon and lead a volunteer unit of troops and command these troops at the front.

It is easy to dismiss this desire as silly machismo. But to do such a thing would be to throw away an opportunity to understand the mind of a figure who could have done much to smooth the way for Republican cooperation with Wilson on the postwar peace—notwithstanding the fact that Roosevelt would die (in January 1919) well before the Versailles treaty was in the hands of Senator Lodge.

Roosevelt's understanding of the imperative to practice what you preach made him feel that his glorification of heroism in combat would be hypocritical if he shrank from the terrors and the lethal risks of war. All of Theodore Roosevelt's sons served in World War I, and by many accounts it almost broke the old man's heart when his youngest and most precocious son, Quentin, was killed in its final months. The old lion had been forced to the sidelines when his youngest cub was sacrificed.

Roosevelt had written to Baker on March 19—just after the three American ships had been sunk on March 18—and proposed to assemble at his own expense a volunteer division to be trained at Fort Sill, Oklahoma, using the Plattsburgh methods that Leonard Wood had pioneered.[93] Baker sent a curt reply on March 20 to the effect that the commanders of volunteer forces would be drawn from the regular army.[94]

Roosevelt would not be put off by such tactics, and on April 10 he went to the White House to see Woodrow Wilson. A White House staff member recorded the visit as follows in his diary:

> At noon the President received Col. Theodore Roosevelt. . . . The President doesn't like Theodore Roosevelt and he was not one bit effusive in his greeting. This did not disconcert the Colonel who in his usual vigorous manner proceeded to outline his plans; but first he commended in the warmest terms the President's message to Congress and gave his entire approval to the administration's program for raising an army by selective conscription. The interview lasted twenty-five minutes and before it closed the President had thawed out and was laughing and "talking back."[95]

Roosevelt later recalled that he had offered—explicitly—to bury the hatchet. He said that all the bad feelings of the past would be "dust in a windy street, if we can make your message [i.e., Wilson's war speech to Congress] good. . . . If we can translate it into fact, then it will rank as a great state paper, with the very great state papers of Washington and Lincoln."[96] Wilson's head was turned by this kind of praise from "TR": Tumulty recalled Wilson musing that Roosevelt "is a great big boy. I was, as formerly"—the two men had met years earlier during Wilson's tenure as president of Princeton—"charmed by his personality. There is a sweetness about him that is very compelling. You can't resist the man."[97]

But Wilson did resist—indirectly. On April 13, Baker wrote to Roosevelt, denying his request. Baker told Roosevelt that the officers of the expeditionary force should be "selected because of their previous military training and, as far as possible, actual military experience." Even though Roosevelt had not attended West Point, he could boast of some spectacular experience under enemy fire in Cuba. But Baker indirectly discounted this qualification, stating that the officers in this war should be men who had "devoted their lives exclusively" to military service.

Whatever the merits of this view, it did insufficient justice to the option of placing Roosevelt in a command position that would have surrounded him with experienced aides with whom he would consult on the newer realities of war.[98] One should not forget that Abraham Lincoln had proven a better strategist than most of his generals, and he grasped the details of war quickly.

Wilson could and arguably should have given Theodore Roosevelt his way. Even if Roosevelt got killed in combat, his political friends, including Henry Cabot Lodge, might have entertained a gratitude to Wilson for overcoming personal animus and allowing the former president to depart this life in glory, as he wished to do. As it was, Theodore Roosevelt would go to his grave in the belief that Wilson had denied him the commission out of spite.[99] And the friends of Theodore Roosevelt never forgot this.

Wilson missed a priceless opportunity to turn an enemy into a friend—and an asset. Again, he had failed to engage in the macropolitical contingency planning that should have anticipated the need for bipartisan alliances to ratify a postwar treaty. Instead, he poured additional poison down the well of Republican animosity.

As with domestic coalition politics, so with international politics. On April 14, Wilson told a visiting member of Parliament, John Howard Whitehouse, that he would stay "detached from the Allies" because he did not agree with the vindictive terms of the Paris economic pact. This was the pact to which Lansing had drawn his attention in the previous year: the pact of June 1916, with its resolutions to continue economic warfare against the Germans even after they were defeated.

In this context, Wilson's preference to keep himself "detached" was revealing: instead of finding ways to sway the Allied leaders—to use leverage to change their position—Wilson held himself aloof, thus effectuating nothing. Wilson did tell Whitehouse that "much could be done in a private or semi-official way in educating public opinion on the problems of the settlement," but this again revealed an aversion to applying much pressure to the people with the power at the bargaining table: the political leaders.[100]

In fact, there is reason to believe that Wilson's abdication was worse. On March 29, House had written to him with very interesting news. Granted, the news was hearsay, but consider the nature of its contents:

[Norman] Hapgood writes that Lloyd George's secretary told him that Lloyd George said—"Great Britain will be fighting for moderate terms at the conference. Some of her allies will be grabbing. We want America to back up England."[101]

If Wilson had wished, he could have followed up. And this is pertinent, since he had not yet given away—for free—the financial relief that the British needed desperately, the relief that he would promise in his war message to Congress. But even after he had relinquished this leverage, he could have managed if he wished during April—especially in April, when British gratitude for the relief might have been manipulated—to engage in intense consultations with Lloyd George on the basis for a nonvindictive peace.

He made no effort to do so.

But the British and the French took action on their own to end his detachment: both governments requested to send delegations to Washington. The British delegation was headed by the new foreign minister, Arthur Balfour. The French delegation was headed by the justice minister, René Viviani, and General Joffre.

When Balfour arrived on April 22, he went into consultations with House. And the result was to end any prospect for short-term *commitments* to "peace without victory." House—sensing, perhaps, the aversion of Wilson to facing up to this task—expressed the opinion, to Balfour and Wilson, that the topic ought to be deferred. Balfour—perhaps taking House's cue in the hope of thus establishing good relations—agreed.

House recorded the details in a letter to Wilson that he sent on the very same date—April 22.

I told Balfour that unless you advised to the contrary, I thought it would be well to minimize the importance of his visit here to the extent of a denial that it was for the purpose of forming some sort of an agreement with the Allies. I find there is a feeling that this country is about to commit itself to a secret alliance with them. . . . I hope you will agree with me that the best policy now is to avoid a discussion of peace settlements. Balfour concurs in this.[102]

House did try to lay the groundwork for a nonvindictive peace by telling Balfour that "he hoped England would consider that a peace which was best for all the nations of the world would be the one best for England. He accepted this with enthusiasm."[103] Of course, such a formulation was vague enough to encompass almost anything, but House told Wilson that Balfour was probably receptive to "peace without victory": "If you have a tacit understanding with him not to discuss peace terms with the other allies, later, this country and England, will be able to dictate broad and generous terms."[104] There is reason to believe that House was genuinely encouraged by the visible attitude of Balfour.

This kindled a new surge of interest in Wilson in regard to the prospect of "dictating broad and generous terms." On April 26, he told House that "it would be a pity to have Balfour go home without a discussion of the subject." House immediately turned on a dime and agreed: "My thought was that there was no harm in discussing it . . . if it was distinctly understood and could be said, that there was no *official* discussion of the subject. . . . It was agreed that this should be done [emphasis added]."[105]

So much for Wilson's professed—and sincerely professed—aversion to secret diplomacy. If the stakes seemed high enough, he could cheerfully (and no doubt unconsciously) toss the principle aside, as this episode illustrates.

On April 28, House met privately again with Balfour, and they discussed territorial settlements. House asked "what treaties were out between the Allies as to the divisions of spoils after the war," and Balfour confirmed that such treaties existed. At one point Balfour spoke with regret at the spectacle of the great nations sitting down and dividing the spoils of war, or, as he termed it, "dividing up the bearskin before the bear was killed." "I asked him if he did not think it proper for the Allies to give copies of these treaties to the President for his confidential information. He thought such a request entirely reasonable and said he would have copies made for that purpose."[106]

House made another pitch for a nonvindictive peace, while staving off the work of discussing a commitment, perhaps because he sensed that he and Wilson might be skating on thin ice:

> I asked if he did not consider it wise for us to keep clear of any promises so that at the peace conference we could exert an influence against greed and an improper distribution of territory. I said to him, as I once said to Grey, that if we are to justify our being in the war, we should free ourselves entirely from petty, selfish thoughts and look at the thing broadly and from a world viewpoint. Balfour agreed to this with enthusiasm.[107]

On April 30, the discussions moved to the White House. Wilson, House, and Edith Wilson had dinner with Balfour, and the president, according to House, "did most of the talking." House recorded the fact that he could "see that he [Wilson] was nervous." House recorded his impression that Wilson "was not at his best because of an apparent eagerness to excel." The upshot of this meeting was to affirm the previous general conclusions reached by Balfour and House.[108]

In May, Wilson met with Viviani, the French minister of justice. The nature of the conference was different: Viviani put pressure on Wilson to send troops and send them quickly. In his report, Viviani recorded the fact that he "insisted on the sending of troops, for moral reasons as much as for material ones—to strike Germany and cheer the Allies." It bears noting that the so-called French mutiny was beginning at the time. Wilson said that "he was resolved to do this; that one division was well on the way toward departure; that he would not give the date in order not to create false hopes."[109]

At another meeting, Wilson tested the waters for his "peace without victory" theme. He asked "whether the French would not remain in a state of uncontrollable hatred of Germany," and Viviani replied that "the atrocities and foreign devastations of war would leave a passionate legacy." Wilson repositioned himself accordingly, altering his formulation of peace without victory as follows—he said he advocated "a peace based on a victory that did not mean the annihilation of a nation, for in that case the desire for revenge was always certain." Viviani replied that he was "in agreement, but that, so long as there was Prussian militarism, there would be no lasting peace."[110]

As a result of these meetings with Viviani, Wilson sensed the weakness of his position and reverted to his first inclination to defer any further discussions of the postwar settlement until later—much later. In July, he told House that it was not yet time to put pressure on the allies:

> England and France have *not the same views with regard to peace that we have* by any means. When the war is over we can force them to our way of thinking, because by that time they will, among other things, be financially in our hands; but we cannot force them now, and any attempt to speak for them or to speak our common mind would bring on disagreements, which would inevitably come to the surface in public and rob the whole thing of its effect. I saw this all too plainly in a conversation with Viviani [original emphasis].[111]

Viviani wanted troops, and the embarrassing truth was that Wilson was averse to creating "false hopes" because he was not in the position to deliver. So what was he to do in the short run except defer? His moment of leverage had come in March—when the British and the French were already "in his hands" for financial reasons—and he let the opportunity go.

He confessed to House that "I have delayed writing to you about this deeply important matter until I could think it out; and I must say that I have not been able to think myself on to safe ground regarding it."[112]

I CANNOT SAY THAT I HAVE ANY CONFIDENCE THAT I KNOW

At the end of May, in consultation with Wilson, the secretary of war selected General John J. Pershing to command the American Expeditionary Force (AEF). Pershing met with the president only once—on May 24—and Wilson told him that he would have a free hand to conduct operations.[113] On May 26,

Baker ordered Pershing to "cooperate with the forces of the other countries employed against [the] enemy; but in so doing the underlying idea must be kept in view that the forces of the United States are a separate and distinct component of the combined forces." Baker told Pershing that "the decision as to when your command, or any of its parts, is ready for action is confided to you, and you will exercise full discretion in determining the manner of cooperation."

On the other hand, as a gesture to the French, Baker's orders also included the following statement: "Until the forces of the United States are in your judgment sufficiently strong to warrant operations as an independent command, it is understood that you will cooperate as a component of whatever army you may be assigned by the French government."[114]

Pershing arrived in France by the middle of June, and he decided that American troops who were beginning to arrive there, even troops from the regular army, were not yet prepared for the fighting: they needed training, so he started to provide it. The 1st Division had arrived on June 28. As a symbolic gesture, he had a battalion from the 16th Infantry Regiment of the 1st Division march through the streets of Paris on the Fourth of July. On July 10, he cabled the war department that thirty divisions, some 1,372,399 men, would be needed eventually in France, far more than the initial draft call would provide.[115]

In the meantime, Pershing refused to send troops to fight under British or French command. Luckily for him, the French commander, Pétain, was disinclined to launch major operations at the time. The British, of course, were about to launch the ill-fated operation in Flanders, but Baker's orders to Pershing had referred to "the French government," not the British. So there was no way that General Haig could put American troops in harm's way during the slaughter at Passchendaele.

Pershing continued to take his time. In September he moved his general headquarters to Chaumont near the headwaters of the Marne. American troops were still not in combat, and Allied consternation at this state of affairs would intensify. This did nothing to improve Woodrow Wilson's bargaining position on war aims.

America's contribution to the naval war, however, came quickly. The most obvious issue was getting not only supply ships but also troop transports through the German submarine blockade. Rear Admiral Sims had arrived in London just after the declaration of war, and in June Wilson instructed Navy Secretary Daniels to write to Sims and review the situation. Sims was instrumental in convincing the British to adopt the convoy system, which was to prove the undoing of the German U-boat campaign. By autumn, the submarine sinkings dropped dramatically. Sims utilized American destroyers for escort duty in the convoys. Augmenting the naval war was a shipbuilding program: Wilson had finally prevailed upon Congress in 1916 to increase the maritime capabilities of the United States. The Shipping Act of 1916 had established a U.S. Shipping Board with authority to purchase ships and to build not only ships but also shipyards.

The ponderous work of mobilization began in earnest after the war declaration. On April 9, Daniels recorded in his diary that Wilson selected George Creel, an investigative journalist and Democratic partisan, as "head" of "censorship" operations, and Bernard M. Baruch, a Democratic activist and financier, to coordinate the production of "munitions."[116]

But the first priorities were to raise the troops and the money for the war. As to the latter, Secretary McAdoo on April 9 requested Congress to legislate authority for the treasury to sell $5 billion worth of bonds. This sum would eventually be tripled, and deficit spending, via war bonds that would soon become known as "Liberty Bonds," would account for two-thirds of the financing of America's role in World War I.

The draft came a few weeks later. Out of reticence (or even squeamishness)—that is to say, a sensitivity to the possible reactions from noninterventionists within the Democratic Party—Wilson neglected to mention the draft in a comprehensive statement on mobilization that he issued on April 15—a statement in which he called upon everyone, farmers, laborers, businessmen, housewives, to rally to the cause. In this "appeal to the American people" he omitted to mention the duty of sacrifice in uniform.[117] But draft legislation was quickly introduced and Congress passed it on April 28 by an overwhelming margin, notwithstanding the opposition of Claude Kitchin and, most notably, Speaker Champ Clark.[118]

The subject of censorship had already arisen as a part of the administration's contingency planning for the possibility of war. The need for protecting military secrets for purposes of national security was obvious. On March 24, the Department of the Navy had hosted a conference with representatives of press associations to come to an agreement.[119] The conference was difficult, and one Wilson staffer recorded that "the newspapermen are up in arms."[120]

Wilson turned to George Creel to help him solve the problem. Creel, a journalist himself, was disinclined to use the word *censorship*; he preferred to speak about control of information, and he strove to win converts to the cause among his colleagues through positive persuasion.[121] He was a consummate salesman, exuding an upbeat tone through campaigns of publicity. On April 13, by executive order, Wilson created a Committee on Public Information, to be headed by Creel. The CPI, as it was known, would supervise huge campaigns of propaganda and persuasion, creating the famous "I Want You" recruiting poster designed by Montgomery Flagg. The CPI also made use of Hollywood stars such as Charlie Chaplin, Douglas Fairbanks Sr., and Mary Pickford in drives to sell bonds. The CPI sponsored a system of speakers committees, through which over seventy-five thousand citizens were recruited to give short speeches around the country—the CPI released a new set every ten days—that justified the war and vilified the enemy.

Creel had been one of the first people whom Wilson had mentioned for service in civilian-side mobilization. The other was Bernard Baruch, who was a close friend of McAdoo.[122] Baruch would eventually run the War Industries Board (WIB), an agency created on July 28, 1917. The existing Council of National Defense had established hundreds of committees, and the work of coordinating production was chaotic. The WIB was created in an effort to improve the situation. Its first chairman was Frank A. Scott, who had headed the War Department's General Munitions Board.

After Baruch had presented some proposals for coordinating production, he was appointed to the WIB, but he was not its chairman yet. In the meantime, production foundered; coordination between the WIB and the military services was poor, and the production of aircraft, artillery, and tanks proceeded at a snail's pace. Such issues would begin to cause Wilson significant political embarrassment by autumn.

Over the summer, the draft went into operation. On registration day, June 5, ten million men reported to their draft boards. Two weeks later, Secretary Baker drew numbers out of a big glass bowl—numbers that were coded to refer to large groups of draft-age men—and the local boards then used these numbers to summon 687,000 men, who reported to training camps in September. The process went smoothly, but September 1917 was just the *beginning* of training—it would take a very long time to augment the army with a group of men large enough to constitute an American Expeditionary Force.

On August 10, Congress passed the Food and Fuel Control Act (the "Lever Act") at the administration's request. The act created two new entities, the Food and Fuel Administrations. To head the food administration, which would coordinate food production, allocation, and rationing, Wilson appointed Herbert Hoover, who had run the Belgian relief operation. To head the fuel administration, Wilson turned to Harry A. Garfield, a friend from academia (he was president of Williams College) and the son of the late president James A. Garfield.

As all of these events unfolded, the preliminary phase of Wilson's censorship policy developed into legislation, the Espionage Act, the first in a series of manifestations of a national security mania resulting in one of the most obnoxious curtailments of civil liberties in American history.

There were several *bona fide* imperatives of national security: protection of military secrets, prevention of enemy sabotage, and the need to guarantee that the operations of the draft and industrial production would be free from improper interference. Wilson, with occasional twinges of ambivalence, was complicit—through a lack of presidential oversight that reached the point of negligence—in policies that took on these challenges by ushering in the very damage to democracy that Wilson had lamented to Frank Cobb would be inevitable. But it was not inevitable: Wilson could have prevented it. Cooper has affirmed that "violations of civil liberties from 1917 through 1919 constituted a great failure for Wilson as a war leader, and they left the ugliest blot on his record as president."[123]

There were hints of what was to come. Months earlier, at a luncheon in Buffalo, New York, Wilson made the following pronouncement: "Variety of opinion among ourselves there may be—discussion, free counsel as to what we ought to do—but, so far as every other nation is concerned, we must be absolutely a unit."[124] And in his second inaugural address he proclaimed that "we are being forged into a new unity amidst the fires that now blaze throughout the world. In their ardent heat we shall, in God's providence, let us hope, be purged of faction and division."[125]

On April 16, Wilson issued a proclamation warning of the penalties for "failure to bear true allegiance to the United States." After reminding citizens that treason as defined in the Constitution included the act of giving "aid and comfort" to the nation's enemies, Wilson listed offenses that would be "vigorously prosecuted," and these included "the performance of any act or the publication of statements of information which will give or supply in any way aid and comfort to the enemies of the United States."[126]

In June, the administration sent to Congress security legislation to effectuate, among other things, censorship of the press and the denial of the use of the mails to publications abetting disloyalty. Wilson's postmaster general (and political enforcer among the Democrats) Albert Burleson worked hard to overcome opposition, but the Senate killed almost every censorship provision except the denial of the use of the mails. Wilson signed the Espionage Act on June 15, and Burleson went to work quickly to use the new powers of his office as postmaster general.

He struck particularly hard at socialist publications, since the Socialist Party and its presidential candidate, Eugene Victor Debs, were opposed to the war, though a substantial minority of socialists supported it. In July, Burleson suspended second-class postage rates (vital to mass circulation) for several publications, including *The Masses*, edited by Max Eastman. When Eastman and others protested to Wilson, the president replied that "I think that a time of war must be regarded as wholly exceptional and that it is legitimate to regard things which would in ordinary circumstances be innocent as very dangerous to the public welfare, but the line is manifestly exceedingly hard to draw and I cannot say that I have any confidence that I know how to draw it."[127]

Wilson forwarded a letter from Eastman, Amos Pinchot, and John Reed to Burleson with a cover note composed as follows: "May I not have your advice as to the enclosed? These are very sincere men and I should like to please them."[128] Burleson replied that he was merely enforcing the Espionage Act, and that if people had grievances, they could take them to court.[129]

In October, Burleson targeted the *Milwaukee Leader*, the *New York Call*, and the *Jewish Daily Forward*. Walter Lippmann wrote to Colonel House asking him to intercede with Wilson. Lippmann wrote, in part, that

> the position taken by Mr. Burleson is brutally unreasonable. . . . [The government] ought to suppress only military secrets and advice to break the law or evade it. . . . Censorship in wartime is one of the most delicate tasks that confronts a government. It should never be intrusted to anyone who is not himself tolerant, nor to anyone who is unacquainted with the long record of folly which is the history of suppression.[130]

House forwarded the letter to Wilson, adding his own observations as follows:

> No matter how much we deplore the attitude of the socialists as to the war, yet more harm may easily be done by repression. Between the two courses, it is better to err on the side of leniency. I have seen for some time that trouble was brewing and I spoke to Burleson when in Washington. I believe you will have to take the matter largely into your own hands for he could never have a proper understanding of it.[131]

Wilson told Burleson that he disagreed about the case of the *Milwaukee Leader*. He also told him that "doubt ought always to be resolved in favor of the utmost freedom of speech."[132] But he did nothing to overturn the actions of Burleson or to place him under supervision. On the contrary, the next act of Congress with implications for press censorship—the Trading with the Enemy Act, which Congress passed on October 6—gave Burleson even greater authority to suppress publications.

Among its other provisions, the earlier Espionage Act gave the Justice Department authority to prosecute those who advocated treason or forcible resistance to the law. In the summer of 1917, a radical labor union, the Industrial Workers of the World (IWW), threatened strikes in several industries critical to mobilization, including copper mining and logging. Vigilante violence against the IWW broke out in several western states, particularly Arizona and Montana, where the IWW organizer Frank Little was lynched. In Bisbee, Arizona, over one thousand copper miners who were members of the IWW were put in cattle cars by a posse and then left in the middle of the desert without food or water. IWW president William D. "Big Bill" Haywood sent cables of protest to Wilson, as did Representative Jeannette Rankin of Montana.[133] On July 31, at a cabinet meeting, Wilson declared that Haywood was only trying to "be a martyr," and the matter was referred to Attorney General Gregory.[134]

Wilson probably knew that Gregory himself intended to crack down on the IWW. To Samuel Gompers, Wilson wrote that while "patriots" in the labor movement could count on his support, "we must oppose at home the organized and individual efforts of those dangerous elements who hide disloyalty behind a screen of specious and evasive phrases."[135]

Gregory had agents of the Bureau of Investigation (precursor to the FBI) raid IWW offices in September, seeking evidence of sedition. Then the Justice Department sought and obtained the indictments of 166 union leaders, including Haywood.

On the other hand, Wilson responded to the "Bisbee deportation" by sending an investigatory commission headed by the secretary of labor, William Bauchop Wilson. The commission reported that the vigilantes ought to be prosecuted, so Wilson had them prosecuted. Wilson also extended the life of this "President's Mediation Commission" and instructed it to help with other labor disputes. This was a wise action, but Wilson should have intervened earlier, instead of letting conditions in various localities get ugly.[136]

The administration's attitude toward vigilantism directed toward Americans of German ancestry was weak in 1917. Despite his pledge in the April war message to make the treatment of German Americans a demonstration—an exemplary demonstration—of America's friendship toward the German *people* (as opposed to their leaders), Wilson said nothing to deplore or condemn the disgraceful incidents that occurred across the country until the summer of the following year. His administration in some ways abetted vigilantism when the Justice Department began to work in cooperation with a new superpatriot group, the American Protective League.

A ludicrous war against German *Kultur* prompted one state, Nebraska, to ban the teaching of the German language, and orchestras refused to play the compositions of Bach and Brahms. Local school boards also banned the teaching of German, and local libraries were sometimes purged of books by Kant and Goethe.[137]

Wilson abdicated one of his most necessary roles as a wartime leader in his failure to mitigate, control, or at least condemn the hysteria. Cooper has affirmed that "despite many entreaties, Wilson declined to speak out against these abuses."[138]

Some of the entreaties were protests that surely made him angry. Charles August Lindbergh, for example—the father of the future celebrity aviator and isolationist—flicked Wilson on the raw when he compared him unfavorably to Lincoln, who "refused to avail himself of a power which he could easily have obtained to fill the northern jails with his calumniators." "Ah no, Mr. President," Lindbergh continued, "your admirers are wrong. You resemble neither Jefferson nor Lincoln unless your actions greatly belie your heart. . . . If Abraham Lincoln was right in allowing the utmost freedom of discussion of his official acts in the midst of the greatest war the world had ever seen up to his time, then every act of your administration, wherein you seek to destroy freedom of thought and conscience, is wrong because diametrically opposed to the course which Lincoln pursued."[139]

No doubt Wilson's thoughts upon reading this missive—if he read it—were unprintable. But he received more circumspect letters from people he admired. Oswald Garrison Villard, for instance, wrote Tumulty warning that suppression of the *Milwaukee Leader* demonstrated that the administration was out of control. Villard passed along this admonition to Wilson's secretary: "I know that you know—from what you have said to me—that the safety of the republic lies in letting the dissatisfied talk; but certainly a republic at war to make a democracy out of an empire cannot go further than either Prussia or Russia ever dared to go, can it?"[140] Tumulty forwarded this letter to Wilson.

Herbert Croly wrote to the president, complaining that "the censorship over public opinion which is now being exercised through the Post Office is, I think, really hurting the standing of the war. . . . Perhaps you might be able to do something or say something which will strengthen the position of those who, like myself, believe profoundly both in you and the work which you are trying to do."[141]

Among the softer entreaties that Wilson received was a letter from Lillian Wald, Roger Baldwin, and others, who suggested that "a public statement from you would tend at once to put a stop to these invasions of established rights at the hands of over-zealous officials."[142]

Wilson silently declined.

There was no excuse for this inaction. In Cooper's opinion, overwork was not the issue, at least in the summer of 1917: "The president stuck to his habits of strictly regulated hours at his desk, tightly rationed meetings and speaking engagements, frequent breaks for golf and rides in the White House limousine, and quiet evenings with family and a few close friends."[143] Something else was going wrong, and only psychological conjecture can tell us what it was.

Wilson was obviously conscious of the need to push mobilization. He was all too well aware of the time he had lost, of his weak position, of his need to put troops in the field. No doubt anxiety would make him inclined to err on the side of overcompensation, or to countenance the overcompensation of others, in reacting to threats, such as strikes, that would slow down the process even more.

No doubt, after all of his soul searching in the weeks before the war declaration—and the indignation that he surely must have felt as he was pushed back and forth by the provocations of the Germans, the British, then the Germans again—it was bracing to have a new clarity. Perhaps the voices of those who called him back to the days of ambivalence, the voices of the dissidents who claimed that he had played his cards wrong, became voices he was glad to have stilled. But to act in a manner that would make his crusade for democracy seem like a sham?

That was pitiful.

NOW, THEREFORE, I, WOODROW WILSON

Notwithstanding his avoidance of overwork—a wise precaution for someone who knew that he suffered from arteriosclerosis—the mental strain on Wilson was enormous. On vacation with Wilson in September, House noted that "once or twice during the conversation I threw the President off his line of thought by interpolations, and he found it difficult to return to his subject. He smiled plaintively and said: 'You see I am getting tired. This is the way it indicates itself.'"[144]

Two simultaneous trends drove Wilson to redouble his efforts in the autumn: (1) the pope called for a negotiated peace, thus reopening the issue of war aims; and (2) the problems with the civilian-side mobilization kept worsening.

In the first week of August, Pope Benedict XV sent a peace note calling for negotiations, reduction in armaments, restoration of occupied territories, and lack of indemnities: each side would pay for its own reconstruction through the money saved on armaments. Some regarded the pope's note as a proposal for restoring the "status quo ante." Lansing, for instance, objected to the note, in part as follows:

> Belgium has been grievously outraged and her people impoverished, brutally treated, even enslaved. Would it be just to deny the Belgians the right to claim full reparation for all they have lost through three years of German occupation? . . . Is the enormous damage done by the German invaders in northern France not even to be paid in part, though much of the damage was the result of wantonness? . . . If I read the Pope's appeal aright, all these questions are to be answered in the affirmative. It is carrying the Christian doctrine of forgiveness a long way, since the burden falls very heavily on one side and very lightly on the other.[145]

Wilson's response was similar. After considering a reply to the pope, he told House that "I do not know that I shall make any reply at all to the Pope's proposals." He added that "a return to the *status quo ante* . . . would leave affairs in the same attitude that furnished a pretext for the war," and that "the autocratic regime still dominant in Germany . . . has made it impossible for other governments to accept its assurances on anything."[146]

But House—typically—urged Wilson to change his mind and try diplomacy. "I believe you have an opportunity to take the peace negotiations out of the hands of the Pope and hold them in your own," he told Wilson. In light of the fact that the president and others had been trying to communicate with German liberals in the hope that the "Kaiser Reich" might be overthrown, House wrote that "a statement from you regarding the aims of this country would bring about almost revolution in Germany."[147]

Wilson took House's advice and began to compose a draft reply to Pope Benedict. With exquisite politeness—he wrote that "every heart that has not been blinded and hardened by this terrible war must be touched by this moving appeal of His Holiness"—Wilson demurred in regard to his proposals. But he also seized the opportunity to restate his own principle of peace without victory: "Responsible statesmen must now everywhere see, if they never saw before, that no peace can rest securely upon . . . any kind of revenge."[148]

House, as usual, stoked the fires with fulsome praise: "You have again written a declaration of human liberty. . . . You are blazing a new path, and the world must follow, or be lost again in the meshes of unrighteous intrigue. I am cabling Balfour expressing my personal hope that England, France, and Italy will accept your answer as also theirs."[149] A few weeks later, House told Wilson that "your reply to the Pope is the most remarkable document ever written."[150] The formal American reply to the pope was sent on August 27 over Lansing's signature.[151]

In early September, Wilson took some new steps of his own to make good on House's idea that he should "take the peace negotiations out of the hands of the Pope." He told House that his letter to the pope had served the useful purpose of undercutting vindictive tendencies among the Allies; after Jusserand, the French ambassador, found out about the letter, he "went up in the air because it seemed to exclude economic punishment of Germany after the war." At this point Wilson found himself glad to have the Allied disagreements flushed into the open: "It will work out as well this way as any. The differences of opinion will be less embarrassing now than they would have been if I had invited them beforehand."

Then Wilson plunged forward and suggested the following to House: "I am beginning to think that we ought to go systematically to work to ascertain as fully and precisely as possible just what the several parties to this war on our side of it will be inclined to insist upon [in] the final peace arrangements, in order that we may formulate our own position . . . and begin to gather the influences we wish to employ,—or, at the least, ascertain what influences we can use." He asked House to coordinate the effort:

> What would you think of quietly gathering about you a group of men to assist you to do this? I could, of course, pay all the bills out of the money now at my command. Under your guidance these assistants could collate all the definite material available and you could make up the memorandum by which we should be guided.[152]

House replied that this was "one of the things I have had in mind for a long while," and declared that he would be "delighted to undertake the work."[153]

Shortly thereafter, Lloyd George sent Wilson a letter. This letter was presented to the president by Lord Reading on September 20. The prime minister discussed "the strategy to be followed in the prosecution of the war during the winter of 1917–18 and the spring and summer of 1918." He did not mince words: the Germans were approaching victory because of "the collapse of Russia." People were "beginning to ask themselves whether victory is obtainable at all." Success would depend "more and more upon the British Commonwealth and the United States." The other Allies had come to "rely upon the British and the Americans to supply that additional effort which is necessary in order to make certain of a just, liberal and lasting peace."

Lloyd George invited Wilson to send a representative to Allied conferences. He said that "the purpose and ideals" of America should be "manifested in the Council Chamber as well as on the battlefield." He flattered Wilson by saying that his speeches had presented a "profound and masterly exposition of the Allied case."[154]

Wilson appointed House as his representative. The next meeting of the group that was known as the Allied War Council was scheduled for November in Paris. Meanwhile, House began to assemble his group of advisers, which would soon become known as "The Inquiry."[155] The participants were drawn heavily from Harvard, Yale, Princeton, Columbia, and the University of Chicago.

When Wilson visited House at the latter's vacation retreat on September 9, a primary topic of conversation was the strain between Wilson and Lansing. Wilson wanted to discuss "the advisability of asking for Lansing's resignation." But House "argued against asking for his resignation," since he "doubted whether he could do better."[156] House did, however, tell Wilson he would find a way to "straighten out" the secretary of state.[157]

Perhaps through House's intercession, things began to improve; Wilson told House on September 19 that "Lansing is not only content that you should undertake the preparation of data for the peace conference but volunteered the opinion that you were the very one to do it."[158] Lansing composed a memorandum on war aims for Wilson to send along to House.

When Reading met the president, he stressed that "American troops should not only be sent to France as quickly as possible, but should take their place on some part of the line." He explained, "French morale required encouragement and there would be some disillusionment on their part if they had to wait until next Spring for active cooperation from Americans." Wilson "expressed himself guardedly, but sympathetically," according to Reading.[159]

No doubt his inability to promise any troops made Wilson's tension much worse. He began to get churlish and petty as he vented his frustration. When news of House's "Inquiry" was published, Wilson reprimanded some editors, who found themselves shocked at the president's attitude: they had thought that they were doing him a favor, since the coverage was positive.[160] But Wilson told David Lawrence that "you newspapermen can have no conception of what fire you are playing with. . . . It is perfectly evident to everyone that what Colonel House is attempting to do neither brings peace nearer nor sets it further off, and that it is my stern and serious judgment that the whole matter ought to be let alone."[161]

House left for Europe in early November with a delegation of assistants.[162] In London, he reported to Wilson, his attempts to elicit definitive statements on war aims led to frustration: "The difficulty with the British I find is that while one can keep in perfect agreement with them, it is exceedingly difficult to have any definite program formulated and put through."[163] In light of the precise inter-Allied agreements that Balfour had acknowledged in the spring, the situation seems curious enough—unless the British were stalling, holding out for the arrival of more American troops.

As to that, General Pershing reported to Baker that his preparations were not to be hurried: "With reference to our entering the trenches for active service, I have emphasized the necessity of thorough preparation, and have been following a logical program leading up to the important final training."[164] Baker forwarded this letter to Wilson on November 23.

House reported to Wilson that the Allies were creating a supreme war council to coordinate their military efforts. In the meantime, a new administration came to power in France: President Poincaré asked Georges Clemenceau to form a government on November 15. In Germany, too, there were changes: Bethmann-Hollweg was no longer chancellor. He had been replaced in July by Georg Michaelis, who, in turn, was replaced on November 1 by Georg von Hertling.

When the Allied War Council met in November, House failed to secure an agreement on a nonvindictive peace. He offered the following resolution (as reported to Wilson): "The Allies and U States declare that they are not waging war for the purpose of aggression or indemnity."[165] The council did not pass this resolution.

Allied leaders viewed the situation as dire: the Germans were winning. The Bolshevik offer of a three-month armistice gave Germany time to consolidate its position on the eastern front. The Germans would then be free to start transferring massive numbers of troops to the western front for offensive operations in the spring. The Italian defeat at Caporetto, combined with the failure of the British campaign in Flanders and the unsuccessful tank attack at Cambrai, created a mood in Paris that was not conducive to talk of a peace without victory. German victory seemed to be approaching.

When House returned, he found Wilson unfazed by the council's refusal to endorse the principle of peace without victory. Wilson intended to proceed—at once—on his own. On December 18, House recorded in his diary that Wilson told him he would forthwith "formulate the war aims of the United States." House wrote that he "never knew a man who did things so casually. We did not discuss the matter more than ten or fifteen minutes when he decided he would take the action." House lamented the fact that he had not been able to persuade the British to join him "in formulating a broad declaration of war aims that would unite the world against Germany. . . . I could not persuade them to do this, and now it will be done by the President. It would have been better if the Interallied Conference had done it for reasons which are apparent."[166]

Wilson asked House for a memorandum summing up the work of the Inquiry. The memorandum was presented to Wilson by House on December 23.

Through all these developments, the home front mobilization had been going badly—going wrong. In July, as Congress deliberated on the measure for regulating food production—the measure that would take the eventual form of the Lever Act—Senator John W. Weeks attached an amendment to the bill that would create a "Joint Committee on Expenditures in the Conduct of the War." Wilson fought back, telling Congressman Asbury Lever of South Carolina, who played the key role in supporting the legislation that would bear his name, that such an entity "would render my task of conducting the war practically impossible. . . . The responsibility rests upon the administration."[167] Wilson got the provision struck from the bill, but the episode was damaging.

Much of the administration's machinery for mobilization proved defective. As Cooper relates, the War Industries Board was "a shell agency"; it "suffered from weak and divided authority" and "could not enter into contracts—a prerogative that the military and naval procurement bureaus jealously guarded. Confusion reigned, and the board's first and second chairmen quit after a few months in exhaustion and frustration."[168]

As with production, so with transportation. A feud broke out between the chairman of the Shipping Board, William Denman (a campaign contributor to Wilson), and General George Washington Goethals, who headed the Emergency Fleet Corporation, a division of the Shipping Board. Among the tasks of the board and the fleet corporation was production of troop transports. The chaos became so great as to prompt the intervention of several congressmen. Wilson convinced both Denman and Goethals to resign, but the fracas had caused more destructive delays and more damage to the administration's credibility in Congress.

Through the summer and fall, the situation of land-based transportation caused alarm. In July, a Railroads War Board had been created to expedite the shipment of strategic materials. A huge foul-up occurred when the board required the tagging of certain items and the order was botched to an extent that created tremendous backups of freight cars in eastern states. The different railroad corporations would not cooperate, strikes were threatened, and the situation kept worsening. At last, under the prompting of McAdoo and Tumulty, Wilson invoked some authority that had been given to him in an army appropriations act that he had signed on August 29, 1916. On December 26, 1917, he nationalized the railroads for the duration of the war. His proclamation stated, in part, that

> WHEREAS, it has now become necessary in the national defense to take possession and assume control of certain systems of transportation and to utilize the same, to the exclusion as far as may be necessary of all other than war traffic thereon, for the transportation of troops, war material and equipment therefor, and for other needful and desirable purposes connected with the prosecution of the war;
>
> NOW, THEREFORE, I, WOODROW WILSON, President of the United States, under and by virtue of the powers vested in me . . . do hereby, through Newton D. Baker, Secretary of War, take possession and assume control at 12 o'clock noon on the twenty-eighth day of December, 1917, of each and every system of transportation and the appurtenances thereof located wholly or in part within the boundaries of the continental United States.

Though Baker, as the secretary of war, was Wilson's preliminary agent for the use of this authority, the proclamation specified that William McAdoo, the treasury secretary, would assume operational control as "Director General of Railroads."[169] The proclamation exempted local streetcar and "interurban" lines and made provision for compensating the railroad corporations for the use of their property.

Wilson's critics in Congress were not impressed, and shortly thereafter—amid continued problems with the railroads, shortages of fuel, and other signs of trouble with the mobilization—senators Henry Cabot Lodge and George E. Chamberlain decided it was time to do something drastic. They began to discuss legislation that would wrest control of the mobilization from Wilson and give it to a war cabinet of "three distinguished citizens" instead. This legislation would trigger a brawl in the early weeks of 1918, when Wilson struck back.

Wilson's mood was increasingly defiant. His sense of certitude had grown since the war declaration. In his annual message to Congress he poured out contempt for his enemies real and imagined, for the critics who had failed to see the moral beauty of America's role in the war as he had come to envision it himself. All previous doubts were cast aside:

> I hear the voices of dissent—who does not? I hear the criticism and the clamour of the noisily thoughtless and troublesome. I also see men here and there

fling themselves in impotent disloyalty against the calm, indomitable power of the nation. I hear men debate peace who understand neither its nature nor the way in which we may attain it. . . . They do not touch the heart of anything. They may safely be left to strut their uneasy hour and be forgotten.

But this intolerable Thing of which the masters of Germany have shown us the ugly face, this menace of combined intrigue and force which we now see so clearly as the German power, a Thing without conscience or honour or capacity for covenanted peace, must be crushed. [170]

And once the "Thing" had been crushed, the promised future—Wilson's future—would follow, like the sun in early morning. And woe to any willful men who tried to stop it.

Chapter Five

1918

In the final year of the war, repression under Wilson worsened with the passage of the Sedition Act, the most clear-cut violation of the First Amendment since the Alien and Sedition Acts of 1798. But as Wilson's punitive tendencies grew, his desire to go down in history as a benign visionary was never greater.

Early in the year, he formulated his Fourteen Points, a set of guidelines for peace that were in certain cases almost utopian. There was no real meeting of minds between Wilson and the Allies on some of these objectives, nor was there any kind of consensus in Congress regarding the most important of them. Wilson just set them forth.

Republicans who were active in the League to Enforce Peace made overtures to Wilson in the hope of hammering out guidelines for American participation in a league of nations. But Wilson spurned them.

American troops at last saw action in the spring and summer of 1918. And as the final campaigns of the war got under way, the campaigns for the congressional elections of 1918 began as well. Wilson made some tremendous blunders in the course of these campaigns, and he bungled the process of negotiating terms for the armistice. These mistakes made the politics of peacemaking dubious.

BEFORE AMERICA CAN THROW STRONG
FORCES INTO THE SCALE

During the three-month truce that the Bolsheviks offered to the Central Powers, the army of the tsar was demobilized.[1] The Bolsheviks tried to procrastinate as Germany demanded a definitive peace, and the negotiations that had started in December in the town of Brest-Litovsk dragged on into the new year. So on February 17, the Germans launched a major new offensive that would force the Russians to accede to their demands. After German troops had plunged 150 miles farther into Russia, the Bolsheviks were forced to capitulate. The Treaty of Brest-Litovsk, signed on March 3, 1918, ceded a vast amount of territory to Germany: roughly a quarter of Russia's population and a third of its agricultural land were given up.[2]

Fighting on the eastern front continued sporadically. The Bolsheviks were hoping that the kaiser would be toppled by a proletarian revolution. Consequently, they cooperated when the Allies began to land troops in Russia for the purpose of keeping the Germans pinned down.[3] Only later did the Allies get involved in the huge civil war that broke out between the Bolsheviks and their enemies.

The terms of the Brest-Litovsk treaty were decisive enough to prompt the Germans to begin their westward shift of troops. This redeployment gave the Central Powers a numerical superiority in France by the spring of 1918: 192 German divisions versus 178 for the Allies. Hindenburg and Ludendorff knew that an early strike was essential. Ludendorff declared that the Allies, especially the British, had to be beaten "before America can throw strong forces into the scale."[4] Ludendorff devised a new plan, code-named "Michael," to unleash an assault along the river Somme that would roll the British back to the sea. The attack was launched on March 21, 1918.

THE CULMINATING AND FINAL WAR FOR HUMAN LIBERTY

Wilson was determined to move ahead—unilaterally—on a war aims statement, despite the fact that he and House had failed to get the Allies to agree to the principle of nonvindictive peace. On January 4, 1918, Wilson and House started working on a draft of a speech to be delivered to Congress a week later. House recorded in his diary that he "did not wish the President to state our case in piecemeal, and . . . was sure that he would not cover the ground I thought necessary."[5]

Their effort continued the next day, and House called the session "remarkable."[6] According to House, the men got busy at 10:30 a.m. and in two hours "finished remaking the map of the world, as we would have it."[7] They worked from the memorandum produced in December by the Inquiry, with a newer addendum that House brought with him.[8]

The memorandum—produced under the aegis of House and written by Sidney Edward Mezes, David Hunter Miller, and Walter Lippmann—was based upon a number of Wilson's presuppositions.[9] A few of its provisions are worthy of note; on the League of Nations, it offered this rumination: "Whether this league is to remain armed and exclusive, or whether there is to be a reduction of armaments and a cordial inclusion of Germany, will depend upon whether the German government is in fact representative of the German democracy."[10] Of equal or greater significance was the observation regarding the leverage that would force the Germans to submit to the Allies' terms. Mezes, Miller, and Lippmann stated that the Allies must "have the power to compel Germany's assent at the peace conference by our ability to bar her indefinitely from access to supplies and to protract the negotiations at her cost and at our own benefit. . . . We might well adopt as our slogan 'No economic peace until the peoples are freed.'"[11] It bears noting that this would be the tool that the French and the British would use to force Germany to sign the Treaty of Versailles.

From the deliberations of Wilson and House on January 5 emerged Wilson's "Fourteen Points." The principles were distilled from provisions of the Inquiry's memorandum and arranged by House to proceed from the general to the specific with the exception of the League of Nations provision, which came at the end.

House's notes of the meeting are quite interesting. He stated, for example, that "I insisted, and made a strong argument, for open diplomacy. I told him there was nothing he could do that would better please the American people and the democracies of the world, and that it was right and must be the diplomacy of the future."[12] It is difficult—nay, impossible—to tell whether House sincerely believed in the proposition himself. If so, he must have been prepared to renounce the kind of secret diplomacy in which he delighted to partake.

When they came to the principle of "freedom of the seas," Wilson, for once, asked House for his "definition of the term." House "answered that I went further than anyone I knew, for I believed that in time of both war and peace a merchantman should traverse the seas unmolested. He agreed to this." And so they laid down the proposition that belligerents should never again be allowed to blockade the supplies of their enemies upon the high seas.[13]

At no point in their deliberations did House or Wilson try to "vet" the propositions with representatives of the Allies, with one minor exception. When they came to territorial matters—issues such as Belgium and Alsace-Lorraine, for example—they turned to the Balkans and decided to consult the head of the Serbian mission, Milenko Vesnić. House's account of the consultation is illuminating:

> I sent for Vesnitch [*sic*] to meet me . . . as I did not think it advisable to have him come to the White House. Much to my surprise, he totally disagreed with what we had written and said it would not satisfy Serbia. . . . The President was rather depressed at this first and only attempt to obtain outside opinion regarding the message. I had not been in favor of going to Vesnitch, and told him so. I have had so much experience with foreigners and others who are obsessed with an idea that I felt it would be hopeless to expect a reasonable viewpoint.

> I advised the President not to change the paragraph in the slightest and to go
> ahead as if no objection had been made, and this he did. [14]

However, House advised Wilson to announce the speech before it was delivered, but Wilson demurred. "No one was consulted," House recounted, "either directly or indirectly, concerning this message on war aims. . . . The thing was done so secretly that his [Wilson's] Private Secretary knew nothing of it until . . . two hours before the message was delivered." [15]

For a president who placed such stress upon open consultations—the word *counsel* reverberated through his rhetoric like a mantra—this action was telling. It was also telling that when Wilson learned that Lloyd George had just given a speech on war aims, a speech in which he coined the term *self-determination*, Wilson—if House's diary is to be believed—was dejected. He feared that Lloyd George had stolen his thunder. House recorded that "when George's speech came out in Washington Saturday afternoon the President was depressed. He thought the terms which Lloyd George had given were so nearly akin to those he and I had worked out that it would be impossible for him to make the contemplated address before Congress." [16] House reassured Wilson that "after the President had made his address, it would so smother the Lloyd George speech that it would be forgotten and that he, the President, would once more become the spokesman for the Entente, and, indeed, the spokesman for the liberals of the world." [17]

Wilson seemed to be treating Lloyd George as a rival instead of an ally with whom effective strategy might be employed. There was still a chance to turn the military situation to advantage in regard to the achievement of a nonvindictive peace. On December 28, the French president, Raymond Poincaré, had written a direct appeal to Wilson as follows:

> The sad events in Russia shall soon liberate a very large number of enemy divisions which are already on the move towards our frontier, and the Anglo-French lines will have certainly to sustain, in the course of the year 1918, a formidable and prolonged pressure. . . . But a number of months will still elapse before the complete formation of the American army. When that army has been entirely transported to Europe, it will of course, if such is your desire, compose an indivisible whole. Until then American valiance would certainly not rest with total inactivity. The troops, landing in succession, would not consent to stand mere spectators of the battles which will be fought and in which our common hope will be at stake. The sooner the American flag will float on the very front by the side of our own tricolor, the sooner will become apparent, in all its significance and grandeur, the historical role assumed by the United States under your guidance. There is therefore a paramount interest in the American troops being engaged with ours, the moment they reach the battle zone. [18]

Here was a new opportunity for Wilson to extract a quid pro quo. Even though Pershing had opposed the deployment of American troops in an international command, it was Wilson's prerogative as commander-in-chief to order him to do so. And one has to remember that American troops would not be launching the kind of suicidal assaults that were ordered by Haig at the Somme and in Flanders. The Americans would just be helping the British and the French repel a *German* assault against the lines of the Allies.

If Wilson had been thinking in terms such as these, he might have answered Poincaré's letter (through confidential channels) in a fashion that might have elicited a reciprocal concession—faster deployment of American troops in return for a French flexibility on a nonvindictive peace.

But Wilson was preoccupied with grandstanding, so another opportunity for power leverage was lost.

Wilson did follow up on Poincaré's letter by conferring with Baker, but when Pershing told the secretary of war that he saw no emergency that would "warrant our putting companies or battalions into British or French divisions," Wilson deferred.[19] When the president answered Poincaré on January 8—the same day that he delivered his Fourteen Points address—the best that he could do was to state that "the judgment of the [Supreme War] Council" would be "conclusively influential" in regard to "the use to which American troops were to be put."[20]

On January 8, Wilson went before Congress and delivered his Fourteen Points address. He began by making reference to the negotiations at Brest-Litovsk. Oversimplifying, he characterized the "Russian representatives" as exemplars of democracy, at least in some of their methods—they had, Wilson proclaimed, "insisted, very justly, very wisely, and in the true spirit of modern democracy, that the conferences they have been holding with the Teutonic and Turkish statesmen should be held within open, not closed doors."[21]

Continuing to oversimplify, he argued (or implied) that the "Russian representatives"—the representatives sent by the Bolsheviks—were tribunes of public opinion compared to the German representatives, who were nothing more than puppets of a ruthless elite. Making reference to some peace-minded resolutions passed by the German Reichstag the previous July, he argued that the kaiser and his military chiefs were imposing their will upon the "liberal" representatives of Germany.

It was true that the Kaiser Reich was semiautocratic: the German Reichstag was in no way equivalent to the British Parliament (though the Reichstag did possess political standing). But Wilson was yielding to the dangerous impulse to set up a Manichaean comparison between Russia as an open society and Germany as an example of democracy thwarted. The truth was more complex.

He oversimplified again by imputing not only an openness of "counsel" but also an unqualified unity of purpose to America and its allies:

> Not only once, but again and again, we have laid our whole thought and purpose before the world, not in general terms only, but each time with suffi-cient definition to make it clear what sort of definitive terms of settlement must necessarily spring out of them. Within the last week Mr. Lloyd George has spoken with admirable candor and in admirable spirit for the people and Government of Great Britain. There is no confusion of counsel among the adversaries of the Central Powers, no uncertainty of principle, no vagueness of detail. The only secrecy of counsel, the only lack of fearless frankness, the only failure to make definite statements of the objects of the war, lies with Germany and her Allies. [22]

One would think that Wilson had succeeded already in establishing a com-plete (or near complete) meeting of minds with the leaders of Britain, France, and Italy, and also with enough congressional leaders to speak with justifica-tion when he used the potent word *we*.

And yet the contents of this speech had been developed in secret—even Lansing was informed as an afterthought, and the rest of the cabinet had been left completely in the dark. The Fourteen Points were the work of Wilson and House, and these men alone could in truth be said to constitute the "we."

The Fourteen Points, as Wilson presented them, consisted—in part—of the following formulations:

1. Open covenants of peace, openly arrived at, after which there shall be no private international understandings of any kind but diplomacy shall proceed always frankly and in the public view.
2. Absolute freedom of navigation upon the seas, outside territorial wa-ters, alike in peace and war, except as the seas may be closed in whole or in part by international action for the enforcement of international covenants.
3. The removal, so far as possible, of all economic barriers and the estab-lishment of an equality of trade conditions among all the nations con-senting to the peace.
4. Adequate guarantees given and taken that national armaments will be reduced to the lowest point consistent with domestic safety.
5. A free, open-minded, and absolutely impartial adjustment of all colo-nial claims, based upon a strict observance of the principle that in determining all such questions of sovereignty the interests of the pop-ulations concerned must have equal weight with the equitable claims of the government whose title is to be determined.
6. The evacuation of all Russian territory and such a settlement of all questions affecting Russia as will secure the best and freest coopera-

tion of the other nations of the world in obtaining for her an unhampered and unembarrassed opportunity for the independent determination of her own political development.

7. Belgium, the whole world will agree, must be evacuated and restored.
8. All French territory should be freed and the invaded portions restored, and the wrong done to France by Prussia in 1871 in the matter of Alsace and Lorraine . . . should be righted.
9. A readjustment of the frontiers of Italy should be effected along clearly recognizable lines of nationality.
10. The peoples of Austria-Hungary, whose place among the nations we wish to see safeguarded and assured, should be accorded the freest opportunity of autonomous development.
11. Rumania, Serbia, and Montenegro should be evacuated; occupied territories restored; Serbia accorded free and secure access to the sea; and the relations of the several Balkan states to one another determined by friendly counsel along historically established lines of allegiance and nationality.
12. The Turkish portions of the present Ottoman Empire should be assured a secure sovereignty, but the other nationalities which are now under Turkish rule should be assured an undoubted security of life and an absolutely unmolested opportunity of autonomous development.
13. An independent Polish state should be erected which should include the territories inhabited by indisputably Polish populations.
14. A general association of nations must be formed under specific covenants for the purpose of affording mutual guarantees of political independence and territorial integrity to great and small nations alike. [23]

Wilson concluded by asserting that "we"—that is to say, "he"—had "spoken now, surely, in terms too concrete to admit of any further doubt or question." To Wilson, there was no doubt at all that "an evident principle runs through the whole programme I have outlined. It is the principle of justice to all peoples and nationalities, and their right to live on equal terms of liberty and safety with one another." He closed with a concise reiteration of his war declaration's conclusion: "The people of the United States could act upon no other principle; and to the vindication of this principle they are ready to devote their lives, their honor, and everything that they possess. The moral climax of this the culminating and final war for human liberty has come." [24]

Cooper has argued that "the Fourteen Points did not express starry-eyed idealism." [25] That assertion is questionable. The "open covenants" provision defied not only strategic prudence but also a crucial provision of Aristotelian ethics: one should *not* always put one's cards on the table, for secrecy in certain situations may well be the only way to deflect malevolent force and save innocent lives.[26] And the provisions in the Fourteen Points for "autonomous" development of "nationalities" appeared to be founded on a starry-eyed presumption that population groups intermingled in a single area—the Austro-Hungarian Empire, for instance, or the Balkans—can be harmonized into perfectly neat, straightforward, and homogeneous polities, notwithstanding the sorts of divisions that result from conflicting religious or ethnic claims to the same land. The pages of history are bloody with assertions of rival nationality, assertions that could never be reconciled (in some cases) without carnage.

One obvious purpose of this famous Wilsonian address was to capture the imagination of the world in a positive way, and Wilson succeeded to a great extent in doing so. But not all of the reactions were positive; Lansing warned Wilson that Italians were incensed by his position on Italian frontiers:

> I presume you have read the telegrams from Rome indicating a measure of dissatisfaction or at least of disappointment on the part of the Italian government and people with the statement in your address of January 8th relative to Italy. . . . If their frontiers are to be rectified only on the basis of nationality, they will be as vulnerable to attack from Austria-Hungary as they have been in the past.[27]

Ambassador Thomas Nelson Page reported from Rome that "newspapers talk of Latin race league or union with Italy as head to counterbalance the power of the Anglo-Saxon peoples and I hear that some leading men have [the] same idea. I hear that French ambassador is very critical of President's last message apparently resenting that he should take so firm and directive a position in European affairs."[28]

Overall, however, the reception of Wilson's speech was positive. Balfour called it "a magnificent pronouncement," and *The Times* called Wilson "the greatest American president since Abraham Lincoln." As Wilson scholar Thomas J. Knock has observed, "The approbation heaped upon the address [in the United States] approached phenomenal proportions. Although a few Republicans took sharp exception to the point on free trade, praise from both parties was generous. Many congressmen and senators expressed the opinion that the address marked a moral turning point of the war."[29]

Perhaps, in the sense of raising giddy expectations, it did. But in the sense that it stiffened Wilson's notion that a venture in mere verbal righteousness could make up for a shortage of power orchestration, this speech was another big step toward the trap that Wilson's runaway ego was setting for itself.

WOOLGATHERERS

The bid by congressional enemies to establish a "war cabinet" to take the prosecution of the war out of Wilson's hands sputtered out. Senator George E. Chamberlain of Oregon—a Democrat—chaired the Senate Military Affairs Committee, and in the middle of January he conducted hearings to prove incompetence in the Wilson administration, especially the war department. Wilson was livid. On January 21, he issued a press release declaring that "Senator Chamberlain's statement as to the present inaction and ineffectiveness of the Government is an astonishing and absolutely unjustifiable distortion of the truth." Wilson admitted that "there have been delays and disappointments," but he claimed that all the problems were over. "Effective measures of reorganization," he declared, had been "thoroughly and maturely perfected."[30]

Wilson also urged the secretary of war to fight back. On January 28, Newton Baker appeared before Chamberlain's committee. A skillful debater, he made a good impression, and the legislation that Chamberlain had introduced went nowhere.[31]

A month later, however, House suggested to Wilson that a "war cabinet" under presidential control might not be a bad idea. So Wilson summoned the secretaries of war and the navy, together with the heads of the mobilization agencies, and began to have weekly meetings with this "war board" or "war cabinet." The meetings were useful.[32]

At last, in the spring of 1918, the mobilization hit its stride. In March, Wilson finally made Bernard Baruch head of the War Industries Board. Smart and flamboyant, he divided the country into production zones and found ways to promote cooperation within them by choosing businessmen to serve on advisory committees to oversee the standardization of processes.[33] Herbert Hoover had already been doing fine work as head of the U.S. Food Administration, and he also found ways to promote voluntary cooperation by publicizing "wheatless" and "meatless" days, becoming a celebrity in his role of benevolent food czar. People spoke of "Hooverizing" their breakfast tables.[34] And William McAdoo was increasingly effective as head of the new U.S. Railroad Administration.[35]

In April, Wilson created a National War Labor Board to improve labor-management relations and to head off conflict. To cochair the new board, Wilson appointed Francis Patrick Walsh, a prominent lawyer and labor advocate, and no less a personage than former president William Howard Taft.[36]

The appointment of Taft was a notable departure from Wilson's tendency to neglect opportunities for bipartisanship, but the position was far below the former president's abilities and Wilson lost a major opportunity to make higher use of Taft in the spring of 1918.

Colonel House was alert to the benefits of bipartisanship. In January, when he and Wilson had discussed what to do about composing a delegation to the peace conference at the end of the war, House had recommended a group of seven, consisting of "four democrats and three republicans." Wilson "immediately announced his intention of not appointing more than two republicans." Then Edith Wilson, who was present at the meeting, "wondered how [Elihu] Root or Taft would do." When Wilson "did not seriously object," House suggested that "Taft would be the more flexible and tractable, for he is good natured and easily led."[37]

House later encouraged Wilson to meet with Taft, since the former president was leader of the League to Enforce Peace and this organization had considerable influence. Taft wanted to help: he and other LEP leaders wished to be of service in advancing the cause of the League of Nations. On March 28, Wilson met with Taft and former Harvard president A. Lawrence Lowell. Taft wrote a memorandum that recorded the substance of the meeting.

Taft and Lowell arrived at the White House, and Wilson said that he was "glad to see" them, but the reason he was glad was his eagerness to *dissuade* them from discussing the details of the proposed League of Nations. Wilson said that "it might embarrass him thereafter in dealing with the subject."[38] He preferred to defer until after the war, and then proceed incrementally with a series of "special conferences." Wilson stated that

> he knew that this would be slow, but that the common law was built up that way, and he thought that by a series of such conferences it would be possible ultimately to reach some form of machinery which experience would suggest; that this might be done by precedents and procedure which custom would formulate.[39]

Then Wilson made a prophetic observation: "He gave it as his opinion that the Senate of the United States would be unwilling to enter into an agreement by which a majority of other nations could tell the United States when they must go to war."[40]

In light of the fact that this issue would be Wilson's undoing, there is no escaping the significance of this choice—this decision to defer any action in discussing the League of Nations. It is true that timing may be hard to second guess when a decision must be made before the fact. And there was a case to be made for letting sleeping dogs lie in the spring of 1918. But in light of what would happen, one cannot avoid wondering whether Wilson should have worked with Taft to sound out Republican opinion, to determine what people like Henry Cabot Lodge might be willing to accept.

We will never know what the results might have been. Wilson was certain that he ought to delay. He told House on March 22 that the "Senate would never ratify any treaty which put the force of the United States at the disposal of any such group or body." Then he continued: "Why begin at the impossible end when there is a possible end and it is feasible to plant a system which will slowly but surely ripen into fruition?"[41]

There was no way for Wilson to know in advance if this scenario would prove to be "feasible." (It would not be feasible when Henry Cabot Lodge began his devastating attack upon the League's enforcement provision and Wilson refused to reach a compromise.) The alternative of working in 1918 with the leaders of the LEP to begin bipartisan discussions that themselves might have "ripened into fruition" seemed to Wilson "impossible."

And the mood in which Wilson made this decision was less than admirable. In a letter to House on March 20, Wilson sneered at the "folly of these League to Enforce Peace butters-in," and declared that "we must head them off one way or another." In another line of this letter, Wilson called the LEP leaders "woolgatherers."[42]

They were nothing of the kind. In May, Lord Bryce sent a message to Theodore Marburg, the former U.S. ambassador to Belgium who was serving at the time as an officer of the LEP. "I fully agree with the President's view that the time has not yet come to discuss (i.e., discuss publicly) the formal constitution of a 'league to enforce peace,'" wrote Viscount Bryce. "But there are so many problems to be solved in constituting any such League . . . that it seems to me that the best jurists and diplomats and historians ought to be studying these problems now, in concert, quite privately, but with the knowledge of their governments. They should be working out alternative plans. . . . These things cannot be extemporized."[43]

In the meantime, the fires of Wilson's expectations for the League were stoked by some admirers who idolized the president. George D. Herron, an American Christian socialist living in Switzerland, encouraged Wilson to create the League right away. Though the call for quick action was unappealing to Wilson, the tone of Herron's letter made the flattery of House seem mild by comparison:

What, or who, is sufficient to save mankind from the ages of iron darkness wherewith Germany is now more nearly overcoming the world than at any hour since she poured her well-nigh cosmical madness through Belgium's gates? No one but yourself, Mr. President. . . . No other than yourself can now speak the word that shall preserve the world from a German darkness and despotism infernal—the word, too, creating as it saves, that renders conscious the common but yet unuttered soul of mankind, and precipitates it upon a new and comparatively divine plan of progress. No one but yourself is sufficient for proposing this world-revolution—this new creation of the world. . . . Let the League of Nations be now, Mr. President. Unto you it is divinely given, and unto you only, to speak the word that shall bring the World-Society into being.[44]

FORCE TO THE UTMOST

And then the German onslaught in France erupted. Wilson had sent Newton Baker to Europe to explore the possibility of short-term American troop commitments. Pershing—after the British finally approached him directly—had agreed to send American troops to serve with the British so the latter would not be forced to reduce the size of their divisions. (Pershing insisted on having his troops commanded by American officers, and he remained opposed to sending troops to the French, since he believed it would be a "dangerous experiment on account of the difference in language.")[45]

Some American troops had been sent to augment the British forces that were destined to bear the brunt of the Germans' assault: the 6th, 12th, and 14th U.S. Engineer regiments were deployed to help the British Fifth Army commanded by General Hubert Gough.[46]

In the early hours of March 21, after a surprise bombardment and gas attack, seventy-six German divisions poured out of their trenches to attack twenty-eight British divisions at St. Quentin, near the old Somme battlefield. The initial result of the battle was a British defeat. There appeared to be serious danger that the Germans would separate the British and French forces, a prelude to driving the British to the sea, as Ludendorff intended.

General Haig conferred urgently with Pétain, and he was not reassured by what the latter had to say. So Haig called for an emergency top-level conference, which occurred on March 26: the French president, Poincaré, attended, as did the prime minister, Clemenceau, and the British war minister, Lord Milner. The upshot was the appointment of the swashbuckling General Ferdinand Foch to coordinate the command of all French and British troops.[47]

Newton Baker, still in Europe, reported to Wilson on March 27 that Pershing would visit Foch "tomorrow and arrange to cooperate fully."[48] Later that day he cabled Wilson again, reporting that "four of our [infantry] divisions"—the 1st, 2nd, 26th, and 42nd (the "Rainbow Division")—were being placed "in the line" of battle to help the French. "General Pershing is in full accord with General Pétain and General Haig and is placing all our men and resources here at their disposal," Baker reported.[49]

But Allied discontent with the level of American military participation continued. Lloyd George wrote to Lord Reading (who had replaced Spring-Rice as the British ambassador to the United States) as follows on March 28:

> It is of paramount importance that American troops should be sent to France with the utmost speed possible and I wish you to urge this on the President. . . . France has no further reserves at her disposal. We are scraping men from every possible side. Our military age is being raised to 50 and possibly to 55, and we are considering whether conscription shall not be applied to Ireland. As we have already raised over five millions of men it is inevitable, however, that the further numbers we can get by this scraping process will be small. It is, there-

fore, of vital importance that American troops of all arms should be poured into France as rapidly as possible. . . . I beg you to impress this fact upon President Wilson with all the force you can.[50]

On the same day, Sir William Wiseman reported to the British foreign office as follows:

> The President never believed that the Germans would attempt the much advertised offensive. He thought the morale of their troops was low and the influence of the military party waning. The success of their present attack has been a great shock to him and necessitates a readjustment of opinions and hopes to which he has stubbornly clung. . . . The first effect here of the recent news has been to let loose a storm of criticism against the Administration which has been brewing for some time. . . . It will be hard for you to realize that anyone should be concerned with the credit of an Administration at a time like this, but . . . the President, at any rate, regards his critics here as little better than traitors.[51]

At a dinner on March 27 at the Lotos Club in New York, Reading recited the text of another telegram from Lloyd George, a telegram addressed to the American people. The British prime minister pleaded publicly for maximum American participation in the war. Then the newspapers published the text of this public message.

Wilson was furious; House recorded that the president considered it "a most discourteous and unusual, as well as an undiplomatic thing, for an ambassador to give out publicly a message from his government directly to the people of another country. . . . He said it was sufficient cause to send an ambassador home." House calmed Wilson down, and the two of them discussed the outline of "the speech we decided he should make soon."[52] In this wrathful state of mind Wilson wrote out a famous battle cry—a war hymn— to prove his commitment to victory was second to none.

On April 6, in a speech in Baltimore to launch the third Liberty Loan campaign, he declared himself "ready even now, to discuss a fair and just and honest peace at any time that it is sincerely purposed,—a peace in which the strong and the weak shall fare alike. But the answer, when I proposed such a peace, came from the German commanders in Russia, and I cannot mistake the meaning of the answer." The answer was distilled within the harsh peace of Brest-Litovsk.

And now America, to rescue the world, would do its share. If the Germans were successful, Wilson warned, then "everything that America has lived for and loved and grown great to vindicate and bring to a glorious realization will have fallen in utter ruin and the gates of mercy once more pitilessly shut upon mankind!"

But the Americans would not let it happen. "The world shall know," the president said, how completely America would mobilize: "We shall give all that we love and all that we have to redeem the world," he promised. The moral terms of the conflict were stark, but Americans were ready to fight German fire with fire:

> Germany has once more said that force, and force alone, shall decide whether Justice and peace shall reign in the affairs of men, whether Right as America conceives it or Dominion as she conceives it shall determine the destinies of mankind. There is, therefore, but one response possible from us: Force, Force to the Utmost, Force without stint or limit, the righteous and triumphant Force which shall make Right the law of the world, and cast every selfish dominion down in the dust. [53]

He meant to prove that all the force at his command would be provided to the British and the French. But it was action, not words, that the Allies were after, and their leaders remained uneasy. The only practical result of this speech would be to make Wilson's mood more strident. He acknowledged this a few days later in remarks to some reporters. This was one of those moments—increasingly rare—when he recognized the danger of his own histrionics and sought to make amends by calming down:

> I would be ashamed to use the knock-down and drag-out language; that is not the language of liberty, that is the language of braggadocio. For my part, I have no desire to march triumphantly into Berlin. . . . It is so difficult in any kind of speech—this kind or any other—to express two things that seem to be going in opposite directions. I wasn't sure that I had succeeded in expressing them on Saturday: the sincere willingness to discuss peace whenever the proposals themselves are sincere and yet, at the same time, the determination never to discuss it until the basis laid down for the discussion is justice. [54]

So Wilson steadied himself. And yet his Baltimore speech had elicited reactions that would worsen his self-righteousness. One admirer wrote that the "message delivered in Baltimore" showed that "God has inspired you to rise to every occasion. The whole world recognizes and acclaims you its Mighty Leader. MAY THE LORD OF HOSTS BLESS YOU AND KEEP YOU!" [55]

In the meantime, the trans-Atlantic tensions in regard to American troop commitments became nothing less than excruciating.

Lloyd George wrote to Reading again, and he observed that "if the struggle should be decided against us without these [American] troops being employed, it is quite possible that the war may be terminated and the cause lost." [56]

House had called upon Reading to explain the displeasure of Wilson with the Lotos Club affair and to urge British finesse. House was stunned when

William Wiseman interjected that the British were prepared to let Wilson take the rap for defeat if the Germans won: "Lloyd George at any time, in order to save himself, might blame the result of the failure in France on the President."[57]

Under these conditions Reading called upon Wilson at the White House on March 30. Reading afterward informed Lloyd George that the president "would issue instructions to the proper authorities to act in accordance with your request." Specifically, Wilson (according to Reading) would "direct that 120,000 infantry be embarked for transport to Europe in each of the months of April May June and July, making a total of 480,000."[58]

Lloyd George would believe it when he saw it. He sent Reading a two-part telegram, a Janus-faced affair that conveyed a dark cynicism in regard to Wilson's credibility. In the first part, meant for the consumption of others, the prime minister asked his ambassador to

> convey to [the] President at once sincere thanks of War Cabinet for his instant and complete response to appeal of British and French Govts. It has come as the greatest relief to all those who have the immediate responsibility for dealing with this crisis to know that, thanks to the President's prompt co-operation allied armies are to receive an indispensable reinforcement of men.[59]

Beneath this paragraph appeared the words *private and confidential*, below which the following displeasure was expressed:

> I feel that unless you can give your personal attention to the measures taken to carry out the President's undertaking the men will not be forthcoming. We have been let down badly once or twice before. In fact we are largely suffering now because the Americans have fallen egregiously short of their programme.[60]

The prime minister's anxiety was such that he wrote the next day to express the opinion that "success or disaster in this battle will be decided by exertions which America puts forth in next few weeks or even days." He added that "we depend greatly on Colonel House and hope that he will devote his great influence and energy to this question until it is certain that 120,000 American infantry are going, in fact and not merely on paper, to arrive in Europe in April and in each succeeding month afterwards."[61]

Lloyd George made sure that the president's ego would be stroked. Coordinated telegrams were sent to Wilson by Poincaré, King George V, Clemenceau, and King Victor Emmanuel of Italy. Each telegram strove to outdo all the others in extolling the American commitment to the cause and praising Wilson as a champion of democracy.[62]

On April 3, Lloyd George and Clemenceau requested Pershing, along with General Tasker H. Bliss—who was serving at the time as both army chief of staff and as American representative to the Supreme War Council of the Allies—to attend a meeting at Beauvais. The purpose of the meeting was to augment the power of General Foch—to give him the authority he needed to coordinate movements of the British, French, and American forces in repelling the German onslaught. Bliss reported that "with perfect unanimity" the conference participants agreed to give Foch "all the powers necessary."[63]

But the "perfect unanimity" expressed at the meeting belied the distrust of Pershing that was haunting the British and French. House wrote to warn Wilson that the Allied concern might be justified:

> The situation in France must be even more critical than we think, for the nervousness of both the French and British Governments cannot otherwise be explained. . . . Outside of the general gravity of the situation, I have still further anxiety because of the effect which a grave disaster in France would have upon your administration. If the German offensive fails, no one can lift a voice in criticism. . . . But if it succeeds, then, there will be no end to the denunciations from such as Roosevelt, Wood, and their kind. Pershing's feeling that an American army under his command should be established and made as formidable as possible is understandable. Nevertheless, the thing to be done now is to stop the Germans.[64]

On April 7, Lloyd George gave a speech to commemorate the anniversary of America's entry into the war. He predicted that America "would give the Prussian military junta the surprise of their lives."[65] The ever-touchy Wilson was insulted; the very next day he told a group of correspondents that he was "rendered a little uneasy by what Mr. Lloyd George was quoted as having said the other day. . . . I, for my own part, don't like the idea of having surprises. I would like people to be surprised that we didn't do our duty, but not surprised that we did." He said Americans were "doing our damnedest."[66]

That was not the opinion of the British. On April 9, Lloyd George told Reading to impress upon Wilson that "all questions of building up an independent American Army in Europe must come second to this imperative necessity whilst crisis lasts," since another "tremendous battle" was "impending."[67] But when Reading met with Wilson, he found him "disinclined to answer specific points [since] he had to consult his military advisers and be guided by them as to details."[68]

The battle to which the prime minister alluded was a new German thrust into Flanders. The Germans had shifted their attack. By April 5 they had advanced twenty miles and were approaching Amiens, but then triumphant German troops began to dally for the purpose of looting and the overall offensive bogged down. Moreover, the Germans were beginning to encounter obstacles on the old Somme battlefield.

And so Ludendorff turned from "Operation Michael" to a subsidiary plan (code-named "George") against the British in Flanders. Commencing on April 9, this attack prompted General Haig to issue a famous admonition to his troops: they would have to fight with their "backs to the wall."

Lloyd George redoubled his efforts to prod the recalcitrant president. On April 14, he wrote to Reading as follows:

> We can do no more than we have done. It rests with America to win or lose the decisive battle of the war. But if it is to be won America will have to move as she has never moved before and the President must overrule at once the narrow obstinacy which would put obstacle[s] in the way of using American infantry in the only way in which it can be used to save the situation. [69]

It is hard to determine the amount of ill will that was created in the minds of British leaders by the inability of Wilson to ease their fears. In all likelihood, their resentment of Wilson was becoming severe. As for Pershing, British anger had reached the boiling point: Wiseman told House that "H.M. Government thinks General Pershing is adopting a narrow and selfish view in the face of a very grave crisis." [70]

On April 18, Reading called upon Baker (who had just returned from Europe) and reminded him of the president's pledge to send a total of 480,000 troops to Europe from April through July. Baker said that there seemed to be a "difference of opinion" as to what the president had promised. He added that planners found it "difficult to pin themselves down definitely to the 480,000 infantrymen." [71]

In the latter part of April, the Allies' luck improved. Early German advances sputtered out. By the end of April, the "George" offensive was over, and the German casualties were high: 303,450 in "Michael" and 120,000 in "George." And the Germans were nearing the end of their manpower reserves. [72]

Still, the situation was grave in the opinion of General Foch. On May 2, he submitted a memorandum to the Supreme War Council. "At this, the most perilous moment of the greatest battle of the war," he wrote, "I have a right to state my views as to how American Infantry should be sent to France." And with all due respect to the wishes of Pershing, "who desires . . . to perfect the formation of the great American army of which he is the chief," the latest German offensive caused "losses in infantry and machine guns out of all comparison with such losses as occurred during the last three years of the war." [73]

Whatever the justifications—and the justifications were obvious—for preserving an American chain of command that was distinct and for protecting American soldiers from the will of foreign commanders whose decisions (especially in the case of Haig) might be open to question, the heedlessness of Wilson and Pershing in regard to the legitimate concerns of the French and the British in the spring of 1918 was astonishing. Surely David Lloyd George and Georges Clemenceau came to feel that their effort to elicit a vigorous partnership with the United States was an exercise in pulling teeth. Pershing seemed callous and Wilson must have seemed like the worst kind of prima donna.[74]

And Wilson's attitude was all the worse when contrasted to his rhetoric. On May 18, in a speech on behalf of the Red Cross in New York, Wilson bragged about the huge American contribution that was coming. "I have heard gentlemen recently say that we must get five million men ready," Wilson proclaimed. "Why limit it to five million? I have asked the Congress of the United States to name no limit, because Congress intends, I am sure, as we all intend, that every ship that can carry men or supplies shall go laden upon every voyage with every man and every supply that she can carry."[75]

On May 27, the Germans swung south, in the hope of menacing Paris. French troops resisting this drive were augmented by Americans: the 2nd and 3rd divisions plus a brigade of U.S. Marines. On June 1, the marines saw action at Chateau Thierry.[76] On June 4, they won an important victory at Belleau Wood.[77] But panic spread in Paris as the long-range guns of the Germans lobbed shells into the city. According to military historian S. L. A. Marshall, "The French government was packing for Bordeaux. Thousands of terrified refugees came streaming through the city. . . . Foch was having his worst hour. . . . Clemenceau bridled at the Americans, railing that though they had three quarters of a million men in France, they were contributing only driblets to the battle; trenchant criticism, beyond answer."[78]

General Bliss wrote to Baker on June 8, informing him that "Boulogne was heavily bombed. . . . I know that General Foch's view is that if it should be necessary to temporarily lose Paris he would let it go and not be diverted from the real purpose of his campaign. . . . In any event, the loss of Paris, temporarily or not, would have a tremendously depressing effect upon the French."[79]

Wilson had finally begun to think seriously about the discontent with Pershing. But he lacked the real strength to command. When Wiseman called upon him on May 29, Wilson said that "if Pershing really stood in the way, he would be ordered to stand out of the way," though "it would, of course, distress him to have to override his Commander-in-Chief [i.e., Pershing] because he felt he ought to be loyal to him, and he did not like overriding a man so far from home and possibly only understanding part of his case."[80]

But events on the battlefield were changing again: the Germans, having lost another one hundred thousand men, called off the attack that threatened Paris.[81] On June 9, Ludendorff attacked in a different direction: along the river Matz. A French and American counterattack on June 14 proved decisive. Moreover, in addition to their battlefield casualties, the Germans were succumbing to the first wave of the catastrophic influenza virus that was soon to spread around the world.

Ludendorff paused to consider his options. By July, the German strategic deliberations would involve the kaiser. The Germans could not replace their losses. And yet the imminence of German defeat was not yet clear. Clemenceau, Lloyd George, and Vittorio Orlando believed that one hundred more American divisions would be needed. Pershing wrote Baker on June 18 to inform him that if eighty more divisions could be sent by the summer of 1919, the war might be won by the autumn of that year.[82] In the meantime, the Allied leaders were convinced that putting Japanese and American troops into Russia in order to exert new pressure on the Central Powers would be necessary.[83]

House came closer to the truth when he suggested to Wilson that the end of the war might be in sight: "Austria is already at the breaking point, and I also believe the German people will take the supreme power away from the military extremists this Autumn if they do not have a decisive victory on the Western front."[84]

And this was one of those times when the views of House would prove prophetic.

THE DESTRUCTION OF EVERY
ARBITRARY POWER ANYWHERE

At the end of 1917, House had forwarded Wilson a memorandum from Lincoln Steffens, the muckraking journalist. Steffens joined the roster of distinguished Americans who tried—discreetly and sympathetically—to guide Wilson away from the excesses of the Espionage Act. Steffens' advice was cogent; he wrote that

> labor and the lower classes are not exactly against the war, but they are not for it; not yet; and the attitude of the upper class and the policy (or some acts) of some parts of the government and press are packing the workers back into a suppressed, sullen opposition. This can be cured. More. I believe this evil tendency can be turned into a force for good. . . . Accept openly the fact that there is this growing feeling. Say so. Call it by its names: doubt, confusion, suspicion, hate. And don't rebuke it. Understand it, sympathetically, and then—melt it into something akin to love and faith. Ask the pro-war people to be more patient with the anti-war folk. Ask the pacifists to be more considerate of the fighters; and to put their minds, not on peace, but the terms of a permanent peace. . . . Ask all editors, writers, and speakers,—all—to remember that the war psychology is a little like a sickness; that it makes men's minds sensitive and sore. . . . Ask the President to practice mercy, as Lincoln did; only, in this later day, more systematically, on a larger scale. . . . He could pick

from among his personal friends . . . to go about for him . . . recommending
pardons, many, many pardons.[85]

But Wilson did precisely the reverse in 1918. In April, 113 IWW leaders
were tried in Chicago, notwithstanding what John Milton Cooper has called
the "flimsy and often ludicrous nature of much of the government's case."[86]
All were convicted. In the meantime, Max Eastman and the other editors of
The Masses were indicted for violating the Espionage Act. When their trial
resulted in a hung jury, the U.S. district attorney for the southern district of
New York moved to have them retried. Several progressives and socialists
urged Wilson to intervene, since Eastman had come to support the war effort.

Upton Sinclair told Wilson that "these men are ready to give real support
to your policies. . . . It seems to me a tragic blunder to drive them into
irritated opposition."[87] Amos Pinchot wrote at greater length about the
"doubtful wisdom of pushing these prosecutions, of their effect on liberal
people and policies—and of the fact that, if rights like that of common
counsel are taken from the public in an emergency, they can never be restored as *rights*. They have become revocable permissions." But above all,
Pinchot contended, "Max Eastman, Art Young, John Reed and the others are
not guilty. I listened to most of the trial myself and read a good deal of the
record; and I know, as a lawyer who has tried many criminal cases, that
evidence proving the charges of the indictment are quite lacking." Pinchot
asserted that Eastman, Young, and Reed—all personal friends, he acknowledged—had no "intent to block the policy of the government." Whatever
their criticism of the war, "they showed no desire to prevent the operation of
the law."[88]

In this one case, Wilson's conscience began to be troubled. He wrote to
Attorney General Gregory as follows: "Here is another letter about the East-
man-Reed prosecutions. Mr. Amos Pinchot is not always very wise, but he is
always very sincere, I believe, and his letter, I must admit, has made some
impression upon me."[89] In another letter to Gregory, Wilson wrote that "I
would be very much obliged to you if you would advise me whether you
think we are in fact pursuing the best and wisest course in these prosecutions."[90]

Gregory met with Wilson on June 6, and he convinced the president to
continue the crackdown on dissent. The prosecution of Eastman and the
others was pushed ahead, though the second trial, which was held from
September 30 to October 5, resulted in a second hung jury.[91]

Later in the summer the attorney general sent Wilson an extended analysis of the situation. Wilson had received a very troubling letter from Upton
Sinclair—a letter requesting that "political prisoners" found guilty of violating the Espionage Act might be jailed in conditions far better than the usual

penal institutions.[92] Wilson sent the letter to Gregory and asked for his comments.

Gregory's answer was a very strange mixture of insight, banality, and something that bordered on cowardice. He acknowledged that many citizens who were targets of the Espionage Act were

> men and women who have not the slightest sympathy with Germany, whose loyalty, in so far as they have national loyalty, is exclusively for the United States, who are intensely sincere, who have no converse whatever with the enemy or agents of the enemy and are guilty of no secret action against the interests of this country, but who, by reason of intense convictions and propagandist temperaments, give public voice to sentiments which are deemed by the Department of Justice and the trial court and jury to be obstructive of the prosecution of the war.

But despite the fact that such dissenters were harmless—and despite what some believed were unequivocal protections in the First Amendment—Gregory told Wilson to reject any notion of clemency (or any disinclination to continue with such prosecutions) for several reasons, and one of them amounted to concern that the previous decisions of elected leaders might be placed in an embarrassing light:

> The Espionage Law may fairly be said to embody the public opinion of the country, speaking through its legislators. . . . The grant of special privileges to persons found guilty . . . would be, if not something in the nature of an apology for the policy embodied in that law, at least a casting of doubt upon the wisdom of that policy.[93]

This advice—to persist in the persecution of harmless people because reconsideration of such behavior might be seen as a confession that Congress and the president had made a mistake—is of secondary importance to the judgment of the president who elicited such advice and chose to follow it, for Wilson had possessed the power to prevent this state of affairs from the beginning.

If Wilson had insisted on changes to the Espionage Act that would have removed the sections of questionable justification, he might have crafted a law that was defensible. If he had chosen to overrule his attorney general, or dismiss him and find someone better, he had the power. Wilson knew better than to do what he was doing, as his twinges of conscience revealed. But he did it just the same—at times in a mood (or in the pose) of ambivalence, and at other times with self-righteous gusto.

And then he did worse.

On May 16, Wilson signed an addition to the Espionage Act that was known before long as the "Sedition Act." This act (which passed the Senate on May 4 and the House on May 7) threatened punishment to anyone who "shall utter . . . any disloyal, profane, scurrilous or abusive language" about the "form of government" of the United States or its "military and naval forces."

When Wilson asked the attorney general about this bill, Gregory replied that its "language is not too broad, because, upon a charge of its violation, the accused . . . must be convicted by proof beyond a reasonable doubt, to the satisfaction of a court and jury." Gregory did, however, object to a provision that would let the postmaster general, upon evidence satisfactory to himself alone, deprive persons "in violation of the act" of all delivery of mail.[94]

Wilson signed the act.

He seemed to be brimming over with resentment; when an antiwar socialist in Kansas City named Rose Pastor Stokes was convicted of sedition, Wilson wrote to Gregory and asked whether the editor of the *Kansas City Star* might also be indicted.[95] The most spectacular prosecution under the Sedition Act was the case against Eugene Victor Debs, the Socialist Party's candidate for the presidency. Debs was indicted on June 29 by the U.S. attorney for northern Ohio, and his trial took place in September. At age sixty-two and in failing health, he was sentenced to ten years in the federal penitentiary for his opposition to the war.

In all, Wilson's record on wartime civil liberties was a history of small-mindedness, myopia, hypocrisy, and—why pull punches?—stupidity.

Ironically, at the very same time that Wilson was silencing critics, he had a new assistant secretary of state, William C. Bullitt Jr.—the very same William C. Bullitt who would later co-author with Sigmund Freud a controversial psychiatric study of Wilson—keep him apprised of the democratic and liberal stirrings in the kaiser's Germany. Wilson had hopes for democratizing Germany, and his advisers tried to send him encouraging news. "Each successive cable which reaches the Department," Bullitt wrote on one occasion in 1918, "indicates more clearly that the President may now make himself leader of the Liberals of Germany and Austria-Hungary."[96]

Wilson clearly had the power to rise above pettiness and live the ideals that he espoused when his mind was working at its best. But his better instincts were stifled by deep inner conflicts most of the time.

The tragedy is shown very clearly by a proclamation in 1918 that shows the man working at his very best for once—a proclamation that condemned the American disgrace of lynching.

Robert P. Prager, a German-born coal miner, had been lynched in Collinsville, Illinois, on April 5, and the case triggered widespread outrage. Congressman Leonidas Dyer of Missouri introduced an anti-lynching law in Congress and asked Wilson to issue a national proclamation supporting it.[97]

And Wilson did. On July 26, he issued a "statement to the American people" that condemned "mob action" and went on to urge Americans to exemplify the decency of democratic institutions in everything they did, lest the world regard this war to make the world safe for democracy as being hypocritical. Wilson on this occasion was forthright and eloquent as he confronted the issues of wartime intolerance head on:

> Germany has outlawed herself among the nations because she has disregarded the sacred obligations of law and has made lynchers of her armies. Lynchers emulate her disgraceful example. . . . We proudly claim to be the champions of democracy. If we really are, in deed and in truth, let us see to it that we do not discredit our own. I say plainly that every American who takes part in the action of a mob or gives it any sort of countenance is no true son of this great Democracy, but its betrayer.[98]

How could a leader with such passion for the protection of life and liberty, a leader so alert to the issue of hypocrisy raised by his own invocations of democracy, a leader who could lead with such nobility and courage, have succumbed to such vindictive spite when it came to a principle as basic to American democracy as free speech? How could he have signed the Sedition Act or urged Gregory to prosecute dissenters and editors? How could he claim that the issues were ambiguous? There is no way around the basic mystery of Wilson's mind, the emotional roots of his impulses, the forces that shaped his rationalizations for the dreadful things he often did, and for the way he lashed out at the people who dared second guess his sense of mission.

Such mysteries defy explanation except through the treacherous and ultimately open-ended process of psychological speculation.

The psychiatric study of Wilson by Bullitt and Freud met with scathing criticism when it was published in the United States.[99] But there is no escaping the fact that Woodrow Wilson had a psychopathology. The mental decline that would lead to many bad judgments in 1919—well before the stroke—was evident at least as early as 1917, and it worsened in 1918. The petulant displays were much greater in frequency and magnitude. Cooper has observed that his contemporaries commented on Wilson's fragile mental condition by the summer of 1918:

> Some observers then and later said that they detected changes in Wilson's psychology around this time. . . . Whether these were signs of a deeper problem—stemming from his long-dormant arteriosclerosis—is impossible to tell. Still, it was clear that this sixty-one-year-old man, who was burdened by responsibilities that he seemed loath to share, was not at the peak of his powers.[100]

Pure stress was a factor, for despite the fact that Wilson included recreation in most of his work days, the aggravation that surged intermittently and with very high velocity through his mind—combined with the exhaustion of mind that the substance of his presidential work entailed—wore him down. Wiseman recorded early in the year that he "could not help noticing that he [Wilson] looked tired, and that his voice was decidedly weak. He admitted that the strain was very great."[101] In February, House wrote that Wilson "does not remember names as well and he does not think to do the things we decide upon. Grayson [Dr. Cary T. Grayson, Wilson's personal physician in his White House years] was talking of this yesterday."[102]

And yet the very same circumstances—physical and mental exhaustion—afflicted Lincoln in the Civil War years, and he was brilliant. There was something else going on—a very different and sinister process—in the stark degeneration of Wilson's judgment, a worsening of preexisting traits combined with the insidious growth of various maladies. Some believe that his arteriosclerosis had led by 1918 to a definite cerebrovascular disease.

It is risky indeed to attempt any "diagnosis" of Wilson's pathology beyond certain medical facts that are established beyond question (such as arteriosclerosis). Many have tried to construct comprehensive psychological theories (in addition to the previously mentioned study of Bullitt and Freud): some have overreached, and then the critics have overreacted.[103] It is probably best at this date to keep the exploration of Wilson's mental shortcomings sketchy. But any treatment of Wilson that neglects the psychological dimension of his bad judgment is an exercise in avoidance.

In a hastily scheduled address to Congress delivered on May 27, Wilson called for extending the congressional session to levy additional taxes. He sought to be inspiring and stern: "Excuses are unavailing," he proclaimed, "we have either done our duty or we have not." Then, to drive home the message of sacrifice, he made another of his impulsive utterances. "Politics is adjourned," he declared. "The elections will go to those who think least of it."[104]

Hyperbole is, of course, to be expected during national emergencies—and disingenuousness about political motivations is in many cases standard procedure, with immense comic value at times, in the cloak-and-dagger world of political maneuver—but in light of the provocative things that Wilson did in the congressional elections of 1918, this statement would soon become farcical to those who remembered it. Worse, after Wilson tried to use the war for partisan advantage in the autumn of 1918, Republicans probably remembered his May declaration with a vindictive sneer.[105]

Just a few weeks before he asserted the adjournment of politics, Wilson said—if House's diary is accurate—that he held most members of the Senate in "contempt," and this applied right across the party lines, though his partisan feelings were keen: House recorded that Wilson expressed his contempt "without going into the republican ranks, most of whom he thoroughly despises."[106]

The very next day, in the Red Cross speech, Wilson tried to pretend that all was blissful: "Not a hundred years of peace could have knitted this nation together as a single year of war has knitted it together," he declared. [107]

But in light of the bitterness that Wilson exuded at the time—bitterness toward Theodore Roosevelt, David Lloyd George, woolgatherers, Republicans in general, and anyone who ruffled his feathers—these lofty generalizations of unity must have rung hollow to the members of Wilson's entourage who knew him best (with the important exception of people such as Newton Baker and Herbert Hoover, who idolized Wilson). And a glimmering of wit from the president—though wrapped in very low humor—gives a hint that Wilson seemed to sense the incongruity in which he was entrapping himself as the off-year elections approached. At the end of the Red Cross speech he told the following joke:

> An Indian was enlisted in the army. He returned to the reservation on a furlough. He was asked what he thought of it. He said: "No much good; too much salute; not much shoot." Then he was asked: "Are you going back?" "Yes." "Well, do you know what you are fighting for?" "Yes, me know; fight to make whole damn world Democratic party." He had evidently misunderstood some innocent sentence of my own. [108]

Wilson still at this point was in a mental condition that his elfin humor could improve. But the greatest release from the anger, frustration, resentment, and spite that kept eating away at his "cool" self-possession was the soaring release that a messianic vision could supply. Just after the "Indian" joke, he spoke of "voices that speak the utter longing of oppressed and helpless people all over the world to . . . hear the feet of the great hosts of liberty going to set them free, to set their minds free, set their lives free, set their children free." He summoned the crowd to join him and "sustain the heart of the world." [109]

In a Fourth of July address at Mount Vernon, Wilson said that the war must result in "the destruction of every arbitrary power anywhere [or] its reduction to virtual impotence." The question must be asked: Was Wilson reflecting to the slightest degree on the literal meaning of such statements? Was he engaging in a pardonable exaggeration that he never expected to be taken literally? If not, what declension in the mind of this former professor of political science could entertain the fantasy of eliminating *every* form of arbitrary power?

This speech, though significant, was only the latest of the millennial declarations that Wilson had been making since the start of the war. If Wilson never meant to have these words taken literally, he was taking a risk—he was surely playing with fire—in raising expectations of utopian magnitude. Listen to him:

On the one hand stand the peoples of the world. . . . Opposed to them, masters
of many armies, stand an isolated, friendless group of governments who speak
no common purpose but only selfish ambitions of their own . . . governments
clothed with the strange trappings and the primitive authority of an age that is
altogether alien and hostile to our own. The Past and the Present are in deadly
grapple and the peoples of the world are being done to death between them.
There can be but one issue. The settlement must be final. There can be no
compromise. No halfway decision would be tolerable. No halfway decision is
conceivable.

It was all or nothing—no halfway measures would suffice. In addition to
destroying "every arbitrary power anywhere," the world's democracies must
create a new order to encompass "the settlement of every question, whether
of territory, of sovereignty, of economic arrangement, or of political relationship, upon the basis of the free acceptance of the settlement by the people
immediately concerned." Again, Wilson's talk was extravagant to the point
of becoming almost childish: he said that *every* question, all over the world,
would be settled the democratic way. He went on, referring to the League of
Nations, and he insisted that the League "shall make it certain that the combined power of free nations will check every invasion of right." Again, he
chose to use the term *every*: not a single aggression in the world would be
allowed to succeed.

These were Wilson's own words, and he could have spoken better ones
by far. He could have spoken in sophisticated terms that would make the
limits of the possible clear to much of his audience. But he refused to do any
such thing; he insisted that the old ambiguities of power balance would
vanish all over the world: "These great ends cannot be achieved by debating
and seeking to reconcile and accommodate what statesmen may wish, with
their projects for balances of power." The great ends would only be achieved
by "forces which, once roused, can never be crushed to earth again; for they
have at their heart an inspiration and a purpose which are deathless and of the
very stuff of triumph!"

When he argued with Taft and the other "butters-in," Wilson posed as a
Burkean gradualist (and he had studied Edmund Burke long before). He
insisted that no quick breakthrough—no millennial covenant, perfect and
pristine at its creation—was likely to emerge as the basis for the League of
Nations; only trial-and-error experience would lead to accretions of precedents. But over and over in 1918, he indulged himself in perfectionist visions
of a new world order with no ambiguities at all.

In his mental confusion, Wilson drifted between these two positions.
Perhaps he had no idea of the deep contradictions in which he was immersing
himself. Or perhaps he sought to bridge the contradictions through a vision of
an incremental process—an accumulation of "precedents" that "custom
would formulate," as he expressed it to Taft—that would still, over time,

reach a critical mass that would *become* the final resolution of history, since God, through his providence, would *make* it all happen in the end. Many statements of Wilson since the onset of war had made the theological nature of his policy premises clear. His speeches in 1919 would make it crystal clear. As political scientist Hans Morgenthau once observed, Wilson's passions were increasingly channeled into "an eschatological hope."[110]

ANY FORCE THAT MAY BE NECESSARY

Notwithstanding his wish to avoid the many practical questions that pertained to the mechanics of the League of Nations, the British forced Wilson's hand and brought him out of avoidance on the day before his Mount Vernon speech. Lord Reading sent Wilson a copy of "an interim report drawn up by a committee appointed by His Majesty's Government to consider the question of a League of Nations." The committee had been chaired by "Sir Walter Phillimore, who commands the highest reputation both as an English lawyer and an international jurist." Wilson was invited to share "any views which you may be kind enough to express with regard to this report."[111]

House had known about the Phillimore Report. House was also aware that the Inquiry had discussed the League's mechanics; indeed, a member of the Inquiry who covered issues of international law (David Hunter Miller) had drafted a sketch for the League.[112] The Phillimore Report was highly tentative. It presented the principle of dispute arbitration among the League's members, but enforcement provisions for collective security were vague. House had received a copy of this report in June.

As Thomas J. Knock has observed, House believed at the time that Wilson was "dragging his feet and ought to put some of his own ideas on paper." When House received the Phillimore Report, he "knew, even if Wilson did not, that the issue could no longer be put off."[113]

So after receiving a letter from Lord Robert Cecil soliciting his views on the League of Nations, House drafted a reply. Before he sent it, he forwarded a copy to Wilson and offered to refrain from sending it if Wilson instructed him to do so. In his cover letter, House told Wilson that "you should guide the movement. It will not wait for the peace conference."[114] With Wilson's tacit consent, House sent the letter to Cecil.

House's letter supported the idea of binding arbitration. Then House proceeded to propose the following enforcement procedure: "If the belligerent against whom the finding is made insists upon going to war, then it shall become obligatory upon every nation in the League to immediately break off all diplomatic, financial and economic relations of every character and, when and where possible, also exert physical force against the offender."[115]

After Wilson had received his own copy of the Phillimore Report, he asked House to respond to the British: "Will you not rewrite the enclosed constitution of a League of Nations as you think it ought to be rewritten,— along the lines of your recent letter to Lord Robert Cecil?"[116]

Wiseman confided to Cecil that Wilson's mental habits were inimical to any exercise along the lines of the Phillimore Report. "The President has not appointed any Committee to deal with the subject [of the League]," Wiseman wrote, "and I do not think he is likely to. He told me quite frankly that he was not able to give much thought to the matter now. He himself claims to have a 'single-track' mind, by which he means that he can only deal with one problem at a time."[117]

Wilson made this statement about his own thought process to many people. It is at odds with his revealing correspondence, which shows him often micromanaging dozens of matters in the course of his workdays. For this reason, the "single-track" explanation appears to be a kind of excuse that Wilson might have talked himself into believing (or else an excuse that he was consciously using as a dodge), when the truth was more complex.

Soon thereafter, the executive committee of the LEP directed A. Lawrence Lowell to request the appointment of an American committee "in connection with similar committees of our Allies to consider the establishment of a League of Nations."[118] Wilson made it clear to the LEP "butters-in" that he wished them to butt out. He told Lowell, "I should consider it very embarrassing to have a private organization like the League to Enforce Peace take this matter up, since [it] . . . constitutes part of the intricate web of counsel now being woven between the associated governments."[119]

In following Wilson's instructions to "rewrite" the Phillimore scheme, House reviewed the League concept *de novo*. He took a bold step when he proposed that the League of Nations be an association whose membership would be limited to the great powers—a concept that might prove inimical to Wilson's notion of "peace among equals."

In other matters, House hewed to the president's proclivities, especially the principle of "open covenants." When he transmitted his draft covenant (comprising twenty-three articles) to Wilson on July 16, he told him "it is necessary I think to do away with the abominable custom of espionage." But he quickly observed that "it would be a mistake" to "leave some dishonorable nation free to surreptitiously prepare for war."[120] How did he resolve this conundrum? Through the proposition that the ethics of gentlemen would shame international offenders. Article 4 of House's draft read as follows:

> Any open or direct inquiry regarding the acts or purposes of a Power may be made by another Power as of course, and shall be regarded as an act of friendship tending to promote frankness in international relations, but any secret inquiry to such end shall be deemed dishonorable.[121]

On the matter of collective security, House's procedure called for blockading frontiers and assisting the victims of aggression.[122]

In August, Wilson—accompanied by Edith Wilson, Dr. Grayson, and Wiseman—travelled to Magnolia, Massachusetts, to visit and converse with House for five days at his vacation home. House recounted that "the President went with me to the beautiful loggia overlooking the sea and we at once plunged into a discussion of the League of Nations."[123] Wilson had at last begun to produce his own version of the League Covenant. He retained a great deal of what House had suggested, while reducing the number of articles to thirteen. According to House, they disagreed about the matter of "equal representation":

> In our discussion I stated that, in my opinion, it seemed impracticable to think of the smaller nations as members of the league on equal terms with the larger ones. He dissented quite warmly and said to exclude them would be to go contrary to all our protestations concerning them. I agreed to this and said when I sat down to write the Covenant I had in mind the participation of every nation both great and small. However, the difficulties were so apparent that I was afraid it was an idealistic dream that could never be made practical.[124]

Wilson began to back down:

> The President was deeply concerned at the attitude I took and yet he was compelled to recognize my argument. . . . I did not push the discussion further . . . having in mind that at the Peace Conference all of the great nations would probably take my view.[125]

Wiseman joined the conversation, and he asked the president to discuss the Phillimore Report. Wilson dismissed it: "'It has no teeth,' he replied. 'I read it to the last page hoping to find something definite, but I could not.'" When Wiseman asked if the president would appoint an American committee to serve as a counterpart to the Phillimore committee, Wilson said that he refused to do such a thing. Wiseman pressed him harder: "'How then,' I asked, 'are we ever to exchange views and urge a common basis.'"

Wilson said that he "would like nothing better than to discuss the whole matter perfectly frankly with MR. LLOYD GEORGE," but "as this is impossible at present," he would discuss the matter with "anyone H.M.G. care to send to him." But in any case, Wilson continued, "he thought the LEAGUE OF NATIONS ought to be constituted at the Peace Conference and not before."[126]

On September 7, Wilson sent House a more definitive draft of his League Covenant. On collective security, Wilson's Article 10 retained House's formula of boycotts, blockades, and assistance to victims of aggression. But Wilson added some important new language: the "Contracting Powers" would employ "jointly any force that may be necessary" to close and block-ade frontiers. [127]

House had been more circumspect: his draft used the word *arrange* in regard to enforcement. The signatory powers would "arrange" to blockade aggressors. Luckily for Wilson, the words *by any means necessary*—the same words that caused such trouble in the armed neutrality fight of March 1917—would not be used in the final League Covenant. But Wilson's League was already in trouble.

And so was his vision of a nonvindictive peace. On August 20, Wiseman cabled Reading to inform him that Wilson was "disturbed . . . on reading the reports of Mr. Lloyd George's speech of July 31st . . . which seemed to recommend the crushing of Germany's trade after the war." Wilson wished to "arrive at some common policy on this important and far-reaching question." [128]

Wilson was right to express such concern, but he had failed to use leverage to push his allies into line when the odds for success had been decent. Now his options were fewer. House observed to Wilson on September 3 that "as the Allies succeed, your influence will diminish." Consequently, House asked, diplomatically, whether "it would not be wise to try to commit the Allies to some of the things for which we are fighting?" [129]

But the time to do that was running out.

WITHOUT ANY ATTEMPT TO SOFTEN WHAT MAY SEEM HARSH WORDS

In August and September, the German position on the western front collapsed. Foch ordered a counteroffensive on the old Somme battlefield, and the importance of the tank in the First World War became decisive. As Keegan has observed, "Germany's failure to match the Allies in tank development must be judged one of their worst military miscalculations of the war." [130] On August 8, an Anglo-French force that employed no less than 530 British tanks and 70 French tanks was unleashed against the Germans. By the end of August, the Germans had retreated to their Hindenburg Line.

Moreover, at the end of August, Pershing finally had his army assembled, and it struck the Germans on September 12 in the "St. Mihiel salient" south of Verdun. The result by September 16 was a significant German defeat. Then Pershing's army was redeployed to the west of Verdun to form the right flank of an attack, in coordination with the French, through the Argonne Forest. Foch's objective was to threaten the German rear. [131] These reverses instilled a mood of shocked demoralization in the German ranks, from the frontline defenders all the way up the chain of command. Keegan summarizes:

After four years of war in which they had destroyed the Tsar's army, trounced the Italians and the Romanians, demoralized the French and, at the very least, denied the British clear-cut victory, they [the Germans] were confronted by an army whose soldiers sprang, in uncountable numbers, as if from soil sown with dragon's teeth. Past hopes of victory had been predicated on calculable ratios of force to force. The intervention of the United States Army had robbed calculation of point. Nowhere among Germany's remaining resources could sufficient force be found to counter the millions America could bring across the Atlantic.[132]

In the final six months of the war, 1.5 million American troops had come to France. In approximately a year and a half, the U.S. Army had increased in size from roughly one hundred thousand men to four million men. As historian Hew Strachan has noted, the American Expeditionary Force by autumn 1918 was finally "comparable in size to both the British imperial forces, which totaled 1.8 million in France, and those of France itself, which had fallen . . . to 1.7 million."[133]

On September 14, the Austrians sent out a peace feeler, and Wilson rejected it. House was appalled by the speed of Wilson's unilateral, shoot-from-the-hip response. In his diary he mused that "the President and Lansing both seem determined that it shall be known to the world that this country is acting independently of our allies. . . . This is well enough if it is our purpose to stand aloof from world politics."[134]

On September 26, Foch ordered a simultaneous attack of all Allied forces, and two days later the hitherto indomitable Ludendorff suffered what by many accounts was a nervous breakdown. After he pulled himself together, he told Hindenburg that there was no alternative to armistice. The next day, September 29, the Hindenburg Line had been breached. The Bulgarians were seeking an armistice. The German high command advised the kaiser that Germany was forced to negotiate peace. At a conference in Spa, the kaiser agreed to a limited democratization of Germany in the hope that such reforms might generate leverage through which the Germans might gain concessions. Chancellor Hertling resigned and the kaiser appointed Prince Maximilian of Baden, a moderate, to take his place on October 3.[135]

The Germans decided as the first order of business to approach Wilson. On October 6, Prince Maximilian sent Wilson a note requesting peace negotiations on the basis of the Fourteen Points.[136] A furor erupted in the Senate the next day; Republicans and several Democrats demanded unconditional German surrender. House advised Wilson to avoid hasty action, but Wilson had Lansing send a cable to the Germans demanding the evacuation of occupied territory and asking whether the German chancellor was "speaking merely for the constituted authorities of the Empire who have so far conducted the war."[137]

On October 12, the Germans sent a note on behalf of both the German government *and* the German people that accepted the Fourteen Points.[138]

It was foolish of Wilson to consider a reply to this overture without consulting other Allied leaders. He would soon pay for this impetuousness.

House had been one of the very few observers among the Allies to foresee the possibility of victory in 1918. In London and Paris, plans for continued military operations in 1919 were under way, and it took the Allied leaders some time to respond to these developments. The British, French, and Italian prime ministers met at Versailles and framed harsh terms for an armistice.[139]

Here, as on other occasions, Wilson found himself behind the flow of events. He had felt no hesitation in acting unilaterally when he rejected the Austrian peace feeler. But when the Allies left him out of their armistice consultations, he was, according to Sir William Wiseman, "very much perturbed."[140]

When Wilson complained to Ambassador Jusserand that he had not been consulted, the French ambassador replied that "a person who knows the President's thinking and would be in a position to take a real part in debates and decisions" should be appointed for that purpose.[141]

There was little doubt as to who that person would be. On October 14, Wilson named House to be "my personal representative . . . to take part as such in the conferences of the Supreme War Council and in any other conferences in which it may be serviceable for him to represent me."[142] "The President certainly gives me the broadest powers," House wrote in his diary. "It virtually puts me in his place in Europe."

House was delighted, especially in light of the fact that, as on previous occasions, Wilson gave him no instructions. Despite his jubilation, House recorded that he "wondered at the strange situation our relations had brought about. I am going on one of the most important missions anyone ever undertook, and yet there is no word of direction, advice or discussion between us."[143]

In the course of their meeting, Wilson openly confessed to a feeling of fecklessness. "I never saw him more disturbed," House wrote. "He said he did not know where to make the entrance in order to reach the heart of the thing." In particular, he "wanted to make his reply [to the latest German note] final . . . [but] it reminded him, he said, of a maze. If one went in at the right entrance, he reached the center, but if one took the wrong turning, it was necessary to go out again and do it over. He said that many times in making extemporaneous speeches he had gone into the wrong entrance and had to flounder out as best he could."

House encouraged Wilson to "get at it," and the two of them conversed as follows:

I thought he should make one condition to a discussion of armistice, and that was the immediate cessation of all atrocities both on land and sea. He agreed to this and it stands in the Note. We went into the question of the German Government and decided to use what he said in his Fourth of July speech about autocracies. This was his suggestion. We were anxious not to close the door, and yet we desired to make the note as strong as the occasion required. . . . At the same time, neither the President nor I desired to make a vengeful peace. [144]

After they had talked, they summoned Lansing, Baker, and Daniels and went over the note with them.

Wilson's note informed the Germans that "the conditions of an armistice are matters which must be left to the judgment and advice of the military advisers of the Government of the United States and the Allied Governments." This would prove to be a mistake, for it led to precisely the vindictive peace that Wilson had been anxious to avoid.

After insisting that the Germans abandon submarine warfare and other acts of "inhumanity, spoliation, and desolation," Wilson laid down the proposition that German autocracy must be overthrown. After invoking his own statements in regard to "the destruction of every arbitrary power anywhere," Wilson stated that "the power which has hitherto controlled the German nation is of the sort here described," and that "it is within the choice of the German nation to alter it." [145]

As Wilson struggled to frame his conditions for peace, he infuriated members of Congress who wanted unconditional surrender. Senator Henry Fountain Ashurst of Arizona (a Democrat) recorded in his diary that

Senators were mystified as the President had not taken any of them into his confidence. Many feared that the President's "altruism" would lead him to a reply to Germany that would lack directness. . . . The strain was enormous; the rumors were that the President's mind was not made up so I resolved upon my own course; I called an automobile and went to the Executive offices of the White House.

Ashurst informed the president that if his reply to the German note "should fail to come up to the American spirit, you are destroyed." Wilson replied that "so far as my being destroyed is concerned, I am willing if I can serve the country to go into a cellar and read poetry the remainder of my life." [146]

Republicans such as Roosevelt and Lodge were even more vociferous in demanding unconditional surrender. Yet Wilson himself had been partially to blame for creating these expectations with his invocation of "force to the utmost," his declaration that "no halfway decision is conceivable," and his promise to achieve "the destruction of every arbitrary power anywhere." David Lawrence came close to revealing the truth of this to Wilson when he wrote that "America has been fed war-hate. . . . The man on the street today doesn't believe Germany 'has been licked enough.'"[147]

As American advocates of unconditional surrender criticized Wilson, the trans-Atlantic tensions with the British and the French got worse. In a cable to Sir Eric Geddes, the first lord of the admiralty, who was visiting the United States, Lloyd George sent instructions on October 12 that "you should be careful to express no approval or disapproval of Wilson's attitude toward Prince Max's Note about which we were not even consulted. As you are aware we cannot accept his views about the Freedom of the Seas and our military advisers including Foch consider that the conditions he seems to contemplate for an Armistice inadequate."[148]

Wilson at last was beginning to pay for his lack of strategic thinking: for his failure to achieve (and, if necessary, force when he possessed the leverage) a meeting of minds with the British and French on war aims, for his failure to consult with the Allies on the Fourteen Points before he issued them, for his failure to establish good will with the British and the French—to send peremptory orders to Pershing—when the Allies felt as if the Germans were winning, and for his failure to maintain a steady liaison with the Allies as the German position fell apart.

After Wilson on October 20 received from Germany a half-conciliatory but half-defensive reply to his note of October 16, he called a cabinet meeting on October 22 and solicited views.[149] After this meeting, he composed a stern message that demanded, in effect, the abdication of the kaiser:

> Feeling that the whole peace of the world depends now on plain speaking and straightforward action, the President deems it his duty to say, without any attempt to soften what may seem harsh words, that the nations of the world do not and cannot trust the word of those who have hitherto been the masters of German policy. . . . The Government of the United States cannot deal with any but veritable representatives of the German people.[150]

Events in Germany were seething, and Wilson's message affected them for better and for worse: better, inasmuch as it hastened the arrival of the armistice, and worse, inasmuch as it hastened the arrival of political chaos in Germany. Any chance that the Germans would be able to hold their own in the peace negotiations was being eroded.

Ludendorff's despair began to yield to second thoughts in October. He began to entertain the idea that continued military action might strengthen the Germans' hand and that an armistice might be used as an advantageous breathing spell. He also initiated machinations to position civilian leaders to bear the blame if surrender became unavoidable. As historian David Stevenson has observed, Ludendorff intended to set up the left-wing politicians as scapegoats.[151]

But Prince Max was alert to this danger; he had taken the precaution of securing from Hindenburg a statement that "there was no further chance of forcing a peace on the enemy."[152] So when Ludendorff composed a proclamation on October 24 rejecting Wilson's terms as demands for surrender, the chancellor moved to get Ludendorff dismissed. The kaiser secured his resignation on October 26 and replaced him with General Wilhelm Groener.

Authority in Germany was tumbling down; the German naval high command, without the kaiser's authorization, planned a sortie against the Royal Navy, to commence on October 30. Rumors spread in the fleet that the attack would be a suicide mission. A naval mutiny began, and it spread to Kiel by November 4. From there it spread across north Germany and the Rhineland. Workers' and soldiers' councils—Soviet-like—appeared in Cologne, Hanover, Stuttgart, and even Berlin. In Munich on November 7, a mass protest against the war led to the proclamation of a republic as troops joined the protests and the king of Bavaria fled.[153] This "German revolution" was abetted by radicals under the leadership of Rosa Luxemburg and Karl Liebknecht.[154]

Prince Max, in his final acts as chancellor, created an armistice delegation that included civilian and military members, thus, as Keegan observes, ensuring that the armistice "would be a joint military and political act, from which the soldiers could not subsequently extricate themselves."[155] Even so, the legend of a "stab in the back" would make the rounds of the German right in the 1920s.

On November 9, Prince Max surrendered the office of chancellor to Friedrich Ebert, leader of Germany's Social Democrats, after mass protests in Berlin were supported by local troops. Ebert told Maximilian that "the Kaiser must abdicate, otherwise we shall have the revolution." Prince Max told the kaiser that his abdication was necessary "to avert Civil War."[156] Wilhelm at first was incredulous, then defiant. But events were unfolding very clearly along the lines of the Russian Revolution in its early phases. General Hindenburg told the kaiser that he could no longer guarantee his safety. It finally took General Groener to persuade the kaiser that the Hohenzollern dynasty was at an end. "The army," he said, "will march home in peace and order under its leaders and commanding generals, but not under the command of Your Majesty, for it no longer stands behind your Majesty."[157] Kaiser Wilhelm abdicated and went into exile in Holland.

"Germany by then was a republic," as Keegan has observed, "yet it was a republic without substance, lacking . . . an armed force to defend itself against its enemies. The last disciplined act of the old imperial army was to march back across the German frontiers with France and Belgium. Once on home territory, it demobilised itself. The soldiers discarded their uniforms and weapons and went home."[158] In the meantime, the Austro-Hungarian Empire was splitting apart, and the Habsburgs followed the Hohenzollerns and Romanovs down the path to political oblivion. By the time a separate armistice between the Austrians and the Italians took effect on November 4, Austria-Hungary had already ceased to exist. Turkey had signed an armistice with the allies on October 30. [159]

A REPUDIATION OF MY LEADERSHIP

As congressional elections approached in November, Wilson blundered on the grand scale, as many critics at the time—and since—have complained. On October 25, he urged the American electorate to vote Democratic. This was hardly on its face an exceptional thing for a president to do for his party in midterm elections, but this particular election was different.

Indeed, Wilson's message, which he drafted on October 19, asserted that the congressional elections "occur in the most critical period our country has ever faced or is likely to face in our time." Then he got down to business: "If you have approved of my leadership and wish me to continue to be your unembarrassed spokesman in affairs at home and abroad, I earnestly beg that you will express yourselves unmistakably . . . by returning a Democratic majority to both the Senate and the House of Representatives."

Wilson hastened to add that he had "no thought of suggesting that any political party is paramount in matters of patriotism." But he charged that the Republican leadership had "sought to take the choice of policy and the conduct of the war out of my hands." He neglected to observe that discontent with his conduct of the war had been to some extent bipartisan. In any case, he warned that "the return of a Republican majority to either House of the Congress would . . . certainly be interpreted on the other side of the water as a repudiation of my leadership." [160]

And so by his very own terms, he stood repudiated—for Republicans took control of the House and Senate in November 1918.

Some people had attempted to talk Wilson out of such a statement, particularly Vance McCormick, the chairman of the Democratic National Committee, and Wilson's wife, Edith. In the aftermath of the elections, several cabinet members condemned Wilson's statement as an act of egregious folly. [161] It certainly reflected a complete lack of worst-case contingency planning. Wilson apparently never gave any thought to what would happen to his power if he stood before the world as a figure who, upon his own say-so, was "repudiated."

What had animated Wilson to take this step was a set of impulsive motivations: a hunger for moral validation and an esoteric notion that a straightforward party appeal was the quintessence of the "parliamentary" culture that for years he had argued, as a scholar of political science, was admirable politics. Cooper has theorized that "the appeal came as a logical outgrowth of

Wilson's studies of parliamentary governments."[162] If true, this was surely intellectual dilettantism of extraordinary magnitude. In any case, Wilson seemed to have forgotten the fact that he had recently told the members of Congress that politics was adjourned.

Republicans began to turn savage. Theodore Roosevelt and Henry Cabot Lodge were in full cry, and the latter would soon become the Senate majority leader and chairman of the Senate Foreign Relations Committee. Roosevelt said, "Let us dictate peace by the hammering guns and not chat about peace to the accompaniment of the clicking of typewriters." He also said that "the language of the fourteen points . . . is neither straightforward nor plain" and charged that most of them were "mischievous."[163]

Cooper has observed that even the "normally milder-mannered Taft—who had now reconciled with Roosevelt—likewise assailed Wilson and his works with venom."[164] Taft wrote that the Fourteen Points were "too vague and indefinite." Observing that "Mr. Wilson has not consulted our Allies as he should," Taft confided to a fellow officer of the LEP that Roosevelt had "come around to favoring the League to Enforce Peace, provided it does not mean universal disarmament." Taft added that he was "in general agreement with Mr. Roosevelt on this subject."[165]

Both Roosevelt and Taft could have been cultivated by Wilson: now both of his presidential predecessors were alienated and hostile. Only six months earlier, Taft had offered to help, but Wilson spurned him.

The Republicans went to work immediately to use their new power. Roosevelt wrote to Balfour in gleeful agreement with Wilson that the voters had "repudiated" him. Roosevelt also wrote to Lloyd George and Clemenceau, encouraging them to be harsh in their armistice terms. Lodge wrote to Balfour condemning the "almost hopelessly impossible" terms for a League of Nations that Wilson had developed.[166]

House had reached Paris on October 27, and he entered into consultations with Clemenceau and Lloyd George. Frank Cobb and Walter Lippmann had accompanied House, and they produced an executive summary of the Fourteen Points for House to use.[167]

The British and the French were not inclined to be easy with Wilson after all that had been passing between them. The discussions with House were quite stormy. House reported to Wilson on October 30 that "the French are inclined not to accept your terms but will formulate their *demands* [original emphasis]."[168] Lloyd George avowed that the British were opposed to such a vague formulation as "freedom of the seas," telling House that "we cannot accept this under any circumstances. It takes away from us the power of blockade. . . . I want to see the character of the League of Nations first before I accept this proposition."[169]

House threatened a breach with the British and French; he told Lloyd George and Clemenceau that "if these views were persisted in the logical consequences would be for the President to say to Germany: 'the Allies do not agree to the conditions of peace proposed by me and accordingly the present negotiations are at an end.'" This implied that the United States might negotiate a separate peace with the Central Powers. House informed Wilson that this threat had "had a very exciting effect upon those present." "Those present" agreed to continue the discussions. [170]

Wilson wrote back to House, informing him that it was his

> solemn duty to authorize you to say that I cannot consent to take part in the negotiation of a peace which does not include freedom of the seas because we are pledged to fight not only to do away with Prussian militarism but with militarism everywhere. Neither could I participate in a settlement which did not include a league of nations because peace would be without any guarantee except universal armament which would be intolerable. [171]

House threatened to make the disagreements public; he also warned that rejection of the freedom-of-the-seas proposition would lead to "the establishment of the greatest naval building program by the United States that the world had ever seen." He told the British, in effect, that America would build a navy bigger than theirs if they did not back down and work with Wilson. [172]

The British and the French remaneuvered; they proposed a reply in which they would "declare their willingness to make peace with the Government of Germany on the terms of peace laid down in the President's address to Congress of January 8, 1918," with the proviso that "clause two, relating to what is usually described as freedom of the seas, is open to various interpretations, some of which they could not accept. They must therefore reserve to themselves complete freedom on this subject when they enter the peace conference." [173] As to the latter, Lloyd George suggested that "the Allies should get together before the Peace Conference and thresh out their differences." [174]

Wilson shot back that while he realized that "freedom of the seas needs careful definition," he would not consent to "British naval control," nor would he "change what our troops are fighting for." And he could "not agree to Lloyd George's program for a general settlement among ourselves before the peace conference." That might violate his principle of open covenants. [175]

In the meantime, the Americans lost credibility when Lloyd George revealed that Pershing sent a message to the Supreme War Council recommending the rejection of an armistice in favor of unconditional victory. Lloyd George called the communication "political not military," and theorized that "someone put him up to it." Clemenceau called the message "theatrical and not in accordance with what he has said to Marshal Foch." House acknowledged that "no allied general has ever submitted a document of this character to the Supreme War Council without a previous request having been made to the civilian authorities." [176] The autonomy that Wilson had granted his general had caused an embarrassment that diminished Wilson's credibility still further.

In the view of Stevenson, the British and the French held a very strong hand in these discussions, though they sensed that time was of the essence: "By late October the evidence reaching Paris was that Germany would accept practically any terms." Consequently, the "Paris and London governments were both willing to stop the war if the conditions were right, though they believed it would be impossible to renew the fighting and therefore needed guarantees now of everything they wanted."[177]

At last, by November 5 (which was election day in the United States) House informed Wilson that "we have won a great diplomatic victory in getting the Allies to accept the principles laid down in your January eighth speech." But House was deceiving both Wilson and himself. The so-called Pre-Armistice Agreement left the League of Nations issue unsettled; House confessed that "both French Prime Minister and George want to make the League of Nations an after-consideration, and not make it part of the Peace Conference." Nonetheless, House rationalized, "I set them right about it but did not press it further at the moment, for in accepting your terms they automatically accept this also."[178]

As to freedom of the seas, House contented himself with the extraction of a noncommittal statement that the British "were quite willing to discuss the freedom of the sea in the light of the new conditions which have arisen in the course of the present war," and that "this most important subject can only be dealt with satisfactorily through the freest debate and the most liberal exchange of views."

And this committed the British to nothing.

In achieving these Pyrrhic victories, House placed secondary emphasis on the military terms of the armistice. But these terms would be harsh enough to put Wilson's hope for a nonvindictive peace in jeopardy. House had sent the details of Foch's armistice proposals to Wilson on October 27.[179] Wilson sent his own detailed preferences on military terms to Pershing (via Baker), but he sent them as opinions, not orders.[180] To House, Wilson merely observed that the military terms should be "as moderate and reasonable as possible."[181]

Contrary to legend, Lloyd George and Clemenceau had considered the dangers of an overly vindictive peace. House advised Wilson on October 30 that the prime ministers regarded Foch's preliminary terms as "too severe."[182] But the Allies were worried about the possibility of German treachery. Consequently, House reported that Lloyd George and Clemenceau would be as "moderate as Foch will permit."[183] Domestic political concerns were important as well; when Lloyd George observed that it "might be unwise to insist on the occupation of the east bank of the Rhine," Clemenceau replied that "he could not maintain himself in the Chamber of Deputies" unless he prevailed on that point.[184]

Without American leverage to push the other way, and with Wilson and House giving more attention to the Fourteen Points and freedom of the seas than to realities of the power balance, events played out as they did. As Stevenson has observed,

> Wilson had conceded that the Allies' military advisers should draft the terms, and failed to prepare conditions of his own. He gave House minimal guidance, rashly sending him without written instructions. . . . The cables he sent during the conference were often garbled in decryption, including a crucial message that too much security for the Allies would complicate negotiations at the peace conference. This became interpreted as an instruction to support Foch's conditions. Although Wilson advised that he opposed an Allied occupation of Alsace and Lorraine, the left bank of the Rhine, and right-bank bridgeheads, and wanted to confine the naval conditions to interning U-boats in a neutral port, the final terms proved far more severe and largely negated his views.[185]

So as Wilson obsessed about "freedom of the seas," his more urgent priority of "peace without victory" was sacrificed. The Pre-Armistice Agreement would strip the Germans of power to resist the definitive peace terms that were coming.

On November 8, the German armistice commission headed by Matthias Erzberger traveled to the Compiègne Forest in France, where they were received at 7 a.m. in a railway car by General Foch. Foch was cold, brusque, and ritualistically formal. At last Foch's aide, General Maxime Weygand, read the terms that his commander had laid down.

The Germans were to intern most of their high seas fleet and surrender 160 U-boats. They were to abandon all territory in France and Belgium, give up Alsace and Lorraine, annul the Treaty of Brest-Litovsk (thereby giving up all German gains on the eastern front), and turn over five thousand artillery pieces, thirty-six thousand machine guns, two thousand airplanes, five thousand locomotives, ten thousand trucks, fifty thousand wagons, and other equipment of war as their troops went home. They were to allow the Allies to occupy the Rhineland and the east bank of the Rhine indefinitely. And the blockade against Germany was to be maintained until the formal peace treaty was concluded.

This latter provision would be used to ensure that the Germans would sign whatever terms were laid down. The continued blockade would use hunger and privation to force them into submission.

When Erzberger asked for an immediate cease-fire, he was turned down. Foch and his colleagues had decided that the armistice would begin at precisely the eleventh hour of the eleventh day of the eleventh month of the year. And so, after several more days of fighting, at precisely 11 a.m., on November 11, 1918, the carnage ended. [186]

This was hardly an auspicious beginning for "peace without victory." As Stevenson has written, these terms had the immediate effect of "thoroughly disorganizing [the Germans'] army and destroying their power to resist." Interestingly, when Lloyd George had attempted to moderate the terms by suggesting that the French would not have to occupy as much territory as Foch had proposed, both Pershing and House supported the French. Stevenson has theorized that "almost certainly Clemenceau obtained House's backing for the military clauses in return for French acquiescence in the Fourteen Points, thus forestalling an Anglo-American front against him on an issue he regarded as much more significant than Wilson's principles; while House . . . misjudged the significance of what he was doing." [187]

Too late, House realized some of it. On November 8, he cabled Wilson and pointed out, "*It is very clear* . . . that the terms of the armistice provide that the blockade shall be continued. The impracticability of this so far as food and other essential supplies are concerned, has already become apparent. . . . I should appreciate very much an expression of your views on this most urgent matter [original emphasis]." [188] But it was too late.

There was nothing "impracticable" about the use of hunger to compel the Germans to accept the Treaty of Versailles. Though the Allies were willing to let some food shipments reach Germany, they retained the power to reduce those shipments at will.

House, who had talked so tough about a separate peace, went soft in his anxiety to secure from the British and the French symbolic assent—symbolic blather, both written and verbal—on behalf of Wilson's sacrosanct agenda.

Distracted when tough-minded strategy was needed, and indignant when confronting any leader who threatened his intuitive readings of "Providence," Wilson was (typically) ill prepared to deal with the British and the French when the German position fell apart.

THE HAND OF GOD IS LAID UPON THE NATIONS

News of the armistice reached Wilson at three o'clock in the morning. Edith recalled that she and her husband "stood mute—unable to grasp the significance of the words." But then Wilson issued one of his religious pronouncements: "A supreme moment of history has come. The eyes of the people have been opened and they see. The hand of God is laid upon the nations." [189] House, at his most sycophantic, cabled Wilson that "autocracy is dead. Long live democracy and its immortal leader." [190] Lloyd George—waxing Wilsonian, at least for the moment—proclaimed that he hoped "we may say that thus, this fearful morning, came to an end all wars." [191]

Wilson made an impromptu speech to Congress. He presented the terms of the armistice and urged patience and forbearance. He exulted that "by unanimous resolution" the Supreme War Council had "assured the peoples of the Central Empires that everything that is possible in the circumstances will be done to supply them with food."[192] But Wilson's understanding of this situation was inaccurate. On November 4 House had proposed a resolution to the council to the effect that the Allies would "cooperate with Austria, Turkey and Bulgaria in the making available as far as possible food and other supplies."[193] But this resolution had not mentioned Germany. The Allies had no intention of giving up this powerful leverage at Wilson's bidding.

Some observers counseled Wilson to abstain from attending the peace conference—to send representatives instead.[194] There was a case to be made for establishing some "distance" from the conference, thus creating some maneuvering room in the give-and-take between the negotiations and congressional politics. But when the British and French suggested to Wilson that he delegate the task of representation, he bristled and decided to go. "I infer that the French and the English leaders desire to exclude me from the Conference for fear I might there lead the weaker nations against them," he fumed.[195]

On November 18, he announced his intention to leave for France in December, just after the opening of the final session of the outgoing Congress.[196] On November 29, the White House announced the composition of the American peace delegation.[197] Republicans exploded, for no member of the Senate was included and the only Republican member was a retired junior diplomat named Henry White. White himself was nonplussed: "I have never been more surprised in my life than when Lansing sent for me . . . and offered me this post," he wrote. "Nobody appears to have suggested my name, and of course I never dreamed of suggesting it myself."[198]

Though Roosevelt and Lodge were quite obviously out of the question as members of the delegation, no Republican leader such as Taft or Hughes had been considered or approached. The delegation (under Wilson's leadership) would consist of House, Lansing, White, and General Tasker H. Bliss.

With the Senate now firmly in Republican hands, and with a dedicated enemy such as Henry Cabot Lodge taking charge as the Senate majority leader and chairman of the Senate Foreign Relations Committee, Wilson should have reassessed his position. Granted, bitterness between the Republicans and Wilson cut both ways—the Republicans could (and arguably should) have been statesmanlike—but Wilson chose to approach this problem in the very same mood of defiance that had typified his overall mentality in 1918.

Cooper has observed that although "Wilson knew he would need Republican support . . . he was balking once more at practicing the kind of partnership with the opposition party that he should have understood from his study of coalition governments under parliamentary systems. . . . The real reason for his failure to reach out to the opposition was that he wanted a free hand in the peace negotiations."[199]

Cooper has attempted to palliate the situation by arguing that Wilson's inability to practice bipartisanship has been "overworked." There is one way alone to agree with this claim: With Wilson being the stubborn and delusional man he had become by the final months of 1918, what good would the presence of leading Republicans in the American delegation have done? Wilson, being Wilson, was his own worst enemy in ways that were far beyond retrieval. Any blunders he committed were the latest missteps in a very long series that were leading him, his country, and the world to disaster.

Before Wilson left for his trans-Atlantic voyage—aboard the USS *George Washington* in the first week of December—his enemies in Congress were working already on a resolution to sever the creation of a League of Nations from the rest of the treaty. The final battle that would bring Wilson down, destroy his health, and lead to world-historical calamity was already brewing.

But he tried to put on a brave front in his annual message to Congress, delivered just before his departure. He used lines from the Agincourt "Crispin's Day" day speech from Shakespeare's *Henry V*. He exulted that American troops had entered battle in the crucial instant, after which it was "back, back, back for their enemies, always back, never again forward!"[200] In light of the congressional elections, he adopted a pose of winsome humility: "May I not hope, Gentlemen of the Congress, that in the delicate tasks I shall have to perform on the other side of the sea . . . I may have the encouragement and the added strength of your united support?" Not for the first time, he tried to disavow the role of ego in his mission: "I can have no private thought or purpose of my own in performing such an errand."[201]

The Republicans gave Wilson "an ice bath," wrote Josephus Daniels.[202] Senator Ashurst wrote that "the applause was meager; his message was long, and surely he must have felt the chilliness of his reception."[203]

On board the *George Washington*, Wilson mused to George Creel—who was one of a large entourage that accompanied the delegation—that he knew at least on some level that his prophecy of a new world epoch had been unrealistic. "You know, and I know," Creel remembered him saying, "that these ancient wrongs, these present unhappinesses, are not to be remedied in a day or with the wave of a hand. What I seem to see—with all my heart I hope I am wrong—is a tragedy of disappointment."[204]

But to his delegation of reporters he spoke in his usual uncompromising terms: "The whole world," he declared, "must be in on all measures designed to end wars for all time."[205] He also observed that he had learned from House's cables that the Allies intended to take a very tough position on reparations. Wilson said (according to Grayson's diary) that he was "absolutely opposed to this." He declared that his peace without victory principle "holds more strongly than ever." He also declared that he would push his Fourteen Points, especially freedom of the seas.[206]

After landing at Brest on December 13, Wilson took his now-legendary tour of Paris, where he rode with Poincaré in an open car and was acclaimed by euphoric throngs. He met with House, met Clemenceau, and checked into his accommodations at the Murat Palace. Then he and Edith crossed the channel to England for a visit on December 26. He met Lloyd George and then he met the king, and he gave a number of interesting speeches. Perhaps the most interesting of all was a speech on his birthday to a delegation of Methodist and Baptist leaders who presented a resolution of support. "I think one would go crazy," he confided, "if he did not believe in Providence. It would be like a maze without a clue. Unless there were some supreme guidance we would despair of the results of human counsel."[207] But since he knew that Providence was guiding the affairs of men, he took heart. Invoking his Presbyterian heritage, he proclaimed that "the stern Covenanter tradition that is behind me sends many an echo down the years."[208]

For years he had been proving that true. And in the year to come, he would prove it true beyond endurance.

Chapter Six

1919

Woodrow Wilson was clearly on the verge of a crack-up in 1919. There were signs he was going to pieces well before the stroke that felled him in October and left him an invalid—half-paralyzed, and at times in the grip of what could well be described as dementia. Though efforts were made by disaffected Democrats to salvage something, Wilson killed all attempts to fix the horrible mess that his own mistakes had created. The last shreds of his rationality were gone. His worst tendencies had taken over as the nation drifted.

THERE IS A GREAT WIND OF MORAL FORCE

Wilson and the other four members of the American peace delegation had copious staff support when they arrived in Paris. House had already brought a group of advisers for the armistice talks. Lansing appointed foreign service officer Joseph C. Grew to head the delegation's staff.[1] Upon House's advice, Wilson appointed twenty-three members of the Inquiry to serve under Grew. Wilson brought his own entourage aboard the *George Washington*, and this group would be expanded to include people such as Ray Stannard Baker, who Wilson hoped would coordinate press coverage, and Herbert Hoover, who had traveled to London to discuss the issue of food relief for Europeans, including the Germans.[2]

An interesting incident aboard the *George Washington* deserves to be related since it sheds significant light on Wilson's interactions with his advisers. William Bullitt told Wilson (just before the members of the entourage were about to watch a motion picture) that "he ought to call together the members of the Inquiry and other important people on board and explain to them the spirit in which he was approaching the conference." Bullitt said that "most of the men with brains on board had been treated like immigrants and felt entirely left out of the game."

Wilson, full of bonhomie at the moment, was stunned by the news. He told Bullitt he was "greatly obliged for the suggestion and that it simply had not occurred to him that such a conference would be necessary." Wilson did most of the talking at the meeting that followed; Bullitt wrote that the president sat at his desk and "talked for an hour, an occasional word being thrown in by one or another of us." Wilson bragged that American troops had won the war, and he did "not intend to let these Europeans forget it. They were beaten when we came in and they know it."

At the end of the meeting, according to Bullitt, Wilson encouraged his advisers to "tell me what is right and I'll fight for it."[3] Another person who attended the meeting, Charles Seymour (a Yale historian who would serve as a negotiator on Austro-Hungarian issues), recorded the very same remark in a letter to his family.[4] Seymour also recorded (a few days later) that Wilson was turning his mind, at long last, to the issue of strategic leverage: "He said several times . . . 'What means, Mr. Seymour, can be utilized to bring pressure upon these people in the interests of justice?'"[5] It was very late indeed— almost too late—for him to think in this way, as events would reveal.

Several people commented on the fact that this voyage was good for Wilson's mood; Raymond Fosdick (an old friend of Wilson's from Princeton) recorded that Wilson "looks much better than when he came on board and talks with his old-time succinctness and lucidity." This interlude appears to have summoned back Wilson's better qualities, at least to an extent. Some of the effect was no doubt the result of relaxation; Fosdick recorded that the crew performed a musical comedy and Wilson "laughed his head off at it."[6]

But Wilson was still in the grip of all his characteristic illusions. He had seemed to believe on the voyage across the Atlantic that moral suasion alone would save the day and deliver the peace without victory to which he was still very much committed. He had heard from Colonel House, he told reporters, "that the representatives of France, Great Britain and Italy are determined to get everything out of Germany that they can. They know that Germany is down and out. Instead of going about the thing in the fair way, namely, determine what they think they are justly entitled to" and then ascertain "how Germany may be expected to meet the demands—if she can meet them at all," the Allies would simply "apportion what Germany has," no matter what the effects might be.[7] Wilson said he was "absolutely opposed" to this scenario.[8] But how did he intend to make this opposition effective? He told the reporters aboard the *George Washington* exactly what he thought would do the trick:

> Upon the first occasion that I have after meeting these gentlemen and letting them know what sort of a fellow I am and giving myself the opportunity of

determining what sort of chaps they are, I will say to them, if necessary, that we are gathered together, not as masters of anyone, but [as] representatives of a new world met together to determine the greatest peace of all time. It must not be a peace of loot and spoliation. . . . I for one shall, if necessary, tell them that if that is the kind of peace they demand, I will withdraw personally and with my commissioners return home and in due course take up the details of a separate peace.[9]

Wilson predicted that the threat would be efficacious at once: "Once they learn that that is my purpose," he declared, "I think that we can come to an agreement promptly."[10]

But the minutes of a British cabinet meeting in late December reveal some tough talk—and some very significant anger—regarding Wilson. William Morris Hughes, the prime minister of Australia—and it should be noted that representatives of the dominions were serving in the war cabinet—spoke of the president with open contempt. He warned his colleagues that "if we were not very careful we should find ourselves dragged quite unnecessarily behind the wheels of President Wilson's chariot." He argued that America's contribution to the war was "not such as to entitle President Wilson to be the god in the machine at the Peace Settlement and lay down the terms on which the world would have to live in the future."

Hughes noted the results of the American off-year elections contrasted to the "overwhelming vote from his fellow countrymen" that Lloyd George had recently received. Consequently, Lloyd George and Clemenceau should "settle the peace of the world as they liked," since it was "intolerable for President Wilson to tell us that the world was to be saved on his terms." As to the League of Nations, Hughes said it constituted for Wilson "what a toy was to a child."[11]

Lord Curzon said "that Mr. Hughes' views were shared by many," and, while admitting that "the fortunes of the world would largely depend on cooperation between Mr. Lloyd George and President Wilson," he felt that the British should go to the conference "with an authority fully equal, and indeed superior, to that of President Wilson's."[12]

Winston Churchill said that "the only point of substance" in his view was to "induce the United States to let us off the debt we had contracted" and "return us the bullion and script we had paid over." If Wilson were "prepared to do that," Churchill continued, "we might go some way towards meeting his view in the matter of indemnity [i.e., reparations]," but "for the rest, we should be civil and insist on our essential terms."[13]

Lloyd George told the cabinet it seemed to him that the League of Nations "was the only thing that he [Wilson] really cared much about," and that it ought to be relatively easy to reach an agreement on the League. That done, the prime minister continued, Wilson's satisfaction "would ease other matters"; indeed, there was reason to hope that the president might leave the conference early if he could "say that he had achieved his purpose with the League of Nations."[14] So the British would agree to make the League the first order of business when the Paris Peace Conference opened.[15]

As soon as Wilson arrived in France, he raised expectations in his usual heedless and inspirational manner. On Christmas Day, he addressed some American troops as follows: "I am happy to say, my fellow countrymen, that I do not find in the hearts of the great leaders with whom it is my privilege now to cooperate any difference of principle or of fundamental purpose." He contended that all the "great leaders" had accepted his Fourteen Points, and so everything was really very easy: "It happened that it was the privilege of America to present the charter of peace [i.e., the Fourteen Points], and now the process of settlement has been rendered comparatively simple by the fact that all the nations concerned have accepted that charter." He went on: "This being a people's war . . . it must be a people's peace."[16]

Wilson had made public statements in support of the League just as soon as he arrived in France. And these statements released the full force of his oracular impulse, with all of its naïve suppositions. At the University of Paris on December 21, for example, he declared that "there is a great wind of moral force moving through the world, and every man who opposes himself to that wind will go down in disgrace." That being the case, the League of Nations would succeed through the force of public opinion:

> My conception of the league of nations is just this, that it shall operate as the organized moral force of men throughout the world, and that whenever or wherever wrong and aggression are planned or contemplated, this searching light of conscience will be turned upon them and men everywhere will ask, "What are the purposes that you hold in your heart against the fortunes of the world?" Just a little exposure will settle most questions. If the Central Powers had dared to discuss the purposes of this war for a single fortnight, it never would have happened.[17]

Lord Derby, the British ambassador to France, met Wilson on December 21, and he reported to Balfour that Wilson's conceptions of the League were "of the haziest description."[18] When Wilson arrived in England, he treated the British to the very same performance, telling King George V and an audience at Buckingham Palace that "the hearts of men have never beaten so singularly in unison before." He proclaimed at the London Guildhall that the soldiers of the Allies had "fought to do away with an old order and to establish a new one," an order without "that unstable thing which we used to call the 'balance of power.'" Wilson claimed that "the men who have fought in this war . . . were determined that that sort of thing should end now and forever."[19]

As usual, Wilson's sense of mission was abetted by admirers. Two days after Lord Derby wrote to Balfour, Wilson received the following message from another Englishman:

> I am . . . conscious that the heart and mind of the common people are with you. . . . I am only writing because my desires & my prayers go with you to France & to the Conference——that you may have the wisdom and the courage to stand against many adversaries. Forgive me if I am impertinent in writing this.
>   Believe me to be
>   Your faithful disciple Charles Gore Bishop of Oxford[20]

Edith Wilson wrote that her husband's speech at the Sorbonne was "a gem, & people were wild about it."[21] There was never any shortage of people in the retinue of Wilson who would keep his sense of certitude charged.

THE HARDEST I EVER TRIED TO DO BUSINESS WITH

In the first week of 1919, Wilson journeyed to Italy with Edith. Then he and Mrs. Wilson returned to Paris, where the preparations for the peace conference were under way. Before the conference began, the Supreme War Council continued to meet—to supervise the armistice—and a "Council of Ten" was created to guide the work of the conference. This council was composed of representatives from each of five Allied powers: France, Great Britain, the United States, Italy, and Japan. Each of these nations was represented on the council by its head of state and by its foreign minister.

Before the first week of 1919 had elapsed, a sudden death changed the course of history: former president Theodore Roosevelt died in his sleep. Roosevelt was in the midst of a remarkable comeback; already, he commanded enough Republican support to be the strong front-runner for the 1920 nomination. He had reconciled with Taft, and—though still as nationalistic as ever and an advocate of unconditional German surrender—he was guardedly willing to consider a League of Nations that was underwritten by the military force of the great powers.[22] Roosevelt's better, more responsible, and more intellectual side had usually been stimulated by the possession of power or the prospect of exercising power. Now he was gone.

Wilson met with the Supreme War Council on January 12 and 13, and he attended meetings of the Council of Ten, which at times occurred twice a day.[23] This was very bad for his health, and his workload was staggering: he was sometimes putting in workdays of ten to fifteen hours' duration. The pressure on Wilson—especially as the weakness of his bargaining position became ever clearer to him—began pounding away at his emotional and mental health.

He was eager to devote himself to the creation of the League of Nations, and he was gratified that it was item number one on the conference's agenda. But the ongoing issues of the armistice (which would expire on January 17 unless renewed by the Supreme War Council), reparations, territorial adjustments, and the organizational questions pertaining to the conference itself demanded attention. As to the latter, Wilson's tenuous bargaining position was revealed right away.

For example, the president had wanted to admit reporters; he had even said that "if I find anything going on in an underhand way I will publish it."[24] Ray Stannard Baker and the other American journalists were livid when they found themselves barred from the sessions of the Council of Ten.[25] Wilson "enquired whether there was any serious objection in the case of the large Conferences to having members of the Press present."[26] Lloyd George retorted that "he feared there would be no end to these Conferences if reporters were there."[27]

Wilson tried again the next day, proclaiming that he "doubted whether anything less than complete publicity would satisfy the American public."[28] But he began to be forced into line by Lloyd George, who condemned the idea of "a peace settled by public clamour." Wilson's principle of open covenants openly arrived at was going down to defeat. But in reality—and for all of his idealistic fantasies—Wilson had always prized the confidentiality of his own "counsels." As we have seen, he would even become quite indignant when editors and reporters poked their noses into the private negotiations of Colonel House when Wilson sent him on an errand. So Wilson quickly proposed that Lloyd George should "draft the message to the Press on the lines explained by him so persuasively in the Meeting."[29] Wilson tried to contain the damage by editing the press release.[30]

Wilson's secretary, Joseph Tumulty, sent a cable to Wilson's friend and physician Dr. Cary Grayson, informing him that "American newspapers [were] filled with stories this morning of critical character about the rule of secrecy adopted for peace conferences, claiming that the first of the fourteen points has been violated."[31]

By the time the conference opened officially, the British and the French had consented to conduct the meetings of the full conference in the open, while reserving the right to keep the meetings of the Council of Ten—which would function as executive committee to the conference—confidential.[32]

Notwithstanding the confidential nature of executive discussions, the Paris press got wind of Wilson's opposition to the harshness of the armistice terms. He had been complaining about this to Clemenceau in meetings of the War Council, which functioned simultaneously with the Council of Ten.[33] It was, of course, too late for Wilson to do much to modify these terms; his inattention during the formulation of the prearmistice agreement left him helpless, except for his rhetoric.

Both he and Herbert Hoover, for example, tried to expedite food relief to Germany, but the British and French representatives to the Committee Appointed by the Allied Premiers to Consider Victualling and Supply of Allied, Neutral, and Enemy Countries—a committee that was formed as an instrumentality of armistice enforcement—kept stalling, thus retaining the leverage to force a vindictive peace on the Germans.[34]

On January 11, Wilson appointed Hoover director general of relief in Europe.[35] He also gave Hoover the job of representing the United States on the Allied committee, which had since been renamed the Supreme Council for Supply and Relief. On January 12, Hoover reported that the Council would recommend that Germany should be allowed "to import a prescribed quantity of foodstuffs" before the next harvest, to wit: "200,000 tons of breadstuffs and 70,000 tons of pork products."[36]

When the Supreme War Council met the next day, the British and French made it clear that they intended to make sure that "the weapon of food would still be left in our hands," as Balfour put it.[37] Wilson argued that "any further delay in this matter might be fatal," adding that "so long as hunger continued to gnaw, the foundations of government would continue to crumble" in Germany.[38] But the British and the French raised the issue of how the Germans would pay for the food. Wilson ceded the point that "Germany must pay," while warning that if the food were not "paid for and supplied immediately there would be no Germany to pay for anything."[39] The council agreed that some food should be provided to stave off hunger for two months' time.

On January 16, the renewal of the armistice provided for shipment of food to the Germans provided that they paid for the food and used their own merchant fleet to ship it. But the details were disputed in a series of conferences at Spa that lasted into March, with the French insisting that food should be provided on a month-to-month basis only, while the Germans wanted a guarantee of food through the next harvest. All the while, the Ebert government in Germany tottered on the brink of collapse.[40] Stevenson has observed that "the blockade was maintained strictly until March and more leniently until July, leading to perhaps a quarter of a million civilian deaths."[41]

As to territorial adjustments, Wilson met with Vittorio Orlando of Italy on January 9 to discuss the territorial spoils that Italy was after.[42] At this point, an astonishing (or not so astonishing) point should be made: Wilson departed for Paris without having read the secret treaties that House had been able to procure from Balfour in 1917. Wilson went to Paris without any knowledge of the Allied plans for "dividing up the bearskin before the bear was killed," to quote Balfour's expression. Arthur S. Link assessed the situation as follows:

Arthur Balfour sent him copies of them [the secret treaties] on May 18, 1917; Wilson acknowledged receipt of them one day later; and the copies are still in his papers. . . . Wilson usually marked up the important documents that he read—by underscoring sentences, drawing vertical lines alongside paragraphs, or making marginal comments. The copies of the treaties in the Wilson papers bear no signs that Wilson had read them. . . . It would seem a reasonable conclusion, in the light of the foregoing, that Wilson filed the treaties that Balfour sent without reading them. [43]

A week after meeting with Orlando, Wilson found himself exasperated by the French position on a buffer zone with Germany. Dr. Grayson recorded in his diary that Wilson "made it very plain . . . that the carrying out of such a program would create new animosities that eventually would turn the sympathy of the world generally against France. He was very tired when he returned home tonight."[44]

When the Peace Conference opened officially on January 18—in the "Hall of the Clock" at the Quai d'Orsay, where the French foreign ministry had its offices—the French president, Poincaré, gave a welcoming speech that neatly parried the thrust of Wilson's demands for nonvindictive "justice." In the nimble hands of Poincaré, the doubled-edged sword of justice was wielded as follows. "You will be therefore seeking nothing but justice," the president of France told the peace conference delegates, "justice that has no favorites, justice in territorial problems, justice in financial problems, justice in economic problems." But what was justice in the context at hand? Poincaré continued:

> Justice is not inert, it does not submit to injustice. What it first demands, when it has been violated, are restitution and reparation for the peoples and individuals who have been despoiled or maltreated. In formulating this lawful claim, it obeys neither hatred nor an instinctive or thoughtless desire for reprisals; it pursues a two-fold object: to render to each his due and not to encourage crime by leaving it unpunished. [45]

Wilson's wartime rhetoric against the Germans left him vulnerable: he had demonized the German authorities too often to prevent these machinations on behalf of a punitive peace. In this opening session of the conference, he was given a slick demonstration of one-upmanship and power preeminence by the French. When Poincaré finished, the French premier, Clemenceau, was elected to serve as the conference's chairman.

Clemenceau twisted the knife in his own remarks. "The League of Nations is here," he intoned, "it is in yourselves; it is for you to make it live; and for that it must be in our hearts. As I have said to President Wilson, there must be no sacrifice which we are not ready to accept." But then—hardly pausing for breath—Clemenceau presented a memorandum "on the responsibility of the authors of the war," adding that "if the conferees wished to establish law in the world, penalties for the breach thereof" should be applied "at once."[46]

Sensing the flow of events (and power), Wilson tried to placate the French; in remarks to the French Senate on January 20, he said that France had "never . . . done a single thing that was aggressive," and then he proceeded to eat humble pie as follows: "France thought us remote in comprehension and sympathy, and I dare say there were times when we did not comprehend, as you comprehended, the danger in the presence of which the world stood."[47] But it was no use: the French position on reparations would not be swayed one inch by such flattery.

The French kept trying to induce Wilson to visit the war-devastated regions of France and Belgium in order to see for himself the destruction that the Germans had committed. The French had a point: as the Germans had withdrawn in 1918, Ludendorff had ordered pure wreckage on an indefensible scale. But Wilson resisted the French entreaties to tour the devastated areas, becoming more and more annoyed as they kept up the pressure.[48] At last, on January 26, he toured Rheims, which the Germans had subjected to a destructive bombardment. Later in the spring, he would see much more devastation.

On January 23, at Clemenceau's bidding, the Council of Ten created a commission to address the issues of war guilt and reparations.[49] Four days later the council further specified that the commission would "examine and report . . . on the amount for reparation which the enemy countries ought to pay" as well as "what they are capable of paying" and the "guarantees that should be obtained for payment." Wilson cogently argued that "Germany could not make reparation unless she had the means therefor," and that "unless German industries were reconstituted, it was clear that Germany could not pay."[50]

More and more, Wilson sensed the hostility of Clemenceau. He confided to some intimates that word had reached him regarding some "double dealing of the French." When a delegation of "French working women" requested a meeting with Wilson, Clemenceau privately "objected to any more demonstrations in favor of the President." He told the women "they could have the meeting but were to make no laudatory remarks about him [Wilson] or about America's part in the war."[51]

In the first week of February, at the prompting of Hoover and Vance McCormick, Wilson made up his mind to propose a relaxation of the blockade.[52] Hoover complained that "the French, by obstruction of every financial measure that we can propose for the feeding of Germany . . . have defeated every step so far for getting them the food which we have been promising for three months."[53] When the Supreme War Council met on February 7, Wilson proposed that the Allies should "relax the blockade." But the British and the French were becoming concerned that the Germans might surreptitiously manufacture more armaments if the treaty were not completed and signed by March. Foch proposed a number of measures to forestall a German power resurgence.[54] The meeting of the council was taken up with new armistice demands that would accelerate German demobilization and disarmament.

Wilson complained that it was "not sportsmanlike" to impose new terms. He contended that "the Council should have known what it was doing when the armistice was drawn up."[55] Lloyd George replied that "he did not think they were necessarily bound either as an obligation of honour, or as sportsmen, to renew the Armistice forever on exactly the same terms," adding that "he and his colleagues were under an obligation to the world and to the people to protect them against a renewal of hostilities."[56] Clemenceau was more blunt. According to the minutes of the meeting, he discoursed as follows:

> There was danger of losing the fruits of victory. It was essential to act quickly. The forces at the call of the Allies had not yet diminished appreciably [but] April would come and find our forces partially scattered. The American and Australian troops would have returned to their homes, and France and Great Britain would be left alone to face the Germans, who, seeing the Allies always giving way, would in turn become more arrogant. . . . Was it forgotten that they were still at war; that the Armistice was a status of war? The Germans had not forgotten it. . . . A state of war still existed, and any appearance of yielding would be construed as evidence of weakness. At any rate, personally he could not accept President Wilson's proposition. He did not wish to starve the Germans, but the blockade must be maintained.[57]

In impotence, Wilson fumed to Grayson that "the French people are the hardest I ever tried to do business with."[58] French press coverage of Wilson's position was harsh, and the president suspected that this "propaganda" was coordinated by the French government.[59] Wilson tried to strike back: he had Ray Stannard Baker plant a story to the effect that the peace conference might have to be moved to a different city.[60] House confided to his diary that he regarded this as "stupid."[61]

Wilson was also offended by the Japanese, who wished to seize the Germans' Pacific colonies. He told Grayson that he "found himself in an absolute minority" regarding such questions as the Council of Ten discussed them, since "the majority of the delegates wanted to 'divide the swag.'"[62]

At last, Wilson forced himself to yield some points to Clemenceau to gain ground for the League of Nations. His work on the League of Nations Covenant—carried out between sessions of the Council of Ten and the Supreme War Council—had approached a critical juncture. He felt that a report to Congress was in order when his schedule required a brief visit to Washington to sign legislation. Congress would adjourn in early March. Perhaps this was the reason why he held out the olive branch to Clemenceau on February 12, three days before he left for America.

He proposed that provisions for German disarmament should precede the provisions for a general peace—that "the Germans could be given short notice to accede to our demands upon pain of having the armistice broken. The main thing was to do this while our forces were so great that our will could not be resisted."[63] Clemenceau was pacified for the moment, and he instructed Foch to prepare "detailed and final naval, military, and air conditions of the preliminaries of peace." After Germany agreed to the conditions, controlled amounts of food and raw materials would be furnished.[64]

But Wilson evidently felt remorse for this concession. On the day before he left for America, he gave some journalists an interview. According to the reporting of Truman Talley of the *New York Herald*, Wilson said that "even the peace treaty and the League of Nations could wait, if necessary, while the wheels of industry were being started up again. . . . He declared the people were more interested in knowing where their next meal was coming from, more interested in work, than they are in who will be their rulers." And he "insisted that the lifting of the blockade is imperative unless we desire to see Germany become another Russia." The headline for Talley's dispatch read as follows: "FEED WORLD AND THEN TALK PEACE SAYS MR. WILSON."[65]

SOME VERY BEAUTIFUL THINGS HAVE COME OUT OF IT

Late in December, two different draft schemes for the League that were created by Lord Robert Cecil and by Jan Christiaan Smuts—a South African statesman who was serving in the British war cabinet—were sent to Wilson.[66] Wilson quickly drafted a new League Covenant, a modified version of the plan that he had sent to House months earlier. He and House discussed the new version on January 8; containing thirteen articles, this document would be known as the "First Paris Draft."[67] It provided for an organization with a "Body of Delegates" containing all member nations of the League and an "Executive Council" of great powers with some rotating seats for other nations. Article 3 stated that "the Contracting Powers unite in guaranteeing to each other political independence and territorial integrity." The enforcement procedure against aggression would consist of blockades, economic boycotts, and the use of military force as recommended by the Executive Council to member nations.

Wilson was at first inclined to draft the Covenant without the involvement of the other American members of the peace delegation. House recorded on January 8 that "the President seems to have no intention of using them [the other commissioners, Lansing, Bliss, and White] effectively. It is the story of Washington over again. We settle matters between the two of us and he begins to consider that sufficient without even notifying the others."[68] But House persuaded him to "notify the others." Wilson read them his draft on January 10. When he discovered they had already formulated points of their own, he was angry, according to Bliss.[69]

In private, Lansing expressed his disdain. "The President astounded us all," he wrote, "by his resistance to every form of criticism or suggestion." He continued as follows:

> I do not like to think that he is so vain of his ability as to think that he can produce so perfect a plan that he really believes it cannot be improved, but it is very hard to find any other excuse sufficient to account for his curt, almost insulting, manner of refuting valid objections to the document which he has drawn. . . . Why he asked us to confer with him I cannot imagine unless it was to have us praise his work.[70]

The bad feelings with the other members of the delegation were smoothed over, and Wilson began to consider their views. Wilson produced a revised version of the text—to be known as the "Second Paris Draft"—on January 18, the very day that the Paris Peace Conference opened.[71]

Wilson had been lobbying the Council of Ten to create a League of Nations Commission that would formulate recommendations for the conference; he had also met with Lord Cecil and Smuts to obtain their agreement and to form a working group that would synthesize the different proposals and create a unified plan.

Wilson pushed these efforts very hard. On January 20, Cecil sent Wilson an updated draft for the League Covenant that he and other British policymakers had prepared.[72] On January 22, the Council of Ten agreed not only to create the League of Nations Commission that Wilson requested but also to make the League "an integral part of the treaty of peace."[73]

Cecil confided to his diary that he found Wilson "a trifle of a bully, and must be dealt with firmly, though with the utmost courtesy and respect—not a very easy combination to hit off." As far as Cecil was concerned, Wilson was "a vain man" who was "very anxious" that "the scheme which we should work on should be, nominally at any rate, his scheme."[74]

On January 25, at a plenary session of the Peace Conference, the commission on the League of Nations was created. Wilson, of course, gave a speech. He said the League of Nations must not be "an occasional thing . . . but always functioning in watchful attendance," the "eye of the nations to keep watch upon the common interest, the eye that does not slumber, an eye that is everywhere watchful and attentive."

He engaged in his usual hyperbole when he imputed support for the League to an undivided American people, who, he proclaimed, "expect their leaders to speak their thoughts and no private purpose of their own. . . . We have no choice but to obey their mandate." By the same token, he said American troops had been fighting "as crusaders, not merely to win the war, but to win a cause . . . and I, like them, must be a crusader for these things." After these assertions, he wound down the speech in a humble pose, avowing that "it is not because we alone represent this idea, but, because it is our privilege to associate ourselves with you."[75]

Wilson worked together with Cecil and Smuts to produce their unified draft in two weeks. On January 30 and 31, House persuaded Wilson to permit two legal experts—David Hunter Miller from the American delegation's staff and C. J. B. Hurst from Great Britain—to fine-tune the language.[76] Wilson disliked what they did: he complained that their text had "no warmth or color."[77] House persuaded him to go along anyway, lest the League deliberations get "stormy."

Lord Cecil was offended by Wilson's behavior; he found himself astonished at the spectacle of Wilson "abruptly tearing up a draft which we had jointly agreed to have prepared as our working text." The incident, Cecil recorded in his diary, seemed to typify "the great tenacity of his mind, and his incapacity for cooperation resulting from a prolonged period of autocratic power."[78] Later Cecil was even more vehement: "Now that I have sat for two or three days with the President I am coming to the conclusion that I do not personally like him. I do not know quite what it is that repels me: a certain hardness, coupled with vanity and an eye for effect. He supports idealistic causes without being in the least an idealist himself, at least so I guess, though perhaps I misjudge him."[79]

The result of these labors would be known as the "Third Paris Draft." When this draft was presented to the League Commission on February 3, disagreements and debates soon erupted.[80] Cecil startled Wilson by arguing that British dominions "do not appreciate the idea of having to fight for the integrity of Bohemia, or some such place."[81] Thomas J. Knock has theorized that Cecil was responding to political shifts in Great Britain.[82]

Wilson assured Cecil that no one would be forced into anything: the League's Executive Council would only have the power to recommend the use of military force against aggression. French delegate Léon Bourgeois proposed the creation of a League army, but Wilson demurred, insisting that "we must all depend on our mutual good faith" to create collective security. "We must make a distinction between what is possible and what is not," Wilson said. "As for us Americans, we cannot consent to control because of our Constitution. . . . All that we can promise . . . is to maintain our military forces in such a condition that the world will feel itself in safety. When danger comes, we too will come, and we will help you, but you must trust us." Wilson did admit that "there would always be a certain inevitable delay in sending [an American military force] to the States where it might be required."[83]

Wilson had presented a very different message on February 3 to the French Chamber of Deputies. He stressed certitude rather than trust; he said the rulers of the world must "make it certain" that France would be safe from another invasion: "there shall never be any doubt or waiting or surmise" for France, as it "stood at the frontier of freedom."[84]

At the final meeting of the League of Nations Commission, Wilson tried (unsuccessfully) to insert a draft article to guarantee freedom of religion in each of the signatory nations. The Japanese requested an additional statement on racial equality, but this request was denied.[85]

"This has been a memorable day," House recorded. "We finished the Covenant for the League of Nations." He wrote that he "did not realize how much time the President took up in talking" until Wilson was called away in midafternoon to attend a meeting of the Council of Ten. Then things speeded up right away. "When I telephoned the President at seven o'clock that we had finished he was astounded and delighted," House wrote.[86]

Wilson sought and received the permission of the Council of Ten to present the League Commission's draft to the Peace Conference, and he did so the very next day.[87] He read the entire document and offered comments. He exulted that League deliberations would effectuate peace by exposing any nation's complaints to the full light of day, to "the cleansing and clarifying and compelling influences of publicity . . . so that intrigues can no longer have their coverts, so that designs that are sinister can at any time be drawn into the open." "Armed force," he declared, "is in the background of this program, but it *is* in the background, and if the moral force of the world will not suffice, the physical force of the world shall. But that is the last resort, because this is intended as a constitution of peace, not as a league of war [original emphasis]." "Many terrible things have come out of this war," he concluded, "but some very beautiful things have come out of it" as well.[88]

The League Covenant contained many things, but the crucial provisions were the ones for collective security. The article that guaranteed territorial integrity against external aggression (Article 3 in the First Paris Draft) was now Article 10. It read as follows:

> The High Contracting Powers undertake to respect and preserve as against external aggression the territorial integrity and existing political independence of all States members of the League. In case of any such aggression or in case of any threat or danger of such aggression the Executive Council shall advise upon the means by which this obligation shall be fulfilled.[89]

Other articles pertained to this purpose. Article 12 mandated arbitration of disputes among members, and, to enforce this provision, it was stated in Article 16 that

Should any of the High Contracting Powers break or disregard its covenants under Article XII, it shall thereby *ipso facto* be deemed to have committed an act of war against all the other members of the League, which hereby undertake immediately to subject it to the severance of all trade or financial relations, the prohibition of intercourse between their nationals and the nationals of the covenant-breaking State, and the prevention of all financial, commercial, or personal intercourse between the nationals of the covenant-breaking State and the nationals of any other State, whether a member of the League or not. It shall be the duty of the Executive Council in such case to recommend what effective military or naval force the members of the League shall severally contribute to the armed forces to be used to protect the covenants of the League.[90]

As Wilson prepared to return to America, he felt a near-euphoric relief: his great mission was nearly accomplished, or so he thought, and his role in history secure. He joked with reporters; when one of them asked him whether freedom of the seas had been included in the League Covenant, he said that he was "glad you asked me about that." He continued:

I have a joke to tell on myself. I admit that I did not realize until I arrived here that with the League of Nations there will be no neutrals. By abolishing neutrality we automatically eliminate the question of neutral rights during war. Then there is no issue over naval or sea rights. The League of Nations will promulgate the rules for naval regulation and disarmament; so, as they say, "there ain't no such" issue as freedom of the seas.[91]

Wilson told the reporters that he hoped to "present an accounting to Washington by March 4 and to leave the United States again on March 6 for Europe, where many grave issues are awaiting determination."[92]

IDEALS, AND NOTHING BUT IDEALS

Just before Wilson left Paris, he conferred with House about a number of things, not least of which was the role that House would be playing in his absence, for House would be staying in Paris. Neither knew that this interlude would lead to the beginning of the end of their friendship. House offered to serve as Wilson's agent and told the president he "thought we could button up everything during the next four weeks." House noted that Wilson "seemed startled and even alarmed by this statement." House remaneuvered in his usual way and "explained that my plan was not to actually bring these matters to a final conclusion but to have them ready for him to do so when he returned. This pleased him."[93]

House also suggested that Wilson should invite the members of the House and Senate foreign relations committees to a White House dinner and ask them to refrain from making comments on the League of Nations until then.

Wilson's reaction boded ill: the fey mood he had displayed with the reporters was replaced by resentment. He said "he would not do it, and that the most he would do would be to make an address to Congress." House told him this was "inadequate," that the members of Congress would "take it that he had called them together as a school master, as they claim he usually does."[94] Wilson grudgingly consented to send the invitation, so House prepared a cable to Tumulty directing him to set up the dinner.

The trip home was rough, and the *George Washington* tossed in heavy seas.[95] But if the bad weather appeared to be a portent, other omens seemed good: Taft decided to cooperate with Wilson and overlook the slights and the snubs of the previous year. Taft and A. Lawrence Lowell wrote to Wilson on February 10 and said "the American people will support you in a really effective League."[96] But Wilson knew that many other Republicans were gunning for him, and he cabled Tumulty to advise Democratic senators "to feel at liberty to answer criticisms of the League of Nations."[97] To Grayson and others, he brooded that "the failure of the United States to back it [the League] would break the heart of the world."[98] He would utter this maudlin sentiment again in the next few months.[99]

House cabled Wilson, informing him that Foch wished to press ahead with settlement terms that amounted to an ultimatum to the Germans.[100] Lloyd George had returned to London while Wilson was away, but Foch and Clemenceau remained active, even though the latter was recovering from an assassination attempt on February 19. Wilson cabled House and warned him to resist any French attempt to "hurry us into an acquiescence" with terms except for purely military and naval peace terms.[101]

When Wilson got to Washington, he found himself cut off from House due to troubles in the latest code that they were employing. "Sorry to say new means of communication so far so unsatisfactory that I really do not clearly know anything that you are trying to tell me," Wilson wrote to House. "Am not in touch with your proceedings and unable to advise. The new code is extremely complicated, is imperfectly transmitted, and . . . when one word is lost it throws out all that follows."[102]

In addition to signing legislation, there was other pressing business for Wilson in his brief visit to Washington. In his message to Congress in December he had mentioned the advisability of public works to employ veterans while industry was retooling for civilian production.[103] As early as the previous July, an adviser had told him that "the Government will be obliged to make a gigantic effort to employ . . . men on living wages in public work."[104] The chief instrumentality for this effort would be the U.S. Employment Service, an agency created within the Department of Labor in 1917.

Late in January, Tumulty had written to Wilson to remind him of this concern. "Many urgent matters await your return," Tumulty wrote. "Business conditions are strange and . . . there are a great many idle men in places."

Tumulty advised that "you should have prepared and considered plans so that you can begin issuing orders as soon as you land. It will be half the battle to act promptly and powerfully." Both the cabinet and the nation's governors ought to be asked for suggestions regarding "the employment of men" and recommendations for putting the plans "into immediate effect."[105]

Wilson cabled Tumulty and told him that since "I cannot remain at home for more than eight days," Tumulty should take the initiative, perhaps summoning a governors conference.[106]

The *George Washington* arrived in Boston on February 23, and the city staged a big parade the next day, with a rally attended by over seven thousand. Wilson spoke extemporaneously. American soldiers had fought, he asserted, with a kind of "religious fervor. They were not like any of the other soldiers. They had a vision; they had a dream; and they were fighting for that dream; and, fighting in that dream, they turned the whole tide of battle, and it never came back." And he could now experience something like "revenge," he said, because all his life he had heard men speak with "condescension of ideals and of idealists," especially those whom they call "academic." Well, events had now proven that idealists—people like Wilson—possessed much greater power than cynics: the power to deliver a victory that powermongers never could.

"In the name of the people of the United States," he chanted, "I have uttered as the objects of this great war ideals, and nothing but ideals, and the war has been won by that inspiration." There was no turning back: Americans were destiny bound to make good on the hope they had given the world.

He paused to conjure up the prospect of failure, calling it unthinkable. "If America were . . . to fail the world," he said, "think of the picture. . . . think of the utter blackness that would fall on the world." But this could never really happen, he continued: "I talk as if there were any question. I have no more doubt of the verdict of America in this matter than I have doubt of the blood that is in me."[107]

This was reckless talk by a man who was in many ways out of control—and out of touch with reality.

When he arrived in Washington, Wilson was told by congressional leaders that Republicans were going to attempt to force a special session of the new Congress—the Congress that they would control—after the adjournment of the lame-duck Congress that was still in session. Their method was to try to postpone action on some uncompleted appropriations in the hope that Wilson's hand would be forced: that he would have to call the new Congress into session. Their intent was to debate the League of Nations behind Wilson's back after he returned to France. Wilson was adamant in his determination to prevent this. He said that he would not call a special session of the new Congress until after the Paris Peace Conference was over.[108]

On February 26, Wilson sponsored the White House dinner with the members of the Senate and House foreign relations committees. They adjourned after dinner to the East Room, where Wilson discussed the League of Nations and answered questions. No transcript of these discussions was produced, and the participants issued very different assessments. In all, the reactions of the congressmen did not bode well.[109]

Some details of the session can be gleaned from press accounts. According to the *New York Times*, when Wilson was "asked whether it was true that the formation of a League of Nations . . . would involve any surrender of sovereignty on the part of this nation," Wilson answered "that in his opinion this nation would relinquish some sovereignty, but asserted that every other nation in the League would make a similar surrender and sacrifice, but for the good of the world."[110] When asked whether any nation could withdraw from the League, Wilson answered—according to Senator Gilbert Hitchcock, who was interviewed by the *Times*—that "any member of it could withdraw, by taking the proper step, at any time," and that the "step" to be taken pertained "to the abrogation of treaties."[111] When asked whether League commitments might "force the United States to participate by 'sending armed forces to Europe,'" Wilson "took the stand that this would be a matter for the United States to decide and that such contribution was not mandatory upon it."[112]

The Republican attack began two days later, with a speech in the Senate by Henry Cabot Lodge. This speech would demonstrate clearly what Wilson was up against.

Lodge savored the occasion; he knew he had the power to thwart Wilson, so he taunted and baited his foe in a relaxed and low-key manner. It was something like a game of cat-and-mouse. "Everybody hates war," the senator proclaimed. "We ought to lay aside once and for all the unfounded and really evil suggestion that because men differ as to the best method of securing the world's peace in the future, anyone is against permanent peace, if it can be obtained." Furthermore, "the question now before us is so momentous that it transcends all party lines. . . . I will follow any man and vote for any measure which in my honest opinion will make for the maintenance of the world's peace."

But the very momentousness of the issue demanded sober judgment, Lodge observed. "No question has ever confronted the United States Senate which equals in importance that which is involved in the league of nations. . . . There should be no undue haste in considering it. . . . If there is any proposition or any plan which will not bear . . . the most thorough and most public discussion, that fact makes it an object of suspicion at the outset. Beware of it; be on your guard against it."

Alas, Lodge continued, the draft League Covenant amounted to a half-baked proposition, at least in its existing form:

In this draft prepared for a constitution of a league of nations, which is now before the world, there is hardly a clause about the interpretation of which men do not already differ. As it stands there is serious danger that the very nations which sign the constitution of the league will quarrel about the meaning of the various articles before a twelvemonth has passed. It seems to have been very hastily drafted, and the result is crudeness and looseness of expression, unintentional, I hope.

This was all the more alarming, Lodge said, despite Wilson's assurance that a nation could withdraw from the League. There was nothing whatsoever in the Covenant that stated this plainly. To Lodge (or so he claimed), there appeared to be no way out of the League of Nations once a nation took the fateful step and joined: "It is evident . . . that this league is intended to be indissoluble, for there is no provision for its termination or for the withdrawal of any signatory. . . . Therefore, before we ratify, the terms and language in which the terms are stated must be as exact and as precise, as free from any possibility of conflicting interpretations, as it is possible to make them."

More troubling still was the fact that the League would force a break in American traditions, as Lodge proceeded to explain:

We abandon entirely by the proposed constitution the policy laid down by Washington in his Farewell Address and the Monroe doctrine. . . . I know that some of the ardent advocates of the plan submitted to us regard any suggestion of the importance of the Washington policy as foolish and irrelevant. Perhaps it is. Perhaps the time has come when the policies of Washington should be abandoned; but if we are to cast them aside I think that at least it should be done respectfully and with a sense of gratitude to the great man who formulated them. . . . Washington declared against permanent alliances. He did not close the door on temporary alliances for particular purposes. Our entry in the great war just closed was entirely in accord with . . . the policy laid down by Washington. . . . Now, in the twinkling of an eye, while passion and emotion reign, the Washington policy is to be entirely laid aside and we are to enter upon a permanent and indissoluble alliance. . . . Let us not overlook the profound gravity of this step.

Most troubling of all, in Lodge's view, was Article 10 as a pathway to war without end for the United States and its people: "In article 10 we, in common, of course, with the other signatories and members . . . guarantee the territorial integrity and the political independence of every member of the league. That means that we ultimately guarantee the independence and the boundaries . . . of every nation on earth." Well, said Lodge, the implications were unmistakable and stark:

There is no need of arguing whether there is to be compulsive force behind this league. It is there in article 10 absolutely and entirely by the mere fact of these guarantees. The ranks of the armies and the fleets of the navy made necessary by such pledges are to be filled and manned by the sons, husbands, and brothers of the people of America. I wish them carefully to consider, therefore, whether they are willing to have the United States forced into war by other nations against her own will. They must bear in mind constantly that we have only one vote in the executive council, only one vote in the body of delegates, and a majority of the votes rules and is decisive. I am not here to discuss the constitutional question of the sole right of Congress to declare war. That is a detail, as it relates only to the Constitution, which we may decide later. In my own opinion, we shall be obliged to modify the Constitution.

Lodge closed this speech, as he began it, in a tone of sweet reason.

I hope the American people will take time to consider this promise before they make it—because when it is once made it can not be broken—and ask themselves whether this is the best way of assuring perfect peace throughout the future years . . . for we all are aiming at the same object. . . . Is it not possible to draft a better, more explicit, less dangerous scheme than the one here and now presented?

Then he made a few suggestions of his own:

Let us put three lines into the draft for the league which will preserve the Monroe Doctrine beyond any possibility of doubt or question. It is easily done. Let us also have, if we enter the league, a complete exclusion from the league's jurisdiction of such questions as are involved in immigration and the right of each country to say who shall come within its borders and become citizens. . . . There should be some definite provision for peaceful withdrawal from the league. . . . Lastly, let us have a definite statement in the constitution of the league as to whether the league is to have an international force of its own or is to have the power to summon the armed forces of the different members of the league. Let it be stated in plain language whether the "measures," the "recommendations," or the suggestions of the executive council are to be binding upon the members of the league and are to compel them. . . . On the question of the use of force, we should not proceed in the dark.

Thus was the gauntlet hurled. Lodge challenged Wilson to come to terms or else court the suspicion that a stealthy agenda lay behind the ambiguous—or supposedly ambiguous—language of the League Covenant: "If those who support the league decline to make such simple statements as these—I mean statements in the body of the instrument, not individual statements—it is impossible to avoid the conclusion that they are seeking to do by indirection and the use of nebulous phrases what they are not willing to do directly." After all, Lodge contended, "we are asked to abandon the policies which we have adhered to during all our life as a Nation."[113] Let Woodrow Wilson prove otherwise.

Wilson faced greater formations of power in the Senate than he cared to acknowledge, for Lodge was a formidable opponent. Not only would he soon be the Senate majority leader and chairman of the Senate Foreign Relations Committee, but he was also a figure of lordly bearing, a match—indeed, an overmatch—for Wilson's aspiration to maintain an Olympian demeanor. Journalist Frederick Lewis Allen reminisced years later as follows: "[Lodge was] a gentleman, a scholar, and an elegant and persuasive figure in the United States Senate. As he strolled down the aisle of the Senate Chamber— slender, graceful, gray-haired, gray-bearded, the embodiment of all that was patrician—he caught and held the eye." About Lodge gathered "a curious combination of men and of influences":

> There were hard-shelled tories like [Frank] Brandegee; there were western idealists like [William] Borah, who distrusted any association with foreign diplomats as the blond country boy of the old-fashioned melodrama distrusted association with the slick city man; there were chronic dissenters like [Robert] La Follette and Jim Reed; there were Republicans who were not sorry to put the Democratic President in a hole. . . . there were Senators anxious to show that nobody could make a treaty without the advice as well as the consent of the Senate and get away with it; and there were not a few who . . . shared Lodge's personal distaste for Wilsonian rhetoric.[114]

Worried Democrats urged the president to bring some friendly congressmen together to help fine-tune the Covenant's language. Senator Thomas Walsh told Wilson that the Covenant contained "language . . . that is obscure and . . . the wisdom of which is seriously questioned by the earnest friends of the project." Consequently, he continued, "I believe incalculable good would result if you could devote just one day of your brief stay to a conference with, say, six members of the Senate and six members of the House, who would sit down with you at the table and go at the draft as one of our committees is accustomed to do with important bills. . . . I appreciate that the demands on your time will be tremendous, but you have no other duty that compares in importance with this."[115]

No, Wilson answered, there was not sufficient time for such a thing: "deliberate conferences seem at this time impossible." He admitted that "many parts of the proposed Covenant" could "with advantage be clarified and rewritten, but on the whole I think that its reasonable interpretation is clear." Without saying that the Senate had to take the Covenant as written, Wilson nonetheless said that "a rewriting of it would be a work of extreme difficulty if indeed it would be possible at all."[116]

Meanwhile, House was having conversations regarding a plan that would activate the League of Nations immediately. "I suggested to Balfour and Cecil this morning," he wrote to Wilson on February 27, "that we make an effort to start the League of Nations functioning at once."[117] It appears that the problems with the trans-Atlantic code—the problems that Wilson had complained about in a message that he sent to House the very same day—did not prevent the transmission of this message, for Wilson replied on March 3, telling House that the plan "disturbs me a little," since Lodge might hurl the accusation that Wilson was trying to outmaneuver the Senate, to "commit the country in some practical way from which it would be impossible to withdraw." So he told House to make sure that any plans were merely "provisional."[118]

There was more going on than Wilson knew until he got back to France on March 13.

In some remarks to the Democratic National Committee—which he urged to drum up support for the League via Democratic state committees—Wilson came close to acknowledging the fact that he was wholly in the grip of his emotions when it came to the subject of the League. "I tried to state in Boston what it would mean to the people of the world if the United States did not support this great ideal with cordiality," he said. Then he confessed that "I was not able to speak when I tried to fully express my thoughts. I tell you, frankly, I choked up; I could not do it. The thing reaches the depth of tragedy."[119]

He told his fellow Democrats to "trot out your orators and turn them loose" because the promise of the League was nothing less than "what once seemed a remote hope of an international miracle."[120] Then Wilson proceeded to pour out his ridicule and wrath toward any who opposed him. "I wish I could stay home and tackle this job with you," he said. "There is nothing I would like to do so much as to really say . . . what I think of the people that are opposing it." He declared that they were imbeciles, pinheads, dolts:

> Of all the blind and little provincial people, they are the littlest and most contemptible. . . . They have not even got good working imitations of minds. They remind me of a man with a head that is not a head but is just a knot providentially put there to keep him from raveling out. But why the Lord should not have been willing to let them ravel out, I do not know, because they are of no use. . . . They are going to have the most conspicuously contemptible names in history. The gibbets that they are going to be erected on by future historians will scrape the heavens, they will be so high. . . . If I did not despise them, I would feel sorry for them.[121]

But it was Wilson who merited pity, for he was not at this point a politician in the best sense of that term. He was close to becoming a fanatic. His descent into mental collapse was occurring fully seven months before the stroke. The extravagant vituperation just quoted reveals this. He was not in a condition to deal with Lodge in any shrewd or practical way. His only recourse was rhetoric: the rhetoric of prophecy, the rhetoric of temper tantrum (as used in the passage above), and the rhetoric of sentimentality ("breaking the heart of the world").

It was all a demonstration of "ideals, and nothing but ideals," for the future historians—and for God—to appreciate. It was not strategy.

Just before the old Congress adjourned, Lodge proved that Wilson was beaten unless he came off his high horse and made a deal. On March 2, Lodge, with assistance from senators Frank Brandegee and Philander Knox, wrote a manifesto denouncing the League. Then Lodge got Republican senators to sign it. On the evening of March 3, Lodge took the floor in the Senate and read the resolution, which stated that the League "in the form now proposed" should be rejected. Then he read the names of thirty-seven Republican senators and senators-elect who had signed the statement. Two others cabled their support, and a Democrat, James Reed, joined their number as well.

The Constitution stipulates that a treaty has to be ratified by a vote of two-thirds in the Senate. The forty senators who signed Lodge's statement were more than enough to defeat the League unless Wilson came to terms. Reporters dubbed the resolution Lodge's "Round Robin."

Republicans proceeded to filibuster further attempts to conduct congressional business unless Wilson would agree to call the new Congress into session. He refused to do so. Among the items of legislative business that perished when the lame-duck Congress adjourned was an appropriation for the U.S. Employment Service. The secretary of labor had warned the president that if appropriations were not forthcoming, the Employment Service "will not only terminate on June 30th but will immediately begin to disintegrate."[122] And more soldiers were returning all the time. Congressional supporters of the service had been seeking $10 million in additional funding.

Tumulty had followed the president's advice and called a conference of governors and mayors to address the unemployment situation. But when the conference met on March 3, the very best that Wilson could do was to express regret that he could not participate, and then shunt the responsibility for dealing with the problem away from the White House: "The primary duty of caring for our people in the intimate matters that we want to discuss here . . . falls upon the states and localities," he said.[123]

Wilson was deceiving himself—averting his eyes from a gathering storm. Within months, Americans would start to experience an economic condition best described by a term from the 1970s: *stagflation*, a recession with high unemployment that occurs at the very same time as inflation. This convulsion, which soon became associated with fierce new labor-management conflict, started that summer and it lasted well into 1921. Wilson's League of Nations predicament—largely self-created by his blunders and posturing— was eclipsing almost every other consideration of presidential leadership. It was preventing him from furnishing the stewardship in demobilization that

Americans urgently needed. The lessons to be learned from this ugly experience would lead later on to the GI Bill in World War II.

Just before he returned to Paris, Wilson made an appearance with William Howard Taft on the stage of the Metropolitan Opera House in New York. They were making a joint appearance on behalf of the League of Nations. Taft took the high road at once: while defending the Covenant, he thanked his fellow Republicans like Henry Cabot Lodge for making "suggestions that should prove especially valuable in the work of revising the form of the Covenant and making changes."[124]

Wilson, however, was militant. He said he knew Americans supported the League by a huge majority: "I have had unmistakable intimations of it from all parts of the country." He imputed his own ideas to American troops without a second's hesitation; he said that all of them had gone off to France "to show . . . that the United States . . . would go anywhere the rights of mankind were threatened." As for his critics, Wilson contradicted Taft by dismissing their ideas out of hand: "I have heard no counsel of generosity in their criticism. I have heard no constructive suggestion."

He pledged to bring back a unified treaty from Paris, a treaty with the League and the terms of the settlement so completely intertwined that no critics could pull them apart: "When the treaty comes back gentlemen on this side will find the Covenant not only in it, but so many threads of the treaty tied to the Covenant that you cannot dissect the Covenant from the treaty without destroying the whole vital structure. The structure of peace will not be vital without the League of Nations, and no man is going to bring back a cadaver with him."[125]

It was the voice of a political dead man that uttered those words.

THEY TALK AND TALK AND TALK

Wilson grudgingly addressed the basic issues that were raised by Lodge on his way back to France aboard the *George Washington*. At first, his mood remained ugly: Ray Stannard Baker wrote at the time that Wilson "is a good hater—& how he does hate these obstructionist Senators. He is inclined now to stand by the Covenant word for word as drawn, accepting no amendments, so that the 37 of the round-robin will be utterly vanquished, will have no chance of saying afterwards, 'Well, we forced the amendments, didn't we?'"[126]

He arrived at Brest on March 13 and was greeted by House, who was chagrined by his friend's waspish attitude. "Your dinner," Wilson told him— the White House dinner with the members of the Senate and House foreign relations committees that House had proposed—was "a failure as far as getting together was concerned." House wrote that "the president comes back very militant."[127]

But this was just the beginning. On the train from Brest to Paris, House shared more details about the plan to jump-start the League. Wilson concluded right away that his friend had been party to an effort to separate the treaty from the League, a scenario that Wilson considered betrayal. House had also indulged the demand of Clemenceau for a Rhenish republic that would serve as a buffer zone between France and Germany, a concept that Wilson opposed.[128]

Wilson was paying once again for giving too much latitude to House.

Wilson's suspicions were in this case well grounded. As Knock has explained, "Before Wilson returned to Paris, the Allied statesmen, having closely followed the politics of the Round Robin, had decided to take the League of Nations hostage. Throughout the spring, each of them would present a different ransom note." Knock continues:

> The first one, appropriately, would be French in origin, and it had at least the partial consent of the British and of Colonel House. Embodied in a short-lived proposal to conclude a preliminary treaty, it presumed to give France perpetual control over the Rhineland by detaching it from Germany, and to uncouple the League from the treaty itself.[129]

Edith Wilson recorded in her memoirs that she was "shocked" by Wilson's appearance right after his meeting with House on the train:

> He seemed to have aged ten years, and his jaw was set in that way it had when he was making a superhuman effort to control himself. . . . He smiled bitterly. "House has given away everything I had won before we left Paris. He has compromised on every side, and so I have to start all over again and this time it will be harder, as he has given the impression that my delegates are not in sympathy with me."[130]

This incident dealt a fatal blow to the House-Wilson friendship. The rupture took the form of a gradual drifting apart as Wilson's attitude toward his erstwhile friend turned distant and then cold. Historian Inga Floto has written that after their talk on the train, "the personal trust of the two men was broken and the friendship damaged beyond repair."[131] For all of the ways in which House had been complicit—through flattery and outright pandering—in Wilson's delusions, it must nonetheless be remembered that House at his best had been capable of giving shrewd advice, as when he urged the necessity of lead time in military matters and also when he urged the development of long-term bipartisan strategies. House was one of the few people in the Wilson entourage who could calm Wilson down and persuade him to reconsider an opinion. That check upon the wild streak in Wilson's nature would gradually be removed in the spring of 1919.

But the breach took time to develop, and in March Colonel House remained active.

Wilson went to work upon the French and the British right away. When Clemenceau and Lloyd George paid a visit on March 15, the president—according to Grayson's diary—told them he "could not agree" to "the side-tracking of the constitution to the League of Nations." He reminded them that "at the initial Plenary Session [of the Peace Conference] all the Allied delegates had agreed that the League of Nations must be the initial compelling paragraph of any peace treaty."

Moreover, in light of the way in which events had been flowing, he would no longer agree with the armistice-related proposition—hammered out in the meetings of the Council of Ten and the Supreme War Council before his departure for Washington—that "military and naval indemnity terms" should be "imposed upon Germany . . . no later than the 20th of March."[132] Since these "terms" had since been inflated into nothing less than a full-fledged (and unacceptable) "preliminary peace treaty," the task of imposing "terms" would have to be postponed.

After finishing with Clemenceau and Lloyd George, Wilson met with the American delegation and brought them into line with regard to the inseparability of the League and the treaty. Then he turned to the subject of revisions to the League, since it was finally dawning on him that he lacked sufficient power to fight both the Allies and his Republican opponents simultaneously.

On March 16, he met with House and Cecil, and, according to House, spent "an hour and a half going over the Covenant . . . and discussing how it should be amended if at all." House recorded that he himself was "in favor of some amendments and clarifications," whereas Wilson, "with his usual stubbornness in such matters, desires to leave it as it is."[133]

Even so, Wilson met again with House and Cecil, joined by David Hunter Miller, on March 18, and he began to consider some revisions. On the very same day, Taft sent him a cable alleging that the "ground will be completely cut from under the opponents of the League in the Senate" if he brought back a treaty containing a "specific reservation of the Monroe Doctrine," along with a requirement for "unanimity of action in Executive Council and Body of Delegates," and other safeguards.[134]

The task of amending the League Covenant proved difficult. On March 18, House recorded that Wilson was "more reasonable than he was the other day as to meeting the wishes of the Senate." But, House continued, "We found it nearly impossible to write what the Senate desires into the Covenant." The Monroe Doctrine reservation caused problems: "If a special reservation of the Monroe doctrine is made, Japan may want a reservation made regarding a sphere of influence in Asia, and other nations will ask for similar concessions, and there is no telling where it would end."[135] Cecil brought the issue to the attention of Lloyd George. As Cooper relates, the prime minister "objected strongly" to recognizing the Monroe Doctrine, but he nonetheless "planned to use the matter as a bargaining chip."[136]

On the evening of March 18, Wilson and Cecil agreed to seek revisions to permit a nation to withdraw from the League, to make the arbitration process in Article 15 noncompulsory, to remove domestic political issues from the League's purview, and to require Executive Council unanimity. But the addition of a Monroe Doctrine reservation was at this point rejected.[137]

The changes were of dubious value in smoothing the way for the League in the U.S. Senate. Henry White, the lone Republican member of the American peace delegation, had cabled Lodge on his own initiative, requesting guidance on revisions to the Covenant. Lodge had no intention of making things easy. So after consultations with Philander Knox, Frank Brandegee, and Elihu Root, Lodge cabled back this noncommittal reply:

> The President expressed no willingness to receive any communication from the Senate while that body was in session. If he now wishes to have amendments drafted which the Senate will consent to, the natural and necessary course is to convene the Senate in the customary way.[138]

As all of these events unfolded, the Council of Ten and the Supreme War Council were meeting. The deliberations bogged down in never-ending variations of proposals for the final surrender terms, territorial adjustments, and the like. On March 19, Lloyd George, Clemenceau, and Wilson decided to scrap the Council of Ten and replace it with a "Council of Four," consisting of themselves and Vittorio Orlando. At first no official minutes were produced, though Clemenceau ordered Paul Mantoux, who was serving as interpreter, to take notes.[139] This Council of Four would meet 148 times in the weeks ahead, often two or three times a day.[140]

But this procedure failed to expedite anything. The discussions dragged: the "Big Four" dealt fitfully with every issue in contention, and they wrestled with scores of them. These jagged and meandering proceedings killed everybody's patience as the weeks rolled on and on.

On March 20 House met privately with Clemenceau and devised a resolution that would guarantee France's security outside the structure of the League of Nations.[141] This idea would be taken up soon by Lloyd George, and it would serve as a significant point of leverage with the French. It was a free-standing and separate Anglo-American initiative to come to the defense of France if Germany attacked again.

Meanwhile, Wilson presided over meetings of the League Commission, which was deluged with proposed amendments. The discussions were exhausting. On March 22, Wilson told Grayson and others that it was "hard to keep one's temper when the world is on fire and we find delegates, such as those of the French, blocking all of the proceedings. . . . They talk and talk and talk and desire constantly to reiterate points that have been already thoroughly thrashed out. . . . This entire afternoon has been wasted because of the stupidity of the French delegates."[142]

On March 24, the big issue of reparations was addressed by the Council of Four. Huge sums were at stake, since there had been talk of making the Germans pay the whole cost of the war. There had also been talk of making the Germans pay for Allied veterans' pensions. The Reparations Committee of the Peace Conference would issue its recommendations—in due time. But the British, French, and Americans would ultimately settle the issue through negotiations—that is, through power politics.[143]

House had proposed a flexible reparations formula, with the sum of $30 billion established as "a maximum figure." He had also proposed to establish a commission that would "meet once a year to determine how much Germany could pay the following year and also determine whether the amount of thirty billions was excessive for reparation demands." "In this way," House explained, "the French and English could let Germany evade an impossible payment."[144]

But Clemenceau said that the Americans and British seemed too lenient. Wilson went after him, declaring that punitive reparations were "impossible," that "the German people could be expected not to stand for a burden that would grind them down for fifty years. . . . Rather than do that they would turn to anything—Bolshevism, or something which would promise them relief."[145] The next day Wilson proposed that the Germans should be forced to pay a prompt one-time indemnity of between $25 and $35 billion.[146]

Lloyd George at this point backed Wilson. In a key memorandum prepared with his advisers—known to historians as the "Fontainebleau Memorandum," since it was prepared on the weekend of March 22–23 in a hotel in the forest of Fontainebleau—he declared that any people who wished to "make Germany so feeble that she will never be able to hit back are utterly wrong." If Germany "feels that she has been unjustly treated," he wrote, "she will find means of exacting retribution."[147] But to pacify Clemenceau, Lloyd George made use of House's suggestion: that "the British Empire and the United States ought to give France a guarantee against the possibility of a new German aggression."[148]

Lloyd George joined Wilson in warning of the Bolshevik threat, and he asked what would happen if the Germans refused to sign the treaty. "A large army of occupation for an indefinite period is out of the question," he stated, and further prolongation of the blockade was problematic: "I am doubtful whether public opinion would allow us deliberately to starve Germany."[149] Though the Allies should extract reparations, they should also "enable the

German people to get upon their legs again. We cannot both cripple her and expect her to pay."[150]

But Lloyd George would prove shifty in the weeks to come as he reacted to political pressures from home to force a more vindictive peace. He alleged to Wilson on March 26 that a majority in Parliament demanded that Germany should be made to pay "to the last cent," and that a vote of no confidence would follow if he tried to resist much longer.[151] And events would soon prove that these concerns were justified.[152] Moreover, Lloyd George's rhetorical support for an altruistic peace concealed a deeper nationalistic agenda of his own that was not at all hard to discern.

The Fontainebleau Memorandum was intended in part to make Wilson back down on his naval building program. There should be "a firm understanding between the British Empire and the United States of America and France and Italy that there will be no competitive building up of fleets or armies between them," the memorandum stated.[153]

To extract this concession from Wilson, Lloyd George revived the threat to uncouple the League from the treaty. The Fontainebleau memorandum stated that the parties to the "Treaty of Peace" would perforce become members of the League—"the Covenant of which will be signed as a separate treaty."[154]

But Wilson had already preempted this particular threat: he had secured the support of the French and Italians to keep the League attached to the treaty.[155] So Lloyd George decided to make the Monroe Doctrine the lever that he hoped would force Wilson to terminate America's naval buildup. Cecil recorded in his diary the fact that Lloyd George admitted his "real reason" for resisting the Monroe Doctrine reservation, which Wilson was beginning to embrace: he wanted "something to bargain with" in order to "induce the Americans to give up their plan of building ships against the British."[156]

Meanwhile, Clemenceau insisted on his territorial agenda, demanding not only the cession of Alsace and Lorraine and the creation of a buffer state on the Rhine but also the annexation of the Saar as retribution for the German destruction of French coal mines. Both Lloyd George and Wilson opposed the buffer state upon the principle of "self-determination." But only Wilson opposed the demand of Clemenceau for the Saar.

Clemenceau was delaying and playing for time: he argued both sides of every question. He agreed to the principles that Wilson espoused, but then he turned the other way and raised doubts. "I agree completely with Mr. Lloyd George and President Wilson about the manner in which to treat Germany," he proclaimed. "We must not abuse our victory." All the same, he continued, "We must not compromise the result of our victory. . . . I implore you to understand our feelings about this. . . . America is very far away, protected by the ocean. Not even Napoleon himself could touch England. You are both sheltered; we are not."[157]

On March 27, in an effort to persuade Clemenceau to give up the buffer state and accept in its place a demilitarized zone in the Rhineland, Wilson offered the "guarantee" that Colonel House and Lloyd George had suggested (with a link to the League of Nations): "If we add . . . a military guarantee by Great Britain and, I hope, the United States, acting under the authority of the League of Nations, to come to the immediate assistance of France in case of aggression committed without provocation by Germany . . . it seems to me that you will have satisfaction."[158]

Wilson was at last beginning to achieve some success with the League of Nations. With support from Cecil, the amendments were being adopted.[159] But in the Council of Four, tempers flared. Wilson and Clemenceau had an angry confrontation over the Saar. "They came close to calling one another names," House recorded.[160] Wilson acknowledged the need to give France compensation for the German destruction of coal mines, but he complained that annexation of the Saar by France lacked "historical basis."[161] Clemenceau retorted that the "excellent intentions" of Wilson ignored "human nature."[162]

At that point, according to several accounts, the two men became openly hostile. According to House's account, the confrontation went like this:

> Clemenceau . . . said that the President favored the Germans. The President replied that such a statement was untrue and that Clemenceau knew that it was. Clemenceau then stated that if they did not receive the Sarre [*sic*] valley, he would not sign the Treaty of Peace. To this the President replied, "Then if France does not get what she wishes, she will refuse to act with us. In that event, do you wish me to return home?" Clemenceau answered, "I do not wish you to go home, but I intend to do so myself," and in a moment he left.[163]

At the same meeting, the issue of reparations came up again, and the French proposed deferring any statement of German obligations since the process of assessing the damage might take many years.[164] Lloyd George introduced the economist John Maynard Keynes, who proposed a plan to "tell the Germans 'Here is what you owe; but we have not yet determined how much you are able to pay.'"[165]

Wilson heatedly objected that the French proposal was tantamount to "asking Germany to place at our disposal all that she possesses indefinitely."[166] On March 29, Lloyd George presented a new plan to create an "Inter-Ally Commission" that would determine "the amounts to be paid, the time and mode of payments and the securities to be given therefore."[167] The plan also included Allied pensions in the reparations.

The stress and exhaustion of these meetings took a toll on all, and this included Clemenceau, who was still recovering from the recent attempt on his life. His resentment of Wilson was obvious: he told a British editor— Henry Wickham Steed, of *The Times*, who was also a personal friend—that Wilson "thought himself another Jesus Christ."[168] Grayson recorded the fact that Wilson tried to use humor to alleviate the tension, telling stories and reciting limericks. But the negotiations dragged on as public criticism mounted and events in Germany seethed. "[Wilson] is working fearfully hard," wrote Ray Stannard Baker on March 31.[169]

On the same date, Wilson proposed a plan to give France ownership of the Saar mines, but without forcing residents of the area to accept French sovereignty.[170]

Clemenceau and Lloyd George persuaded Wilson to consider the pressures they were under: they convinced him that their governments would fall if they could not fulfill promises and satisfy public opinion. Wilson told some advisers on March 31 that "we should try to meet Lloyd George's and Clemenceau's suggestions as otherwise, he was told by them, their ministries might fall and we would have no governments to make peace with for some time to come."[171] The next day, in a meeting with a larger group of reparations advisers—Bernard Baruch, John William Davis, Thomas William Lamont, Vance McCormick, and John Foster Dulles—Wilson agreed to include Allied pensions in the reparations plan, as Lloyd George had demanded.[172]

On April 3, Wilson's health gave out: he fell ill. Dr. Grayson diagnosed influenza. In light of what would happen to Wilson's health in the latter part of April—and in light of his catastrophic stroke in October—the experts have been debating the nature of this episode for years.[173]

During Wilson's convalescence, he appointed House to represent him. As Cooper has observed, while this gesture "could have been taken as a sign of trust, it was not."[174] The reason for the selection of House was simple: the British, the French, and the Italians insisted upon it.[175]

THE TIME HAS COME TO BRING THIS THING TO A HEAD

John Maynard Keynes—disgusted by the economic terms of the Treaty of Versailles—wrote a scathing book about the subject that became a best seller in 1919. For years, Keynes's book (*The Economic Consequences of the Peace*) was invoked to support the view that the peace terms of 1919 were foolish or worse.

In recent years, revisionists (including Arthur S. Link) have challenged the idea that the Versailles treaty was as bad as many have believed. These issues and controversies will be duly considered. In the meantime, Keynes's estimation of Wilson is pertinent to assessing the strategic situation at the Paris Peace Conference.

Keynes believed that Wilson had thrown away an economic weapon of vast power, for even though Wilson had failed to use the leverage he intermittently possessed in 1917 and 1918 to compel a "peace without victory," a final form of leverage remained if Wilson had used it. When Wilson came to France, Keynes wrote,

> Europe was in complete dependence on the food supplies of the United States; and financially she was even more absolutely at their mercy. Europe not only already owed the United States more than she could pay; but only a large measure of further assistance could save her from starvation and bankruptcy. Never had a philosopher held such weapons wherewith to bind the princes of this world.[176]

Other British observers—such as Winston Churchill at the end of 1918—had made the same point. On March 26, Cecil wrote that "the great want of the future is money, and the only one of the Associated Governments that has money at its command is the United States."[177] Lloyd George sent a powerful hint to Wilson on April 23 in a memorandum on European postwar reconstruction. "The United Kingdom enters upon the peace . . . with the question as to how we are to pay what we owe to the United States Treasury as the chief problem of our external finance," he wrote.[178]

Strangely enough, it was precisely this leverage that Wilson himself had anticipated using as he pondered the issue of peace without victory during the summer months of 1917: "When the war is over," he had written to House, "we can force them [the Allies] to our way of thinking, because by that time they will . . . be financially in our hands."[179] But in the intervening months he rejected the idea of a debt moratorium for the British and the French—a financial package to be dangled at the end of the war. "Both Britain and France had hoped that the Americans would write off their wartime Treasury loans," David Stevenson has written, but Wilson "ruled out cancellation because of concerns that Congress would object and because of America's own fiscal burdens."[180] This decision left Wilson unfortunately weak when he might have been strong in 1919. Stevenson has argued that "the French would have moderated their reparation demands if the Americans had been more forthcoming over war debts."[181]

Though Keynes's estimation of the character of Wilson was in some ways inaccurate, he hit the mark when he described Wilson's temperament as essentially "theological, not intellectual."[182] With only slight exaggeration, Keynes contended that Wilson "had no plan, no scheme . . . for clothing with the flesh of life the commandments which he had thundered from the White House."[183]

Due to a series of missed opportunities, Wilson lurched back and forth between threats and concessions during April 1919. He was fit to be tied as he grappled with the increasing shiftiness of Lloyd George, the tenacity of

Clemenceau, and the territorial ambitions of the Italians and Japanese. Keynes summed up Wilson's dilemma as he tried to cut a decent deal in April without many options for maneuver:

> What then was he to do in the last resort? He could let the Conference drag on an endless length by the exercise of sheer obstinacy. He could break it up and return to America in a rage with nothing settled. Or he could attempt an appeal to the world over the heads of the Conference. These were wretched alternatives, against each of which a great deal could be said. They were also very risky,—especially for a politician. The President's mistaken policy over the Congressional elections had weakened his personal position in his own country, and it was by no means certain that the American public would support him in a position of intransigeancy [*sic*]. . . . Thus, if he threw down the gage publicly he might be defeated. And if he were defeated, would not the final Peace be far worse than if he were to retain his prestige and endeavor to make it as good as the limitations of European politics would allow him? But above all, if he were defeated, would he not lose the League of Nations? [184]

So Wilson entered the final phase of the conference in a posture of damage control:

> As the President had thought nothing out, the Council [of Four] was generally working on the basis of a French or British draft. [Wilson] had to take up, therefore, a persistent attitude of obstruction, criticism, and negation. . . . Compromise was inevitable, and never to compromise on the essential, very difficult. [185]

So, in Keynes's view, he talked himself into believing in the essential rightness of his compromises:

> Now it was that what I have called his theological or Presbyterian temperament became dangerous. . . . He would do nothing that was not honorable; he would do nothing that was not just and right. . . . Thus, without any abatement of the verbal inspiration of the Fourteen Points, they became a document for gloss and interpretation and for all the intellectual apparatus of self-deception, by which, I daresay, the President's forefathers had persuaded themselves that the course they thought it necessary to take was consistent with every syllable of the Pentateuch. [186]

It was not quite as bad as Keynes thought: there were times when Wilson would acknowledge, openly or privately—at the time of the conference and afterward—that some compromises were regrettable, the results of some bargains imperfect. But Ray Stannard Baker, an ardent admirer of Wilson (and his future biographer), asserted that with Wilson

the League of Nations is a matter of *faith*: and the President is first of all a *man
of faith*. He believes in the L. of N. as an organization that will save the world.
On the Commission House is the only one who supports this view & House
only *feels* it, where the President *sees it, grasps it, feels it*, with the mighty
tenacity of a great faith. He is willing even to compromise desperately for it,
suffer the charge of inconsistency for it—He is the only Man here [original
emphasis].[187]

During his convalescence in early April, Wilson reflected on his alternatives. Clemenceau's resistance to compromising on the issues of the Saar and
the Rhineland caused Wilson to contemplate a rupture with the French. Ray
Stannard Baker, House, and others had encouraged him to consider this. On
April 2, House offered to tell the French that "unless a conclusion was
reached within the next ten days . . . [Wilson] would probably go back to
America and that we would all go with him," adding that a pretext vis-à-vis
"the necessity for calling in Special Session Congress and passing appropriation bills" could be added to convince the French that the threat of Wilson's
departure was real.[188] Wilson liked this idea: On the evening of April 3, from
his sickbed, he told advisers that he was "threatening to go home as he must
call Congress in May."[189]

On April 6, he told Cary Grayson to have the USS *George Washington*
sent to Brest. "I do not intend it as a bluff," Wilson said. "When I decide to
carry this thing through I do not want to say that I am going as soon as I can
get a boat. I want the boat to be here."[190] News of this development leaked to
the press, quite possibly with Grayson's connivance.[191] When a French reporter asked Grayson whether the ship was coming because of Wilson's
health or otherwise, Grayson said he "took great pleasure in telling him it
was 'otherwise.'"[192]

This threat would soon prove effective: Clemenceau became more flexible regarding the Saar and the Rhineland. Colonel House had given Wilson
sage advice.[193]

Both House and Wilson were impatient with the endless give-and-take of
the conference. But House, more than Wilson, was inclined to make haste at
the expense of casuistry. In a meeting of the Council of Four, House said that
"it was more important to bring about peace quickly than it was to haggle
over details."[194] Small wonder that the British and the French wanted House
as Wilson's representative. Notwithstanding their own inclination to haggle,
they could see that it was relatively easy to get their own way with House—
more often than not.

So despite the fact that House could talk tough on occasion—as he did
when he recommended the threat to pack up and go home—he continued to
sink in Wilson's eyes. On April 7, Wilson asked Grayson whether he saw
"any change in House," since he seemed "to act distant with me as if he has

something on his conscience." No doubt Wilson worried that House was "selling out" again.

By April 8, Wilson felt well enough to rejoin the negotiations—in a fighting mood. According to Baker, Wilson said that he was "going to fight. . . . He will win for the principles though he lose the peace & lose his own prestige—& this is what matters." Baker mused that the president "can die for faith . . . he can bring down the world around him before giving over his convictions." "The time has come to bring this thing to a head," Wilson declared.[195]

But what followed were more weeks of give-and-take—some successful for Wilson, some not.

On the Saar, Wilson made headway in convincing Clemenceau to put the region under French control for fifteen years, and then hold a plebiscite to determine the inhabitants' wishes.[196] On the Rhineland, he pushed the idea of a demilitarized zone, augmented by the Anglo-American "guarantee" of assistance to France in the event of future German aggression.[197] On April 10, House and Cecil worked out a memorandum calling for an Anglo-American conference on naval limitations; in return, Lloyd George agreed to include the reservation on the Monroe Doctrine—which Wilson had at last decided to embrace—as a revision to the League Covenant.[198] So Wilson introduced the following revision: "Nothing in this Covenant shall be deemed to affect the validity of international engagements such as Treaties of arbitration or regional understandings like the Monroe Doctrine for securing the maintenance of peace."[199]

The League of Nations Commission accepted the Monroe Doctrine reservation—but only after Wilson overcame the objections of the French delegates.[200] Once again, the Japanese introduced their racial equality amendment, and, again, it was voted down.[201]

On the matter of reparations, he continued to struggle. He hoped to limit the damage to Germany by imposing a fixed sum and a fixed schedule of payments. But the arguments on these matters swung back and forth.[202] Moreover, Wilson confronted new problems, as Italy asserted territorial claims that clashed as openly with his principle of "self-determination" as the French demands in the Rhineland and the Saar. In particular, the Italians wanted the city of Fiume on the Adriatic coast and the South Tirol.[203] Soon enough, the demands of the Japanese in Asia would add to this problem.

Wilson was under severe pressure almost every single day; "the strain he is going through is almost beyond superhuman endurance," Grayson wrote.[204] Grayson told him to get some relaxation, to delegate more, but Wilson feared mistakes and betrayals. After all, this was the grand consummation for him: this was the role he had rehearsed almost constantly since 1914, the supreme role of helping the world to wake up from its nightmare.

Vittorio Orlando was pressing the Italian claims hard. A secret treaty—the 1915 Treaty of London with the British and French—gave Italy territorial concessions in Trentino, Istria, and Dalmatia. It was useless for Wilson to try to overturn that existing treaty. On April 14, he agreed to let the Italians have the South Tirol, thus giving them future protection against the Austrians but at the expense of putting thousands of German-speaking Austrians under Italian sovereignty. He later regretted this lapse from the principle of "self-determination."[205]

Perhaps to compensate for this lapse, he dug in his heels in opposing the Italian demand for Fiume, which was not included in the 1915 treaty. On April 19, Orlando began an incessant campaign to get Wilson to agree to the cession of Fiume, but Wilson refused to budge. According to Baker, Wilson said that "the Italians had worked themselves up to the point of insanity."[206] When House proposed deferring the matter, Baker noted that "the rift between the President & Col. House seems to be widening. The Colonel compromises everything away. He has gone so far with the Italians that they are now heralding him as the great man of the conference & comparing him favorably with the President."[207] When Wilson refused to make a deal, Orlando and the rest of the Italian delegation stormed out of the peace conference on April 24.

Before they did, Wilson appealed to the Italian people. He issued a statement urging them to "exhibit to the newly liberated peoples across the Adriatic that noblest quality of greatness, magnanimity, friendly generosity, the preference of Justice over interest."[208] The ploy backfired spectacularly: all over Italy Wilson was vilified.[209] Here, surely, was a classic refutation of the long-standing Wilsonian presumption that the people of the world, if properly informed, would be immune from bellicose nationalism, since war was supposed to be the fault of the ruling elites.

Just after the Italians walked out, the Japanese confrontation began. A secret 1917 treaty with the British, French, and Italians had promised the Japanese control of the Shantung Peninsula in China, which had been a German sphere of influence.[210] Wilson opposed the move on the grounds of Chinese self-determination. For a week Wilson agonized, knowing that if the Japanese walked out, Japan might decline to join the League of Nations. So he temporized; he struggled with his conscience. He went through the sort of casuistry that John Maynard Keynes described. According to Baker's diary, Wilson "remarked, with a smile, that he had been reading over the 14 points to refresh his memory!" The following colloquy with Baker ensued:

> "The opinion of the world," I [Baker] said, "supports the Chinese claims." "I know that," he said. "Especially American public opinion," I added. "I know that, too," he replied, "but if Italy remains away & Japan goes home, what becomes of the League of Nations?"[211]

In misery, Wilson went along with the Japanese, and he was later excoriated for it.

The conference was approaching its conclusion, and plans to summon the Germans were discussed. On April 28, at a plenary session, Wilson unveiled the revised League of Nations Covenant.[212] Cooper has noted that "the president confined himself to a drab recital [of the revisions], and he made some factual slips in discussing them, which caused him to backtrack. Those slips were not like Wilson, nor were his abrupt delivery and his failure to toss out even a morsel of eloquence."[213]

Something had apparently happened.

Several decades ago, Arthur S. Link and the editors of the Wilson papers theorized that Wilson had suffered a stroke on April 28, 1919. "It became obvious to us," they wrote, "while going through the documents from late April to about mid-May 1919, that Wilson was undergoing some kind of a crisis in his health. . . . Whatever happened to Wilson seems to have occurred when he was signing letters in the morning of April 28," when his handwriting suddenly changed. "Wilson's handwriting continued to deteriorate even further. It grew increasingly awkward, became more heavily slanted to the right, was more and more heavily inked, and became almost grotesque."[214]

The specialists consulted by the editors concurred, and they theorized that Wilson's more irrational behavior—well before 1919—had all been attributable to this condition. The rigidity, the petulance: all had been the symptoms of a cerebrovascular dysfunction. Dr. Bert E. Park concluded that "a deterioration in the President's mind-set was occurring during the years 1918–1919 on the basis of hypertensive cerebrovascular disease, to the extent that, by mid-May 1919, a recognizable syndrome compatible with multi-infarct dementia had emerged."[215] Edwin A. Weinstein, already the author of articles and a major book about Wilson's neurological condition, concurred: "There is a great deal of evidence that Wilson suffered from progressive cerebral vascular disease which affected his behavior even before his incapacitating strokes of 1919."[216]

Contemporaneous evidence abounded. At the end of May, Baker noted that Wilson "looked very much worn & the left side of his face twitched sharply, drawing down the under lid of his eye. . . . Often recently he has had trouble in recalling . . . exactly what the Four did during the earlier part of the day."[217] Cooper has affirmed that Wilson increasingly displayed "forgetfulness, inarticulateness, irritability, and suspicion bordering on paranoia."[218]

The collapse that would render him an invalid was just months away. In the meantime, as Link and his colleagues suggest, "something very serious did happen to Wilson on or about April 28, 1919, so serious that, at times, it rendered him incompetent."[219]

THAT MAKES ME VERY SICK

On May 7—the anniversary of the *Lusitania* sinking—at the Trianon Palace at Versailles, the preliminary terms of the treaty were presented to a German delegation. They gradually leaked to the public as well, and a widespread reaction was one of shock. Several members of the American delegation were stunned, and members of the delegation staff resigned in protest. Ray Stannard Baker called the treaty "a terrible document: a document of retribution, . . . such a dispensation of hard justice as I never read before."[220] Herbert Hoover went out for a walk to consider the situation, and he encountered John Maynard Keynes, who shared his views on the likely economic consequences—an odd encounter in light of the opposing positions they would take on economic issues in the Great Depression.[221]

The Germans were confronted by the following terms: by signing the treaty they would formally admit that the guilt for the war was theirs alone. They would agree to pay a reparations bill that had not been worked out, but as of May 1, 1921, they would owe a preliminary sum of $5 billion. Who could say how high the eventual total might soar? They would agree to demilitarize the east bank of the Rhine to a depth of thirty miles. They would agree to the internationalization of German rivers. They would agree to give up Alsace and Lorraine and give the French sole use of the coal in the Saar valley for fifteen years. The loss of coal might severely handicap German economic recovery.

The German delegation was headed by the new foreign minister, Count Ulrich von Brockdorff-Rantzau. The count peremptorily declared that the admission of sole war guilt would constitute "a lie."[222] The Germans were given two weeks to respond to the preliminary terms of the treaty.

Liberal opinion in the United States was generally outraged. *The Nation* and *The New Republic* printed scathing editorials. The Fourteen Points seemed to have been vitiated—witness the Shantung clause and the fact that the terms of the treaty had been drafted in secret—and besides, the treaty seemed so vindictive that Wilson's goal of peace without victory appeared to have been tossed overboard. Some liberals condemned Article 10 of the League Covenant as a covert deal to uphold the status quo, in the name of maintaining the peace, against justified revolutionary movements.[223]

Keynes, who went to work right away on his book *Economic Consequences*, epitomized the views of many who regarded the treaty as a Carthaginian peace that was pregnant with the seeds of future war. Keynes was particularly outraged by the reparations policy, which failed to set a definite sum and thus opened up the prospect of open-ended German misery. "The policy of reducing Germany to servitude for a generation, of degrading the lives of millions of human beings, . . . should be abhorrent and detestable," he wrote.[224] He continued in greater detail:

There is a great difference between fixing a definite sum, which though large is within Germany's capacity to pay and yet to retain a little for herself, and fixing a sum far beyond her capacity, which is then to be reduced at the discretion of a foreign Commission acting with the object of obtaining each year the maximum which the circumstances of that year permit. The first still leaves her with some slight incentive for enterprise, energy, and hope. The latter skins her alive year by year in perpetuity, and . . . it would represent a policy which, if it were really entertained and deliberately practiced, the judgment of men would soon pronounce to be one of the most outrageous acts of a cruel victor in civilized history.[225]

For a long time, such views have created the feeling that the treaty made Nazism and the onset of World War II inevitable. In more recent years, a revisionist school of thought has challenged this view. Link, for instance, argued in the 1970s that Wilson's concessions on reparations were made "in the conviction that it would not matter much in the long run," and this conviction proved justified in Link's opinion:

[Wilson] knew that the Allies would never be able to collect the astronomical sums that they expected. . . . He also knew that passions would eventually cool. And he must have thought that the Reparations Commission, under American leadership, would gradually handle the reparations problem in a sensible and realistic way. This, in fact, is what did occur in the 1920s with the establishment of the Dawes and Young commissions of 1923–1924 and 1929. Finally, in 1932, the European powers, meeting in Lausanne, Switzerland, ended the problem altogether. They reduced Germany's obligations to some $700 million and tacitly acknowledged that this sum would never have to be paid.[226]

As for World War II, Link wrote that it was "time to stop perpetuating the myth that the Paris settlement made inevitable the rise to power of Mussolini, the Japanese militarists, and Hitler, and hence the Second World War." The Second World War was result of the global depression and the politics of appeasement on the part of the Western democracies, Link argued.[227]

More recently, David Stevenson has written that the Paris peace settlement

was more flexible than its critics acknowledged and could either have accommodated a lasting reconciliation with the new republican regime in Germany or ensured that it remained militarily harmless. The real tragedy of the interwar years was that it did neither, with the result that in 1939 France and Britain had to take up the task they had left off in 1918, and in much less favourable circumstances. The main reason for this tragedy was not that the treaty terms were impractical or unjust. Nor did the Allies lack the adequate military strength. The more fundamental problem was their disunity.[228]

These are large claims—disputable claims—and the controversies go on.

Turning to the other side of the question, there is reason to believe that the early critics of the treaty were astute. In the 1970s, for instance, economist John Kenneth Galbraith argued that the reparations terms of the treaty could be linked to the hyperinflation that beset the German economy in the 1920s. When the overall bill for reparations was established in 1921 (with the possibility of later reductions to be based upon Germany's ability to pay), it came to 132 billion prewar marks or roughly $33 billion.

Worst-case planning led policymakers and investors in Germany to brace for the worst. And "there was no particular mystery," Galbraith wrote, "as to what payment would have required." Draconian taxes and budget cuts would be in store: "Public expenditures in Germany would have had to be rigorously limited [and] taxes, especially on consumer goods, would have had to be ruthless."[229] Furthermore, worst-case thinking—the expectation that the full amount would be collected—prompted investors to "conclude that the prospect was hopeless and to begin turning in their spendable assets for goods." As the "spendable assets" got dumped, the value of money itself began to change in an inflationary direction:

> [German] domestic prices went from 14 times the 1913 level at the middle of 1921 to 35 times that level at the end of the year. The increase continued in 1922; at the end of the year they were 1,475 times higher than before the war. Then in 1923, things became serious. By November 27, 1923, domestic prices stood at 1,422,900,000,000 times the prewar level.[230]

In 1923 Germany defaulted on its reparations. The Dawes Plan was devised in response: American bankers helped the Germans to meet their obligations. But in 1930, as the Wall Street crash hit the banking sector, dependence on American banks began to backfire. When American banks withdrew loans, an economic contraction started and unemployment in Germany skyrocketed. Then the rise of Hitler began in earnest.[231]

Enough: the verdict on the Treaty of Versailles is a complicated matter that will never be settled by historians. Wilson's options for affecting the outcome of the Paris Peace Conference appeared to be gone by the time the preliminary terms were presented to the Germans on May 7, 1919.

But that was not the case at all. The process continued: the Council of Four continued to meet, the Italians had rejoined the negotiations, and the issues remained in play for weeks to come. The Germans asked for a week's extension, so their deadline became May 28. But fatigue was wearing everyone down; at one point Clemenceau and Lloyd George appeared to be headed for a physical confrontation amid accusations of lying.[232]

Wilson continued to attend the Council of Four, but he did some sightseeing and made some speeches—took some time off. On May 30, he spoke at the Suresnes Cemetery—the first cemetery for American war dead in France. And he could not help speaking in the tones of the Gettysburg Address: "The League of Nations is the covenant of governments that these men shall not have died in vain," Wilson proclaimed. If the honored dead could be buried in America, their dust would "mingle with the dust of the men who fought for the preservation of the Union. . . . Those men gave their lives to secure the freedom of a nation. These men have given theirs to secure the freedom of mankind." These American soldiers, said Wilson, came to France "to see to it that there should never be a war like this again. . . . This can be done. It must be done."[233]

In the course of this speech Wilson vented his scorn for the European politicians with whom he had been forced to deal: "You are aware, as I am aware, that the airs of an older day are beginning to stir again, that the standards of an old order are trying to assert themselves again. There is here and there an attempt to insert into the counsel of statesmen the old reckonings of selfishness and bargaining and national advantage which were the roots of this war." But "let these gentlemen not suppose that it is possible for them to accomplish this return to an order of which we are ashamed and that we are ready to forget. They cannot accomplish it."[234]

One might get the impression from these remarks that Wilson was prepared to fight to the end for his principle of peace without victory. But this was not so.

Smuts, the South African, wrote to Wilson on May 14 warning that it was "impossible for Germany to carry out the provisions of the Treaty." He asked Wilson to try to make the terms more "moderate and reasonable."[235] But Wilson replied that while the terms were "undoubtedly very severe indeed," he did not find them "unjust," because of the "offense against civilization which the German State committed."[236]

On May 29, the German delegation returned. The German foreign minister, Brockdorff-Rantzau, refused to sign the treaty, calling it a "death sentence."[237] The effect of this refusal was stunning, and it caused the British to reconsider the treaty.

After the German reply, Smuts tried again. He wrote to both Wilson and Lloyd George. To Wilson, he wrote that "we are under solemn obligation to them to make a Wilson Peace, a peace in accordance with your Fourteen Points and other Principles enunciated in 1918. To my mind there is absolutely no doubt that this is so."[238]

Lloyd George was stricken, so he called his delegation together. The result was unanimous on June 1: the British delegation decided that the terms of the treaty should be softened. Here was Wilson's chance to exert some Anglo-American leverage on Clemenceau.

He did not wish to do so. When the American delegation (and its staff) met on June 3, the general sentiment was one of scorn for the British "loss of nerve." According to one account of the meeting, Wilson said, "We ought not to be sentimental. Personally I do not want to soften the terms for Germany. I think that it is a good thing for the world and for Germany that the terms should be hard, so that Germany may know what an unjust war means." "If the Germans won't sign the treaty as we have written it," he added, "then we must renew the war."[239]

According to the transcript of the meeting, Wilson said that "the time to consider all these questions was when we were writing the treaty, and it makes me a little tired for people to come and say now that they are afraid the Germans won't sign, and their fear is based upon things that they insisted upon at the time of the writing of the treaty; that makes me very sick."[240] The only thing that mattered to Wilson was whether the terms were "unjust."[241] But what was "just" in 1919? As S. L. A. Marshall once observed, the treaty "would have fitted the Germany of 1914," not the bankrupt entity of 1919 that was "trying to make democracy work under a semisocialist government."[242]

Admirers of Wilson have puzzled over his behavior in the course of this episode—this missed opportunity (the latest in a very long series). Cooper, for instance, concedes that this episode raises "a pertinent question," since, "after all, [Lloyd George] was trying to rewrite the treaty along lines that were closer to the president's own thinking." Cooper has concluded that the reason for Wilson's lapse was "his ever-present bane—fatigue."[243]

On June 16, the treaty with some very slight revisions was returned to Brockdorff-Rantzau, and the Germans were given three more days to make up their minds. They refused to sign.[244] The German government that Brockdorff-Rantzau represented fell; the chancellor, Philipp Scheidemann, resigned. German sailors manning seized vessels of the German navy scuttled their ships instead of letting the French and the British possess them. The German president, Ebert, asked Hindenburg if there were any realistic chance of renewing hostilities. Hindenburg said that there was none.

So on June 23, a newly formed German government led by Gustav Bauer cabled its acceptance: two minor figures, Hermann Mueller and Johannes Bell, were dispatched to sign the treaty. The famous ceremony took place on June 28—the anniversary of the assassination at Sarajevo—in the Hall of Mirrors at the Palace of Versailles. As the "Big Four"—Wilson, Lloyd George, Clemenceau, and Orlando—stepped out of the palace into sunlight, crowds surged up, crying "Vive Wilson," and women tried to reach out and touch him.

In the evening, the Wilsons went to La Gare des Invalides to take the overnight train to Brest, where the *George Washington* waited. Colonel House met Wilson at the station, where he urged him to work with his critics in the Senate when he got back home. "House," Wilson said, "I have found one can never get anything in life that is worth while without fighting for it."[245] It was the very last time they ever met.[246]

Back home in America, Henry Cabot Lodge was waiting.

THE LIGHT STREAMS UPON THE PATH AHEAD

In February—during his whirlwind visit to America—Wilson was courted by civil libertarians. They besieged him with requests to grant pardons to "political prisoners." On February 24, he was petitioned as follows by John Palmer Gavit:

> There seems to me a golden opportunity, while you are here these few days, to declare immediate and unconditional amnesty for all those persons who have been convicted of expression of opinion. I can think of nothing that would so uplift and electrify the liberal forces in this and other countries. . . . I have nothing to ask for those found guilty of acts of violence. . . . What I do desire is to show our people by this signal act of Americanism, that they can speak and be heard.[247]

Wilson paid attention; he told his secretary, Tumulty, that he "would be very much obliged if you would tell me your own judgment about this suggestion of Gavit's."[248]

The moment seemed to be propitious, since Attorney General Gregory would retire in March. In his place Wilson was appointing former congressman A. Mitchell Palmer of Pennsylvania.

In addition to pardons or a general amnesty, there were calls to repeal the Espionage Act (and its addendum, the "Sedition Act"). Civil liberties advocate Dudley Field Malone wrote Wilson as follows on February 28:

> Many radical groups in the United States who supported you in 1916 are opposed to your leadership now because the Government and its agents continue to act as if we were still at war. . . . I respectfully suggest that before you sail for Europe next Wednesday . . . announce that you will urge upon the new Congress the repeal of the Espionage Law. It is no longer needed, Mr. President, and its enforcement . . . is causing profound unrest. . . . Have the new Attorney General Mitchell Palmer drop all political cases from the Court Calendars.[249]

The soon-to-be ex–attorney general was also receiving petitions. And Gregory was finally prepared to admit that some injustices had occurred. While protesting that none of the persons who were charged under the Espionage Act had been convicted for "mere expression of an opinion," he acknowledged that in some cases "because of the all-prevalent condition of intense patriotism and aroused emotions on the part of jurors . . . the severity of the sentence imposed would sometimes be out of proportion to the intrinsic character of the offense committed."[250] He was prepared to recommend commutations of sentences.

Tumulty supported the idea of a general amnesty. Instead of mere commutations of sentences, he advocated outright pardons.[251] There was insufficient time to resolve the matter in the days before Wilson left for Paris. In the meantime, a major blow against civil liberties was meted out by the Supreme Court. On March 3, the court ruled in the case of *Schenck v. United States.* The case was a challenge to the constitutionality of the Espionage Act. Writing for a unanimous court, Justice Oliver Wendell Holmes Jr. declared that in regard to free speech,

> The question in every case is whether the words used are used in such circumstances and are of such a nature as to create a clear and present danger that they will bring about the substantive evils that Congress has a right to prevent. When a nation is at war many things that might be said in time of peace are such a hindrance to its effort that their utterance will not be endured so long as men fight and that no Court could regard them as protected by any constitutional right.[252]

Holmes was heatedly denounced for taking this position, and he shifted in subsequent cases to greater scrupulousness regarding the First Amendment. In any case, the Espionage Act would never be repealed, though the Sedition Act addendum was repealed by Congress in 1920.

After the *Schenck* decision, a steady flow of petitions for the pardon of Eugene V. Debs flowed into the White House.[253] In April, the new attorney general sent to Paris a packet of pardons for Wilson to consider.[254]

Wilson at last began to come around to a decent position. On June 28, he wired Tumulty from Paris, instructing him to tell both Palmer and Burleson that it was his "earnest desire to grant complete amnesty and pardon to all American citizens in prison or under arrest on account of anything they have said in speech or in print concerning their personal opinions with regard to the activities of the Government during the period of the war. . . . I think it would be a very serious mistake to continue to detain anyone merely for the expression of opinion."[255]

During the summer, Wilson was approached by several people—Upton Sinclair and Clarence Darrow, for example—who reiterated the call to pardon Debs, but none carried greater weight with Wilson than the Reverend John Nevin Sayre, the brother-in-law of Wilson's daughter Jessie.[256] Wilson told Palmer to address the matter, but Palmer had already recommended against any pardon for Debs until the peace treaty was ratified.[257] As Cooper has written, Wilson's "failure to move" in the summer of 1919 "toward freeing Debs and other dissenters was a fateful missed opportunity."[258]

In the meantime, a series of events had erupted that would make the year one of the most hideous and nightmarish in American history, especially for civil liberties.[259]

On April 28, a bomb was discovered in the mail of Mayor Ole Hanson of Seattle. Hanson had decried the "Red Menace" in the aftermath of a general strike led by remnants of the IWW. On the following day, a bomb exploded at the home of former senator Thomas R. Hardwick in Atlanta. Senator Hardwick had been crusading for immigration restrictions to keep out "Reds." On April 30, sixteen bombs were discovered in the New York City post office. The bombs were in packages addressed to Attorney General Palmer, Postmaster General Burleson, and Justice Holmes, among others.

On May 1, in Cleveland, Ohio, a socialist leader named Charles Ruthenberg organized a May Day parade to protest the jailing of Debs. His marchers were attacked by a group of Liberty Loan workers, and massive fighting broke out. Ruthenberg's headquarters was sacked by a mob.

On the same day in New York the owners of the *New York Call*, a socialist paper, were holding a reception in their office. A crowd of soldiers and sailors broke in, destroyed the premises, and forced the throng of men, women, and children who attended the reception out into the streets, where they were clubbed. This "May Day Riot" would be memorialized in fiction by F. Scott Fitzgerald in his short story *May Day*.

On June 2, a bomb exploded at the home of Attorney General Palmer. Though Palmer and his family were unhurt—they were upstairs when the bomb exploded—the blast was powerful enough to blow the windows out of homes nearby. A mangled corpse was found amid the wreckage.

This was the beginning of the so-called Red Summer in America. The "red" referred not to leftist radicals, but rather to the blood that would be spilled in the streets. Some of the violence was racial. Civil rights leaders had attempted to capitalize on the service of blacks in uniform by launching a "New Negro Movement" that would parlay the crusade to make the world safe for democracy into a drive for black voting rights. As black soldiers returned, a white backlash assumed gigantic proportions, not only in the South—where lynchings occurred at a furious pace—but also in northern cities, including Chicago, Philadelphia, and Washington, D.C., where "race riots" occurred. These riots were in no way similar to the black inner-city protests of the 1960s. American "race riots" from the 1890s onward were essentially pogroms directed at black neighborhoods. One of the worst was the Chicago race riot of July 17 to August 3, in which thirty-eight people died and over five hundred were injured.[260]

Some of the violence stemmed from economic insecurity and the fear of losing one's job. Without the public works spending that Wilson had endorsed but then neglected, the American economy began a slow contraction—the worst came in 1920—and thousands of demobilized soldiers found themselves unemployed. As factories retooled for civilian production, more workers were thrown out of jobs. As the government's intervention in labor-management relations ceased, unions lost a great deal of power. Strikes broke out around the country as workers saw their paychecks reduced. In 1919, over two thousand strikes—involving over four million workers—occurred, the largest wave of strikes in the nation's history. And due to Wilson's decision to lift wartime price and profit controls, the cost of living rose due to temporary shortages of civilian goods. An interlude of "stagflation" ensued, though inflationary pressures would ease in the full-fledged (though brief) depression that began in 1920.

It was against this background of turbulence that Wilson returned from France to gain the ratification of the Treaty of Versailles. Americans were in an ugly mood. In the background as well was the killer flu: as the lethal epidemic of influenza hit America, some twenty million Americans came down with it during the winter of 1918–1919.

Wilson had intended to address domestic issues upon his return. When he finally convened the new Congress in May (before leaving Paris), he sent a message urging, among other things, legislation to improve the lot of organized labor. Also, he wrote, "We must see to it that our returning soldiers are assisted in every practicable way to find the places for which they are fitted in the daily work of the country."[261]

On August 8, he addressed a joint session of Congress—the very last time that he would do this—on domestic matters. He gave prominent attention to inflation, arguing that "the prices the people of this country are paying for everything that is necessary for them to use in order to live are . . . in many cases artificially and deliberately created by vicious practices which ought immediately to be checked by law."[262] In general, however, this speech was unfocused. "Wilson had great difficulty in writing" the speech, according to Link and the editors of the Wilson papers.[263] The problem, they suspected, was another small stroke that Wilson seemed to have suffered on July 19.[264] Earlier in the month, Senator Ashurst observed that Wilson displayed "a contraction in the back of his neck and a transparency of his ears; infallible indicia of a man whose vitality is gone."[265] Link and his colleagues have suggested that "the transparency of the ears was an indication of a lack of proper blood supply to the head."[266]

Wilson presented the Treaty of Versailles to the Senate on July 10. This was a big occasion, and crowds had been gathering about the Capitol for hours. Most of the Republicans in the Senate sat silent during the speech and afterward.[267]

Wilson did not go into great detail about the treaty, though he did discuss some of its provisions. Once again, he paid tribute to American troops and called them "crusaders": "As their thousands swelled into millions," he proclaimed, "their strength was seen to mean salvation."[268] But people were used to this sentiment by 1919; Wilson had said the same thing so many times before that this rhetoric had lost its effect.

He acknowledged that the treaty was far from perfect. "Old entanglements of every kind stood in the way," he reported, "and these could not always be honourably brushed aside. It was not easy to graft the new order of ideas on the old, and some of the fruits of the grafting may, I fear, for a time be bitter."[269] "The treaty," he admitted, "is not exactly what we would have written."[270]

But when he got to the League of Nations, he asserted once again the prophetic vision that everyone had come to expect:

> War had lain at the heart of every arrangement of Europe,—of every arrangement of the world,—that preceded the war. Restive peoples . . . knew that no old policy meant anything else but force, force,—always force. And they knew that it was intolerable. Every true heart in the world . . . demanded that, at whatever cost to independent action, every government that took thought for its people or for justice or for ordered freedom should lend itself to a new purpose and utterly destroy the old order of international politics. . . . A war in which they had been bled white to beat the terror that lay concealed in every Balance of Power must not end in a mere victory of arms and a new balance. The monster that had resorted to arms must be put in chains that could not be broken.[271]

The League of Nations could do this, he said, and the people of the world saw it "as the main object of the peace, as the only thing that could complete it and make it worthwhile. They saw it as the hope of the world, and the hope they did not dare to disappoint. Shall we or any other free people hesitate to accept this great duty? Dare we reject it and break the heart of the world?"[272]

He closed with another iteration of his religious vision: "The stage is set, the destiny disclosed. It has come about by no plan of our conceiving, but by the hand of God who led us into this way. We cannot turn back. We can only go forward, with lifted eyes and freshened spirit, to follow the vision. It was this that we dreamed at our birth. America shall in truth show the way. The light streams upon the path ahead, and nowhere else."[273]

This "destiny" had come about "by no plan of our conceiving," Wilson said. It was certainly true that no plan of his own conceiving—since he rarely planned much of *anything*—had led to these results. As to the providence of God, the results remained to be seen.

The response to this speech was in general terms uncharitable. Republicans were derisive, and Democratic critics of Wilson such as Senator Henry Ashurst were embarrassed. Ashurst recorded these reactions:

> Here was the President just home from Europe where he had met and matched wits with cunning men. Here were the League supporters, hungry for arguments in support of the League, whilst supporter and opponent alike, expected

explanations of obscure portions of the Covenant. . . . The League opponents
were in state of felicity; they winked, thrust tongue against cheek, and whis-
pered that Wilson had failed to "make good." Wilson's speech was as if the
head of a great Corporation, after committing his company to enormous under-
takings, when called upon to render a statement as to the meanings and extent
of the obligations he had incurred, should arise before the Board of Directors
and tonefully read Longfellow's Psalm of Life.[274]

Cooper has acknowledged that "the speech was a flop," but then he says
that this fact is rather "puzzling." But *why* should it be puzzling? Was this not
the very same Wilson—the quintessential Wilson—who foretold the coming
of "that final league of nations which must, in the providence of God, come
into the world"?[275] He had said this in 1916. Was this not the very same
Wilson who said that the First World War was nothing less than "the culminating and final war for human liberty"?[276] He had said this in 1918. Was
this not the same Wilson who had so often let religious inspirations interfere
with his thinking?

The speech in Cooper's opinion was clearly "the wrong speech at the
wrong time in the wrong place." It showed "impaired political judgment."
Cooper relates it to the overall state of Wilson's health. And there can be
little doubt that Wilson's mental condition was worsening. Cooper notes the
fact that he "skipped several words in reading from his typewritten text and
then reread the sentences." [277]

To his credit, Wilson began to meet privately with senators to line them
up behind the treaty. Between July 18 and August 1, he met with twenty-six
of them, mostly Republicans. But though most of the meetings were cordial
in tone, many senators were to some extent dissatisfied with the League
revisions that Wilson, at the cost of so much time and stress and blood
pressure, hammered into place during April.[278] And Lodge—well, Lodge
made it obvious that the humbling of Wilson would now be a long-drawn-out
affair. As chairman of the Senate Foreign Relations Committee, he packed
that body with opponents of the treaty and the League: Frank Brandegee,
Philander Knox, Hiram Johnson, William Borah. The latter two were intransigent isolationists who were known in the course of the League fight as
"irreconcilables."

Lodge began to hold hearings on the treaty in August. One of the prime
witnesses was the secretary of state, Robert Lansing. Lansing's testimony
was predictably weak, and for two reasons: (1) he had taken little part in the
negotiations since Wilson gave him little to do in Paris, and (2) he felt bound
at this point to conceal his disagreements with Wilson, at least to some
extent, for Lansing at heart was opposed to the League of Nations.[279] Wilson
was beginning to pay—really pay—for his inability from 1916 onward to
replace Lansing with a secretary of state who was more to his liking.[280] On

August 9, Lodge wrote to his daughter, asking, rhetorically, "What do you suppose Lansing did while he was in Paris?"[281]

The partisan politics concerning the League were becoming more complex. Even though Lodge's Round Robin ploy had been grounded in Republican politics, there were powerful friends of the League in the Republican Party, most prominently former president William Taft, who ran the League to Enforce Peace (LEP). An anti-League organization had been founded to oppose the LEP: the League for the Preservation of American Independence, usually known as the Independence League for short.[282] It was headed by an elderly Democrat, Henry Watterson, a newspaper publisher.

In early August, there were nine Republican senators known as "mild reservationists." They supported the League but wanted further revisions. In Cooper's opinion, they "needed political cover for siding with a Democratic president."[283] Bipartisan talks were in progress—the Democrat Key Pittman of Nevada was one of the facilitators—and on August 6 Wilson met with two LEP representatives to discuss bipartisan strategy.[284] At first he expressed a willingness to consider some reservations. But on August 11, when Lansing offered to help, Wilson's mood abruptly changed. He "would have none of it," Lansing recalled, and his face took on a "stubborn and pugnacious expression."[285] A few days later, news coverage reported that Wilson would adopt an intransigent stand.[286] Pittman wrote to Wilson in distress, informing him that "the desire on the part of a number of Democratic Senators to pass the treaty with reservations is steadily, if not rapidly, growing."[287]

Wilson was already flirting with the notion of appealing to "the people"—taking to the road as he had done when he gave his preparedness speeches back in 1916. He could not let go of the romantic Jeffersonian idea that "the people" would see the truth and rise with a powerful voice to overrule the little groups of willful men. He should have learned from his experience with Italy and Fiume that this notion was extremely risky. But he would never really learn that lesson.

Cooper has concluded that when "Wilson dashed these hopes for bipartisan cooperation. . . he was making a serious mistake," since "an accommodation with the mild reservationists could have strengthened his hand with the Senate and put pressure on other Republicans. This was another significant missed opportunity."[288]

On August 14, Lodge wrote to Wilson telling him that the members of the Foreign Relations Committee wished to meet with him personally to discuss the treaty.[289] Wilson told his ally Senator Gilbert Hitchcock—the ranking Democrat on Lodge's committee—to announce that he (the president) would meet with the committee right away. This unprecedented meeting took place at the White House on August 19.[290]

The meeting was a nightmare, even though Wilson managed to maintain his self-possession and poise (often under keen provocation) throughout.[291]

Wilson began with a statement he had written on the subject of League reservations. Since Lodge's concerns about the Monroe Doctrine and withdrawal from the League had been substantially addressed (or so Wilson thought), the major bone of contention was the meaning of Article 10, the prime collective security provision.

Wilson began with a note of dignified defiance: "Nothing, I am led to believe, stands in the way of the ratification of the treaty except certain doubts of the covenant of the league of nations, and I must frankly say that I am unable to understand why such doubts should be entertained."[292] Article 10 "is in no respect of doubtful meaning when read in the light of the covenant as a whole. The council of the league can only 'advise upon' the means by which the obligations of that great article are to be given effect to." Consequently, military participation in a League enforcement action involved "a moral, not a legal, obligation."[293]

Wilson said he had no objection to drafting further reservations so long as they were not "embodied in the instrument of ratification." If they were, he contended, "long delays would be the inevitable consequence, inasmuch as all the many governments concerned would have to accept, in effect, the language of the Senate."[294]

However logical Wilson's position might have seemed (at least to himself), it ignored the political realities. Cooper has it right when he contends that it was simply "inadequate to the occasion." He continues:

> Agreeing to reservations that were not part of the instrument of ratification was a meager sop that did not satisfy even the mild reservationists. If Wilson had been willing to work with them earlier, he might have been able to unveil an agreement on a specific set of reservations. That would have been a stupendous coup and would have sent his critics and opponents reeling. Instead, he was adding to the pile of missed opportunities.[295]

Lodge contended that a reservation within the instrument of ratification would not require any action by other signatories; only an outright amendment to the treaty would require such action, he said. Wilson admitted there was a "difference of opinion among the authorities" regarding that issue, but he had not had time to research it.[296]

Brandegee brought up the proposition that he knew was anathema to Wilson: the idea of completely severing the League Covenant from the treaty. He asked if it were not feasible to "cut the Gordian knot which ties us to the covenant"; would it not be possible for the United States to "establish peace with Germany" without consenting to the League? Wilson replied, "We could, sir; but I hope the people of the United States will never consent to it." Brandegee inserted the knife and twisted it: "There is no way by which the people can vote on it."[297]

Brandegee also taunted Wilson on the clarity of Article 10. "You think now that everything in the treaty is plain," the senator observed, whereas he personally harbored "grave doubt about many of the provisions." Wilson stolidly maintained his ground: the "meaning of the wording is plain." But Brandegee kept right on: no, he contradicted, the meaning was anything but plain. The mere fact that Wilson happened to be clear in his opinion that the language was plain was no guarantee at all against the likelihood that "there will be a dispute between nations as to what the treaty means after we have passed from the scene."[298]

Wilson was repeatedly baited (with exquisite politeness) as the meeting went on. Borah and Johnson asked Wilson whether the United States had tried to set a fixed sum for German reparations. When Wilson replied in the affirmative, his questioners asked him to explain why this view did not prevail with the British and the French. Could he explain?

> Wilson: No, Senator, I can not; and yet I dislike to decline, because it may create a misapprehension on your part. . . . I would be very glad, gentlemen, to tell you all about it, if you will leave it out of the notes. May I do that?

> Borah: I am content to have it left out of the notes upon your request; but I am afraid it would still get to the public. . . .

> Wilson: It is not an explanation discreditable to anybody, but it is an international secret.[299]

Naturally this showed up the fact that Wilson's principle of open covenants had been surrendered in Paris.

At the end of the ordeal, Wilson simpered pathetically as follows: "Will you gentlemen take luncheon with me? It will be very delightful."[300]

Events moved swiftly in the aftermath of this meeting. Pittman drafted some reservations that, as mere interpretations, would not be part of the instrument of ratification. But the mild reservationists would not accept this.[301] Then Lodge and his friends got busy. On August 23, the Senate Foreign Relations Committee removed all references to Japan in the Shantung clause of the treaty and substituted "China" instead, thus reversing the outcome at Paris.[302] If adopted by the Senate, this amendment would force the reopening of the Paris negotiations. Lodge called for a reservation of Article 10 that would be "much more drastic than anything hitherto drafted."[303]

The upshot was clear: Lodge was demanding nothing less than full participation by the U.S. Senate—and of course himself—in the making of the peace. It was time for Wilson to be taught a big lesson in regard to the cost of his high-and-mighty ways. He would be humbled—forced to back down.

Wilson (or a designated representative of his) might have to go right back to Europe and do things over again.

Wilson's response was predictable: on August 27, he announced that he would go on his speaking tour in September. Both his wife and Dr. Grayson tried to talk him out of it, but he was committed.[304]

Just before he left, he wavered a bit. He drafted his own text for four possible reservations that might be inserted in the instrument of ratification (as opposed to amendments that would change the text of the treaty), including one on Article 10 maintaining that League Council action was to be regarded "only as advice and leaves each Member State free to exercise its own judgment as to whether it is wise or practicable to act upon that advice or not."[305] Wilson called Senator Hitchcock to the White House and showed him the text, but he instructed Hitchcock to keep the matter to himself.

The politics continued to erode. Wilson's delay in pardoning dissenters cost him crucial support among progressives. Socialist John Spargo wrote to him in late August as follows: "Many thousands of Liberals and Radicals . . . fully expected . . . a general amnesty. . . . They have been grievously disappointed. . . . Their support is still needed—perhaps more than ever. It is needed to help fight for ratification of the Peace Treaty, especially the League of Nations." But "*the overwhelming majority of Liberals and Radicals who supported the war* [were in] *revolt* [against] *what they have come to regard as a reactionary and oppressive government* [original emphasis]."[306]

"Spargo is right," Wilson wrote to his attorney general.[307] He replied to Spargo, promising to "deal with the matter as early and in as liberal a spirit as possible."[308] And yet he put it off—again. He seemed to be no more capable of issuing a direct order to A. Mitchell Palmer than he had been able to issue an order to Thomas Watt Gregory—or, for that matter, to General John J. Pershing. Too often—though by no means always—he seemed to lack the simple power to *command*.

Why was this so?

PASTURES OF QUIETNESS AND PEACE

Only a month or so of relatively normal existence remained for Wilson. The speaking tour destroyed his health, both physical and mental. He would never recover from the horrible blow that was coming.

The caliber of the speeches that he gave in September varied greatly. All of the speeches were delivered from typed outlines that Wilson prepared from day to day. He gave an average of two speeches per day. Some were given in packed auditoriums and others from the rear platform of his train, whistle-stop fashion. Stenographers took down the speeches and Tumulty, who accompanied Wilson (as did Edith and Dr. Grayson), had the copies circulated to newspapers.

On the evening of September 3 the trip began. The first stop was Columbus, Ohio, on September 4. At the municipal auditorium he told four thousand people that he owed no one an explanation of the treaty except for the American people: "The only people I owe any report to are you and the other citizens of the United States."[309] This was a clear slap at the prerogatives of the Senate. He discoursed at length on the treaty and the League, and then announced that he had "not come to debate the treaty. It speaks for itself, if you will let it."[310]

Then he spoke in Indianapolis to a crowd of almost twenty thousand. Wilson's voice was already being strained, and the strain got worse as he gave forty speeches before the tour was over. This particular speech was not bad, at least as pure rhetoric goes: at the end, he told the crowd that his critics should "put up or shut up," since "a great plan is the only thing that can defeat a great plan," and "the only thing that equals an organized program is a better program. . . . If we must reject this way, then I beg that, before I am sent to ask Germany to make a new kind of peace with us, I should be given specific instructions."[311]

When the train reached St. Louis, he said that if Article 10 of the League were impaired, he would feel like telling the troops who fought in the war that all was in vain:

I would stand up before them and say, "Boys, I told you before you went across the seas that this is a war against wars, and I did my best to fulfill that promise, but I am obliged to come to you in mortification and shame and say that I have not been able to fulfill the promise. You are betrayed. You fought for something that you did not get." And the glory of the armies and navies of the United States is gone like a dream in the night, and there ensues upon it, in the suitable darkness of night, the nightmare of dread which lay upon the nations before this war came. And there will come some time, in the vengeful Providence of God, another struggle in which not a few hundred thousand fine men from America will have to die, but as many millions as are necessary to accomplish the final freedom of the peoples of the world.[312]

This was a rhetorical and a conceptual departure for Wilson, who had almost always asserted that the First World War was *itself the final war*. He began now to warn that another war might be coming.

In St. Louis, he ridiculed his critics: "I wonder if some of the gentlemen who are commenting upon this treaty ever read it! . . . It is the plainest English that you would desire. . . . There isn't a phrase of doubtful meaning in the whole document."[313]

The train worked its way through Kansas City and Des Moines (September 6), Omaha and Sioux Falls (September 8), on its way toward the West

Coast. In Kansas City Wilson flayed his opponents; they were men who "think only of some immediate advantage to themselves," and "when at last, in the annals of mankind, they are gibbeted, they will regret that the gibbet is so high."[314]

In Des Moines he made the remarkable assertion that the treaty "is drawn along the specifications laid down by the American government, and now the world stands at amaze because an authority in America hesitates whether it will endorse an American document or not."[315] What on earth could he have meant when he said this? His fatigue was getting worse. And his rhetoric at times became insipid. America, he said, was going "to those distant heights upon which will shine at last the serene light of justice, suffusing a whole world in blissful peace."[316]

As his train roared across the prairies, he was starting to experience headaches that lasted for several days. The train was uncomfortable and hot. And Wilson's work of preparing notes for every speech never ended.

Back in Washington, D.C., his enemies were active. Speeches on the Senate floor were to some degree hostile to the League by a margin of two-to-one, according to Cooper.[317] Lodge introduced four reservations and then pushed them through his committee.[318] Three covered issues that Wilson had already addressed in the revisions that were put into place back in April. But *Lodge* had not been consulted back in April, so everything would have to be revised—*new* language on withdrawing from the League and exempting the Monroe Doctrine would have to be crafted.

A major reservation on Article 10 was adopted to stipulate that military action could never occur without the consent of Congress. By September 10, Lodge presented these four reservations to the Senate, along with no less than forty-five outright amendments to the treaty.[319]

Two days later, Wilson's enemies achieved a psychological coup. In testimony before Lodge's committee, William Bullitt, who resigned in Paris to protest against the terms of the treaty, read the text of a memorandum recording a conversation he had with Robert Lansing. He quoted Lansing as saying that the League of Nations was useless, and that if the Senate understood the treaty correctly, it would be defeated.[320] This testimony made newspaper headlines all over the country.

Lansing was silent for the next five days, and then he cabled Wilson. He said that Bullitt had misquoted him in a way that was "despicable and outrageous."[321] But he confided later on that Bullitt's statement contained "enough truth" that he could "not flatly deny" the testimony of the "little traitor."[322]

Wilson's long-standing hatred of Lansing was such that he presumed the man was lying. Tumulty recalled this reaction from Wilson when he got Lansing's cable:

Were I in Washington I would at once demand his resignation. Think of it! This from a man whom I raised from the level of a subordinate to the great office of Secretary of State of the United States. My God! I did not think it was possible for Lansing to act in this way.[323]

Wilson gave speeches in St. Paul and Minneapolis (September 9) in Bismarck, North Dakota (September 10), in Billings and Helena, Montana (September 11), in Coeur d'Alene, Idaho, and Spokane, Washington (September 12), in Tacoma and Seattle (September 13), and in Portland, Oregon (September 15). The quality of these speeches varied.

In Minneapolis he used a bit of humor. He said the League would be as effective as a proverbial Irishman who walked into a saloon, saw a fight, and asked, "Is this a private fight, or can everybody get in?" In this spirit, Wilson said, "we are abolishing private fights," so that dangerous wars would henceforth be "everybody's business."[324] He said that America was free to stay out of the League, just as anyone was perfectly "free to go up to the top of this building and jump off." He said Americans would have to choose between acting like "ostriches or eagles."[325]

In St. Paul he admitted that "nothing guarantees us against human passion and error," but if the League "increases the probability of peace by, say, 10 per cent, don't you think it is worthwhile? ('Yes,' cheers) And in my judgment, it increases it about 90 per cent."[326] His subsequent speeches in the high plains tended to ramble. In Bismarck, however, he made a cogent point—a point he would repeat—in regard to the fears that America might be forced into war against its will.

Article 10, he pointed out, gave the Council of the League only power to *advise* "what steps are necessary." "Now the Council cannot give that advice without a unanimous vote," he explained. "It can't give that advice, therefore, without the affirmative vote of the United States, unless the United States is party to the controversy in question." But what about the latter case? In the latter case, the point was moot: "Suppose that somebody does attempt to grab our territory, or that we do attempt to grab somebody else's territory? Then the war is ours anyhow. So what difference does it make what advice the Council gives?" The United States would already be at war. So "unless the war is our own, we can't be dragged into a war without our own consent."[327]

In Coeur d'Alene he agreed to League reservations designed to avert "misunderstanding," so long as that was done "without changing the document."[328] In Spokane, he declared that he was "ready to fight from now until all the fight has been taken out of me by death."[329] In Portland, he declared America "the savior of the world!"[330]

Two days later he reached California. He spoke in San Francisco (September 17 and 18) and in Oakland (September 18). "Why do we debate details," he asked in Oakland, "if the heart of the thing is sound?"[331] In San Diego on September 19, he spoke before a crowd of thirty thousand in an amphitheater equipped with a microphone and loudspeakers. "One of the most important verdicts of history is now to be rendered by the great people of the United States," he said,[332] going on to state, "The heart of humanity beats in this document."[333] He concluded this speech with a warning of the consequences should his efforts fail: if America did not join the League, he said, it would mean a "death warrant" for the children who would fall in the next and "final war."[334]

After several more speeches by Wilson in Los Angeles on September 20 and in Sacramento on September 21, the presidential train swung east. As the return leg of this exhausting trip started, Wilson reached the end of his stamina. He spoke in Reno on September 22 and in Salt Lake City on September 23. Grayson noted that the trip used "every possible bit of vitality that the President had." His "constantly recurring headaches" were causing the doctor great concern.[335]

Wilson's speech at Salt Lake City went badly. The Mormon Tabernacle, where he spoke, was badly ventilated, so badly that Edith recalled feeling close to fainting in the "fetid air."[336] After Wilson read the text of Lodge's proposed reservation to Article 10, the crowd cheered. This was not, of course, what Wilson wanted, so he lost his composure: "Now wait a minute!" he yelled. "You want to applaud that? Wait until you understand the meaning of it, and if you have a knife in your hands with which you intend to cut out the heart of this Covenant, applaud."[337]

After speeches in Cheyenne (September 24) and Denver (September 25), Wilson's train reached Pueblo, Colorado. It was there that he was destined to give his final speech. And it was there that his religious streak produced one of his most striking pronouncements:

> Now that the mists of this great question have cleared away, I believe that men will see the truth, eye to eye and face to face. . . . We have accepted that truth, and we are going to be led by it, and it is going to lead us, and through us, the world, out into pastures of quietness and peace such as the world never dreamed of before.[338]

This was nothing less than revelation inspired by the book of Isaiah, with its imagery of "last days" when the penitent would "beat their swords into plowshares and spears into pruninghooks" (Isaiah 2:2 and 2:4). The desert would "blossom as the rose" (Isaiah 35:1). Isaiah was also a book of messianic prophecy: "For unto us a child is born, unto us a son is given, and the government shall be upon his shoulder" (Isaiah 9:6).

Wilson "never thought of himself as a messiah," in John Milton Cooper's opinion.[339] In an obvious sense, this was true: as an orthodox Christian,

Woodrow Wilson would never—ever—allow himself to harbor the blasphe-
mous thought that he was somehow equivalent to Christ.

But the religious heart of Wilson's sensibility cannot be denied. Historian
Richard Hofstadter once theorized that Wilson was shaped by an early child-
hood vision inspired by his clergyman father: "When young Tommy Wilson
sat in the pew and heard his father bring the Word to the people, he was
watching the model upon which his career was to be fashioned."[340] Subsequently, a psychological theory suggested that intergenerational *competition*
might also have been involved: Alexander and Juliette George argued that
Wilson's demanding father instilled feelings of inadequacy in young Wilson
that bred an urge to *outdo* the father.[341]

Other politicians displayed religiosity as great as Wilson's at the time.
Indeed, the power of Christian imagery in American political culture is obvious, now as in the past. But Wilson's brand of Christianity was heavily (and
perhaps unusually) *millennial*. When Clemenceau had sneered that Wilson
thought himself another Jesus Christ, he was only slightly off the mark:
Wilson thought of himself as a prophet like Isaiah or John the Baptist who
could *see* the course of Providence and *herald* the glory to come.

And yet, since the very beginning of the war, he had felt that *he himself*
might be destined by God to play the central role in putting an end to the
horror: he himself would find a way to create the new dispensation. So was
Cooper essentially right or was he wrong when he claimed that Wilson never
thought of himself as a messiah? It is all a matter of nuance, and informed
Wilson scholars may permissibly agree to disagree.

After he had finished his speech in Pueblo, Wilson knew that something
was wrong—very wrong—and he could *feel* it. He told Grayson that night
that his headache was so severe "that he could hardly see."[342] As the night
wore on, his condition got worse: "The muscles of his face were twitching,"
Grayson wrote, "and he was extremely nauseated."[343] The doctor told Tumulty it was time to cancel the remainder of the trip and head home.

Later on, the doctor told Ray Stannard Baker he had noticed "a curious
drag or looseness at the left side of [Wilson's] mouth—a sign of danger that
could no longer be obscured."[344] When the train paused in Wichita, Wilson
was able to discuss his condition with Grayson. He confessed that he knew
something terrible was happening to him. "I have never been in a condition
like this," he said, "and I just feel as if I am going to pieces." Then he broke
down and burst into tears.[345]

In excruciating pain, Wilson braced himself as he tried to endure the long
miles.

When the Wilsons returned to the White House, Edith recalled that her
husband "wandered like a ghost between the study at one end of the hall and
my room at the other. The awful pain in his head that drove him back and
forth was too acute to permit work."[346] On October 1, things seemed to

improve, and Wilson read aloud from the Bible. But on the morning of the next day, he said that he had no feeling at all in his left hand. He asked Edith to help him to the bathroom. Then he collapsed as Edith called Grayson. Wilson had suffered the crippling stroke that would end his career and leave the United States leaderless for over a year.

I WILL RESIGN THE PRESIDENCY

Even if Wilson had finished his speaking tour—and then conducted the follow-up tour that he had planned for New England—it might not have made much difference in the politics of ratifying the treaty. He was building up public support in some quarters, but his opponents were also on the stump. He was further alienating the worst of his senatorial enemies. Even his highly successful preparedness speeches of 1916 had not by themselves turned the tide in Washington. It was his strategies for pushing the legislation through Congress that had won the day.

He was in no condition to do that again. His preexisting emotional and mental deterioration was worsened immeasurably by the stroke. Much of his left side was paralyzed as well.

Wilson was examined by a neurologist, Dr. Francis X. Dercum, and the stroke diagnosis was confirmed. Wilson was bedridden; then he suffered an additional crisis—a prostate infection that became life threatening. Edith became the White House gatekeeper, reading and forwarding correspondence, forbidding press releases that mentioned any illness other than "nervous exhaustion," and discouraging talk of Wilson's resignation. She idolized her husband and wanted him to get better. She was determined to spare him any stress. She talked Grayson into agreeing with these policies. But a number of outside observers guessed the truth: Wilson had suffered a stroke.[347]

Lansing explored the possibility of having the vice president—a pleasant nonentity, Thomas R. Marshall (who was mostly known for his quip that what America really needed was a good five-cent cigar)—take over, pursuant to Article II, Section 1 of the Constitution, which provides, in part, that in the case of the president's "inability to discharge the powers and duties of the said office, the same shall devolve on the Vice President." A cabinet meeting was held on October 6 to discuss the situation, and Wilson was enraged when he found out about it later.

Wilson was out of action for the rest of October and early November.[348] On October 24, a caucus of Democratic senators decided to take no position on League reservations without Wilson's consent. This left Republican "mild reservationists" isolated in their fight against "irreconcilables."[349]

The Senate had already rejected the amendments to the treaty that the foreign relations committee had proposed because full-fledged amendments would require the renegotiation of the treaty. So Lodge and his allies converted the most important of these amendments into reservations. On October 24, a total of fourteen reservations were sent to the full Senate by the Foreign Relations Committee. The committee recommended that four of the Allies in the war—Britain, France, Italy, and Japan—should assent to these reservations in the Senate's ratification.[350]

On November 7, Senator Hitchcock, Wilson's point man in the League fight, was allowed by Edith to visit Wilson's sickbed. On November 13, the senator outlined in a letter to Edith a Democratic strategy for dealing with the League reservations:

> One by one we are voting on the Lodge reservations. The republicans are supporting those reservations solidly. We are offering substitutes which are being supported by the democrats with three or four exceptions. . . . It is our plan at the proper time to offer a resolution of unqualified ratification of the treaty as a substitute for Lodge's resolution of ratification with reservations. We shall be beaten on that and shall then offer interpretive reservations to take the place of the drastic reservations proposed by Lodge. We expect, of course, to be beaten also on this vote but will make the democratic record clear. Senator Lodge will thereupon present for final vote a resolution of ratification including his reservations and it is then proposed by us to cast enough votes against it to prevent it from receiving the necessary two-thirds vote for ratification.[351]

Hitchcock included the text of the substitute "interpretive" reservations he intended to offer. Importantly, they were based upon Wilson's own memorandum of early September: the memorandum he presented to Hitchcock containing his own proposals for a possible compromise. Hitchcock's proposed reservation on Article 10 read as follows:

> That the advice mentioned in Article X of the covenant of the league which the council may give to the member nations as to the employment of their naval and military forces is merely advice which each member nation is free to accept or reject according to the conscience and judgment of its then existing government and in the United States this advice can only be accepted by action of the Congress at the time in being, Congress alone under the Constitution of the United States having the power to declare war.[352]

On November 15, Hitchcock wrote again and requested a definite decision as to the strategy that he had proposed. He included the text of the Lodge reservations, which now stood at fifteen.[353] Edith wrote back (on the envelope of Hitchcock's letter) that Hitchcock's plan had Wilson's approval. Hitchcock was therefore free to propose his reservation on Article 10.

As the showdown approached, Hitchcock met with Wilson again on November 17. Wilson ruled out any acceptance of the Lodge reservations. Cooper has put it correctly in saying that Wilson's "emotions were unbalanced, and his judgment was warped."[354] According to Grayson, who sat in on the meeting, the president declared that Lodge's reservation on Article 10 "cuts the very heart out of the treaty." It was "nullification"—"impossible" to accept.[355] Wilson's mind was set on defiance and vengeance, not negotiation. He said that

> if the Republicans were bent on defeating this Treaty, I want the vote of each, Republican and Democrat, recorded, because they will have to answer to the country in the future for their acts. They must answer to the people. I am a sick man, lying in this bed, but I am going to debate this issue with these gentlemen in their respective states whenever they come up for re-election if I have breath enough in my body to carry on the fight. I shall do this even if I have to give my life to it. And I will get their political scalps.[356]

All of this might seem understandable—even reasonable—if the Lodge reservation on Article 10 would indeed have "nullified" the League. But that was not the case at all, in the opinion of Arthur S. Link, who has written that "the great mystery is why Wilson rejected the Lodge reservation to Article 10."[357] Remembering the text of Hitchcock's reservation, which Wilson had accepted, it is time now to read the actual text of the Lodge reservation as it stood on November 17. Here it is:

> The United States assumes no obligation to preserve the territorial integrity or political independence of any other country or to interfere in controversies between nations—whether members of the league or not—under the provisions of article 10, or to employ the military or naval forces of the United States under any article of the treaty for any purpose, unless in any particular case the Congress which, under the Constitution, has the sole power to declare war or authorize the employment of the military or naval forces of the United States, shall by act or joint resolution so provide.[358]

Without a doubt, the language of this Lodge reservation was grudging. The assertion that Congress has the sole power not only to declare war but also to authorize any use of military force was at odds with the prerogative of the president as commander-in-chief to commit U.S. forces to military action short of full-fledged war. But so what? The Lodge reservation was essentially the Hitchcock reservation framed in the negative. Both of them said substantially the same thing: that only Congress can declare war, as everybody knows. So Link puts the question (as a purely logical proposition) as follows: "Why, when the two sides were so close together, did Wilson reject the Lodge reservation to Article 10?"[359]

Many League supporters were ready to accept this reservation, including Taft and the LEP. Taft said that the Lodge reservation to Article 10 "does not modify the original article nearly so much as a good many people have supposed it did."[360]

If this had been the Wilson of six months earlier, haggling with Clemenceau to find language on the Saar and the Rhineland that might be minimally suitable, the results might have been very different. But this was Wilson at his worst psychologically—full of gall—Wilson in the aftermath of a brain injury exceeding anything caused by the years of inadequate blood flow that had preceded it. Link affirms that Wilson's "whole emotional balance had been shattered. He was sick, petulant, and rigid."[361]

Hitchcock drafted a letter for Wilson to sign and then released it on November 18. Wilson told the Democrats in the Senate that he hoped "the friends and supporters of the treaty will vote against the Lodge resolution of ratification."[362]

On November 19, events in the Senate played out as they had to play out. Lodge defeated the compromise reservations of Hitchcock in favor of his own. He called for a vote on the treaty with his own reservations attached. It failed to pass. Then he permitted a vote on the treaty with no reservations. This, too, failed to get the necessary two-thirds vote and was defeated.

The U.S. Senate had failed to ratify the Treaty of Versailles, and the United States was technically still at war with Germany. As for the League of Nations, the United States would not join.

In any case, as Link has observed, "the vote on November 19 was not the end of the struggle, for during the following months an overwhelming majority of the leaders of opinion in the United States refused to accept the vote as the final verdict."[363] Taft and the leaders of the LEP were distraught.

As Cooper has observed, by the end of 1919, "Democratic and Republican party leaders wanted to put the controversy behind them before the next election. . . . Senators themselves made the most important moves. . . . Now the mild reservationists took more initiative, and Democrats started talking about concessions."[364]

But Wilson would have none of it. On December 14, he issued a statement declaring he had "no compromise or concession of any kind in mind, but intends, so far as he is concerned, that the Republican leaders of the Senate shall continue to bear the undivided responsibility for the fate of the treaty."[365]

Then he proposed a ludicrous scheme—outlandish, if not grotesque—in which fifty-six senators who opposed him would resign and run for reelection. He promised that "if all of them or a majority of them are re-elected, I will resign the presidency."[366] But there was no constitutional provision for anything of this sort. Wilson was beginning to approach the brink of what might be called outright insanity.

One other horror unfolded before the year was over. With the president incapacitated, Attorney General A. Mitchell Palmer unleashed the worst assault yet upon American civil liberties. Early in November, he had Justice Department agents raid the offices of leftist organizations in twelve cities. They seized records, destroyed property, and arrested over 250 radicals. Palmer succeeded in deporting most of them to the Soviet Union. On December 21, the steamer *Buford*, soon dubbed the "Soviet Ark," left for Russia.[367]

These "Palmer Raids" would continue and intensify in 1920. The "Big Red Scare" was far from over. Wilson's record on civil liberties sank to its lowest depths as state and local officials around the country, joined by right-wing superpatriotic vigilantes, followed the lead of "the Feds." On November 11, 1919, in Centralia, Washington, members of the American Legion attacked an IWW office. Four were cut down by gunfire and killed. Ten members of the IWW were arrested. One of them, Wesley Everest, was taken from the jail by a mob.

Then he was lynched.

Chapter Seven

1920–1924

Wilson hovered at the brink of a condition that was very close to madness in 1920. In the following years, he drifted back and forth between delusional fantasies and a better perception of his own condition and that of the world.

The United States never did join the League of Nations. A separate peace with Germany would eventually be worked out by Wilson's successor, Warren G. Harding. Right up to the moment of his death in 1924, Wilson toyed with the fantasy of running for the presidency again. When he died, his many admirers around the world regarded him as a visionary—and a martyr. But his many detractors regarded him as a fool.

THE DIFFERENCE BETWEEN A NULLIFIER
AND A MILD NULLIFIER

In the first week of January 1920, Wilson committed the next in the very long series of errors that followed his stroke. He sent a letter to the Democrats, who gathered for their annual Jackson Day dinner on January 8. The letter proposed that the Democrats turn the election of 1920 into a "great and solemn referendum" on the League of Nations.[1] As Link has observed, "The Jackson Day letter spelled disaster for ratification of the treaty in any form. Wilson committed the supreme error of converting what had really not been a partisan issue, except in the parliamentary sense, into a hostage of party loyalty and politics."[2] But that didn't matter to Wilson: this was theater. He was obsessed with finding some—finding any—method of referring this issue to the voters, allowing the people to choose once and for all between virtue and vice. The *vox populi* would vindicate him, and nothing else mattered.

On January 15, some renegade Democrats in the Senate met with Lodge and other Republicans to work out a bipartisan compromise. They were close to an agreement by January 23, but then Republican irreconcilables threatened Lodge with a revolt of their own, and so he retreated.[3]

At the same time, Tumulty drafted a letter for Wilson to consider sending to Hitchcock, a letter "interpreting" many issues in regard to League reservations that might facilitate the negotiation of a settlement.[4] But the effort led nowhere. Ray Stannard Baker, in misery, expressed the frustration that was growing all over Washington: "This sick man, with such enormous power, closed in from the world, & yet acting so influentially upon events! It is plain that Grayson cannot move him: and also clear from what Mrs. Wilson says that she can do nothing either. . . . Was there ever such a situation in our history!"[5] Then Wilson came down with the flu, and the situation worsened even more.

On January 31, a veteran British participant in these events joined the fray: Lord Edward Grey, the former foreign minister who had worked so closely with House in 1915. Grey sent a letter to *The Times* stating that American participation in the League would be welcome regardless of the terms of any reservations that the Senate might choose adopt.[6] Wilson was enraged. He wrote a press release stating that if Grey had possessed the temerity to try to "influence the President and Senate" as a British ambassador in Washington, "his government would have been promptly asked to withdraw him."[7]

Lansing, however, thought Grey's letter was wonderful. Baker recorded in his diary that Lansing "hardly concealed his satisfaction in the thought that it might hasten action in the Senate, however it might offend the president."[8] Wilson got wind of what Lansing was saying, so he forced a confrontation with his long-suffering secretary of state. On February 7, he picked a fight with Lansing by sending him a letter demanding to know if he had called cabinet meetings in Wilson's absence (as Lansing had indeed done in the immediate aftermath of the stroke).[9]

Lansing was delighted to have this occasion for resigning. Early in January, he had unburdened himself as follows in a private memorandum:

> Ever since the way the President ignored me in Paris and openly humiliated me I have longed to resign. . . . I confess that I cannot fathom the President's mind. I have endured many mortifications only out of a sense of duty. . . . But I cannot subordinate my independence of thought or refrain from telling him that I do not agree with him. This mental independence he seems to resent. With an appearance of suavity he arrogantly demands that his Secretary of State shall be merely a rubber stamp, who accepts his declarations as those of a divinely-inspired superman. . . . No man, convinced of this intolerance of contrary opinion and possessed of any self-respect, could continue in office

under him longer than a sense of public duty required. I certainly cannot and do not intend to do so.[10]

After he received Wilson's letter of February 7, Lansing wrote that it "sounded like a spoiled child crying out in rage at an imaginary wrong." Wilson was suffering from "mania," Lansing wrote, and, regardless of his illness, he had always been "a tyrant." "Thank God I shall soon be a free man," he exulted.[11] Then Lansing sent Wilson an extremely dignified reply, explaining that when "deprived of your guidance and direction, it has been my constant endeavor to carry out your policies as I understood them. . . . If, however, you think that I have failed in my loyalty to you . . . I am of course ready, Mr. President, to relieve you of any embarrassment by placing my resignation in your hands."[12]

Lansing's letter was so obviously a successful gesture in one-upmanship that Grayson, Tumulty, and Edith pleaded with Wilson not to accept the resignation. Edith told him that his letter to Lansing "as written made him look small."[13] This only made Wilson more enraged, and he declared that he would "not have disloyalty about me."[14] So he compounded the embarrassment by engaging in a rapid-fire exchange of more accusatory letters with Lansing, who did resign after several more days. Then Lansing released the entire correspondence to the press on Friday the thirteenth, which he deemed a very lucky day.[15] It was indeed a lucky day for him, for, as Cooper has observed, "The Lansing affair cast [Wilson] in a terrible light," and it increased the speculation that he might not be fit to govern any longer.[16] And in Cooper's opinion, he was indeed no longer fit to govern:

> At times in the first three months of 1920 [Wilson] did seem on the verge of mental instability, if not insanity. Edith Wilson, Dr. Grayson, and Tumulty did the best they could by their lights, but they were frightened, limited people who should not have been trying to keep Wilson's presidency afloat. He should not have remained in office.[17]

The Senate was about to reopen the debate on the treaty. Late in February, Tumulty warned Wilson that the treaty with the Lodge reservations might soon be approved by a two-thirds majority comprised of many Democrats.[18] Wilson was in no mood to take such tidings philosophically; he was digging in his heels even more. On February 29, he started drafting a letter to Hitchcock, reiterating his position that the Lodge reservation on Article 10 would "nullify the treaty."[19]

The final draft of the letter, as sent and released to the press on March 8, expressed contempt for any Democrat who wavered: "I have been struck by the fact that practically every so-called reservation was in effect a nullification of the terms of the treaty itself. I hear of reservationists and mild reservationists, but I cannot understand the difference between a nullifier and a mild nullifier."[20]

Democrats, newspaper editorial writers, and public opinion began to recoil from Wilson, who appeared more and more as he truly was at that point: a peevish, irrational, obstructive, and broken old man. The final vote on the treaty took place on March 19. Twenty-one Democrats rebelled against Wilson and voted for the treaty with the Lodge reservations. But that was seven votes shy of the necessary two-thirds majority. The Treaty of Versailles, with the League Covenant grafted within it, was killed in the Senate on that spring day in 1920.

Wilson killed it.

He still entertained the ludicrous hope of being nominated for the presidency again in 1920. But the Democrats nominated Governor James Cox of Ohio. His running mate was Franklin Delano Roosevelt. Both campaigned for the League in the hope that the fight was not actually over. The Republicans, after a stalemate among front-runners Hiram Johnson, Governor Frank Lowden of Illinois, and General Leonard Wood, fell back upon the "dark horse" candidacy of a political hack, Senator Warren Harding of Ohio. Harding won in a landslide. And though Republicans in 1920 were torn between League supporters such as Taft and the irreconcilable isolationists, Harding slowly revealed that he was one of the latter. He wanted nothing to do with the League.

This is not the place in which to discuss at length the Harding presidency or the state of Europe after World War I. Germany drifted through recurrent economic crises as its Weimar Republic struggled to survive. In 1923, Adolf Hitler staged his abortive "Beer Hall Putsch" in Munich with support from General Erich Ludendorff. But the rise of Nazism in Germany was far from inevitable. So was the appeasement of the Nazi regime by the Western democracies, appeasement that rendered the League of Nations—with or without the United States—laughable. None of these developments was in and of itself inevitable. Things could and should have been different, just as events in the 1910s could have been different if a better man had occupied the White House during World War I.

Woodrow Wilson retired to a house in Washington, D.C., and tried to practice law. He continued to indulge himself in the fantasy of a presidential comeback. As the election of 1924 approached, he started work on his nomination acceptance speech and his third inaugural address. But on February 3, 1924, he passed away. He is buried in the National Cathedral in Washington, D.C.

TRAGEDY OR PATHOS?

After such knowledge, what forgiveness? Think now
History has many cunning passages, contrived corridors
And issues, deceives with whispering ambitions,
Guides us by vanities. . . .
These tears are shaken from the wrath-bearing tree.
— T. S. Eliot, "Gerontion," 1920

After such knowledge of Wilson's errors, what forgiveness? He was great in certain obvious and undeniable ways: not only in audacity but also in his widely recognized and absolutely genuine potential—unfulfilled, alas—to improve the situation of the world.

But he possessed too many fatal flaws. His capacity for competence was drowned too often in naïve and narcissistic fantasy. His ego—and we all have this worm in our apple—was out of control. Yet heroic ego, when present in a better personality (Lincoln, for example), can constitute a necessary prerequisite for genius.

Wilson was a very sick man—sick with arteriosclerosis, which, in the view of many competent observers, caused a cerebrovascular condition that warped his judgment, twisting it into ugly and irrational patterns. He was often, because of this condition, little better than a fool, and yet his basic intelligence and capacity for judgment might have made him a very wise person.

It is terrible to have to assert such things, and they are not asserted out of malice. It just seems from the record that in Wilson's case they were true— too obviously true to be denied.

He will always have his admirers. And many of these admirers are astute. Recent Wilson scholarship is rife with admiration from scholars who are also trenchant critics of Wilson when they feel that his actions deserve it. They all command respect:

- Arthur S. Link: "It is Wilson the prophet and the pivot of the twentieth century who survives in history, in the hopes and aspirations of mankind for a peaceful world, and in whatever ideals of international service that the American people still cherish. . . . The prophet of 1919–1920 was right in his vision."[21]
- Thomas J. Knock: "Woodrow Wilson's significance continues to inhere in his inclusive comprehension of the unfolding epoch, in his eloquence, and in the enduring relevance of his vision."[22]
- John Milton Cooper Jr.: "For all their decency and intelligence, Wilson's opponents were wrong. For all his flaws and missteps, Wilson was right. He should have won the League fight. His defeat did break the heart of the world."[23]

It is tempting to agree with these people. But after looking at the documented record of Wilson's misjudgments and follies during World War I, at what point does admiration for the man become an exercise in special pleading, especially in light of the fact that there were other American leaders at the time who shared Wilson's better values and might, if they had only been in power, have done a decent job of delivering viable results?

At what point in the career of a leader (or a would-be leader) does the inability to deliver good results—strategic incompetence—vitiate the effort by "giving a good cause a bad name"? Wilson's failure helped to set off a huge and cynical isolationist backlash in the 1920s. And this backlash might never have occurred if Wilson had not been in the White House—if, for example, Theodore Roosevelt had survived and returned to the presidency in 1920. But TR died as Wilson lived on to fail wretchedly—and he failed in a manner that played into the hands of the cynics. It was Wilson, with all of his absurd histrionics, who gave H. L. Mencken the basis for flaying "the Wilsonian buncombe," with its "ideational hollowness, its ludicrous strutting and bombast, its heavy dependence upon greasy and meaningless words, its frequent descents into mere sound and fury."

Mencken continued: "The Woodrovian style, at the height of the Wilson hallucination, was much praised by cornfed connoisseurs." He reduced "all the difficulties of the hour to a few sonorous and unintelligible phrases, often with theological overtones." He knew "how to arrest and enchant the boobery with words that were simply words, and nothing else. The vulgar like and respect that sort of balderdash." But "reading the speeches in cold blood offers a curious experience. It is difficult to believe that even idiots ever succumbed to . . . so vast and obvious a nonsensicality."[24]

Was this an oversimplification of Wilson's weaknesses, a cruel satirical cartoon? Of course it was. Yet Wilson himself was to blame for the fact that this cartoon had a basis in reality.

A more temperate literary caricature at the time was Frederick Lewis Allen's account of Wilson's self-hypnosis—his *supposed* self-hypnosis—as he talked himself into the supposed perfection of the Treaty of Versailles in the months that followed its creation:

> He had signed the Treaty, and must defend it. Could he admit that the negotiations at Paris had failed to act in the unselfish spirit which he had proclaimed in advance that they would show? To do this would be to admit his own failure and kill his own prestige. Having proclaimed before the Conference that the settlement would be righteous, how could he admit afterward that it had not been righteous? The drift of events had caught him in a predicament from which there must be one outlet of escape. He must go home and vow that the Conference had been a love feast . . . that the salvation of the world depended on the complete acceptance of the Treaty as the charter of a new and idyllic world order. That is what he did—and because the things he said about the

Treaty were not true, and he must have known—sometimes, at least—that they were not true . . . he fell into the pit that is digged for every idealist. . . . Having failed to embody his ideal in the fact, he distorted the fact. . . . He said that if the United States did not come to the aid of mankind by indorsing all that had been done at Paris, the heart of the world would be broken. But the only heart which was broken was his own.[25]

Was this an oversimplification? Surely. Wilson acknowledged on a number of occasions that the treaty was far from perfect. But when he talked about the *League*, he most certainly did portray the outcome at Paris in millennial terms, in extravagant terms, in terms of prophecy, as Mencken said. That being the case, he was vulnerable to Lewis's caricature. And this caricature of the naïve, credulous idealist would give a bad name to the many idealists who touted an internationalist program in the 1920s and 1930s.[26]

This was Wilson's fault. Should he be forgiven?

Wilson set back his own cause through his miserable judgment, his naïve suppositions, his petulance, his rhetorical excess—all of it.

At his worst, he was dreadfully incompetent. But not all of the idealists are. Lincoln also talked in an oracular manner: he brooded on the providence of God. He set standards that he hoped would guide events. He often kept his own counsel, like Wilson. But he dealt with the power realities, he shaped effective coalitions, he consulted with people as he tested the best-case and worst-case scenarios, and he reveled in all the fine distinctions. He was a virtuoso in the art of orchestrating power.

Wilson was not. To put it harshly, he was a disaster. He was not the right leader for America during the First World War, and he confessed this plainly to House.

But if the medical theories on Wilson are right, should he be blamed? At what point do genetic or biological or medical or psychological predispositions shade over into what we call the character flaws—arrogance, stupidity, and so on—that deserve condemnation, not pity? Should Wilson be the object of our castigation or our pity?

If pushed far enough, such questions take us down metaphysical paths that the human mind is not really structured to comprehend. The catastrophe of Wilson is an object lesson in the mysteries of the human mind.

We will leave it at that.

Notes

PREFACE

1. John Milton Cooper Jr., *Woodrow Wilson: A Biography* (New York: Alfred A. Knopf, 2009). The literature on Wilson in the fields of history and political science is vast. Two earlier studies by Cooper are important: *The Warrior and the Priest: Woodrow Wilson and Theodore Roosevelt* (Cambridge, MA: Belknap Press of Harvard University Press, 1985) and *Breaking the Heart of the World: Woodrow Wilson and the Fight for the League of Nations* (Cambridge: Cambridge University Press, 2001). Among the more important earlier works on Wilson by historians are the books by the preeminent Wilson scholar Arthur S. Link. Link wrote a five-volume series on Wilson's career before the United States entered World War I: the titles of the volumes, all published by Princeton University Press, are *Wilson: The Road to the White House* (1947), *Wilson: The New Freedom* (1956), *Wilson: The Struggle for Neutrality, 1914–1915* (1960), *Wilson: Confusions and Crises, 1915–1916* (1964), and *Wilson: Campaigns for Progressivism and Peace, 1916–1917* (1965). The wartime years and their aftermath are covered in Link's later volume, *Woodrow Wilson: Revolution, War, and Peace* (Arlington Heights, IL: Harlan Davidson, 1979). Link also edited the *Papers of Woodrow Wilson*, a majestic sixty-nine-volume series that provides the most indispensable source of primary documents to Wilson scholars. Other major scholarly studies of Wilson include Robert H. Ferrell, *Woodrow Wilson and World War I, 1917–1921* (New York: Harper & Row, 1985), Thomas J. Knock, *To End All Wars: Woodrow Wilson and the Quest for a New World Order* (Princeton: Princeton University Press, 1992), and Ronald J. Pestritto, *Woodrow Wilson and the Roots of Modern Liberalism* (Lanham, MD: Rowman & Littlefield, 2005). Thomas Fleming's *The Illusion of Victory: America in World War I* (New York: Basic Books, 2004) is a negative account of Wilson's wartime leadership that sometimes overgeneralizes. Jim Powell's *Wilson's War: How Woodrow Wilson's Great Blunder Led to Hitler, Stalin, and World War II* (New York: Crown Forum, 2005) is an oversimplified critique of Wilson's leadership in World War I from a conservative isolationist standpoint.

2. See Thomas J. Knock, "Kennan vs. Wilson," in John Milton Cooper Jr. and Charles E. Neu, eds., *The Wilson Era: Essays in Honor of Arthur S. Link* (Arlington Heights, IL: Harlan Davidson, 1991), 302–26; Hans J. Morgenthau, *Scientific Man vs. Power Politics* (Chicago and London: University of Chicago Press, 1946, Phoenix edition, 1965), 52–53; Reinhold Niebuhr, *The Irony of American History* (New York: Charles Scribner's Sons, 1952), 36; Robert E. Osgood, *Ideals and Self-Interest in American Foreign Relations* (Chicago: University of Chicago Press, 1953); John Morton Blum, *Woodrow Wilson and the Politics of Morality* (Boston: Little, Brown, 1956); Roland Stromberg, *Collective Security and American Foreign Policy:*

From the League of Nations to NATO (New York: Praeger, 1963); and Garry Wills, *Nixon Agonistes: The Crisis of the Self-Made Man* (Boston: Houghton Mifflin, 1970), 456–80, which, notwithstanding the title, contains a significant amount of critical analysis relating to Wilson's ideas and statecraft. See also Eyal J. Naveh, *Reinhold Niebuhr and Non-Utopian Liberalism* (East Sussex, UK: Sussex Academic Press, 2002).

1. 1914

1. John Keegan, *The First World War* (New York: Alfred A. Knopf, 1999), 135–36.
2. Ibid., 52.
3. Ibid., 63–65.
4. Ibid., chapter 2.
5. Ibid., 45.
6. Ibid., 47.
7. Fischer's indictment, *Grasp for World Power: The War Aims of Imperial Germany* (*Griff nach der Weltmacht: die Kriegszielpolitik des kaiserlichen Deutschland*), appeared in 1961. David Stevenson, one of the most prominent historians to analyze the causes of the First World War in recent years, wrote in 2004 that "the fundamental contention of the Versailles 'war guilt' article was justified, and the work of writers such as Albertini [Luigi Albertini, author of the three-volume *Origins of the War of 1914*] and Fischer has confirmed it. . . . At the root of everything that followed was Germany's decision to march 2 million men westwards across industrial and rural landscapes that had known decades of peace." However, Stevenson admitted that Fischer "overstated the unanimity within the Berlin elite and understated the resemblances between Germany's war aims and those of the Allies." David Stevenson, *Cataclysm: The First World War as Political Tragedy* (New York: Basic Books, 2004), 484–85, 480. Generalizations regarding the First World War, its origins, the emotions of its participants, and the culpability (or lack thereof) of the leaders involved must be delineated with care, and the historical literature is rife with disagreements. For mid-twentieth-century opinions, see Barbara W. Tuchman, *The Guns of August* (New York: Macmillan, 1962), and A. J. P. Taylor, *The First World War: An Illustrated History* (New York: Perigee Trade, 1963). For more recent opinions, see James Joll, *The Origins of the First World War* (Essex: Longman/Pearson Education, 1984), and Holger W. Herwig, ed., *The Outbreak of World War I: Causes and Responsibilities* (Boston: Houghton Mifflin, 1997). On World War I generally, see Hew Strachan, *The First World War* (London: Simon & Schuster UK, 2003), and Eric Dorn Brose, *A History of the First World War* (New York: Oxford University Press, 2010).
8. Jacques Barzun, *From Dawn to Decadence, 1500 to the Present: 500 Years of Western Cultural Life* (New York: HarperCollins, 2000, Perennial edition, 2001), 700; Roland N. Stromberg, *Redemption by War: The Intellectuals and 1914* (Lawrence: University Press of Kansas, 1982).
9. Germany's attempt to blame the incidents on Belgian "guerrillas" is illustrated by a telegram sent by the kaiser via diplomatic channels to Wilson on September 7, 1914; the text alleged that "the atrocities committed even by women and priests in this guerrilla warfare . . . were such that my generals finally were compelled to take the most drastic measures in order to punish the guilty and to frighten the blood-thirsty population." Enclosure, William Jennings Bryan to Woodrow Wilson, September 9, 1914, *Papers of Woodrow Wilson*, ed. Arthur S. Link, 69 vols. (Princeton, NJ: Princeton University Press, 1966–1993), vol. 31, 17.
10. Keegan, *The First World War*, 82–83.
11. Woodrow Wilson, speech at Independence Hall, Philadelphia, July 4, 1914, *Papers*, vol. 30, 248–55.
12. From the Diary of Colonel House, December 2, 1913, *Papers*, vol. 29, 12.
13. Wilson to House, June 16, 1914, *Papers*, vol. 30, 187. See also Wilson to House, June 22, 1914, ibid., 201, and House, diary entry for August 30, 1914, ibid., 465.
14. House to Wilson, June 3, 1914, ibid., 139–40.
15. From the Diary of Colonel House, August 30, 1914, ibid., 462.

16. Woodrow Wilson, An Appeal to the American People, August 18, 1914, ibid., 394.

17. Woodrow Wilson, Remarks at a Press Conference, August 3, 1914, ibid., 331.

18. Wilson to House, August 17, 1914, ibid., 390.

19. Wilson to House, August 18, 1914, ibid., 395.

20. Woodrow Wilson to Mary Allen Hulbert, September 6, 1914, *Papers*, vol. 31, 3–4.

21. House to Wilson, August 22, 1914, *Papers*, vol. 30, 432–33.

22. Sir Cecil Arthur Spring-Rice to Sir Edward Grey, September 3, 1914, ibid., 472. Wilson's ambassador to Great Britain, Walter Hines Page, encouraged Wilson to think in this way; he wrote Wilson that the Germans were driven by "a dream of universal conquest. Sir Edward remarked to me the other day that if this thing succeeds, Europe will become a place in which life will not be worth living. . . . I see no hope of the world's going on towards ends and ideals that we value except on the hypothesis that Prussian militarism be utterly cut out, as surgeons cut out a cancer. And the Allies will do it—must do it, to live. It would dash our Monroe doctrine to the ground. It wd. even invade the U.S. in time." Walter Hines Page to Woodrow Wilson, September 6, 1914, *Papers*, vol. 31, 7–8.

23. Arthur S. Link, *Woodrow Wilson and the Progressive Era, 1910–1917* (New York: Harper & Row, 1954, Harper Torchbooks edition, 1963), 150.

24. Stockton Axson, interview by Ray Stannard Baker, February 8, 10, 11, 1925, Ray Stannard Baker papers, box 99, cited by John Milton Cooper Jr., *Woodrow Wilson: A Biography* (New York: Alfred A. Knopf, 2009, Vintage edition, 2011), 266.

25. From the Diary of Colonel House, September 30, 1914, *Papers*, vol. 31, 109.

26. Wilson to House, August 3, 1914, *Papers*, vol. 30, 336.

27. House to Wilson, August 3, 1914, ibid., 341.

28. Wilson to House, August 4, 1914, ibid., 342.

29. Wilson to House, August 5, 1914, ibid., 345.

30. A Press Release, August 4, 1914, ibid., 342.

31. House to Wilson, August 5, 1914, ibid., 349.

32. Wilson to House, August 6, 1914, ibid., 352.

33. Link, *Woodrow Wilson and the Progressive Era*, 160–61.

34. Edward Mandell House to Arthur Zimmermann, September 5, 1914, *Papers*, vol. 30, 488–89.

35. Count Johann Heinrich von Bernstorff to the German Foreign Office, September 7, 1914, *Papers*, vol. 31, 9–10.

36. Jean Jules Jusserand to the French Foreign Ministry, September 8, 1914, ibid., 15–16.

37. William Jennings Bryan to Woodrow Wilson, September 19, 1914, ibid., 56.

38. A Memorandum by Herbert Bruce Brougham, December 14, 1914, ibid., 458–59.

39. House to Wilson, September 18, 1914, ibid., 45.

40. House to Wilson, September 19, 1914, ibid., 55.

41. From the Diary of Colonel House, September 28, 1914, ibid., 95.

42. See Keegan, *The First World War*, chapter 6.

43. House to Wilson, October 8, 1914, *Papers*, vol. 31, 137. House continued: "He asked me to read up on the diplomatic correspondence between England and his country during the years of '62 and '63 and note the reply which Lincoln's Government gave Great Britain when she proposed mediation."

44. Wilson to Mary Allen Hulbert, September 20, 1914, ibid., 59–60.

45. Link, *Woodrow Wilson and the Progressive Era*, 152–53.

46. William Jennings Bryan, statement published in the *New York Times*, August 16, 1914, quoted in Ibid., 151.

47. Ibid., 151.

48. Keegan, *The First World War*, 267.

49. See Cecil Arthur Spring-Rice to Edward Grey, October 1, 1914, *Papers*, vol. 31, 117–18.

50. *Papers*, vol. 31, 154–55; Cooper, *Woodrow Wilson*, 265–66.

51. Spring-Rice to Wilson, October 20, 1914, *Papers*, vol. 31, 194.

52. Wilson to Walter Hines Page, October 28, 1914, ibid., 242–43.

53. *New York Times*, October 16, 1914, cited in Cooper, *Woodrow Wilson*, 267.

54. This letter has been lost. See *Papers*, vol. 31, 358–59, n. 1.
55. A News Report and Statement, "Wilson Against Defense Inquiry," December 7, 1914, ibid., 409.
56. Woodrow Wilson, An Annual Message to Congress, December 8, 1914, ibid., 421–23.
57. Cooper, *Woodrow Wilson*, 268.
58. From the Diary of Colonel House, December 16, 1914, *Papers*, vol. 31, 468–69.
59. Link, *Woodrow Wilson and the Progressive Era, 1910–1917*, 161.
60. From the Diary of Colonel House, December 3, 1914, *Papers*, vol. 31, 384–85.
61. From the Diary of Colonel House, November 4, 1914, ibid., 265–66.
62. House to Wilson, December 11, 1914, ibid., 452–53.
63. Jacob Henry Schiff to Woodrow Wilson, November 19, 1914, ibid., 333–34.
64. From the Diary of Colonel House, November 25, 1914, ibid., 355.
65. Wilson to Jacob Henry Schiff, December 8, 1914, ibid., 425.

2. 1915

1. John Keegan, *The First World War* (New York: Alfred A. Knopf, 1999), 230.
2. Ibid., 265.
3. Arthur S. Link, *Woodrow Wilson and the Progressive Era, 1910–1917* (New York: Harper & Row, 1954, Harper Torchbooks edition, 1963), 156.
4. William Jennings Bryan to Woodrow Wilson, January 6, 1915, *Papers of Woodrow Wilson*, Arthur S. Link, ed., 69 vols. (Princeton, NJ: Princeton University Press, 1966–1993), vol. 32, 24.
5. Woodrow Wilson, "A Jackson Day Address in Indianapolis," January 8, 1915, ibid., 41.
6. William Gibbs McAdoo to Woodrow Wilson, August 21, 1915, *Papers*, vol. 34, 275.
7. Robert Lansing, draft of a note to Johann von Bernstorff, April 12, 1915, *Papers*, vol. 32, 511.
8. Edward Mandell House to Woodrow Wilson, January 15, 1915, ibid., 75.
9. Ibid.
10. From the Diary of Chandler Parsons Anderson, January 9, 1915, ibid., 44–50.
11. Paul Samuel Reinsch to Woodrow Wilson, January 4, 1915, ibid., 11.
12. Message from James W. Gerard, January 24, 1915, ibid., 145.
13. House to Wilson, January 29, 1915, ibid., 161.
14. From the Diary of Colonel House, January 25, 1915, ibid., 121.
15. Wilson to House, January 29, 1915, ibid., 157.
16. Stockton Axson, interviewed by Ray Stannard Baker, February 8, 10, and 11, 1925, Ray Stannard Baker Papers, Box 99, cited by John Milton Cooper Jr., *Woodrow Wilson: A Biography* (New York: Alfred A. Knopf, 2009), 276. See also Thomas J. Knock, *To End All Wars: Woodrow Wilson and the Quest for a New World Order* (Princeton, NJ: Princeton University Press, 1995), 35–36.
17. Lansing to Wilson, February 5, 1915, *Papers*, vol. 32, 193.
18. Robert Lansing, A Draft of a Note to Germany, February 6, 1915, ibid., 194–95.
19. See Keegan, *The First World War*, 265, and John Morton Blum, *Woodrow Wilson and the Politics of Morality* (Boston: Little, Brown, 1956), 99–100.
20. Associated Press report of German government announcement, enclosure from Lansing to Wilson, February 7, 1915, *Papers*, vol. 32, 196, n. 1.
21. John Morton Blum, *Woodrow Wilson and the Politics of Morality*, 100.
22. Walter Hines Page to Woodrow Wilson, February 10, 1915, *Papers*, vol. 32, 212.
23. Gerard's message was quoted by Wilson in a letter to House dated February 16, 1915, ibid., 234.
24. House to Wilson, February 15, 1915, ibid., 237.
25. House to Wilson, February 18, 1915, ibid., 253.
26. Remarks at a Press Conference, February 9, 1915, ibid., 200.
27. Woodrow Wilson, A Statement, March 4, 1915, ibid., 316.

28. House to Wilson, March 8, 1915, ibid., 340.
29. Woodrow Wilson, Outline Sketch of a Note to Great Britain, March 19, 1915, and draft of Note, March 28, 1915, ibid., 399–401 and 443–49. See also Bryan to Wilson, March 22, 1915, and Wilson's replies to Bryan, March 24 and March 25, 1915, ibid., 412–13, 424–25, 432–33.
30. See Link, *Woodrow Wilson and the Progressive Era*, 160–61. As late as January 28, 1917, the head of the German War Food Office admitted in a *New York Times* interview that the Germans had enough food. See ibid., 159. On the German offer, see William Jennings Bryan to Woodrow Wilson, February 15, 1915, *Papers*, vol. 32, 235.
31. House to Wilson, March 26, 1915, *Papers*, vol. 32, 438.
32. Lansing to Bryan, April 2, 1915, ibid., 465.
33. Bryan to Wilson, April 6, 1915, ibid., 487.
34. Bryan to Wilson, April 7, 1915, ibid., 488–90.
35. Woodrow Wilson, Remarks to the Associated Press in New York, April 20, 1915, *Papers*, vol. 33, 40.
36. House to Wilson, April 11, 1915, *Papers*, vol. 32, 504–6.
37. Wilson to Bryan, April 22, 1915, *Papers*, vol. 33, 61–62. For subsequent give-and-take among Wilson, Bryan, and Lansing on the Thrasher case, see Bryan to Wilson, April 23, 1915; Bryan to Wilson, April 27, 1915; Lansing to Bryan, April 27, 1915; Wilson to Bryan, April 28, 1915; Lansing to Bryan, May 1, 1915; Lansing to Bryan, May 3, 1915; Lansing to Bryan, May 5, 1915, ibid., 66–68, 71–72, 72–77, 85–86, 91–93, 94–95, 107–8.
38. Wilson to Bryan, April 28, 1915, ibid., 85.
39. Facsimile of German embassy notice reproduced in Link, *Woodrow Wilson and the Progressive Era*, 165.
40. In 2008 divers found the hulk of the sunken *Lustitania* full of thousands of rounds of ammunition. See Sam Greenhill, "Secret of the *Lusitania*," *Daily Mail*, December 19, 2008. On the *Lusitania* case, see Thomas A. Bailey, "The Sinking of the *Lusitania*," *American Historical Review* 41, no. 1 (October 1935), 54–73; Thomas A. Bailey and Paul B. Ryan, *The Lusitania Disaster: An Episode in Modern Warfare and Diplomacy* (New York: Free Press, 1975); and Diana Preston, Lusitania*: An Epic Tragedy* (Waterville: Thorndike Press, 2002).
41. Theodore Roosevelt, quoted in Joseph Bucklin Bishop, ed., *Theodore Roosevelt and His Time: Shown in His Own Letters* (New York: Charles Scribner's Sons, 1920), vol. 2, 376.
42. Woodrow Wilson, An Address in Philadelphia to Newly Naturalized Citizens, May 10, 1915, *Papers*, vol. 33, 147–50.
43. Woodrow Wilson to Edith Bolling Galt, May 11, 1915, ibid., 160–61.
44. Woodrow Wilson to Edith Bolling Galt, May 11, 1915, ibid., 162. Edith replied that "when I went to market this morning [I] heard this greeting from my butcher. 'Well! Mrs. Galt have you read the President's speech made in Philadelphia? He is the greatest man this country has ever produced and he is going to stay right where he is another four years.'" Ibid., 162.
45. Ibid., 149, n. 3.
46. Theodore Roosevelt to Archie Roosevelt, *The Letters of Theodore Roosevelt*, vol. 8, ed. Elting E. Morison (Cambridge, MA: Harvard University Press, 1954), 922.
47. House to Wilson, May 9, 1915, *Papers*, vol. 33, 134.
48. House to Wilson, May 11, 1915, ibid., 158–59.
49. William Howard Taft to Woodrow Wilson, May 10, 1915, ibid., 150–52.
50. Lansing to Bryan, May 10, 1915, ibid., 144–45.
51. Woodrow Wilson, A Draft of the First *Lusitania* Note, May 11, 1915, ibid., 155–58.
52. Wilson attempted to placate Bryan in two letters written and sent the same day. See Wilson to Bryan, May 11, 1915, ibid., 154–55.
53. See Bryan to Wilson, May 12, 1915, ibid., 165–67, 167–68, 173–74. Bryan instructed Lansing to prepare a note protesting the British blockade. See Lansing to Bryan, with enclosure, May 15, 1915, ibid., 206–9.
54. Wilson to Bryan, May 13, 1915, enclosure, ibid., 181–82.
55. See Cooper, *Woodrow Wilson*, 288–89. See also Wilson to Bryan, May 13, 1915, *Papers*, vol. 33, 183–84. Arthur S. Link expressed the belief that Wilson nonetheless sent this "tip" to the press verbally in a meeting with David Lawrence, at that time Washington corre-

spondent for the *New York Evening Post*. See *Papers*, vol. 33, 191–92, n. 1. Lawrence, indeed, had a meeting with the German ambassador, Bernstorff, and reported the results to Wilson. Ibid., 199–201.

56. Oswald Garrison Villard to Woodrow Wilson, May 14, 1915, ibid., 201–2.

57. Woodrow Wilson, Remarks at a Luncheon in New York, May 17, 1915, ibid., 209–12.

58. Woodrow Wilson, A Statement on the Condition of the Atlantic Fleet, May 18, 1915, ibid., 216–17. For Dewey's statement, see ibid., n. 1.

59. See House to Wilson, May 19, 1915; Wilson to House, May 20, 1915; Wilson to Bryan, May 20, 1915; House to Wilson, May 20, 1915; House to Wilson, May 21, 1915; Wilson to Bryan, May 23, 1915; House to Wilson, May 25, 1915, *Papers*, vol. 33, 222, 223, 223–24, 226–27, 229, 237–38, 253. Gerard's message was included in House's telegram to Wilson of May 25.

60. Count Johann von Bernstorff to Theobald von Bethmann-Hollweg, May 29, 1915, ibid., 279–84. For commentary on the meeting between Wilson and Bernstorff that seems to have occurred at the White House on May 28, see ibid., 280–82, n. 1.

61. Bryan to Wilson, June 3, 1915, ibid., 321–26.

62. Bryan to Wilson, June 4, 1915, and June 5, 1915, ibid., 337, 342–43.

63. Wilson to Bryan, June 5, 1915, ibid., 343.

64. Woodrow Wilson, quoted in David F. Houston, *Eight Years with Wilson's Cabinet, 1913 to 1920*, vol. 1 (Garden City, NY: Doubleday, Page, 1926), 141.

65. From the Diary of Colonel House, June 14, 1915, *Papers*, vol. 33, 397, and Edward Mandell House to Woodrow Wilson, June 16, 1915, ibid., 409.

66. Cooper, *Woodrow Wilson*, 295.

67. Robert Lansing, "The Mentality of Woodrow Wilson," November 20, 1921, Diary of Robert Lansing, Library of Congress, quoted in Link, *Woodrow Wilson and the Progressive Era*, 33, n. 18.

68. See Press Release, July 21, 1915; Woodrow Wilson to Lindley Miller Garrison, July 21, 1915; Woodrow Wilson to Josephus Daniels, July 21, 1915, *Papers*, vol. 34, 3–5.

69. Press Release, July 21, 1915, ibid., 3–4.

70. In a speech to the Gridiron Club on December 11, 1915, he spoke of the supposed "disappearance of party lines in Great Britain and France and Germany and Italy," and then asked "shall we omit to do the same handsome thing and combine all counsels in order that the nation may be served?" But a few weeks earlier, he had proclaimed to the Chamber of Commerce in Columbus, Ohio, that he was a "militant Democrat" because "I think Republicans are mistaken and Democrats right, and I hope and believe that I hold that conviction in no narrow partisan spirit." *Papers*, vol. 35, 341, 323.

71. See John Garry Clifford, *The Citizen Soldiers: The Plattsburg Training Camp Movement, 1913–1920* (Lexington: University Press of Kentucky, 1972).

72. Woodrow Wilson to Edith Bolling Galt, August 15, 1915, *Papers*, vol. 34, 209.

73. Link, *Woodrow Wilson and the Progressive Era*, 169.

74. On the second and third *Lusitania* notes, see Wilson to Lansing, July 9, 1915; House to Wilson, July 10, 1915; Wilson to Lansing, July 13, 1915; Lansing to Wilson, July 14, 1915; Lansing to Wilson, July 15, 1915; Lansing to Wilson, with enclosure, July 16, 1915; Lansing to Wilson, with enclosure, July 19, 1915; Memorandum by Lindley Miller Garrison, July 20, 1915; Lansing to Wilson, July 21, 1915; Wilson to Lansing, with enclosure, July 21, 1915; *Papers*, vol. 33, 490, 490–91, 499–500, 507–8, 509–10, 527–29, 529–32, 536–37, 544, 545–48; House to Wilson, July 25, 1915; Lansing to Wilson, July 29, 1915, *Papers*, vol. 34, 24–25, 44.

75. For correspondence on the cotton issue, see Morris Sheppard to Woodrow Wilson, July 22, 1915; House to Wilson, with enclosure, July 27, 1915; Lansing to Wilson, July 28, 1915; House to Wilson, August 2, 1915; Wilson to House, August 5, 1915; Bernstorff to Lansing, August 6, 1915; Wilson to Lansing, August 9, 1915; House to Wilson, August 14, 1915; Sir Cecil Spring-Rice to Sir Edward Grey, August 23, 1915, *Papers*, vol. 34, 13–14, 32, 34–35, 62–63, 98, 123, 142, 200, 295–96.

76. See Lansing to Wilson, August 20, 1915, ibid., 264–66.

77. Wilson to Edith Bolling Galt, August 19, 1915, ibid., 257.

78. Wilson to Edith Bolling Galt, August 22, 1915, ibid., 288.
79. Wilson to House, August 21, 1915, ibid., 271.
80. Joseph Patrick Tumulty to Woodrow Wilson, August 21, 1915, ibid., 274.
81. House to Wilson, August 22, 1915, ibid., 298–99.
82. Count Johann Heinrich von Bernstorff to Edward Mandell House, August 21, 1915, ibid., 297–98.
83. Bernstorff to Lansing, August 24, 1915, ibid., 308–9.
84. Lansing to Wilson, August 24, 1915, ibid., 318–19.
85. See ibid., 333, n. 1.
86. Link, *Woodrow Wilson and the Progressive Era*, 169.
87. Wilson to Edith Bolling Galt, August 26, 1915, *Papers*, vol. 34, 333.
88. Lansing to Wilson, August 26, 1915, ibid., 339–40.
89. House to Wilson, August 30, 1915, ibid., 368–69.
90. Wilson to House, August 31, 1915, ibid., 381–82.
91. Bernstorff to Lansing, September 1, 1915, ibid., 400.
92. House to Wilson, August 31, 1914, ibid., 388.
93. From the Diary of Colonel House, June 24, 1915, *Papers*, vol. 33, 448.
94. Edith Bolling Galt to Wilson, August 26, 1915, *Papers*, vol. 34, 338.
95. Wilson to Edith Bolling Galt, August 28, 1915, ibid., 352–53.
96. Wilson to Edith Bolling Galt, August 29, 1915, ibid., 359.
97. Josephus Daniels to Wilson, September 3, 1915, ibid., 410–11.
98. Herbert Clark Hoover to Wilson, September 3, 1915, ibid., 409–10.
99. Oswald Garrison Villard to Wilson, September 3, 1915, ibid., 411–12. Villard reiterated his anti-preparedness message on October 30. See *Papers*, vol. 35, 141–43.
100. For analysis of these recommendations, see Arthur S. Link, *Wilson: Confusions and Crises, 1915–1916* (Princeton, NJ: Princeton University Press, 1964), 15–18. See also Lindley Miller Garrison to Wilson, August 12, 1915, and Garrison to Wilson, September 17, 1915, *Papers*, vol. 34, 173–74, 482–85, and Wilson to Edith Bolling Galt, August 31, 1915, ibid., 392. In this letter Wilson confided to Edith that he was relying on the views of General Hugh Scott, the army chief of staff, in regard to preparedness planning, as opposed to Secretary of War Garrison, whom Wilson disparaged as a "solemn, conceited ass."
101. See House to Wilson, August 10, 1915, ibid., 158–59 and 159, n. 1. See also Arthur S. Link, *Wilson: The Struggle for Neutrality* (Princeton, NJ: Princeton University Press, 1960), 555–56.
102. See Link, *Woodrow Wilson and the Progressive Era*, 200, n. 1 and n. 2.
103. Wilson to House, August 4, 1915, *Papers*, vol. 34, 79.
104. Wilson to Edith Bolling Galt, August 24, 1915, ibid., 309.
105. See Memorandum from James Gerard, September 7, 1915; Bernstorff to Lansing, September 8, 1915; Lansing to Wilson, September 11, 1915; Lansing to Wilson, September 13, 1915, ibid., 439–40, 436, 449–51, 461–62.
106. Wilson to Edith Bolling Galt, September 14, 1915, ibid., 468.
107. From the Diary of Colonel House, September 22, 1915, ibid., 506.
108. On October 2 Bernstorff gave Lansing a draft letter to this effect and then Lansing and Wilson made emendations to the draft to render it more acceptable. See Bernstorff to Lansing, October 2, 1915; A Memorandum by Robert Lansing, October 5, 1915; Bernstorff to Lansing, October 5, 1915, *Papers*, vol. 35, 13, 25–26.
109. See Lansing to Wilson, November 2, 1915, November 11, 1915, November 19, 1915; Wilson to Lansing, November 21, 1915; Lansing to Wilson, December 1, 1915, ibid., 158–59, 189–90, 218–19, 233–34, 276–78.
110. Lansing to Wilson, September 12, 1915, *Papers*, vol. 34, 454–55.
111. Wilson to House, October 4, 1915, *Papers*, vol. 35, 19.
112. See Cooper, *Woodrow Wilson*, 301–2, also Woodrow Wilson, An Outline and Two Drafts of Statements, c. September 20, 1915, Edith Bolling Galt to Wilson, September 19, 1915; Wilson to Edith Bolling Galt, September 19, 1915, *Papers*, vol. 34, 496–97, 490, 491–92.
113. Cooper, *Woodrow Wilson*, 306.

114. From the Diary of Colonel House, October 8, 1915, *Papers*, vol. 35, 43–44.

115. Link, *Woodrow Wilson and the Progressive Era*, 198, n. 4.

116. In his letter to House of July 14, 1915, Grey had observed that "I see that it will naturally take very great provocation to force your people into the war. If they do go to war, I believe it is certain that the influence of the United States on the larger aspects of the final conditions of peace will prevail, and I am very doubtful whether anything short of being actually involved in the war will stir your people sufficiently to make them exercise, or enable the President to exercise, on the terms of peace all the influence that is possible. Personally, I feel that the influence of the President would be used to secure objects essential to future peace that we all desire." Then Grey made the following point, which became the basis for the House-Grey agreement that the Central Powers must, as it were, "negotiate or else": "If neutral nations and the opinion of the world generally had been sufficiently alert to say that they would side against the party that refused a Conference [in the summer of 1914 as the crisis of Serbia and Austria-Hungary developed], war might have been avoided. Peace in future years, after this war is over, seems to me to depend greatly upon whether the world takes this lesson to heart." *Papers*, vol. 34, 145–46.

117. Enclosure, Wilson to House, October 18, 1915, *Papers*, vol. 35, 81–82.

118. Enclosure, House to Wilson, November 10, 1915, ibid., 186–87.

119. Ibid. See also House Diary entry, October 15, 1915, ibid., 71, n. 3.

120. House to Wilson, November 10, 1915, ibid., 186.

121. House to Wilson, November 25, 1915, with enclosure, Grey to House, November 11, 1915, ibid., 254–56.

122. From the Diary of Colonel House, November 27, 1915, ibid., 257.

123. Ibid., November 28, 1915, 260.

124. Wilson to House, December 24, 1915, ibid., 387–88.

125. Woodrow Wilson, An Address on Preparedness to the Manhattan Club, November 4, 1915, ibid., 167–73. The details of the War Department's proposals were released to the press two days later, on November 6.

126. Link, *Woodrow Wilson and the Progressive Era*, 193.

127. Woodrow Wilson, Annual Message to Congress, December 7, 1915, *Papers*, vol. 35, 300.

128. Ibid., 306–7. Just two months earlier, in an address to the Daughters of the American Revolution, Wilson had taken a very different tack; he said on that occasion that "we ought to be very careful about some of the impressions that we are forming just now. There is too general an impression, I fear, that very large numbers of our fellow citizens, born in other lands, have not entertained with sufficient intensity and affection the American ideal. But the number of such is, I am sure, not large." Woodrow Wilson, An Address to the Daughters of the American Revolution, October 11, 1915, ibid., 50. Wilson adopted a similarly calm tone in his November 4 address to the Manhattan Club (ibid., 172). Possibly letters from House on November 19 and Lansing on the following day might have changed Wilson's mood for the worse; House wrote that "many of our people are becoming restive because of the continued exposures of the German propaganda, and it is becoming increasingly difficult to refrain from drastic action. This is a cause for much concern as it is clear that something should be done to put an end to it." Lansing wrote that "there has been an unfortunate and probably an unavoidable lack of coordination between the different Departments of the Government charged with the investigation of violations of law, growing out of the activity of agents of the belligerent Governments in this country." Ibid., 221, 227–28. On November 27, after showing House a draft of the address, Wilson confided that "he thought he had not done his best because he had not been well." House Diary entry, November 27, 1915, ibid., 257–58.

129. From the Diary of Colonel House, December 15, 1915, ibid., 356.

3. 1916

1. John Keegan, *The First World War* (New York: Alfred A. Knopf, 1999), 312–16.

2. Ibid., 298–99.

3. Ibid., 270.

4. David Stevenson, *Cataclysm: The First World War as Political Tragedy* (New York: Basic Books, 2004), 486.

5. Arthur S. Link, *Woodrow Wilson and the Progressive Era, 1910–1917* (New York: Harper & Row, 1954, Harper Torchbooks edition, 1963), 206.

6. Edward Mandell House to Woodrow Wilson, December 22, 1915, *Papers of Woodrow Wilson*, Arthur S. Link, ed., 69 vols. (Princeton, NJ: Princeton University Press, 1966–1993), vol. 35, 382.

7. Wilson to House, December 24, 1915, ibid., 387.

8. House to Wilson, January 7, 1916, ibid., 453.

9. House to Wilson, January 15, 1916, ibid., 484–86.

10. House to Wilson, February 3, 1916, *Papers*, vol. 36, 123.

11. House to Wilson, February 3, 1916, ibid., 125.

12. Robert Lansing to Woodrow Wilson, January 2, 1916, *Papers*, vol. 35, 420–22.

13. Lansing to Wilson, January 7, 1916, ibid., 448.

14. Enclosure, Lansing to Wilson, January 7, 1916, ibid., 448–49.

15. See Deborah Lake, *Smoke and Mirrors: Q-Ships Against U-Boats in the First World War* (London: History Press, 2009).

16. Lansing to Wilson, with enclosure, January 17, 1916, *Papers*, vol. 35, 495–98.

17. Wilson to Lansing, January 17, 1916, ibid., 498.

18. Enclosure, Lansing to Wilson, January 27, 1916, ibid., 531–33.

19. See Lansing to Wilson, January 7, 1916; Wilson to Lansing, January 10, 1916; Lansing to Wilson, January 11, 1916; Lansing to Wilson, January 24, 1916, ibid., 450, 457–58, 463–64, 512–13.

20. Lansing to Wilson, with enclosures, January 24, 1916, ibid., 512–15.

21. House to Wilson, January 15, 1916, ibid., 483.

22. Wilson to Lansing, January 24, 1916, ibid., 516.

23. Lansing to Wilson, with enclosure, February 4, 1916, *Papers*, vol. 36, 127–29.

24. "Conversation du Colonel House avec M. Jules Cambon," February 2, 1916, ibid., 126, n. 1.

25. House to Wilson, February 9, 1916, ibid., 147–48.

26. "Deuxième Entrevue du Colonel House," February 7, 1916, ibid., 148–50, n. 1.

27. See Link, *Woodrow Wilson and the Progressive Era*, 209, n. 27.

28. Robert Lansing, Desk Diary, January 26, 1916, Memorandum by the Secretary of State, February 9, 1916, quoted in Link, *Woodrow Wilson and the Progressive Era*, 209, n. 28.

29. Wilson to Lansing, February 16, 1916, *Papers*, vol. 36, 184.

30. Wilson to House, February 16, 1916, ibid., 185.

31. House to Wilson, February 15, 1916, ibid., 180.

32. See Link, *Woodrow Wilson and the Progressive Era*, 210.

33. Ibid. For further analysis of the tangled *modus vivendi* episode, see Patrick Devlin, *Too Proud to Fight: Woodrow Wilson's Neutrality* (New York: Oxford University Press, 1975), 410–50.

34. For accounts of this meeting, see David Lloyd George, *War Memoirs of David Lloyd George*, vol. 2 (Boston: Little, Brown, 1933–1937), 137–39, and Arthur S. Link, *Wilson: Confusions and Crises, 1915–1916* (Princeton, NJ: Princeton University Press, 1964), 131–33.

35. *Papers*, vol. 36, 180, n. 2.

36. *New York Times*, February 24, 1916, and William Joel Stone to Woodrow Wilson, February 24, 1916, *Papers*, vol. 36, 209–11.

37. Woodrow Wilson to William Joel Stone, February 24, 1916, ibid., 213–14.

38. See Link, *Woodrow Wilson and the Progressive Era*, 212–13, n. 34.

39. Much of the documentation for these German policy debates can be found in *Official German Documents Relating to the World War* (New York: Oxford University Press, 1923), vol. 2, 1116–30.

40. For an example of a German radiogram intercepted by the navy, see Lansing to Wilson, with enclosure, April 17, 1916, *Papers*, vol. 36, 498–99.

41. John Milton Cooper Jr., *Woodrow Wilson: A Biography* (New York: Alfred A. Knopf, 2009, Vintage edition, 2011), 318.

42. Lansing to Wilson, March 27, 1916, *Papers*, vol. 36, 371–73.

43. Lansing, Suggested insertion at the beginning of *Draft of Instruction to the American Ambassador—Berlin*, April 6, 1916, ibid., 449.

44. From the Diary of Colonel House, March 30, 1916, ibid., 388.

45. Woodrow Wilson, A Draft of a *Sussex* Note, April 10, 1916, ibid., 452–56.

46. From the Diary of Colonel House, April 11, 1916, ibid., 460.

47. Lansing to Wilson, with enclosure, April 12, 1916, ibid., 466–71.

48. For the final text of Wilson's *Sussex* note, see ibid., 490–96.

49. Woodrow Wilson, An Address to a Joint Session of Congress, April 19, 1916, ibid., 506–10.

50. On the German deliberations, see Link, *Wilson: Confusions and Crises, 1915–1916*, 257–79.

51. Lansing to Wilson, May 6, 1916, with enclosure, May 4, 1916, *Papers*, vol. 36, 621–26.

52. Woodrow Wilson, Draft of Answer to German Note of May 4, 1916, May 8, 1916, ibid., 650–51.

53. Woodrow Wilson, A Jefferson Day Address, April 13, 1916, ibid., 472–76.

54. Woodrow Wilson, A Welcome to the Daughters of the American Revolution, April 17, 1916, ibid., 489–90.

55. Woodrow Wilson, An Address in Washington to the League to Enforce Peace, May 27, 1916, *Papers*, vol. 37, 113–16.

56. Alfred Lord Tennyson, "Locksley Hall" (1842), in *Tennyson: Selected Poems* (London: Penguin Books, 1941), 1985 edition, 66. This vision had a power that extended far beyond the generation of Wilson. Harry Truman, for instance, was so captivated by these Tennyson lines that he copied them out for himself at the age of sixteen and then kept them close at hand for the rest of his life.

57. Lindley Miller Garrison to Woodrow Wilson, January 12, 1916, and Garrison to Wilson, January 14, 1916, *Papers*, vol. 35, 468–71, 480–81. See also Wilson to James Hay, January 18, 1916, ibid., 499–500.

58. Joseph Patrick Tumulty to Woodrow Wilson, January 17, 1916, ibid., 492–94.

59. Woodrow Wilson, An Address in New York on Preparedness, January 27, 1916, *Papers*, vol. 38, 8.

60. John Morton Blum, *Woodrow Wilson and the Politics of Morality* (Boston: Little, Brown, 1956), 110–11.

61. Wilson, An Address in New York on Preparedness, January 27, 1916, *Papers*, vol. 35, 11.

62. Ibid., 13.

63. Ibid.

64. Woodrow Wilson, After-Dinner Remarks in New York to the Motion Picture Board of Trade, January 27, 1916, ibid., 16–19.

65. Woodrow Wilson, An Address in Pittsburgh on Preparedness, January 29, 1916, ibid., 26–35.

66. Woodrow Wilson, Address in Pittsburgh to an Overflow Meeting, January 29, 1916, ibid., 35–41.

67. Woodrow Wilson, An Address in Cleveland on Preparedness, January 29, 1916, ibid., 41–48.

68. Woodrow Wilson, An Address in Chicago on Preparedness, January 31, 1916, ibid., 63–73.

69. Ibid.

70. Ibid.

71. Woodrow Wilson, An Address in Des Moines on Preparedness, February 1, 1916, ibid., 77–85.

72. Ibid.

73. Ibid.

74. Ibid.

75. Woodrow Wilson, An Address on Preparedness in Topeka, February 2, 1916, ibid., 87–96.

76. Woodrow Wilson, An Address to an Overflow Meeting in Topeka, February 2, 1916, ibid., 96–100.

77. Woodrow Wilson, An Address on Preparedness in Kansas City, February 2, 1916, ibid., 100–110.

78. Ibid.

79. Ibid.

80. Woodrow Wilson, An Address in St. Louis on Preparedness, February 3, 1916, ibid., 114–21.

81. Claude Kitchin to William Jennings Bryan, February 9, 1916, quoted in Link, *Woodrow Wilson and the Progressive Era*, 186.

82. Newton Diehl Baker to Woodrow Wilson, April 7, 1916, *Papers*, vol. 36, 431–34.

83. See News Release, July 28, 1916; Press Release, October 10, 1916; and Luncheon Address to the Chicago Press Club, October 19, 1916, *Papers*, vol. 37, 491–92 and vol. 38, 387–88, 479–80.

84. Claude Kitchin, quoted in Link, *Woodrow Wilson and the Progressive Era*, 190.

85. For coverage of the 1916 revenue and taxation debate, see ibid., 192–96.

86. Edward Mandell House to Edward Grey, May 7, 1916, *Papers*, vol. 36, 652–53.

87. House to Grey, May 11, 1916, *Papers*, vol. 37, 21.

88. Grey to House, May 12, 1916, ibid., 43–44.

89. Wilson to House, May 16, 1916, ibid., 57–58.

90. From Edward Mandell House, with enclosure, May 17, 1916, ibid., 63–64, 68, n. 1.

91. Wilson to House, May 18, 1916, ibid., 68–69.

92. Woodrow Wilson, An Address in Charlotte, North Carolina, May 20, 1916, ibid., 82.

93. A Memorandum by Ray Stannard Baker of a Conversation at the White House, May 12, 1916, ibid., 32, 35. Baker went on to write an important early biography of Wilson.

94. House to Wilson, with enclosure, May 21, 1916, ibid., 88–91.

95. Frank Lyon Polk to Woodrow Wilson, May 22, 1916, ibid., 93–94. See also Jean Jules Jusserand to Aristide Briand, June 1, 1916, and Polk to Wilson, June 6, 1916, ibid., 135, n. 2, 164. Jusserand told the French premier that "the status of Mr. House remains truly extraordinary. Especially with regard to Europe, the President does nothing without consulting him. The State Department is constantly in communication with him by a telephone service specially controlled to avoid indiscretions."

96. Walter Hines Page to House, June 2, 1916, ibid., 227.

97. House to Wilson, July 12, 1916, ibid., 411.

98. Lansing to Wilson, May 20, 1916, ibid., 83.

99. Lansing to Wilson, June 23, 1916, ibid., 287.

100. Wilson to House, July 23, 1916, *Papers*, vol. 37, 466–67.

101. To the British Foreign Office, July 26, 1916, ibid., 476–79.

102. See Link, *Woodrow Wilson and the Progressive Era*, 221, and Lansing to Wilson, with enclosure, September 18, 1916, *Papers*, vol. 38, 184–85.

103. Grey to House, August 28, 1916, ibid., 89–92.

104. Ibid.

105. A Draft of the National Democratic Platform of 1916, *Papers*, vol. 37, 196.

106. Woodrow Wilson, A Campaign Speech to Young Democrats at Shadow Lawn, September 30, 1916, *Papers*, vol. 38, 306.

107. Woodrow Wilson, A Campaign Address to Farmers at Shadow Lawn, October 21, 1916, ibid., 506–7.

108. Woodrow Wilson, An Address in Indianapolis, October 12, 1916, ibid., 418.

109. Woodrow Wilson, A Campaign Address at Shadow Lawn, October 14, 1916, ibid., 437.

110. Woodrow Wilson, A Luncheon Address to Women in Cincinnati, October 26, 1916, ibid., 531.

111. Woodrow Wilson, A Nonpartisan Address in Cincinnati, October 26, 1916, ibid., 538, 541.

112. Ibid., 542.

113. Woodrow Wilson, An Address on Abraham Lincoln, September 4, 1916, ibid., 144–45.

114. An Interview by Ida Minerva Tarbell, October 3, 1916, ibid., 326–27.

115. See Lansing to Wilson, September 21, 1916; Wilson to Lansing, September 29, 1916; Lansing to Wilson, September 30, 1916; Lansing to Wilson, October 2, 1916, ibid., 194–95, 294–95, 315, 320.

116. James Watson Gerard to Robert Lansing, September 25, 1916, ibid., 313–14.

117. See Link, *Woodrow Wilson and the Progressive Era*, 255, n. 10.

118. From the Diary of Colonel House, October 19, 1916, *Papers*, vol. 38, 493.

119. Bernstorff to House, with enclosure, October 18, 1916, ibid., 494–96.

120. Ibid., 453, n. 1.

121. House to Wilson, November 6, 1916, ibid., 619.

122. From the Diary of Colonel House, November 14, 1916, ibid., 645–46.

123. From the Diary of Colonel House, November 15, 1916, ibid., 657. See Lansing to Wilson, November 15, 1916, and Lansing to Wilson, November 21, 1916, ibid., 650–53 and *Papers*, vol. 40, 24–27.

124. House Diary, November 15, 1916, *Papers*, vol. 38, 657–58.

125. Ibid., 658.

126. Ibid.

127. Ibid.

128. Wilson to House, November 24, 1916, *Papers*, vol. 40, 62–63.

129. Woodrow Wilson, An Unpublished Prolegomenon to a Peace Note, c. November 25, 1916, ibid., 67–70.

130. Ibid., 70.

131. Woodrow Wilson, A Draft of a Peace Note, c. November 25, 1916, ibid., 70–74.

132. From the Diary of Colonel House, November 26, 1916, ibid., 84–86.

133. Woodrow Wilson to William Proctor Gould Harding, November 26, 1916, ibid., 77–78. See also Link, *Woodrow Wilson and the Progressive Era*, 258–59.

134. Diary of Robert Lansing, December 3, 1916, cited in *Papers*, vol. 40, 258.

135. Robert Lansing to Woodrow Wilson, May 25, 1916, *Papers*, vol. 37, 106–8.

136. Wilson to House, December 8, 1916, *Papers*, vol. 40, 189.

137. Lansing to Wilson, December 8, 1916, ibid., 190–91.

138. Lansing to Wilson, December 10, 1916, ibid., 209–11.

139. Lansing to Wilson, December 14, 1916, enclosure dated December 12, 1916, ibid., 230–32.

140. Drafts of Notes, December 13, 1916, Wilson to Lansing, with enclosure, December 15, 1916, ibid., 222–29, 241–43.

141. From the Diary of Colonel House, December 14, 1916, ibid., 238–39.

142. Woodrow Wilson to Pleasant Alexander Stovall, December 19, 1916, ibid., 277.

143. Link, *Woodrow Wilson and the Progressive Era*, 260, n. 23.

144. Wilson to Lansing, with enclosure, December 17, 1916; Lansing to Wilson, with enclosure, December 17, 1916, *Papers*, vol. 40, 256–59, 259–62.

145. An Appeal for a Statement of War Aims, December 18, 1916, ibid., 273–76.

146. Joseph Patrick Tumulty to Woodrow Wilson, December 21, 1916, with enclosure, ibid., 306.

147. Cooper, *Woodrow Wilson*, 366–67.

148. Wilson revealed to House that he "came very near to asking for his [Lansing's] resignation when he gave out the statement regarding the last note." House diary entry, January 11, 1917, *Papers*, vol. 40, 445.

149. Wilson to Lansing, December 21, 1916, ibid., 307. See also ibid., 307–11, n. 1, for extended commentary on this affair.

150. James Watson Gerard to Robert Lansing, with enclosure, December 26, 1916, ibid., 331.

151. Link, *Woodrow Wilson and the Progressive Era*, 260, n. 23.

4. 1917

1. John Keegan, *The First World War* (New York: Alfred A. Knopf, 1999), 332.
2. Ibid., 365.
3. Ibid., 369, 368.
4. Hew Strachan, *The First World War* (New York: Viking, 2004), 221.
5. Ibid., 352–53.
6. Ibid., 372.
7. Edward Mandell House to Woodrow Wilson, December 27, 1916, *Papers of Woodrow Wilson*, ed. Arthur S. Link, 69 vols. (Princeton, NJ: Princeton University Press, 1966–1993), vol. 40, 337.
8. Count Johann Heinrich von Bernstorff to the German Foreign Office, December 29, 1916, ibid., 364–65.
9. From the Diary of Colonel House, January 3, 1917, ibid., 403–4.
10. Ibid., 404.
11. From the Diary of Colonel House, January 4, 1917, ibid., 409.
12. From the Diary of Colonel House, January 11, 1917, tbid., 445–46.
13. William Graves Sharp to Robert Lansing, January 10, 1917, ibid., 441–42, n. 1.
14. Ibid., 439–41.
15. Bernstorff to Theobald von Bethmann-Hollweg, January 16, 1917, ibid., 505–6. "We can allow no difficulties in the old question of submarines," Bernstorff wrote. "Our enemies in this country have gone stark raving mad and try in every conceivable way to put obstacles in Wilson's path."
16. Zimmermann's message is printed in *Official German Documents relating to the World War, Translated under the supervision of the Carnegie Endowment for International Peace* (New York: Carnegie Endowment, 1923), I, 1012–13.
17. House to Wilson, January 15, 1917, *Papers*, vol. 40, 477–78.
18. House to Wilson, January 18, 1917, ibid., 516–17.
19. Wilson to House, January 19, 1917, ibid., 524.
20. Bernstorff to House, January 18, 1917, ibid., 525–26.
21. House to Wilson, January 20, 1917, ibid., 526–28.
22. Ibid.
23. Bernstorff to House, January 20, 1917, ibid., 528–29.
24. Woodrow Wilson, An Address to the Senate, January 22, 1917, ibid., 534.
25. Ibid., 534–35.
26. Ibid., 535.
27. Ibid., 536.
28. Ibid., 537–38.
29. Ibid., 539.
30. Ibid., 538.
31. House to Wilson, January 22, 1917, ibid., 539.
32. William Jennings Bryan to Wilson, January 26, 1917, *Papers*, vol. 41, 29.
33. John Milton Cooper Jr., *Woodrow Wilson: A Biography* (New York: Alfred A. Knopf, 2009), 371.
34. Ibid., 372.
35. Henry Cabot Lodge, 64th Congress, 2nd Session, *Congressional Record*, 2364–70, February 1, 1917, quoted in ibid., 372.
36. Cooper, *Woodrow Wilson*, 371.
37. Arthur S. Link, *Woodrow Wilson and the Progressive Era, 1910–1917* (New York: Harper & Row, 1954, Harper Torchbooks edition, 1963), 265–66.
38. See, for instance, William Bower Fleming to Wilson, January 24, 1917, and Cleveland Hoadley Dodge to Wilson, January 24, 1917, *Papers*, vol. 41, 5, 6–7.
39. Link, *Woodrow Wilson and the Progressive Era*, 263, n. 29. It is interesting to note that Wilson and Lansing were passing back and forth a memorandum titled "Bases of Peace" that attempted to spell out in a rudimentary way some principles to govern a nonvindictive peace.

One of these principles was "mutual guarantee against such economic warfare as would in effect constitute an effort to throttle the industrial life of a nation or shut it off from equal opportunities of trade with the rest of the world." See Lansing to Wilson, February 8, 1917, with enclosures, *Papers*, vol. 41, 160–64.

40. Arthur S. Link, *Woodrow Wilson: Revolution, War, and Peace* (Wheeling, IL: Harlan Davidson, 1979), 55.

41. Wilson to House, January 24, 1917, *Papers*, vol. 41, 3–4.

42. Link, *Woodrow Wilson and the Progressive Era*, 264, n. 31.

43. Cooper, *Woodrow Wilson*, 368–69.

44. House to Wilson, January 25, 1917, *Papers*, vol. 41, 17–18.

45. House to Wilson, January 26, 1917, ibid., 26.

46. House to Wilson, January 26, 1917, ibid., 24.

47. Bernstorff to Robert Lansing, January 31, 1917, ibid., 74–79.

48. Bernstorff to House, January 31, 1917, ibid., 80–82.

49. Bernstorff to Bethmann-Hollweg, January 27, 1917, ibid., 51–52.

50. Link, *Woodrow Wilson: Revolution, War, and Peace*, 60.

51. Robert Lansing, Memorandum on the Severance of Diplomatic Relations with Germany, February 4, 1917, *Papers*, vol. 41, 120–21.

52. David F. Houston, *Eight Years with Wilson's Cabinet, 1913 to 1920*, 229–30, quoted in Cooper, *Woodrow Wilson*, 375.

53. From the Diary of Colonel House, February 1, 1917, *Papers*, vol. 41.

54. Woodrow Wilson, An Address to a Joint Session of Congress, February 3, 1917, ibid., 108–12.

55. Hugh L. Scott to D. Hunter Scott, February 15, 1917, Papers of Hugh L. Scott, Library of Congress, cited in Link, *Woodrow Wilson and the Progressive Era*, 269, n. 43. See also Newton Diehl Baker to Wilson, with enclosure, February 3, 1917, *Papers*, vol. 41, 114. Secretary of War Newton Baker was nonetheless active in contingency war planning throughout February. See Baker to Wilson, February 7, 1917, and Baker to William Howard Taft, February 7, 1917, *Papers*, vol. 41, 151–52, 155–56.

56. Woodrow Wilson, Annual Message to Congress, December 5, 1916, *Papers*, vol. 40, 156.

57. See Baker to Wilson, February 8, 1917, *Papers*, vol. 41, 169–70.

58. Franklin K. Lane to George W. Lane, February 25, 1917, *The Letters of Franklin K. Lane, Personal and Political*, ed. Anne W. Lane and Louise H. Wall (Boston: Houghton Mifflin, 1922), 239–41.

59. Josephus Daniels, *The Wilson Era*, vol. 1 (Chapel Hill: University of North Carolina Press, 1944), 582.

60. Wilson to Samuel Seabury, January 25, 1917, *Papers*, vol. 41, 12.

61. Wilson to House, February 12, 1917, ibid., 201.

62. Cooper, *Woodrow Wilson*, 89.

63. See Walter Hines Page to Wilson, February 24, 1917, *Papers*, vol. 41, 280–82.

64. Woodrow Wilson, An Address to a Joint Session of Congress, February 26, 1917, ibid., 283–87.

65. Woodrow Wilson, A Statement, March 4, 1917, ibid., 318–20.

66. On the consultations concerning the arming of merchant ships, see Lansing to Wilson, February 22, 1917; Wilson to McAdoo, with enclosure, February 24, 1917; Lansing to Wilson, March 5, 1917; Lansing to Wilson, March 8, 1917; Diary of Josephus Daniels, March 8, 1917; Lansing to Wilson, with enclosures, March 9, 1917; Daniels to Wilson, with enclosure, March 9, 1917; Daniels to Wilson, March 11, 1917; Daniels to Lansing, March 11, 1917; Daniels memorandum, March 13, 1917, ibid., 263–66, 279–80, 341–44, 360–61, 364, 368–72, 376–79, 387, 387–88, 395–98.

67. Page to Wilson, March 5, 1917, ibid., 336–37.

68. See Lansing, A Memorandum of the Cabinet Meeting, March 20, 1917, ibid., 436–44.

69. Frank Irving Cobb, *Cobb of "The World": A Leader in Liberalism*, ed. John L. Heaton (New York: E. P. Dutton, 1924), 268–70.

70. See Cooper, *Woodrow Wilson*, 642, n. 51. See also Arthur S. Link, "That Cobb Interview," *Journal of American History* 72 (June 1985): 7–17.

71. Cooper, *Woodrow Wilson*, 389.

72. From the Diary of Colonel House, March 27, 1917, *Papers*, vol. 41, 482–83.

73. See also House to Wilson, March 29, 1917, ibid., 501.

74. Keegan, *The First World War*, 119.

75. Woodrow Wilson, An Address to a Joint Session of Congress, April 2, 1917, *Papers*, vol. 41, 519–20.

76. Ibid., 520.

77. Ibid., 521.

78. Ibid.

79. Ibid., 521–22.

80. Ibid., 522.

81. Ibid., 523.

82. Ibid., 525.

83. Ibid.

84. Ibid., 524. Both Lansing and House made this point, Lansing telling Wilson that "no League of Peace would be of value with a powerful autocracy as a member," and House had said that "the United States would not be willing to join a league of peace with an autocracy as a member." Lansing memorandum, March 20, 1917; House Diary, March 29, 1917, ibid., 440, 498. House made this suggestion as a direct contribution to the text of Wilson's war message.

85. Ibid., 526–27.

86. Cooper, *Woodrow Wilson*, 411, passim.

87. Ibid., 387.

88. Ibid., 390–91.

89. Wilson to Carter Glass, April 9, 1917, *Papers*, vol. 42, 21.

90. Blum, *Woodrow Wilson and the Politics of Morality* (Boston: Little, Brown, 1956), 136.

91. Newton Diehl Baker to Wilson, February 7, 1917, *Papers*, vol. 41, 151–52.

92. Ibid.

93. See ibid., 470, n. 1.

94. Ibid.

95. From the Diary of Thomas W. Brahany, April 10, 1917, *Papers*, vol. 42, 31.

96. Theodore Roosevelt to J. Callan O'Laughlin, April 13, 1917, *The Letters of Theodore Roosevelt*, vol. 8, ed. Elting E. Morison (Cambridge, MA: Harvard University Press, 1954), 1173.

97. Joseph Patrick Tumulty, *Woodrow Wilson as I Know Him* (Garden City, NY: Doubleday, Page, 1921), 286–88.

98. Baker to Roosevelt, April 13, 1917, *Papers*, vol. 42, 56–57. Wilson later revealed that Roosevelt himself suggested such a plan. Reminiscing in 1919, Wilson recalled that he asked Roosevelt "whether he thought he had sufficient military training to justify his being placed in command of a body of men and be responsible for their lives. Roosevelt said that he would select, and in fact, he told the President that he had already had the promise of all the best officers of the Regular Army, that they would accompany him and pilot him, in order that there would be no cause for fear because of his lack of military training. The President told Colonel Roosevelt that it was his viewpoint that this was the very reason why he ought not be sent to France inasmuch as these very officers would be badly needed to train the vast army . . . that the United States must raise." Diary of Cary P. Grayson, March 19, 1919, *Papers*, vol. 56, 87. This was nonsensical reasoning, since there was no inherent reason why the training of Roosevelt's unit would have impaired or diminished the training of other units. It bears noting that when he learned of Theodore Roosevelt's plans, young Dwight D. Eisenhower expressed the wish to serve under him.

99. John J. Leary Jr., *Talks with T.R.: From the Diaries of John J. Leary, Jr.* (Boston: Houghton Mifflin, 1920), 95–98.

100. A Memorandum by John Howard Whitehouse, April 14, 1917, *Papers*, vol. 42, 65–69.

101. House to Wilson, March 29, 1917, *Papers*, vol. 41, 501.

102. House to Wilson, April 22, 1917, *Papers*, vol. 42, 120.

103. Ibid.

104. Ibid.

105. From the Diary of Colonel House, April 26, 1917, ibid., 142–43.

106. From the Diary of Colonel House, April 28, 1917, ibid., 155–58.

107. Ibid.

108. From the Diary of Colonel House, April 30, 1917, ibid., 168–73.

109. Jean Jules Jusserand to the Foreign Ministry, May 1, 1917, ibid., 184–85.

110. Jean Jules Jusserand to the Foreign Ministry, May 3, 1917, ibid., 212–13.

111. Wilson to House, July 21, 1917, *Papers*, vol. 43, 237–38.

112. Ibid.

113. On Pershing, see Frank E. Vandiver, *Black Jack: The Life and Times of John J. Pershing* (College Station: Texas A&M University Press, 1968), especially 682–96.

114. Baker to John J. Pershing, May 26, 1917, *Papers*, vol. 42, 404–5.

115. S. L. A. Marshall, *World War I* (New York: American Heritage Press, 1964), 287–88.

116. From the Diary of Josephus Daniels, April 9, 1917, *Papers*, vol. 42, 23.

117. Woodrow Wilson, An Appeal to the American People, April 15, 1917, ibid., 71–75.

118. On the draft, see John Whiteclay Chambers II, *To Raise an Army: The Draft Comes to Modern America* (New York: Free Press, 1987), 151–67. Wilson discoursed on the principles of selective service in a letter to Guy Tresillian Helvering on April 19, 1917, *Papers*, vol. 42, 97–98.

119. See *Papers*, vol. 41, 475, n. 2.

120. From the Diary of Thomas W. Brahany, March 26, 1917, ibid., 474.

121. Creel's autobiography, *Rebel at Large: Recollections of Fifty Crowded Years* (New York: G. P. Putnam's Sons, 1947), is revealing.

122. On Baruch, see Jordan A. Schwartz, *The Speculator: Bernard M. Baruch in Washington, 1917–1965* (Chapel Hill: University of North Carolina Press, 1981).

123. John Milton Cooper Jr., *Pivotal Decades: The United States, 1900–1920* (New York: W. W. Norton, 1990), 312–13. See also Harry N. Scheiber, *The Wilson Administration and Civil Liberties, 1917–1921* (Ithaca, NY: Cornell University Press, 1960).

124. Woodrow Wilson, A Luncheon Address in Buffalo, November 1, 1916, *Papers*, vol. 38, 577.

125. Woodrow Wilson, second inaugural address, March 5, 1917, *Papers*, vol. 41, 335.

126. Woodrow Wilson, A Proclamation, April 16, 1917, *Papers*, vol. 42, 77–78.

127. Wilson to Max Eastman, September 18, 1917, *Papers*, vol. 44, 210–11. See Max Eastman, Amos Pinchot, and John Reed to Wilson, July 12, 1917, and Amos Pinchot to Wilson, July 25, 1917, *Papers*, vol. 43, 165, 276–78. Subsequently, Eastman wrote a letter to Wilson claiming that U.S. troops had tried to lynch him when he visited Fargo, North Dakota. See Eastman to Wilson, September 8, 1917, *Papers*, vol. 44, 169–72.

128. Wilson to Albert Sidney Burleson, July 13, 1917, *Papers*, vol. 43, 164.

129. Burleson to Wilson, July 16, 1917, ibid., 187–88.

130. Walter Lippmann to House, October 17, 1917, *Papers*, vol. 44, 393–94.

131. House to Wilson, October 17, 1917, ibid., 393.

132. Wilson to Burleson, October 18, 1917, ibid., 396–97.

133. See Jeannette Rankin to Wilson, August 1, 1917, *Papers*, vol. 43, 339–40. A report on the condition of the refugees from Bisbee was sent to Wilson in early September. See George Wylie Paul Hunt to Wilson, September 3, 1917, *Papers*, vol. 44, 134–39. On the findings of the "President's Mediation Commission" on the Bisbee incident, see William Bauchop Wilson and Others to Woodrow Wilson, with enclosure, November 6, 1917, ibid., 516–20.

134. From the Diary of Josephus Daniels, July 31, 1917, *Papers*, vol. 43, 336.

135. Wilson to Samuel Gompers, August 31, 1917, *Papers*, vol. 44, 101–12.

136. See Melvyn Dubofsky, *We Shall Be All: A History of the Industrial Workers of the World* (Chicago: Quadrangle, 1969), 385–92. See also Thomas Watt Gregory to Wilson, August 21, 1917, *Papers*, vol. 44, 17–18, esp. n. 2.

137. See Frederick C. Luebke, *Bonds of Loyalty: German-Americans and World War I* (DeKalb, IL: Northern Illinois University Press, 1974).

138. Cooper, *Woodrow Wilson*, 399.

139. Charles August Lindbergh to Wilson, August 27, 1917, *Papers*, vol. 44, 108–16.
140. Oswald Garrison Villard to Joseph Patrick Tumulty, September 26, 1917, ibid., 271–72.
141. Herbert David Croly to Wilson, October 19, 1917, ibid., 408–10.
142. Lillian D. Wald, Crystal Eastman, Roger Baldwin, and L. Hollingsworth Wood to Wilson, August 10, 1917, *Papers*, vol. 43, 420–24.
143. Cooper, *Pivotal Decades*, 297.
144. From the Diary of Colonel House, September 10, 1917, *Papers*, vol. 44, 185.
145. Lansing to Wilson, August 20, 1917, *Papers*, vol. 43, 523–25.
146. Wilson to House, August 16, 1917, ibid., 488–89.
147. House to Wilson, August 17, 1917, ibid., 508–9.
148. Wilson to House, with enclosure, August 23, 1917, *Papers*, vol. 44, 33–36.
149. House to Wilson, August 24, 1917, ibid., 40–41.
150. House to Wilson, September 4, 1917, ibid., 149.
151. Ibid., 57–59.
152. Wilson to House, September 2, 1917, ibid., 120–21.
153. House to Wilson, September 4, 1917, ibid., 149.
154. David Lloyd George to Wilson, September 3, 1917, ibid., 125–30.
155. See House to Wilson, September 20, 1917, ibid., 226. See also Lawrence E. Gelfand, *The Inquiry: American Preparations for Peace* (New Haven, CT: Yale University Press, 1963). For a preliminary report of the Inquiry, see Sidney Edward Mezes to Wilson, with enclosure, November 9, 1917, *Papers*, vol. 44, 549–51.
156. From the Diary of Colonel House, September 9, 1917, *Papers*, vol. 44, 176.
157. From the Diary of Colonel House, September 10, 1917, ibid., 184.
158. Wilson to House, with enclosure, September 19, 1917, ibid., 216–19.
159. Lord Reading to the War Cabinet, September 21, 1917, ibid., 237–38.
160. See Herbert Bruce Brougham to Wilson, September 28, 1917; Wilson to Brougham, September 29, 1917; David Lawrence to Wilson, October 3, 1917, ibid., 275–76, 279, 299–301.
161. Wilson to Lawrence, October 5, 1917, ibid., 309.
162. On events leading up to the meeting of the Council, see Lord Reading to the War Cabinet and Others, October 12, 1917; Diary of Colonel House, October 13, 1917; House Diary, October 22, 1917, October 23, 1917, October 24, 1917; and House to Wilson, with enclosures, October 27, 1917, ibid., 369–70, 378–82, 426–27, 433, 437–39, 454–57.
163. House to Wilson, November 11, 1917, *Papers*, vol. 45, 3–4.
164. Pershing to Baker, November 13, 1917, ibid., 107–11.
165. House to Wilson, November 30, 1917, ibid., 166. For other reports on House's role in London and Paris in 1917, see House to Wilson, November 14, November 28, November 29, ibid., 47, 151, 156–57.
166. From the Diary of Colonel House, December 18, 1917, ibid., 323–27.
167. Wilson to Asbury Francis Lever, July 23, 1917, *Papers*, vol. 43, 245.
168. Cooper, *Woodrow Wilson*, 407.
169. Woodrow Wilson, A Proclamation, December 26, 1917, *Papers*, vol. 45, 358–61.
170. Woodrow Wilson, An Annual Message to Congress, December 4, 1917, ibid., 195.

5. 1918

1. John Keegan, *The First World War* (New York: Alfred A. Knopf, 1999), 382.
2. Ibid., 342, 382.
3. Ibid., 385–86.
4. Ibid., 393–94.
5. From the Diary of Colonel House, January 4, 1918, *Papers of Woodrow Wilson*, ed. Arthur S. Link, 69 vols. (Princeton, NJ: Princeton University Press, 1966–1993), vol. 45, 458–59.
6. From the Diary of Colonel House, January 9, 1918, ibid., 550.

7. Ibid., 551.

8. Ibid., n. 1.

9. Mezes, a brother-in-law of House, was president of the City College of New York. Miller was a New York lawyer with expertise in treaties.

10. A Memorandum by Sidney Edward Mezes, David Hunter Miller, and Walter Lippmann, "The Present Situation: The War Aims and Peace Terms It Suggests," *Papers*, vol. 45, 472.

11. Ibid., 473.

12. House Diary, January 9, 1918, *Papers*, vol. 45, 551.

13. Ibid., 551.

14. Ibid., 553–54.

15. Ibid., 554–55.

16. Ibid., 556. Lloyd George's speech had been delivered on January 5 before the Trades Union Conference in London.

17. Ibid., 556–57.

18. Raymond Poincaré to Wilson, December 28, 1917, ibid., 372–73.

19. Newton Diehl Baker to Wilson, with enclosures, January 3, 1918, ibid., 438–40.

20. Wilson to Poincaré, January 8, 1918, ibid., 539–40.

21. Woodrow Wilson, An Address to a Joint Session of Congress, January 8, 1918, ibid., 534–35.

22. Ibid., 535.

23. Ibid., 536–38.

24. Ibid., 539.

25. John Milton Cooper Jr., *Woodrow Wilson: A Biography* (New York: Alfred A. Knopf, 2009, Vintage edition, 2011), 424.

26. Aristotle, *Nichomachean Ethics*, Book 4, chapter 7, in *The Ethics of Aristotle*, trans. J. A. K. Thomson (Baltimore: Penguin Classics, 1953), 132.

27. Lansing to Wilson, January 25, 1918, *Papers*, vol. 46, 96–97.

28. Wilson to House, with enclosure (telegram from Thomas Nelson Page), January 31, 1918, ibid., 178. Germany and Austria-Hungary both responded to the Fourteen Points speech; their responses were delivered in speeches by the German chancellor, Hertling, and the Austrian foreign minister, Count Ottokar von Czernin. Wilson in turn responded to the Germans and Austrians in another speech to Congress on February 11, 1918, a speech in which he dismissed the German position but reacted to the Austrians in a guardedly positive manner. Wilson would make a number of attempts to drive a wedge between Germany and Austria-Hungary. Woodrow Wilson, An Address to a Joint Session of Congress, February 11, 1918, ibid., 318–24. The Austro-Hungarian emperor sent a peace feeler to Wilson via the king of Spain in late February, but Lansing advised Wilson to use the overture to redouble the pressure on Germany. House regarded the situation as "one of the most delicate and difficult situations with which [Wilson] has yet had to deal." Wilson played for time by asking the king of Spain to probe the Austrian positions much further. See Lansing to Wilson, February 23, 1918; Alfonso XIII to Wilson, February 25, 1918; House Diary, February 26, 1918; draft telegram to Alfonso III, February 28, 1918; Prince Fürstenberg to Count Ottokar von Czernin, March 5, 1918; Czernin to Fürstenberg, March 23, 1918, ibid., 424, 440–42, 467, 486–87, 551–53; vol. 47, 124–26.

29. Thomas J. Knock, *To End All Wars: Woodrow Wilson and the Quest for a New World Order* (Princeton, NJ: Princeton University Press, 1992), 145–46.

30. Woodrow Wilson, Press Release, January 21, 1918, *Papers*, vol. 46, 55–56.

31. See Seward W. Livermore, *Politics Is Adjourned: Woodrow Wilson and the War Congress, 1916–1918* (Middletown, CT: Wesleyan University Press, 1966), 65–104. See also "A News Report: Wilson Summons Senators to Beat War Cabinet Bill," February 1, 1918, *Papers*, vol. 46, 204–5.

32. See Robert D. Cuff, "We Band of Brothers—Woodrow Wilson's War Managers," *Canadian Review of American Studies* 5 (Fall 1974): 135–38, and House Diary, February 25, 1918, *Papers*, vol. 46, 444–45. The members of the War Cabinet were Newton Baker, Josephus Daniels, Bernard Baruch, Harry Garfield, Herbert Hoover, William G. McAdoo, and Edward Hurley.

33. See Robert D. Cuff, *The War Industries Board: Business-Government Relations during World War I* (Baltimore: Johns Hopkins University Press, 1973). For an account of a meeting between Baker and Baruch on reorganizing the WIB, see Baker to Wilson, with enclosure, February 2, 1918, *Papers*, vol. 46, 215–17. See also Wilson to Baruch, March 4, 1918, ibid., 520–22.

34. See Witold S. Sworakowski, "Herbert Hoover, Launching the Food Administration," in Lawrence E. Gelfand, ed., *Herbert Hoover: The Great War and its Aftermath, 1914–1923* (Iowa City: University of Iowa Press, 1979), 40–60.

35. McAdoo and Hoover did not get along; the latter criticized the performance of the former in ways that prompted complaints to Wilson. See McAdoo to Wilson, February 23, 1918, *Papers*, vol. 46, 424–26.

36. See Valerie Jean Conner, *The National War Labor Board: Stability, Social Justice, and the Voluntary State in World War I* (Chapel Hill: University of North Carolina Press, 1983). The genesis of this board may be found in part in the work of William Bauchop Wilson, secretary of labor, who, in the course of his work as chair of the President's Mediation Commission, summoned a War Labor Conference Board including representatives of American manufacturers and representatives of labor (the latter selected by Samuel Gompers). Taft was recruited for service on this board by the manufacturers' representatives. See William Bauchop Wilson to Woodrow Wilson, March 8, 1918, *Papers*, vol. 46, 578, and William Bauchop Wilson to Woodrow Wilson, April 4, 1918, with enclosures, and April 6, 1918, *Papers*, vol. 47, 247–53, 272–74. See also Woodrow Wilson, A Proclamation, April 8, 1918, ibid., 282–84.

37. House Diary, January 27, 1918, *Papers*, vol. 46, 114–17.

38. William Howard Taft, A Memorandum, c. March 29, 1918, *Papers*, vol. 47, 200.

39. Ibid.

40. Ibid., 200–201.

41. Wilson to House, March 22, 1918, ibid., 105–6.

42. Wilson to House, March 20, 1918, ibid., 85–86. See also Ruhl J. Bartlett, *The League to Enforce Peace* (Chapel Hill: University of North Carolina Press, 1944).

43. James Viscount Bryce to Theodore Marburg, undated, received May 1, 1918, *Papers*, vol. 47, 507.

44. George Davis Herron to Wilson, May 31, 1918, *Papers*, vol. 48, 210–17.

45. Baker to Wilson, with enclosure, January 16, 1918, *Papers*, vol. 46, 8–11. See also Pershing to Henry Pinckney McCain, January 31, 1918, ibid., 196–98.

46. S. L. A. Marshall, *World War I* (New York: American Heritage Press, 1964), 345. In the course of this give-and-take, Wilson fretted and equivocated. Sir William Wiseman reported to Balfour on a meeting with Wilson on February 3 in which the president stated that "an American army should be created under American leaders and American flag in order that the people of America shall solidly and cheerfully support the war," and that "the placing of American troops in small bodies under foreign leaders would be taken as proof that the recent criticism of the War Department was justified and that the American military machine had broken down." Nonetheless, Wilson proclaimed he was willing to "risk any adverse public criticism in order to win the war and he has told Pershing that he may put American troops by battalions in the British line, or use them in any way which in his, Pershing's, judgment may be taken by the necessities of the military situation." Wiseman to Balfour, February 3, 1918, *Papers*, vol. 46, 231–32. See also Wiseman to Sir Eric Drummond and Balfour, February 4, 1918; Baker to Wilson, with enclosure from Pershing, February 13, 1918; Lord Reading to Foreign Office, February 15, 1918, ibid., 247–50, 337–38, 353–57, as well as W. B. Fowler, *British-American Relations, 1917–1918: The Role of Sir William Wiseman* (Princeton, NJ: Princeton University Press, 1969), 139–40, and Eric Dorn Brose, *A History of the Great War* (New York: Oxford University Press, 2010), 337.

47. Keegan, *The First World War*, 396–403, and Marshall, *World War I*, 346–53.

48. Baker to Wilson, March 27, 1918, *Papers*, vol. 47, 160–61.

49. Baker to Wilson, March 27, 1918, ibid., 166.

50. David Lloyd George to Lord Reading, March 28, 1918, ibid., 181–83.

51. Sir William Wiseman to the Foreign Office, March 28, 1918, ibid., 184–85.

52. House Diary, March 28, 1918, ibid., 185–86.

53. Woodrow Wilson, An Address, April 6, 1918, ibid., 267–70.

54. Woodrow Wilson, Remarks to Foreign Correspondents, April 8, 1918, ibid., 284–89.

55. William Bowyer Fleming to Woodrow Wilson, April 8, 1918, ibid., 295–96.

56. Lloyd George to Reading, March 29, 1918, ibid., 203–5.

57. House Diary, March 29, 1918, ibid., 206.

58. Reading to Lloyd George, March 30, 1918, ibid., 213–14.

59. David Lloyd George to Lord Reading, April 1, 1918, ibid., 221.

60. Ibid.

61. Lloyd George to Reading, April 2, 1918, ibid., 229.

62. See Lansing to Wilson, with enclosure (Poincaré telegram), April 4, 1918, and Reading to Wilson, with enclosure (telegram from George V), April 5, 1918; Clemenceau to Wilson, April 6, 1918; Victor Emmanuel II to Wilson, ibid., 257, 265–66, 277–78, 278.

63. Tasker Howard Bliss to Peyton Conway March, April 3, 1918, ibid., 237–38.

64. House to Wilson, April 9, 1918, ibid., 302–3.

65. See ibid., 284, n. 2.

66. Woodrow Wilson, Remarks to Foreign Correspondents, April 8, 1918, ibid., 284–89.

67. Lloyd George to Reading, April 9, 1918, ibid., 307.

68. Reading to Balfour, April 10, 1918, ibid., 314.

69. Lloyd George to Reading, with enclosure, April 14, 1918, ibid., 338–41.

70. House to Wilson, with enclosure, April 25, 1918, ibid., 433–35.

71. Reading to Lloyd George, April 18, 1918, ibid., 369–72.

72. Keegan, *First World War*, 405–6.

73. A Memorandum by Ferdinand Foch, May 2, 1918, *Papers*, vol. 47, 497–98.

74. Pershing claimed to Newton Baker that Lloyd George and General Foch had expressed complete satisfaction to him (verbally) regarding troop deployments as of May 15, 1918. If Pershing's claim was accurate, then perhaps Lloyd George and Foch were being "diplomatic" due to lack of other leverage. They might also have feared that real candor, let alone bluntness, with Pershing might have made his attitude worse. See Baker to Wilson, with enclosure, May 16, 1918, *Papers*, vol. 48, 32–34. Just three days later, Lloyd George cabled Lord Reading to urge Colonel House to attend the next meeting of the Supreme War Council in June. The prime minister said that "in regard to use of United States troops . . . I do not think it is possible to come to satisfactory conclusions unless a political authority representing U.S. Government is present with whom we can deal on equal terms and who can come to a decision on the spot." Lloyd George to Reading, May 18, 1918, ibid., 61–62. According to House, in a letter to Wilson, Reading quietly undermined the prime minister as follows: "Reading confessed to me that he thought it would be a mistake for me to go, or for you to send anyone, because it is so evident that what Lloyd George wants is someone to over-rule Pershing." House to Wilson, May 20, 1918, ibid., 79. House recorded in his diary that "what Lloyd George wants is for me to supercede General Pershing and to dominate our military action over there. He knows my views and intimated in the cable that I was the only one who would be able to act with authority. He said there was no use sending someone who would have to refer matters back to Washington." House Diary, May 20, 1918, ibid., 94–95. Reading met with Wilson and conveyed Lloyd George's request, but agreed off the record when Wilson demurred. House Diary, May 23, 1918, ibid., 135.

75. Woodrow Wilson, An Address in New York on Behalf of the American Red Cross, May 18, 1918, ibid., 53–54.

76. Marshall, *World War I*, 370–71.

77. Ibid., 376–83.

78. Ibid., 373.

79. Baker to Wilson, with enclosure, June 21, 1918, *Papers*, vol. 48, 383–90.

80. Sir William Wiseman to Sir Eric Drummond, May 30, 1918, ibid., 203–6.

81. Keegan, *First World War*, 407.

82. Marshall, *World War I*, 384.

83. The landing of Allied troops in Russia during 1918 is a complicated story. Wilson eventually sent troops to Vladivostok in August for the purpose of transporting some newly freed Czech prisoners of war who wished to fight on the western front. At first relations

between the Allies and the Bolsheviks were cordial, but for various reasons this situation gradually changed. On August 3, Wilson issued a press release on the military action in Russia. See Press Release, August 3, 1918, *Papers*, vol. 49, 170–72. See also Keegan, *The First World War*, 385–92, and Knock, *To End All Wars*, 154–57. See also George F. Kennan, *Soviet-American Relations, 1917–1920*, vol. 2, *The Decision to Intervene* (Princeton, NJ: Princeton University Press, 1958).

84. House to Wilson, June 23, 1918, *Papers*, vol. 48, 400.

85. A Memorandum from Lincoln Steffens, c. December 28, 1917, *Papers*, vol. 45, 381–84.

86. Cooper, *Woodrow Wilson*, 432.

87. Upton Beall Sinclair to Wilson, May 18, 1918, *Papers*, vol. 48, 59.

88. Amos Richards Eno Pinchot to Wilson, May 24, 1918, ibid., 146–47.

89. Wilson to Thomas Watt Gregory, June 1, 1918, ibid., 220.

90. Wilson to Gregory, May 31, 1918, ibid., 209.

91. Gregory to Wilson, June 6, 1918, ibid., 251, n. 2.

92. Upton Beall Sinclair to Wilson, August 7, 1918, *Papers*, vol. 49, 207–9.

93. Gregory to Wilson, August 21, 1918, ibid., 306–8.

94. Thomas Watt Gregory to Wilson, May 14, 1918, *Papers*, vol. 48, 12–14.

95. Wilson to Gregory, June 24, 1918, ibid., 405.

96. Gordon Auchincloss to Wilson, with enclosure, Memorandum for Colonel House, by William C. Bullitt, January 31, 1918, *Papers*, vol. 46, 183–93.

97. Leonidas Carstarphen Dyer to Wilson, July 23, 1918, *Papers*, vol. 49, 61–62.

98. Woodrow Wilson, A Statement to the American People, July 26, 1918, ibid., 97–98.

99. Sigmund Freud and William C. Bullitt, *Thomas Woodrow Wilson, Twenty-Eighth President of the United States: A Psychological Study* (Boston: Houghton Mifflin, 1966). Available in Europe in the 1930s, this book met a scathing reception when published in America; see, for example, the review by psychologist Erik Erickson in the *New York Review of Books*, February 9, 1967, 3–6, and Arthur S. Link, "The Case for Woodrow Wilson," *Harpers*, April 1967, 85–93. See also Peter Gay, *Freud for Historians* (New York: Oxford University Press, 1985).

100. Cooper, *Woodrow Wilson*, 440–41.

101. A Memorandum by Sir William Wiseman, January 23, 1918, *Papers*, vol. 46, 85.

102. House Diary, February 27, 1918, ibid., 485.

103. See, for example, Alexander L. George and Juliette L. George, *Woodrow Wilson and Colonel House: A Personality Study* (New York: Dover Publications, 1956, 1964). For an overview of psychological studies of Wilson in the 1970s, see Edwin A. Weinstein, James William Anderson, and Arthur S. Link, "Woodrow Wilson's Political Personality: A Reappraisal," *Political Science Quarterly* 93, no. 4 (Winter 1978): 585–98. For a contemporaneous exploration of underlying medical issues, see Edwin A. Weinstein, "Woodrow Wilson's Neurological Illness," *Journal of American History* 57, no. 2 (September 1970): 324–51. Weinstein gradually developed the theory that Wilson's mental shortcomings were all derived from an underlying cerebral vascular disease involving hypertension. See Edwin A. Weinstein, *Woodrow Wilson: A Medical and Psychological Biography* (Princeton, NJ: Princeton University Press, 1981).

104. Woodrow Wilson, An Address to Congress, May 27, 1918, *Papers*, vol. 48, 162–65.

105. Wilson's political agenda for 1918 was in fact complex; though he sometimes came across as a heavy-handed partisan, he also engaged in the challenge of purging the Democratic Party of Southern reactionaries. In February, he had mused to House regarding "the necessity of forming a new political party," since "he did not believe the Democratic Party could be used as an instrument to go as far as it might be needful to go and largely because of the reactionary element in the South." House Diary, February 24, 1918, *Papers*, vol. 46, 436. On the 1918 purge, see Cooper, *Woodrow Wilson*, 435–37.

106. House Diary, May 17, 1918, *Papers*, vol. 48, 51.

107. Woodrow Wilson, An Address in New York on Behalf of the American Red Cross, May 18, 1918, ibid., 54.

108. Ibid., 57.

109. Ibid.

110. Hans Morgenthau, *Scientific Man vs. Power Politics* (Chicago: University of Chicago Press, 1946), 52.

111. Reading to Wilson, July 3, 1918, *Papers*, vol. 48, 501–2.

112. Knock, *To End All Wars*, 150–54, Cooper, *Woodrow Wilson*, 439–40.

113. Knock, *To End All Wars*, 151.

114. House to Wilson, with enclosure, June 25, 1918, *Papers*, vol. 48, 424–26.

115. Ibid., 426.

116. Wilson to House, July 8, 1918, ibid., 549–50.

117. Wiseman to Lord Robert Cecil, with enclosures, July 18, 1918, *Papers*, vol. 49, 12.

118. House to Wilson, with enclosure, July 8, 1918, and Abbott Lawrence Lowell to Wilson, July 10, 1918, *Papers*, vol. 48, 561–62, 586.

119. Wilson to Lowell, July 11, 1918, ibid., 590–91.

120. House to Wilson, July 16, 1918, ibid., 630–31.

121. Ibid., 633.

122. Ibid., 635.

123. House Diary, August 15, 1918, *Papers*, vol. 49, 265.

124. Ibid., 266.

125. Ibid., 267.

126. Ibid., 273–74.

127. Wilson to House, with enclosure, September 7, 1918, ibid., 470.

128. Wiseman to Reading, August 20, 1918, ibid., 300–301.

129. House to Wilson, September 3, 1918, ibid., 428–29.

130. Keegan, *The First World War*, 410.

131. Keegan, *The First World War*, 412; Hew Strachan, *The First World War* (London: Simon & Schuster UK, 2003), 313; Brose, *A History of the Great War*, 353.

132. Keegan, *The First World War*, 411–12.

133. Strachan, *The First World War*, 304.

134. House Diary, September 16, 1918, *Papers*, vol. 51, 23–24.

135. Keegan, *The First World War*, 412–13; Strachan, *The First World War*, 314.

136. Friedrich Oederlin to Wilson, October 6, 1918, with enclosure, *Papers*, vol. 51, 252–53.

137. House to Wilson, October 6, 1918; A Draft of a Note to the German Government, October 7, 1918; A Draft of a Note to the German Government, October 8, 1918; Penultimate Draft of a Note to the German Government, October 8, 1918; Lansing to Oederlin, October 8, 1918, ibid., 254, 255–57, 263–64, 264–65, 268–69. On the crimes committed by retreating German troops, see Lansing to Wilson, October 4, 1918, ibid., 215. On the drafting of Wilson's reply to the Germans, see House Diary, October 9, 1918, ibid., 275–80.

138. See ibid., 317, n. 6.

139. Tasker Howard Bliss to Robert Lansing and others, October 8, 1918, ibid., 272–75.

140. Wiseman to Reading, October 9, 1918, ibid., 290–91.

141. A Translation of a Letter from Jean Jules Jusserand to Colville Adrian de Rune Barclay and its Enclosure, October 11, 1918, ibid., 307–9.

142. House Diary, October 15, 1918, ibid., 342.

143. Ibid.

144. Ibid., 340–41.

145. Woodrow Wilson, A Draft of a Note to the German Government, October 14, 1918, ibid., 333–34. The note was sent on October 16.

146. From the Diary of Henry Fountain Ashurst, October 14, 1918, ibid., 338–39.

147. David Lawrence to Wilson, October 13, 1918, ibid., 320–24.

148. Lloyd George to Sir Eric Geddes, October 12, 1918, ibid., 313.

149. For a summary of the cabinet meeting of October 22, see Memorandum by Franklin Knight Lane, October 23, 1918, ibid., 413–15.

150. Wilson to Lansing, with enclosures, October 23, 1918, ibid., 417–19. For the text of the German note that Wilson received on October 20, see ibid., 402, n. 1. It is interesting to note that in Lane's account of the October 22 cabinet meeting, Wilson had allegedly said that "he was afraid of Bolshevism in Europe, and the Kaiser was needed to keep it down—to keep some order." Ibid., 415.

151. David Stevenson, *Cataclysm: The First World War as Political Tragedy* (New York: Basic Books, 2004), 381–82.

152. Keegan, *The First World War*, 413.

153. Stevenson, *Cataclysm*, 403.

154. On the Kiel mutiny and the German revolution generally, see Stevenson, *Cataclysm*, 399–404; Brose, *A History of the Great War*, 358.

155. Keegan, *The First World War*, 417.

156. Keegan, *The First World War*; Stevenson, *Cataclysm*, 403–4.

157. Strachan, *The First World War*, 320.

158. Keegan, *The First World War*, 419.

159. Stevenson, *Cataclysm*, 394–99.

160. Woodrow Wilson, An Appeal for a Democratic Congress, October 19, 1918, *Papers*, vol. 51, 381–82. For an early and very different draft of this appeal prepared by Joseph Tumulty on October 11, see ibid., 304–6. For earlier drafts by Wilson, see ibid., 317–18, 343–44, 353–55.

161. See Cooper, *Woodrow Wilson*, 445–46.

162. Ibid., 446.

163. Ibid., 455–56, n. 1.

164. Ibid.

165. William Howard Taft to Thomas Walter Bickett, October 30, 1918, in *Papers*, vol. 53, 29–30.

166. See Theodore Roosevelt to Arthur James Balfour, December 15, 1918, *The Letters of Theodore Roosevelt*, vol. 8, ed. Elting E. Morison (Cambridge, MA: Harvard University Press, 1954), 1415; Henry Cabot Lodge to Balfour, November 25, 1918, Henry Cabot Lodge Papers, cited in Cooper, *Woodrow Wilson*, 649, n. 54.

167. For Cobb and Lippmann's executive summary, see House to Wilson, October 29, 1918, *Papers*, vol. 51, 495–504.

168. House to Wilson, October 30, 1918, ibid., 511.

169. House to Wilson, October 30, 1918, ibid., 512.

170. Ibid.

171. Wilson to House, October 30, 1918, ibid., 513.

172. House to Wilson, October 30, 1918, ibid., 514. This threat reflected Wilson's own thinking. He wrote House that "if the British cannot, relying upon our friendship and good faith, accept the principle of freedom of the seas, they can count upon the certainty of our using our present great equipment to build up the strongest navy our resources permit, as our people have long desired." Wilson to House, November 4, 1918, ibid., 575.

173. House to Wilson, October 30, 1918, ibid., 515.

174. House to Wilson, October 30, 1918, ibid.

175. Wilson to House, October 31, 1918, ibid., 533.

176. House to Wilson, October 31, 1918, ibid., 532.

177. Stevenson, *Cataclysm*, 388.

178. House to Wilson, November 5, 1918, *Papers*, vol. 51, 594–95.

179. House to Wilson, October 27, 1918, ibid., 463–64.

180. See, for instance, Baker's message to Pershing, drafted on October 27. Some extracts: "The President raises the question as to whether it is necessary for Allied or American Army to actually occupy Alsace and Lorraine when evacuated under armistice. . . . The President doubts advisability of requiring Allied or American occupation on eastern side of Rhine, as that is practically an invasion of German soil under armistice." A Draft of a Telegram from Newton Diehl Baker to John Joseph Pershing, October 27, 1918, ibid., 470–71. The cable was sent on October 28. On October 15, Navy Secretary Daniels solicited suggestions for naval armistice terms from Admiral Sims. Sims replied on October 25 and Daniels sent the terms to Wilson on October 28. See Naval Terms for an Armistice, October 28, 1918, ibid., 474–75. Wilson edited the terms and sent them to House. See ibid., 475, notes 1–3. See also Franklin D. Roosevelt to Wilson, with enclosures, October 29, 1918, ibid., 486–95.

181. Wilson to House, October 28, 1918, ibid., 473.

182. House to Wilson, October 30, 1918, ibid., 515–17.

183. House to Wilson, November 1, 1918, ibid., 542.

184. House to Wilson, October 30, 1918, ibid., 516.

185. Stevenson, *Cataclysm*, 389–90.

186. Marshall, *World War I*, 443–44; Brose, *A History of the Great War*, 359.

187. Stevenson, *Cataclysm*, 391. See also Harry R. Rudin, *Armistice, 1918* (New Haven, CT: Yale University Press, 1944).

188. House to Wilson, November 8, 1918, *Papers*, vol. 51, 638–39.

189. Woodrow Wilson, A Statement, November 11, 1918, *Papers*, vol. 53, 34.

190. House to Wilson, November 11, 1918, ibid.

191. David Lloyd George, *Parliamentary Debates, House of Commons*, 110, 2463, cited in Cooper, *Woodrow Wilson*, 649, n. 60.

192. Woodrow Wilson, An Address to a Joint Session of Congress, November 11, 1918, *Papers*, vol. 53, 41.

193. House to Wilson, November 5, 1918, *Papers*, vol. 51, 595. On November 12, the new German chancellor, Ebert, sent a message via Switzerland requesting American assistance in supplying the German people with food. Lansing's answer cited Wilson's faulty understanding of the Allied position. Hans Sulzer to Robert Lansing, November 12, 1918, Lansing to Sulzer, November 12, 1918, *Papers*, vol. 53, 63, 64. The very next day, House reported that "Clemenceau informs me that the Allies feel, now that the armistice is signed, that the German authorities should address their official communications to them rather than to the United States exclusively." House to Wilson, November 13, 1918, ibid., 69.

194. House broached the subject, though cautiously, on November 14, when he wrote that "Americans here whose opinions are of value are practically unanimous in the belief that it would be unwise for you to sit in the Peace Conference. They fear that it would involve a loss of dignity and your commanding position." Frank Cobb advised against attending as early as November 4, and Lansing recommended against it on November 12. House to Wilson, November 14, 1918; Cobb to House, November 4, 1918; Lansing to Wilson, November 12, 1918, *Papers*, vol. 53, 71–72; vol. 51, 590–91; vol. 53, 65–66. Lansing recorded that when he advised Wilson not to go, the reaction was one of stony silence: "The President did not like what I had said. His face assumed that harsh, obstinate expression which indicates resentment of unacceptable advice. He said nothing, but looked volumes. If he goes, he will some day be sorry. He will probably not forgive me." See also Lansing, A Memorandum on the President's Going to the Peace Conference, November 18, 1918, *Papers*, vol. 53, 127–28: Lansing wrote, "I prophesy trouble in Paris and worse than trouble here. Congress will resent his leaving and without a guiding hand will act very badly."

195. Wilson to House, November 16, 1918, *Papers*, vol. 53, 96–97.

196. Wilson to House, November 18, 1918, ibid., 108–9.

197. A Press Release, November 29, 1918, ibid., 243.

198. Henry White to Wilson, November 20, 1918, ibid., 147, n. 1.

199. Cooper, *Woodrow Wilson*, 457–58.

200. Woodrow Wilson, An Annual Message on the State of the Union, December 2, 1918, *Papers*, vol. 53, 276.

201. Ibid., 285–86.

202. Josephus Daniels Diary, December 2, 1918, ibid., 301.

203. Ashurst Diary, December 2, 1918, ibid., 305. The next day Ashurst called upon Wilson, who asked him the following question: "What are those **** on the hill doing today?" Ashurst told him that "the House of Representatives would impeach you and the Senate convict you if they had the courage. Their lack of nerve is all that saves your removal from office; Congress opposes your going to Europe." Ashurst Diary, December 3, 1918, ibid., 313.

204. George Creel, *The War, the World, and Wilson* (New York: Harper and Brothers, 1920), 163.

205. Cary T. Grayson Diary, December 4, 1918, *Papers*, vol. 53, 314.

206. Grayson Diary, December 8, 1918, ibid., 336–40. According to Grayson's diary, Wilson told reporters aboard the *George Washington* that "England . . . very seriously infringed on America's rights before we became a belligerent through the improper use of her blockade,—in fact did the same thing on the seas as Germany did to Belgium, and on the same grounds—

necessity." Grayson's summary continues: "He [Wilson] declared that at one time if it had not been for his realization that Germany was the scourge of the world, he would have been ready to have it out with England."

207. Woodrow Wilson, Remarks in London to Free Church Leaders, December 28, 1918, *Papers*, vol. 53, 530.

208. Woodrow Wilson, An Address at Mansion House, December 28, 1918, ibid., 533–34.

6. 1919

1. Lansing appointed Grew without consulting Wilson, who was furious when he learned about it. When Wilson reached Paris, House found him "in an ugly mood about Lansing. . . . He thought I was building up an organization and that when they got here we would determine together who would officer it." House advised him to let Grew keep the job: "I told him that Grew while not the man for the place, was a gentleman, was honest and trustworthy and I hope he would not remove him." House continued his diary entry as follows: "Sometime ago I determined to let Lansing carry his own fortunes without help or hindrance from me. He has not been entirely considerate, after what I have done for him. On the other hand, I always appreciate the fact that I have been what Gerard once termed 'Super-Secretary of State,' and Lansing has played a minor part and has done it without complaint." House Diary, December 14, 1918, *Papers of Woodrow Wilson*, ed. Arthur S. Link, 69 vols. (Princeton, NJ: Princeton University Press, 1966–1993), vol. 53, 389–90. On House's role in the Paris Peace Conference, see Inga Floto, *Colonel House in Paris: A Study of American Policy at the Paris Peace Conference 1919* (Princeton, NJ: Princeton University Press, 1980), original Danish edition published 1974. On the Paris Peace Conference overall, see Margaret MacMillan, *Paris 1919: Six Months that Changed the World* (New York: Random House, 2003).

2. As to Hoover's discussions, see Memorandum and Statement by Herbert Clark Hoover and John William Davis, December 10, 1918, and Hoover to Wilson, December 20, 1918, *Papers*, vol. 53, 360–64, 453–54. See also Edward Nash Hurley to Wilson, with enclosure, December 23, 1918, ibid., 480–85.

3. From the Diary of William Christian Bullitt, December 9 [10], 1918, ibid., 350–53.

4. Charles Seymour to His Family, December 10, 1918, ibid., 356–57.

5. Charles Seymour to His Family, December 12, 1918, ibid., 377–78.

6. Raymond Blaine Fosdick Diary, December 11, 1918, ibid., 365.

7. Grayson Diary, December 8, 1918, ibid., 336–37.

8. Ibid., 337.

9. Ibid.

10. Ibid.

11. A Memorandum, Secret, Imperial War Cabinet 47, Draft Minutes of a Meeting held at 10 Downing Street, S.W., on Monday, December 30, 1918, at 3–30 p.m., ibid., 565.

12. Ibid., 566–67.

13. Ibid., 567.

14. Ibid., 558–59.

15. Even so, some French political leaders went along in a mood of resentment. In late January, Paul Cambon, the French ambassador to Great Britain, complained to Lord Curzon that he and many others were experiencing "irritation at the slow progress that was being made with the business of the Conference, and he attributed this in the main to the unfortunate lead of which had been given to the proceedings by President Wilson. Of the latter he spoke in very critical terms. He regarded him as an academic lecturer with considerable literary gifts, but out of touch with the world, giving his confidence to no one, unversed in European politics, and devoted to the pursuit of theories which had little relation to the emergencies of the hour." Cambon avowed that "all such questions as the Freedom of the Seas and the League of Nations" had "nothing whatever to do either with the war or with the immediate task of concluding peace" and should have been "postponed to a later stage." Lord Curzon to Lord Derby, January 23, 1919, *Papers*, vol. 54, 235.

16. Woodrow Wilson, Remarks at Humes to American Soldiers, December 25, 1918, *Papers of Woodrow Wilson*, vol. 53, 505–7.

17. Woodrow Wilson, An Address at the University of Paris, December 21, 1918, ibid., 461–62.

18. Lord Derby to Arthur James Balfour, December 22, 1918, ibid., 470–72. Derby also reported that Wilson's conception of Freedom of the Seas was "equally vague."

19. Woodrow Wilson, After-Dinner Remarks at Buckingham Palace, December 27, 1918, and Wilson, An Address at Guildhall, December 28, 1918, ibid., 522–24, 531–33. As his visit in England continued, Wilson's speeches were often simplistic. On December 29, he declared in the church where his grandfather had preached that the war was like the action of a posse: "The knowledge that wrong was being attempted has aroused the nations. They have gone out like men upon a crusade. No other cause could have drawn so many nations together. They knew that an outlaw was abroad who purposed unspeakable things." Woodrow Wilson, Remarks in His Grandfather's Church in Carlisle, December 29, 1918, ibid., 541.

20. From the Right Reverend Charles Gore to Wilson, December 23, 1918, ibid., 486–87.

21. Edith Bolling Galt Wilson to Sallie White Bolling and Others, December 24, 1918, ibid., 499–501.

22. A former congressman named Alfred Lucking wrote the following to Tumulty in mid-December 1918: "I happened to be in the same train with former President Taft yesterday, and had quite a visit with him. We got to talking about the League of Nations. . . . I said to him 'it looks as if Mr. Roosevelt is commencing to hedge on the question, notwithstanding his former bitter enmity to it, and that before long he will be on the other side of the question.' Mr. Taft laughed very heartily and said that he had noticed his change of sentiments as shown in the newspapers. . . . He then told me that Mr. Roosevelt had signified recently in a conversation with him that Roosevelt would be with him (Taft) on the question, but that he must give him time to turn the corner. This communication is wholly confidential. . . . I would expect that in case of any mishap, that Mr. Roosevelt will be carrying the flag of the League of Peace in the front line of the campaign of 1920." Alfred Lucking to Joseph Patrick Tumulty, December 13, 1918, ibid., 382.

23. For minutes of the meetings of the Council of Ten, see *Papers*, vol. 54, 7–26, 35–50, 64–76, 96–103, 108–21, 155, 179–89, 204–11, 218–26, 247–54, 283–301, 310–31, 334–45, 350–78, 415–25, 461–63, 490–93, 505–9; vol. 55, 104–13, 140–48; vol. 56, 88–95, 148–52, 165–69, 209–22. One humorous feature of these meetings was the fact that Lansing constantly doodled. Charles Seymour reported that "Lansing draws all the time the session goes on, with his left hand; caricatures and grotesque figures, really very well done. When one is finished he drops it on the floor and begins another. . . . Lloyd George was filled with admiration for the drawings: 'I say,' he said, 'could I have one of those; they're awfully good.' So Lansing gave him one and he folded it carefully and put it in his pocket with gratitude." Charles Seymour to His Family, February 8, 1919, *Papers*, vol. 55, 34–35.

24. Edward Price Bell to Lawrence Lanier Winslow, with enclosure, December 31, 1918, *Papers*, vol. 53, 575.

25. Ray Stannard Baker to Cary Travers Grayson, with enclosure, January 14, 1919, *Papers*, vol. 54, 59–60.

26. Ibid., 66.

27. Ibid., 66–67.

28. Hankey's Notes of a Meeting of the Council of Ten, January 16, 1919, ibid., 97.

29. Hankey's Notes of Two Meetings of the Council of Ten, January 17, 1919, ibid., 111–14. Months later, toward the close of the conference, by which time the Council of Ten had been replaced by an elite Council of Four, Ray Stannard Baker set forth in his diary the following rationalization for Wilson's position: "One reason the President so dislikes publicity while events are in the making is due to a certain artistic repugnance to expose half-done work to the light of day. He wants to present a workmanlike result (in his messages & speech not alone, but in his decisions in conference). He honestly does not believe in the old diplomacy, or secret diplomacy, for he is conscious in no way of desiring any dishonest end, or to be working for any selfish interest. He honestly thinks this method of settling the world by secret confer-

ences of 4 men is the best & only way. He does it because it is *his* way of working & he knows no other." Ray Stannard Baker Diary, May 17, 1919, *Papers*, vol. 59, 245.

30. A Memorandum on Publicity, January 17, 1919, *Papers*, vol. 54, 121–22.

31. Tumulty to Grayson, January 16, 1919, ibid., 105.

32. See Ray Stannard Baker to Wilson, with enclosure, ibid., 191–92.

33. On January 30, Wilson complained to the Council of Ten that "each morning in the Paris press, printed in English, appeared a great deal more information regarding the meetings than was given in the official communiques. He referred especially to the comments on President Wilson's idealistic views. It was stated, for instance, that, as regards President Wilson's ideals, he (President Wilson) did not know how his ideals would work." Hankey's Notes of Two Meetings of the Council of Ten, January 30, 1919, ibid., 351.

34. Thomas Francis Logan, a special commissioner of the U.S. Shipping Board, took part in these Allied discussions and reported both the position of Herbert Hoover, which he defended, and the polemical give-and-take in response to it. The Allies demanded an equal role with the United States in controlling food relief (thus protecting, in effect, their power to stall deliveries to Germany). Hoover tried unsuccessfully to cut the red tape (and shenanigans) by acting on his own. Logan reported as follows to Edward Nash Hurley, who chaired the Shipping Board: "Since we supply the food and most of the finances, the American Food Administrator should be left unrestricted, as Mr. Hoover bluntly told them. This has been used as an indication that we want to retain for ourselves all the credit for feeding Europe; that we want to keep France and England and Italy out of it so that it will appear that they have held aloof from the aid given to the enemy countries and the liberated peoples. You will remember the shrewd way in which Reading put forward this idea in the conferences which we attended with the French, British and Italians. He repeated, until it became rather tiresome, that 'the hand that feeds Europe will control its destinies.'" Logan to Hurley, December 23, 1918, *Papers*, vol. 53, 480–85.

35. Wilson to Hoover, January 11, 1919, ibid., 714.

36. Hoover to Wilson, with enclosure, January 12, 1919, *Papers*, vol. 54, 29–31.

37. Hankey's Notes of a Meeting of the Supreme War Council, January 13, 1919, ibid., 37.

38. Ibid., 40.

39. Ibid., 40–41.

40. For the details of this situation, see *Papers*, vol. 55, 459, n. 1.

41. David Stevenson, *Cataclysm: The First World War as Political Tragedy* (New York: Basic Books, 2004), 416.

42. Grayson Diary, January 9, 1919, *Papers*, vol. 53, 696–97.

43. Arthur S. Link, *Woodrow Wilson: Revolution, War, and Peace* (Wheeling, IL: Harlan Davidson, 1979), 78, asterisked footnote.

44. Grayson Diary, January 15, 1919, *Papers*, vol. 54, 64. For a long exposition by Foch on the need to bar Germany from access to the west bank of the Rhine, see *Papers*, vol. 55, 502–10. Foch argued that the "Prussianizing" of German political culture would continue to make Germany (even in the form of a republic) a menace, especially with the long-term German advantage in the size of its population.

45. Protocol of a Plenary Session of the Inter-Allied Conference for the Preliminaries of Peace, January 18, 1919, *Papers*, vol. 54, 129.

46. Ibid., 131.

47. Woodrow Wilson, An Address to the French Senate, January 20, 1919, ibid., 156–58.

48. Diary of Edith Benham, January 20, 1919, ibid., 175. Benham was Edith Wilson's secretary. Wilson and his wife took an extensive tour of French battle sites in late March. See Grayson Diary, March 23, 1919, *Papers*, vol. 56, 194–200.

49. Hankey's Notes for a Meeting of the Council of Ten, January 23, 1919, *Papers*, vol. 54, 223.

50. Hankey's Notes for Two Meetings of the Council of Ten, January 27, 1919, ibid., 283–84.

51. Edith Benham Diary, January 27, 1919, ibid., 307.

52. From the Diary of Vance Criswell McCormick, February 2, 1919, ibid., 440: "Went to the President's house at 6 o'clock. Got him to present at Supreme War Council tomorrow

program for a considerable relaxation of embargo." The Supreme War Council did not meet until February 7.

53. Hoover to Wilson, with enclosure, February 4, 1919, ibid., 477–79.

54. Foch was at this point less inclined than Clemenceau to take a hard line. House recorded the following: "Much to my surprise, Foch expressed the opinion that an immediate peace should be made with Germany so the wheels of industry should be started in motion throughout the world." House Diary, February 5, 1919, ibid., 499–500. And Grayson recorded that Foch, in the Supreme War Council meeting of February 7, clashed openly with Clemenceau: "A controversy between Clemenceau and Marshal Foch—a real fight developed over whether German prisoners shall be returned to Germany to work—those with dependent families—also to help put machinery in working order and help pay debt of war indemnities. Foch got up and left the room stiffly; his aide gathered up the papers and followed. No disturbance or notice taken by other Peace Commissioners. Clemenceau went on with the business of the Peace Commission as if nothing had occurred out of the ordinary—not even looking at Foch or in his direction as he left the room." Grayson Diary, February 8, 1919, *Papers*, vol. 55, 3. Wilson told members of his entourage that Foch and Clemenceau had been "spitting at each other like cats" before Foch walked out of the meeting. Edith Benham Diary, February 9, 1919, ibid., 40–41. Clemenceau and Foch composed their differences afterward and agreed to a compromise position at the next meeting of the Supreme War Council. See Hankey's Notes of a Meeting of the Supreme War Council, February 8, 1919, ibid., 9–11.

55. Hankey's Notes for a Meeting of the Supreme War Council, February 7, 1919, *Papers*, vol. 54, 531.

56. Ibid.

57. Ibid., 533–34.

58. Grayson Diary, February 10, 1919, *Papers*, vol. 55, 41.

59. Wilson's suspicion was recorded by Grayson as follows: "It developed that the French newspaper proprietors had been tipped off by the Government that it would be a good thing for them to play up to the skies all of the Republican opposition in the United States to the President's plans." Grayson Diary, February 12, 1919, ibid., 94. Ray Stannard Baker recorded the following on March 13: "[Wilson] said to us that he had positive evidence of the control of many of the papers by the French government, this in the form of an order (written instructions, of which he had a copy) issued through the Maison de la Presse (given to him personally by a French editor whose name, or course, could not be disclosed) in which the papers were advised regarding three items of policy: 1. To emphasize the opposition to him (Mr. Wilson) in America by giving all the news possible of Republican & other opposition; 2. To emphasize the disorder & anarchy in Russia, thereby, to provoke allied intervention; 3. To publish articles showing the ability of Germany to pay a large indemnity." *Papers*, vol. 55, 489–90.

60. Edith Benham Diary, February 10, 1919, ibid., 66–67.

61. House Diary, February 11, 1919, ibid., 88–89.

62. Grayson Diary, January 28, 1919, *Papers*, vol. 54, 308. Regarding issues pertaining to colonies and the League of Nations "mandate" system, see Thomas J. Knock, *To End All Wars: Woodrow Wilson and the Quest for a New World Order* (Princeton, NJ: Princeton University Press, 1992), 210–13.

63. Hankey's Notes of Meetings of the Council of Ten and of the Supreme War Council, February 12, 1919, *Papers*, vol. 55, 104–5.

64. Ibid., 108.

65. A News Report of a Press Conference, February 14, 1919, ibid., 161–63.

66. For Cecil's scheme, see Memorandum by Lord Robert Cecil, December 17, 1918, *Papers*, vol. 53, 415–17. For Smuts's scheme, see Memorandum: League of Nations, December 26, 1918, ibid., 515–19. Smuts wrote a longer treatise, *The League of Nations: A Programme for the Peace Conference*, which was given to Wilson in London on December 26, 1918. See ibid., 515, n. 1.

67. Woodrow Wilson, A Draft of a Covenant, c. January 8, 1919, ibid., 678–86. House was busily consulting with Clemenceau, Lansing, Sir Robert Cecil, and Herbert Hoover regarding the structure of the League. See House Diary, January 7, 1919, and January 8, 1919, ibid., 652–54, 693–96.

68. House Diary, January 8, 1919, ibid., 695.

69. Tasker Howard Bliss to Newton Diehl Baker, January 11, 1919, ibid., 719–21.

70. Robert Lansing, A Memorandum, January 11, 1919, *Papers*, vol. 54, 3.

71. Wilson's Second "Paris Draft" of the Covenant, January 18, 1919, ibid., 138–48.

72. Cecil to Wilson, with enclosure, January 20, 1919, ibid., 160–70.

73. Hankey's Notes for a Meeting of the Council of Ten, January 22, 1919, ibid., 206, 208–11.

74. Cecil Diary, January 19, 1919, ibid., 152.

75. Protocol of a Plenary Session of the Inter-Allied Conference for the Preliminaries of Peace, January 25, 1919, ibid., 264–68.

76. House Diary, January 31, 1919, ibid., 407–8. See Hurst-Miller Draft of the Covenant of the League of Nations, February 2, 1919, and its revision, February 3, 1919, ibid., 433–39, 449–58.

77. House Diary, February 3, 1919, ibid., 459.

78. Cecil Diary, February 3, 1919, ibid., 460.

79. Cecil Diary, February 6, 1919, ibid., 514.

80. For minutes of the meetings of the League of Nations Commission, see *Papers*, vol. 54, 463–64, 481–84, 495–99, 509–13, 545–48; vol. 55, 4–9, 41–51, 70–80, 120–40; vol. 56, 170–78, 223–33, 298–303; vol. 57, 218–32, 248–66.

81. Cecil Diary, February 6, 1919, *Papers*, vol. 54, 514.

82. Knock, *To End All Wars*, 213–15. For extended analysis of the League Commission's deliberations, see ibid., 213–26.

83. Minutes of a Meeting of the Commission on the League of Nations, February 11, 1919, *Papers*, vol. 55, 74–75, 79–80.

84. Woodrow Wilson, An Address to the French Chamber of Deputies, February 3, 1919, *Papers*, vol. 54, 464–67.

85. Minutes of Two Meetings of the Commission on the League of Nations, February 13, 1919, *Papers*, vol. 55, 137–40. Stevenson comments on the politics of this initiative: "Eleven out of sixteen countries represented [on the League Commission] voted for the amendment, but Britain and America abstained and Wilson, as chairman, ruled that in the absence of unanimity it was lost. The most vocal objections came from the Australian premier, Hughes, but both Lloyd George and Wilson let him take the lead, because British imperial unity might be threatened unless Australia and New Zealand maintained the right to exclude Japanese immigrants, and because the American Senate might reject the Covenant if the Pacific coast states were forbidden to discriminate against them." Stevenson, *Cataclysm*, 414. It bears noting that House had tried to help the Japanese; he recorded in his diary that "Baron Makino and Viscount Chinda came for advice concerning what Japan had best do regarding the race question. There is a demand in Japan that the Peace Conference through the League of Nations should express some broad principle of racial equality. Chinda and Makino do not desire to bring it up themselves if they can avoid doing so. I advised them to prepare two resolutions, one which they desired, and another which they would be willing to accept in lieu of the one they prefer. I promised I would then see what could be done. . . . I took occasion to tell them how much I deprecated race, religious or other kinds of prejudice. I insisted, however, that it was not confined to any one country or against any particular class of people." House Diary, February 4, 1919, *Papers*, vol. 54, 484–85. In the final deliberations of the League of Nations Commission, House made a final attempt to get the race equality clause. At 8:30 p.m. on February 13 (the last day of the commission's work), House got the commission to reconsider the previously defeated Article 21: "Makino and I agreed upon a form the other day which the President accepted and which was as mild and inoffensive as possible, but even that the British refused." House Diary, February 13, 1919, *Papers*, vol. 55, 155–56.

86. House Diary, February 13, 1919, *Papers*, vol. 55, 155–56.

87. Hankey's Notes of a Meeting of the Council of Ten, February 13, 1919, ibid., 147–48.

88. Woodrow Wilson, An Address to the Third Plenary Session of the Peace Conference, February 14, 1919, ibid., 175, 177.

89. Ibid., 167.

90. Ibid., 169.

91. A News Report of a Press Conference, February 14, 1919, ibid., 162.

92. Ibid., 162–63.

93. House Diary, February 14, 1919, ibid., 193.

94. Ibid., 194.

95. Grayson noted one day that "the seas were so high that they were breaking clear over the top of the escorting destroyers' stacks, and one wave carried away a Lieutenant and a Quartermaster from one of the destroyers." Assistant Secretary of the Navy Franklin D. Roosevelt, on board the *George Washington* with Wilson, ordered the destroyers to break off the escort. Grayson Diary, February 19, 1919, ibid., 207.

96. William Howard Taft and Abbott Lawrence Lowell to Wilson, February 10, 1919, ibid., 65.

97. Wilson to Tumulty, February 21, 1919, ibid., 222.

98. Grayson Diary, February 22, 1919, ibid., 224.

99. Wilson uttered the sentiment again aboard the *George Washington* in the course of a lunch attended by Franklin and Eleanor Roosevelt, both of whom were on board. Grayson Diary, February 22, 1919, ibid., 224–25.

100. House to Wilson, February 19, 1919, ibid., 212–13.

101. Wilson to House, February 23, 1919, ibid., 229–30.

102. Wilson to House, February 27, 1919, ibid., 299.

103. Men "will be at a loss where to gain a livelihood unless pains are taken to guide them and put them in the way of work," Wilson said, and "there will be a large floating residuum of labor which should not be left wholly to shift for itself. It seems to me important, therefore, that the development of public works of every sort should be promptly resumed." Wilson, State of the Union Address, December 2, 1918, *Papers*, vol. 53, 280.

104. Robert Latham Owen to Wilson, July 18, 1918, *Papers*, vol. 49, 6–8.

105. Tumulty to Wilson, January 30, 1919, *Papers*, vol. 54, 390.

106. Wilson to Tumulty, February 20, 1919, *Papers*, vol. 55, 219.

107. Woodrow Wilson, An Address in Boston, February 24, 1919, ibid., 238–45.

108. Grayson Diary, February 25, 1919, ibid., 254.

109. See John Milton Cooper Jr., *Woodrow Wilson: A Biography* (New York: Alfred A. Knopf, 2009, Vintage edition, 2011), 478.

110. A News Report, February 26, 1919, *Papers*, vol. 55, 268.

111. Ibid., 275.

112. Ibid., 274.

113. Henry Cabot Lodge, Speech in the Senate, February 28, 1919, in Richard N. Current and John A. Garraty, eds., *Words That Made American History* (Boston: Little, Brown, 1962), 251–62. This speech can also be found in the *Congressional Record*, 65th Congress, 3d session, 4520–28.

114. Frederick Lewis Allen, *Only Yesterday: An Informal History of the 1920s* (New York: Harper and Brothers, 1931, Perennial Library edition, 1964), 24–25.

115. Thomas James Walsh to Wilson, February 25, 1919, *Papers*, vol. 55, 262–63.

116. Wilson to Walsh, February 26, 1919, ibid., 280.

117. House to Wilson, February 27, 1919, ibid., 304–5.

118. Wilson to House, March 3, 1919, ibid., 392.

119. Woodrow Wilson, Remarks to Members of the Democratic National Committee, February 28, 1919, ibid., 313.

120. Ibid., 319.

121. Ibid., 323.

122. William Bauchop Wilson to Woodrow Wilson, February 26, 1919, ibid., 291–92. On March 5, and again on March 11, the secretary of labor tried to persuade Wilson to keep the employment service going with an allotment from his own discretionary National Security and Defense Fund (ibid., 447, 478). No response to these pleas can be found in Wilson's *Papers*.

123. Woodrow Wilson, An Address to a Conference of Governors and Mayors, March 3, 1919, ibid., 389–90.

124. William Howard Taft, Speech in New York, March 4, 1919, in *Taft Papers on League of Nations*, eds. Theodore Marburg and Horace Flack (New York: Macmillan, 1920), 262–80.

125. Woodrow Wilson, An Address at the Metropolitan Opera House, March 4, 1919, *Papers*, vol. 55, 413–21.

126. Ray Stannard Baker Diary, March 8, 1919, ibid., 465.

127. House Diary, March 14, 1919, ibid., 499.

128. Ray Stannard Baker, an admirer of Wilson, was ready to take Wilson's side, as was Cary T. Grayson. See Ray Stannard Baker, *Woodrow Wilson and World Settlement* (New York: Doubleday, Page, 1922–1923), I, 306–10, and Cary T. Grayson, "The Colonel's Folly and the President's Distress," *American Heritage* XV (October 1964), 4–7. For commentary on the Wilson-House rupture, see *Papers*, vol. 55, 488, n. 2.

129. Knock, *To End All Wars*, 246.

130. Edith Bolling Galt Wilson, *My Memoir* (Indianapolis and New York: Bobbs-Merrill, 1938), 245–46.

131. Inga Floto, *Colonel House in Paris: A Study of American Policy at the Paris Peace Conference* (Princeton, NJ: Princeton University Press, 1980), 164–70.

132. Grayson Diary, March 15, 1919, *Papers*, vol. 55, 529–30.

133. House Diary, March 16, 1919, ibid., 538–39.

134. Taft to Wilson, March 18, 1919, *Papers*, vol. 56, 83. Taft followed up on March 21 with some more detailed suggestions (ibid., 157–59).

135. House Diary, March 18, 1919, ibid., 82–83.

136. Cooper, *Woodrow Wilson*, 485.

137. Knock, *To End All Wars*, 247; Grayson Diary, March 18, 1919, *Papers*, vol. 56, 75–81.

138. Lodge to White, March 15, 1919, quoted in Cooper, *Breaking the Heart of the World: Woodrow Wilson and the Fight for the League of Nations* (Cambridge: Cambridge University Press, 2001), 74. For an extended discussion of Republican machinations during this episode, see ibid., 72–74.

139. Cooper, *Woodrow Wilson*, 485.

140. For records of these meetings, see Paul Mantoux, *The Deliberations of the Council of Four (March 24–June 28, 1919): To the Delivery to the German Delegation of the Preliminaries of Peace*, ed. Arthur S. Link (Princeton, NJ: Princeton University Press, 1992).

141. House Diary, March 20, 1919, *Papers*, vol. 56, 126, n. 1. House's text read as follows: "Because of the havoc which Germany has brought upon the world by her attack upon France and Belgium in 1914, and in order to prevent as far as (humanly) possible such another disaster to humanity, we hereby solemnly pledge to one another our immediate military, financial, economic and moral support of and to one another in the event Germany should at any time make a like unprovoked and unwarranted (invasion of) *attack against* the territories of either one or more of the subscribing powers."

142. Grayson Diary, March 22, 1919, ibid., 164–65.

143. For deliberations on the reparations issue among the American delegation's staff, see Norman Hezekiah Davis to Wilson, March 25, 1919, ibid., 270–72. See also Philip M. Burnett, *Reparation at the Paris Peace Conference: From the Standpoint of the American Delegation* (New York: Columbia University Press, 1940).

144. House Diary, March 17, 1919, ibid., 4–5.

145. Grayson Diary, March 24, 1919, ibid., 246–49.

146. Mantoux's Notes of Two Meetings of the Council of Four, March 25, 1919, ibid., 250–51.

147. A Memorandum by Lloyd George, March 25, 1919, ibid., 259–60.

148. Ibid., 264–65.

149. Ibid., 262–63.

150. Ibid., 262.

151. Grayson Diary, March 26, 1919, ibid., 285. Link has pointed out that Lloyd George did not in fact receive a formal message from Parliament to this effect until April 8 (ibid., 286, n. 1).

152. For commentary on the "punitive" rebellion in the House of Commons, see *Papers*, vol. 57, 6–7, n. 7 and 147, n. 1.

153. A Memorandum by Lloyd George, March 25, 1919, *Papers*, vol. 56, 264.

154. Ibid., 265.

155. Mantoux's Notes for Two Meetings of the Council of Four, March 25, 1919, ibid., 249–50.

156. Cecil Diary, March 26, 1919, ibid., 297.

157. Mantoux's Notes of Two Meetings of the Council of Four, March 27, 1919, ibid., 316, 319.

158. Ibid., 323.

159. Minutes of a Meeting of the League of Nations Commission, March 26, 1919, ibid., 298–303.

160. House Diary, March 28, 1919, ibid., 349.

161. Mantoux's Notes of Two Meetings of the Council of Four, March 28, 1919, ibid., 365.

162. Ibid., 366.

163. House Diary, March 28, 1919, ibid., 349–51. For variant accounts of this confrontation, see Memorandum by Robert Lansing, March 28, 1919, and Ray Stannard Baker Diary, March 28, 1919, ibid., 351–52, 353–54.

164. Mantoux's Notes of Two Meetings of the Council of Four, March 28, 1919, ibid., 355–57.

165. Ibid., 357.

166. Ibid., 358.

167. Hankey's and Mantoux's Notes of a Meeting of the Council of Four, March 30 [29], 1919, ibid., 418–20.

168. House Diary, April 1, 1919, ibid., 517. On another occasion, Clemenceau said that "When I talk with President Wilson, I feel as if I were talking to Jesus Christ. . . . The Almighty gave us Ten Commandments, but Wilson has given us Fourteen." House Diary, April 28, 1919, *Papers*, vol. 58, 186.

169. Baker Diary, March 31, 1919, *Papers*, vol. 56, 441.

170. For background on the ensuing negotiations on the Saar issue, see Charles Homer Haskins to Wilson, with enclosure, April 1, 1919, and Henry Wickham Steed to Edward Mandell House, with enclosure, April 1, 1919, ibid., 513–14, 515–17.

171. Vance Criswell McCormick Diary, March 31, 1919, ibid., 444.

172. A Memorandum by John Foster Dulles, April 1, 1919, ibid., 498–99.

173. See ibid., 557–58, n. 2, for an extended analysis of these diagnoses. In the course of this footnote, Link and the other editors of the Wilson papers present retrospective diagnoses pointing to a viral infection. One scholar, Edwin A. Weinstein, has argued that Wilson also suffered an attack of encephalitis after the supposed influenza subsided. See Edwin A. Weinstein, *Woodrow Wilson: A Medical and Psychological Biography* (Princeton, NJ: Princeton University Press, 1981), 328.

174. Cooper, *Woodrow Wilson*, 488.

175. *Papers*, vol. 56, 558, n. 2.

176. John Maynard Keynes, *Economic Consequences of the Peace* (New York: Harper, Brace, and Howe, 1919), 34.

177. Cecil Diary, March 26, 1919, *Papers*, vol. 56, 297.

178. David Lloyd George to Wilson, with enclosure, April 23, 1919, *Papers*, vol. 58, 8–14.

179. Wilson to House, July 21, 1917, *Papers*, vol. 43, 237–38.

180. Stevenson, *Cataclysm*, 420–21.

181. Ibid., 423. See also Wilson to Lloyd George, May 5, 1919, *Papers*, vol. 58, 446–48.

182. Keynes, *Economic Consequences of the Peace*, 35.

183. Ibid., 36.

184. Ibid., 37–38.

185. Ibid., 37.

186. Ibid., 39. An example of such casuistry was recorded by John Foster Dulles on April 1. Dulles and other advisers objected to including the cost of pensions in German reparations, arguing that pensions were not within the scope of the armistice declarations in regard to reparation for "damage to the civilian population." Wilson answered that "he did not regard this as a matter for decision in accordance with strict legal principles," adding that he was "continuously finding new meanings and the necessity of broad application of principles previously enunciated even though imperfectly." Dulles Memorandum, April 1, 1919, *Papers*, vol. 56,

499. See also First Draft of an Anglo-American Accord on Reparations, April 1, 1919, and Second Draft of an Accord on Reparations, April 2, 1919, ibid., 504–5, 536–39.

187. Baker Diary, April 30, 1919, *Papers*, vol. 58, 270–71.

188. House Diary, April 2, 1919, *Papers*, vol. 56, 540.

189. Vance Criswell McCormick Diary, April 3, 1919, ibid., 580.

190. Grayson Diary, April 6, 1919, *Papers*, vol. 57, 50–52.

191. Ibid., 63, n. 1.

192. Grayson Diary, April 7, 1919, ibid., 63–65.

193. It bears noting, however, that Wilson's gesture led to negative repercussions in the United States. Tumulty wrote Grayson on April 9 that Wilson's summoning of the *George Washington* was perceived as "an act of impatience and petulance" that "puts upon the President the responsibility of withdrawing when the President should by his own act place the responsibility for a break of the Conference where it properly belongs." Tumulty to Grayson, April 9, 1919, ibid., 177. Grayson answered Tumulty as follows: "From your side of the water your points are well taken but [Wilson] has formed his ideas through immediate contact with actual conditions on this side. The French are the champion time killers of the world. The *George Washington* incident has had a castor oil effect on them all. More progress has been made in the last two days than has been made for the last two weeks." Grayson to Tumulty, April 10, 1919, ibid., 194.

194. House Diary, April 4, 1919, *Papers*, vol. 56, 587.

195. Baker Diary, April 7, 1919, *Papers*, vol. 57, 68.

196. On the Saar negotiations, see Council of Four minutes, April 8, 1919; David Hunter Miller to House, April 8, 1919; Council of Four minutes, April 8, 1919; André Tardieu memorandum, April 9, 1919; Baruch to Wilson, April 9, 1919; Council of Four minutes, April 9, 1919; Secret Memorandum, April 9, 1919; Council of Four minutes, April 10, 1919; Council of Four minutes, April 11, 1919; Charles Homer Haskins to Wilson, with enclosure, April 16, 1919, ibid., 113–17, 117–20, 128–30, 155–59, 159–60, 161–65, 196–99, 199–202, 242–47, 407–15.

197. Woodrow Wilson, Memorandum on the Amendments proposed by France to the Agreement suggested by President Wilson regarding the Rhine Frontier, April 12, 1919, ibid., 296–98. The "guarantee" read as follows: "I should lay before the Senate of the United States and urge for adoption a treaty with France containing a pledge by the United States, subject to the approval of the Executive Council of the League of Nations, to come immediately to the assistance of France so soon as any unprovoked movement of aggression against her is made by Germany, this agreement to remain in force until it shall be recognized by the contracting powers that the League of Nations itself gives sufficient guarantee in these matters." See also Memorandum by Georges Clemenceau, April 20, 1919; Council of Four minutes, April 22, 1919; Appendices III–V, ibid., 525, 591–92. See also Council of Four minutes, May 6, 1919, *Papers*, vol. 58, 480. For the final text of the "guarantee," see Agreement Between the United States and France, signed at Versailles, June 28, 1919, *Papers*, vol. 61, 311–13.

198. On the quid pro quo regarding naval construction and the Monroe Doctrine reservation, see Cecil Diary, April 8, 1919; Cecil to House, April 8, 1919; House to Cecil, April 9, 1919; William Shepherd Benson to Wilson, April 9, 1919; House Diary, April 10, 1919; Cecil to House, with enclosures, April 10, 1919; League of Nations Commission meeting, April 10, 1919, *Papers*, vol. 57, 142, 143–44, 179–80, 180–88, 215, 216–18, 218–32.

199. Minutes of a Meeting of the League of Nations Commission, April 10, 1919, ibid., 226.

200. League of Nations Commission meetings, April 10, 1919, and April 11, 1919, ibid., 226–32, 254–57.

201. League of Nations Commission meeting, April 11, 1919, ibid., 259–65.

202. On the continuing problem of hammering out the reparations policy, see, for example, Council of Four minutes, April 5, 1919; House Diary, April 7, 1919; Council of Four minutes, April 7, 1919; Council of Four minutes, April 10, 1919; Council of Four minutes, April 12, 1919; Council of Four minutes, May 6, 1919; A Memorandum by Norman Hezekiah Davis, June 1, 1919; Council of Four minutes, June 2, 1919; Council of Four minutes, June 9, 1919; Council of Four minutes, June 10, 1919; Council of Four minutes, June 11, 1919; Norman Hezekiah Davis to Wilson, June 11, 1919; Council of Four minutes, June 11, 1919; appendix,

Reparation: Reply to German Counter Proposals, Finally Approved by the Council of the Principal Allied and Associated Powers on afternoon of June 11, 1919, *Papers*, vol. 57, 5–21, 71–72, 79–89, 203–15, 293–95; vol. 58, 481; vol. 60, 4–7, 22–33, 318–27, 345–51, 389–99, 399–401, 406–11.

203. On the Fiume issue, see Council of Four minutes, April 3, 1919, *Papers*, vol. 56, 562–65, as well as Wilson to House, April 7, 1919; Memorandum, April 14, 1919; Wilson, Memorandum Concerning the Question of Italian Claims on the Adriatic, April 14, 1919; House Diary, April 15, 1919; Isaiah Bowman and others to Wilson, April 17, 1919; Thomas Nelson Page to House, April 17, 1919; Baker Diary, April 18, 1919; Grayson Diary, April 19, 1919; Council of Four minutes, April 19, 1919; Edith Benham Diary, April 19, 1919; House Diary, April 19, 1919; Grayson Diary, April 20, 1919; Council of Four minutes, April 20, 1919; House Diary, April 20, 1919; Baker Diary, April 20, 1919; Mantoux's Notes of a British-French-Italian Meeting, April 21, 1919; Draft of a Statement, April 21, 1919; Council of Four minutes, April 21, 1919; Orlando to Wilson, April 21, 1919; Baker Diary, April 21, 1919; Benham Diary, April 21, 1919; Baker Diary, April 22, 1919; Council of Four minutes, April 22, 1919; Grayson Diary, April 23, 1919; Wilson, A Statement on the Adriatic Question, April 23, 1919; Council of Four minutes, April 23, 1919; Grayson Diary, April 24, 1919; Council of Four minutes, April 24, 1919; Council of Four minutes, April 24, 1919; Thomas Nelson Page to Wilson, April 24, 1919; News Report, April 24, 1919; A Memorandum by Robert Lansing, April 24, 1919; House Diary, April 24, 1919; Baker Diary, April 25, 1919; Page to American Commissioners, April 25, 1919; Page to American Mission, April 28, 1919; Tumulty to Wilson, April 28, 1919; Page to American Mission, April 29, 1919; Page to American Mission, May 1, 1919; Page to American Mission, May 2, 1919; Council of Four minutes, May 3, 1919; House Diary, May 3, 1919; Council of Four minutes, May 3, 1919; Page to American Mission, May 3, 1919, *Papers*, vol. 57, 90, 337–43, 343–45, 352, 432–33, 434–37, 467–68, 477–78, 479–94, 502–3, 504, 512–13, 514–21, 527, 527–28, 536–42, 542–44, 545–56, 562–65, 575, 576–77, 585, 610–14; vol. 58, 3–5, 5–8, 14–24, 53–56, 57–61, 74–90, 91–93, 97–101, 102, 104, 142–43, 143–44, 210–11, 215, 238–41, 321–22, 357–59, 369–78, 379–80, 390–402, 413–15. Further discussions of Fiume occurred in May. The city would eventually be seized by the Italian poet and agitator Gabriele D'Annunzio in September 1919. D'Annunzio's forces were ejected the following year, and then Fiume became an autonomous city-state until 1924 when Italy annexed it. On the south Tirol, see Archibald Cary Coolidge to the American Commissioners, April 7, 1919, *Papers*, vol. 57, 96–97.

204. Grayson to McAdoo, April 12, 1919, ibid., 304–6.

205. Woodrow Wilson, Memorandum Concerning the Question of Italian Claims on the Adriatic, April 14, 1919, ibid., 343–45.

206. Baker Diary, April 21, 1919, ibid., 575.

207. Baker Diary, April 19, 1919, ibid., 508–9.

208. Woodrow Wilson, A Statement on the Adriatic Question, April 23, 1919, *Papers*, vol. 58, 5–8.

209. See Thomas Nelson Page to Wilson, April 24, 1919, ibid., 91–93: "The tone of the press last night and this morning is one of intense anger," the American ambassador reported. "The tenseness of the situation created can hardly be exaggerated. The attitude of the press and people daily becomes more threatening and the newspapers are full of violent attacks on the President." See also ibid., 97–101, in which the *New York Times* coverage of this story bore the following headline: "Orlando Makes Protest: Accuses the President of Breach of Diplomatic Usage."

210. On the Shantung question, see House Diary, April 15, 1919; Council of Four meeting, April 15, 1919; Lansing to Wilson, April 21, 1919; A Translation of a Telegram from Keishiro Matsui to Viscount Yasuya Uchida, April 22, 1919; Viscount Sutemi Chinda to Lansing, April 21, 1919; Council of Four minutes, April 22, 1919; Council of Four minutes, April 22, 1919; Lu Cheng-hsiang to Wilson, April 24, 1919; Edward Thomas Williams to Wilson, April 24, 1919; Council of Four minutes, April 25, 1919; Memorandum by Edward Thomas Williams, April 26, 1919; Memorandum by Arthur James Balfour, April 27, 1919; Council of Four minutes, April 28, 1919; Balfour to Baron Nobuaki Makino, April 28, 1919; Lansing Memorandum, April 28, 1919; Grayson Diary, April 29, 1919; Council of Four meeting, April 29,

1919; Balfour to Wilson, April 29, 1919; House Diary, April 29, 1919; Baker Diary, April 29, 1919; Baker Memorandum, April 29, 1919; Tasker Howard Bliss to Wilson, April 29, 1919; Wilson to Balfour, April 30, 1919; Balfour to Makino, April 30, 1919; Vi Kyuin Wellington Koo to Wilson, April 30, 1919; Council of Four minutes, April 30, 1919; Baker Diary, April 30, 1919; Wilson to Tumulty, April 30, 1919; Baker Diary, May 1, 1919, *Papers*, vol. 57, 354–55, 358–59, 560–62, 581–85, 597–98, 599–610, 615–26; vol. 58, 68–70, 70–73, 129–33, 165–68, 175–76, 177–83, 183–84, 185, 215–16, 216–27, 228, 228–29, 229, 230–32, 232–34, 245–46, 246–47, 247, 257–61, 270–71, 272–73, 327, 419, n. 1.

211. Baker Diary, April 25, 1919, *Papers*, vol. 58, 142–43. A few days later, Wilson told Baker, "Anything he might do was wrong! He gave me a copy of the cablegram he had just sent to Tumulty giving the gist of the decision. He said it was 'the best that could be gotten out of a dirty past.' He had considered every possible contingency. His sympathies were all with the Chinese. . . . But if he made such a decision that the Japanese went home, he felt that the whole Peace Conference would break up. . . . It might mean that everyone would return home & begin to arm—wars everywhere. And this would not force Japan out of Shantung; it would only encourage deeper penetration. The only hope was, somehow, to keep the world together, get the League of Nations with Japan in it & then try to secure justice for the Chinese not only as regards Japan but as regarding England, Russia, France & America." Baker Diary, April 30, 1919, ibid., 270–71.

212. The Covenant of the League of Nations, April 28, 1919, and Wilson, Remarks to a Plenary Session of the Paris Peace Conference, April 28, 1919, ibid., 188–99, 199–202.

213. Cooper, *Woodrow Wilson*, 494.

214. Arthur S. Link et al., Appendix, Wilson's Neurological Illness at Paris, *Papers*, vol. 58, 607–40. For dissenting opinions, see Juliette L. George, Michael F. Marmor, and Alexander L. George, "Issues in Wilson Scholarship: References to Early 'Strokes' in the *Papers of Woodrow Wilson*," *Journal of American History* 70, no. 4 (1984): 845–53.

215. Bert E. Park, MD, MA, "The Impact of Wilson's Neurological Disease during the Paris Peace Conference," in Appendix, *Papers*, vol. 58, 611–30.

216. Edwin A. Weinstein, MD, "Woodrow Wilson's Neuropsychological Impairment and the Paris Peace Conference," ibid., 630–35. See also Edwin A. Weinstein, "Woodrow Wilson's Neurological Illness," *Journal of American History* 57 (September 1970): 324–51, and Weinstein, *Woodrow Wilson: A Medical and Psychological Biography* (Princeton, NJ: Princeton University Press, 1981). Weinstein attributes much of the behavior of Wilson critiqued in this study to the neurological illness: "Throughout 1918, Wilson grew increasingly egocentric, suspicious, and secretive, and less discreet in his public references to people. He became extremely proprietary about the proposed League of Nations: he refused to discuss it with anyone but Colonel House, rejected the ideas of a committee to coordinate plans with the British, and spoke scathingly of 'butters-in' . . . Wilson used intemperate language in turning down the suggestion that William Howard Taft and Elihu Root—both strong League supporters—be appointed Peace Commissioners. Aboard the *George Washington*, Wilson, apparently still smarting from his defeat in the congressional elections, charged that David Lloyd George and Georges Clemenceau did not truly represent their people. In Paris, in January, after Lloyd George had brought Wilson the news of the death of Theodore Roosevelt, he was horrified by the 'outburst of acrid detestation' in which Wilson denounced the former President." *Papers*, vol. 58, 632–33. If House is to be believed, Wilson was extraordinarily irrational at times before he left Paris. Consider the following from House's diary on June 23:

> Wallace and Jusserand were among my early morning callers. They came about the dinner President Poincaré wishes to give to President Wilson and which he absolutely refuses to accept. It bids fair to become an international episode. . . . The President became stubborn and when Jusserand called, he refused to see him although Jusserand sent word by Grayson that he had a personal message from the President of France. The matter has become so serious that Poincaré called a meeting of the Council of State. . . . The President's attitude is an affront to France and will be so considered unless I can move him to reconsider his decision. . . . I had Jusserand and Wallace wait in my study while I went into another room to call

up Grayson and find how matters stood. Grayson was not disposed to speak to the President further. He evidently wanted to "stand from under." . . . The President came to the Crillon around twelve o'clock and we had it out in great shape. He said he had no notion of eating with Poincaré, that he would choke if he sat at the table with him. I replied that if I were in his place I would go to the dinner and choke. He looked at me but made no reply. I am glad he did not, as it probably would not have been pleasant. I called his attention to the fact that Poincaré was representing the French people, and that he, the President, had been a guest of the Nation for nearly six months. He said it made no difference, that he would not eat with him; that Poincaré was "no good" and had tried to make trouble by sending a message to the Italian people, showing that he was in sympathy with them, and out of sympathy with him, Wilson. (*Papers*, vol. 61, 111–15)

For commentary, see ibid., 112, n. 1, which includes an extract of a memoir by Irwin Hood ("Ike") Hoover, who was White House head usher. Hoover recalled that Wilson was convinced at the time that "every French employee" serving him was a "spy." Many other incidents attest to Wilson's imminent breakdown. See Bert E. Park, "Wilson's Neurologic Illness during the Summer of 1919," *Papers*, vol. 62, 628–38. Ray Stannard Baker recorded that, upon their return from France, "although I had been seeing him daily—& intimately—for months—had occupied a confidential position—not one word did he say about it, either commendatory or otherwise, or intimate that he cared ever to see me again. He said good-bye to me just as he would have said it to a visitor of an hour." Baker Diary, July 9, 1919, *Papers*, vol. 61, 416. On July 12, the *Washington Post* reported that Senator Hitchcock, the Senate minority leader and Wilson's chief Senate ally on the League of Nations and Versailles treaty, would leave town for several weeks because of "some lack of warmth between the President and the Nebraska senator. . . . Friends of the senator admitted frankly that Mr. Hitchcock was not altogether pleased with the signs of recognition of his leadership which came from the President." Ibid., 468–69.

217. Baker Diary, May 28, 1919, *Papers*, vol. 59, 574–75.

218. Cooper, *Breaking the Heart of the World*, 89.

219. Link et al., April 3, 1919, *Papers*, vol. 56, 557–58, n. 2.

220. Baker Diary, May 3, 1919, *Papers*, vol. 58, 418–19.

221. Baker reported Hoover's views a few weeks later as follows: "Hoover . . . says that the treaty is wholly unworkable & that if the economic terms are enforced it will mean ruin in Germany & probably Bolshevism, to say nothing of the impossibility of getting Reparations of the Germans." Baker Diary, May 23, 1919, *Papers*, vol. 59, 447–48. Hoover later developed his views in a memorandum. See Memorandum by Herbert Clark Hoover, June 5, 1919, *Papers*, vol. 60, 194–96.

222. Remarks at a Plenary Session by Count Ulrich von Brockdorff-Rantzau, May 7, 1919, *Papers*, vol. 58, 514–17.

223. For liberal and progressive attacks upon the treaty, see Knock, *To End All Wars*, 252–56, and Cooper, *Breaking the Heart of the World*, 85–86, 97–100.

224. Keynes, *Economic Consequences of the Peace*, 121.

225. Ibid., 95.

226. Link, *Woodrow Wilson: Revolution, War, and Peace*, 91–92.

227. Ibid., 103.

228. Stevenson, *Cataclysm*, 411–12. For other works casting doubt upon the causal link between the Treaty of Versailles and World War II, see Etienne Mantoux, *The Carthaginian Peace* (Pittsburgh: University of Pittsburgh Press, 1952), Gerhard Weinberg, *A World at Arms: A Global History of World War II* (New York: Cambridge University Press, 1994), and Correlli Barnett, *The Collapse of British Power* (London: Pan, 2002).

229. John Kenneth Galbraith, *Money: Whence It Came, Where It Went* (Boston: Houghton Mifflin, 1975), Bantam edition, 188.

230. Ibid., 190.

231. For an overview, see Harold James, "Economic Reasons for the Collapse of the Weimar Republic," in *Weimar: Why Did German Democracy Fail*, ed. Ian Kershaw (London: Weidenfeld & Nicolson, 1990), 30–57.

232. Grayson recorded the incident this way: "Before the meeting had much more than started Clemenceau and Lloyd George got into a very serious clash, the question of the secret treaties which had been entered into during the war precipitating it. Clemenceau declared that Lloyd George had made serious misrepresentations, and had in effect charged him with having lied. Finally, Lloyd George declared that he would not allow any such statement to be made and addressing himself directly to Clemenceau he demanded that he apologize and take back his charges. Lloyd George angrily demanded of Clemenceau: 'Will you take back your charges?' In reply Clemenceau said: 'That's not my style of doing business.' President Wilson finally straightened them out." Grayson Diary, May 21, 1919, *Papers*, vol. 59, 321–22.

233. Woodrow Wilson, Remarks at Suresnes Cemetery on Memorial Day, May 30, 1919, *Papers*, vol. 59, 607–8.

234. Ibid., 608.

235. Jan Christiaan Smuts to Wilson, May 14, 1919, ibid., 149–50.

236. Wilson to Smuts, May 16, 1919, ibid., 187–88.

237. Count Ulrich Karl Christian von Brockdorff-Rantzau to Georges Clemenceau, May 29, 1919, ibid., 579–84.

238. Smuts to Wilson, May 30, 1919, ibid., 616–18.

239. Charles Seymour to His Family, June 3, 1919, *Papers*, vol. 60, 75–79.

240. A Discussion with the American Delegation, June 3, 1919, ibid., 71. The give-and-take on this issue between Wilson and Lloyd George became intense in the ensuing weeks. On June 4, House reported that Wilson "said that George was very offensive not only to Clemenceau but to him, and that he took occasion to be ugly himself." House Diary, June 4, 1919, *Papers*, vol. 60, 144. See also Council of Four minutes, June 2, 1919; Council of Four minutes, June 9, 1919; Council of Four Minutes, June 10, 1919; Council of Four minutes, June 11, 1919; Reparation: Reply to German Counter Proposals, Finally Approved by the Council of the Principal Allied and Associated Powers on afternoon of June 11, 1919, ibid., 22–33, 318–27, 345–51, 389–99, 406–11. On June 13, Grayson recorded that Wilson "said that rather than weaken the terms in the slightest degree he would welcome Germany's refusing to sign them. He said that the terms were very hard, it was true, but at the same time every one must realize that the Germans themselves had brought on this horrible war, and that they had violated all ethics of international law and international procedure, and had created a series of crimes that had amazed and shocked beyond belief all of the peoples of the world. He declared that under no circumstances would he be a party to any position to entice the Germans to sign. After the President made his position clear, Clemenceau said that he was well satisfied; that as far as he was concerned he did not even want to talk to the Boche at all at any time." Grayson Diary, June 13, 1919, ibid., 488–89.

241. *Papers*, vol. 60, 67.

242. S. L. A. Marshall, *World War I* (New York: American Heritage Press, 1964), 459.

243. Cooper, *Woodrow Wilson*, 501.

244. In the aftermath, the Allies discussed the options for renewing the war, occupying Germany, and reimposing the blockade in all its rigor. See Council of Four minutes, June 17, 1919, *Papers*, vol. 60, 619–21.

245. House Diary, June 29, 1919, *Papers*, vol. 61, 354–55. House wrote, "My last conversation with the President yesterday was not reassuring. . . . I said a fight was the last thing to be brought about, and then only when it could not be avoided. My own plan in negotiations had been to get all I could by friendly methods, but if driven to fight, then it was to do it so effectively that no one would wish to drive me to it again."

246. House's diary for some time had been replete with signs that he understood the estrangement. On the emotional level, House began to reciprocate Wilson's displeasure with this turn of events, as he had done in earlier years when he felt his influence diminish. On May 6, for instance, he wrote, "The President is the most prejudiced man I ever knew and likes but few people." On May 30, he wrote that "I seldom or never have a chance to talk with him [Wilson] seriously and, for the moment, he is practically out from under my influence." On June 10, he

wrote that Wilson "is one of the most difficult and complex characters I have ever known. . . . He has but few friends and the reason is apparent to me. He seems to do his best to offend rather than to please, and yet when one gets access to him, there is no more charming man in all the world. . . . He could use this charm to enormous personal and public advantage if he would, but in that, he is hopeless. . . . We must work collectively if we are to work effectively. The President understands this intellectually, for he is always saying what he does not practice. He speaks constantly of 'teamwork' but seldom practices it." *Papers*, vol. 58, 482; vol. 59, 623–24; vol. 60, 373. Once the House-Wilson rupture became decisive, Wilson disposed of House by assigning him minor tasks that effectively sidetracked him for the rest of the year.

247. John Palmer Gavit to Wilson, February 24, 1919, *Papers*, vol. 55, 255.

248. Wilson to Tumulty, February 25, 1919, ibid., 254.

249. Dudley Field Malone to Wilson, February 28, 1919, ibid., 337.

250. Gregory to Wilson, March 1, 1919, ibid., 345–47.

251. Tumulty to Wilson, March 1, 1919, ibid., 344–45.

252. 249 U.S. 47.

253. See, for example, Francis Patrick Walsh and others to Wilson, March 24, 1919, and Charles Edward Russell and others to Wilson, March 25, *Papers*, vol. 56, 245, 282–83.

254. Alexander Mitchell Palmer to Wilson, April 4, 1919, *Papers*, vol. 56, 619.

255. Wilson to Tumulty, June 28, 1919, *Papers*, vol. 61, 351–52.

256. John Nevin Sayre to Wilson, August 1, 1919, *Papers*, vol. 62, 126–28. Indeed, Sayre was the Episcopal clergyman who had married Jessie Wilson to his brother, Frank Sayre.

257. Palmer to Wilson, July 30, 1919, ibid., 58. Palmer wrote that "Debs' sentence of ten years is too long and ought to be commuted, but I am firmly of the opinion that the time is not yet ripe for such action. . . . When we release Debs, we shall have to release also two or three other leaders of the same class. Their release now would be used by many opponents of the peace treaty as evidence of too great leniency toward law violators of the radical element in the labor classes, in a way that would prejudice many people against the liberal labor provisions of the treaty. My own judgment is that we should wait until the peace treaty is ratified and out of the way and conditions in the country have settled down."

258. Cooper, *Woodrow Wilson*, 512.

259. For commentary on these trends, see John Milton Cooper Jr., *Pivotal Decades* (New York: W. W. Norton, 1990), 320–33.

260. See William M. Tuttle, *Race Riot: Chicago in the Red Summer of 1919* (New York: MacMillan, 1972).

261. Woodrow Wilson, A Special Message to Congress, May 20, 1919, *Papers*, vol. 59, 289–97.

262. Woodrow Wilson, An Address to a Joint Session of Congress, August 8, 1919, *Papers*, vol. 62, 209–19.

263. Ibid., 209, n. 1.

264. On Wilson's illness (whatever it was), see News Report, July 21, 1919, and July 22, 1919, *Papers*, vol. 61, 569–70, 578–79.

265. Henry Fountain Ashurst Diary, July 11, 1919, ibid., 445–46.

266. Ibid., 446, n. 1.

267. Cooper, *Woodrow Wilson*, 508.

268. Woodrow Wilson, An Address to the Senate, July 10, 1919, *Papers*, vol. 61, 428.

269. Ibid., 429.

270. Ibid., 434.

271. Ibid., 433–34.

272. Ibid., 434.

273. Ibid., 436.

274. Ashurst Diary, ibid., 445–46.

275. Wilson, Campaign Address at Shadow Lawn, October 14, 1916, *Papers*, vol. 38, 437.

276. Wilson, An Address to a Joint Session of Congress, January 8, 1918, *Papers*, vol. 45, 539.

277. Cooper, *Woodrow Wilson*, 509.

278. For coverage of these discussions in the *Washington Post* and the *New York Times*, see *Papers*, vol. 61, 544–47, 563–65; *Papers*, vol. 62, 11–13, 16–20, 66–69, 112–14. See also Tumulty to Wilson, July 18, 1919, *Papers*, vol. 61, 534. For coverage of this entire interlude, see Cooper, *Breaking the Heart of the World*, 121–41.

279. Baker made the following entry in his diary on May 17: "Lansing told me he thought there was no hope even in the League of Nations, if it passed the Senate: for it was founded upon an unjust settlement: & that the provision requiring unanimous consent in the Council made it an impossible document to change. With section 10, he said, we were called upon to guarantee all the mistakes of the treaty. But then, Mr. Lansing has never really believed in the League!" Baker Diary, May 17, 1919, *Papers*, vol. 59, 285–86.

280. See Cooper, *Breaking the Heart of the World*, 138–40. For Lansing's testimony, see U.S. Senate, Committee on Foreign Relations, *Treaty of Peace with Germany Hearings*, 66 Cong., 1st Sess. (Washington, D.C., 1919), 139–214.

281. Henry Cabot Lodge to Constance Lodge Gardiner, August 9, 1919, cited in Cooper, *Breaking the Heart of the World*, 140, n. 54.

282. See Cooper, *Breaking the Heart of the World*, 80–81.

283. Cooper, *Woodrow Wilson*, 513.

284. Ibid., 513–14.

285. Lansing Diary, August 11, 1919, *Papers*, vol. 62, 258–59.

286. "Reports Wilson Bound to Carry Treaty Unaltered, Hitchcock says the President Won't Concede Even the Crossing of a 'T,'" *New York Times*, August 16, 1919, *Papers*, vol. 62, 305–9.

287. Pittman to Wilson, August 15, 1919, *Papers*, vol. 62, 310–12.

288. Cooper, *Woodrow Wilson*, 514.

289. Lodge to Wilson, August 14, 1919, *Papers*, vol. 62, 275–76.

290. A Conversation with Members of the Senate Foreign Relations Committee, August 19, 1919, ibid., 339–411.

291. For coverage and analysis of this meeting, see Cooper, *Breaking the Heart of the World*, 141–47.

292. *Papers*, vol. 62, 341.

293. Ibid., 343.

294. Ibid., 343–44.

295. Cooper, *Woodrow Wilson*, 515–16.

296. Lodge said that there was a "distinction between a textual amendment, which changed the treaty for every signatory, and a reservation, which changed it only for the reserving power. In that I may be mistaken, however." Wilson replied that "there is some difference of opinion among the authorities, I am informed," but he had "not had time to look them up myself." *Papers*, vol. 62, 353.

297. Ibid., 406.

298. Ibid., 385.

299. Ibid., 378–79.

300. Ibid., 411.

301. Cooper, *Woodrow Wilson*, 517–18.

302. Cooper, *Breaking the Heart of the World*, 147.

303. Henry Cabot Lodge, quoted in Chandler P. Anderson Diary, entry for August 22, 1919, cited in Cooper, *Woodrow Wilson*, 518, n. 28.

304. Edith Wilson later recalled that her husband said something like this at the time: "I promised our soldiers, when I asked them to take up arms, that this was a war to end wars; and if I do not do all in my power to put the Treaty into effect, I will be a slacker and never able to look those boys in the eye. I must go." Edith Bolling Wilson, *My Memoir* (New York: Bobbs-Merrill, 1938), 274. Link and the editors of the Wilson papers have argued that this decision was "made without much thought, in anger, and on the spur of the moment." *Papers*, vol. 62, 507, n. 2. Cooper dissents from this view in "Fool's Errand or Finest Hour? Woodrow Wilson's Speaking Tour in September 1919," in *The Wilson Era: Essays in Honor of Arthur S. Link*, eds. John Milton Cooper Jr. and Charles E. Neu (Arlington Heights, IL: Harlan Davidson, 1991), 199–205.

305. Wilson, A Memorandum: Suggestion, September 3, 1919, *Papers*, vol. 62, 621.

306. John Spargo to Wilson, with enclosure, August 25, 1919, ibid., 555–59. See also Clarence Darrow to Wilson, July 30, 1919, ibid., 58–59.

307. Wilson to Palmer, August 29, 1919, ibid., 555.

308. Wilson to Spargo, August 29, 1919, ibid., 559.

309. Wilson, An Address to the Columbus Chamber of Commerce, September 4, 1919, *Papers*, vol. 63, 7.

310. Ibid., 17.

311. Wilson, An Address in the Indianapolis Coliseum September 4, 1919, ibid., 29.

312. Wilson, A Luncheon Address to the St. Louis Chamber of Commerce, September 5, 1919, ibid., 42.

313. Wilson, An Address in the St. Louis Coliseum, September 5, 1919, ibid., 48.

314. Wilson, An Address in Convention Hall in Kansas City, September 6, 1919, ibid., 72.

315. Wilson, An Address in the Des Moines Coliseum, September 8, 1919, ibid., 77.

316. Ibid., 88.

317. Cooper, *Breaking the Heart of the World*, 164.

318. Cooper, *Woodrow Wilson*, 524.

319. Cooper, *Breaking the Heart of the World*, 165.

320. Ibid., 168–71. See also *Papers*, vol. 63, 338–39, n. 1.

321. Lansing to Wilson, September 17, 1919, *Papers*, vol. 63, 337–38.

322. Lansing to Frank Lyon Polk, October 1, 1919, ibid., 539–41.

323. Joseph Patrick Tumulty, *Woodrow Wilson as I Know Him* (1921), 442. Poor House cabled Wilson, offering to testify before the committee, "tell a different story," and "put your position and your attitude while in Paris in a better light." House to Wilson, September 15, 1919, *Papers*, vol. 63, 299–300.

324. Wilson, An Address in the Minneapolis Armory, September 9, 1919, ibid., 136.

325. Ibid., 138.

326. Wilson, An Address in the St. Paul Auditorium, September 9, 1919, ibid., 146.

327. Wilson, An Address in Bismarck, September 19, 1919, ibid., 158–59.

328. Wilson, An Address at Coeur d'Alene, September 12, 1919, ibid., 220.

329. Wilson, An Address in Spokane, September 12, 1919, ibid., 234.

330. Wilson, A Luncheon Address in Portland, September 15, 1919, ibid., 283.

331. Wilson, An Address in Oakland, September 18, 1919, ibid., 360.

332. Wilson, An Address in the San Diego Stadium, September 1919, ibid., 371.

333. Ibid., 373.

334. Ibid., 382.

335. Grayson Diary, September 23, 1919, ibid., 446.

336. Edith Wilson, *Memoir*, 282.

337. Wilson, An Address in Salt Lake City, September 23, 1919, *Papers*, vol. 63, 451.

338. Wilson, An Address in Pueblo, September 25, 1919, ibid., 513.

339. Cooper, *Woodrow Wilson*, 529.

340. Richard Hofstadter, *The American Political Tradition—And the Men Who Made It* (New York: Alfred A. Knopf, 1948), Vintage edition, 308.

341. Alexander L. George and Juliette L. George, *Woodrow Wilson and Colonel House: A Personality Study* (New York: Dover Publications, 1956).

342. Grayson Diary, September 25, 1919, *Papers*, vol. 63, 489.

343. Grayson Diary, September 26, 1919, ibid., 518.

344. Baker Diary, November 5, 1919, ibid., 620.

345. Grayson Diary, September 26, 1919, ibid., 519.

346. Edith Wilson, *Memoir*, 266–88. See also Bert E. Park, MD, MA, "Woodrow Wilson's Stroke of October 2, 1919," *Papers*, vol. 63, 639–46.

347. House recorded on October 21 that "there is much discussion in Washington and elsewhere as to whether the president has suffered a stroke." House Diary, October 21, 1919, *Papers*, vol. 63, 585–86.

348. For coverage of this crucial period in the League fight, see Cooper, *Breaking the Heart of the World*, 212–70.

349. See Herbert F. Margulies, *The Mild Reservationists and the League of Nations Controversy in the Senate* (Columbia: University of Missouri Press, 1989).

350. On these reservations, see Lloyd E. Ambrosius, *Woodrow Wilson and the American Diplomatic Tradition: The Treaty Fight in Perspective* (New York: Cambridge University Press, 1987), 199–201.

351. Gilbert Monell Hitchcock to Edith Bolling Galt Wilson, with enclosure, November 13, 1919, *Papers*, vol. 64, 28–30.

352. Ibid., 30.

353. Gilbert Monell Hitchcock to Edith Bolling Galt Wilson, with enclosure, November 15, 1919, ibid., 37–41. For the text of the Lodge reservations, see ibid., 38–41.

354. Cooper, *Woodrow Wilson*, 544.

355. A Memorandum by Cary Travers Grayson, November 17, 1919, *Papers*, vol. 64, 43–45.

356. Ibid.

357. Link, *Woodrow Wilson: Revolution, War, and Peace*, 122.

358. *Papers*, vol. 64, 39.

359. Link, *Woodrow Wilson: Revolution, War, and Peace*, 122.

360. Taft to Casper S. Yost, November 13, 1919, quoted in Cooper, *Breaking the Heart of the World*, 248.

361. Link, *Woodrow Wilson: Revolution, War, and Peace*, 122.

362. Wilson to Hitchcock, November 18, 1919, *Papers*, vol. 64, 58.

363. Link, *Wilson: Revolution, War, and Peace*, 124. For coverage of this interlude, see Cooper, *Breaking the Heart of the World*, 283–96.

364. Cooper, *Woodrow Wilson*, 549.

365. Wilson, A Statement, December 14, 1919, *Papers*, vol. 64, 187.

366. Wilson, A Draft of a Public Letter, December 17, 1919, ibid., 199–202.

367. Cooper, *Pivotal Decades*, 327–28. See also Robert K. Murray, *Red Scare: A Study in National Hysteria* (Minneapolis: University of Minnesota Press, 1955), and Stanley Coben, *A. Mitchell Palmer: Politician* (New York: Columbia University Press, 1963).

7. 1920–1924

1. Woodrow Wilson, A Jackson Day Message, January 8, 1920, *Papers of Woodrow Wilson*, Arthur S. Link, ed., 69 vols. (Princeton, NJ: Princeton University Press, 1966–1993), vol. 64, 257–59.

2. Arthur S. Link, *Woodrow Wilson: Revolution, War, and Peace* (Arlington Heights, IL: Harlan Davidson, 1979), 125–26.

3. John Milton Cooper Jr., *Woodrow Wilson: A Biography* (New York: Alfred A. Knopf, 2009), 550. See also *New York Times* coverage, January 23, 1920: A News Report, "Senate Conferees Near Compromise on Resolutions," January 22, 1920, *Papers*, vol. 64, 311–12. For a progress report on these negotiations, see Hitchcock to Tumulty, January 16, 1920, *Papers*, vol. 64, 283–84.

4. Tumulty to Edith Bolling Galt Wilson, with enclosure, January 15, 1920, *Papers*, vol. 64, 276–82.

5. Baker Diary, January 23, ibid., 320–22.

6. On Grey's letter, see ibid., 355–57, n. 1.

7. Wilson, A Press Release, February 5, 1920, ibid., 363–64.

8. Baker Diary, February 5, 1920, ibid., 365.

9. Wilson to Lansing, February 7, 1919, ibid., 383.

10. Lansing, Memorandum, January 7, 1919, ibid., 255–56.

11. Lansing, Memorandum, February 9, 1920, ibid., 385–86.

12. Lansing to Wilson, February 9, 1920, ibid., 388–89.

13. Edith Bolling Galt Wilson, *My Memoir* (Indianapolis and New York: Bobbs-Merrill, 1938), 301.

14. Joseph Patrick Tumulty, *Wilson as I Know Him* (New York: Doubleday, Page, 1924), 445.

15. Lansing, Memorandum, February 13, 1920, *Papers*, vol. 64, 415–19.

16. Cooper, *Woodrow Wilson*, 555.

17. Ibid., 560. For detailed coverage of the final episode of the League fight, see Cooper, *Breaking the Heart of the World: Woodrow Wilson and the Fight for the League of Nations* (Cambridge: Cambridge University Press, 2001), 297–375.

18. Tumulty to Wilson, February 27, 1920, *Papers*, vol. 64, 479–80.

19. Wilson, First Draft of a Letter to Senator Hitchcock, February 28, 1920, *Papers*, vol. 65, 7–9.

20. Wilson to Hitchcock, March 8, 1920, ibid., 67–71.

21. Link, *Woodrow Wilson: Revolution, War, and Peace*, 128.

22. Thomas J. Knock, *To End All Wars: Woodrow Wilson and the Quest for a New World Order* (Princeton, NJ: Princeton University Press, 1992), 276.

23. Cooper, *Breaking the Heart of the World*, 433.

24. H. L. Mencken, "The Archangel Woodrow," *Smart Set*, 1921, in Alistair Cooke, ed., *The Vintage Mencken* (New York: Vintage Books, 1955), 116–20.

25. Frederick Lewis Allen, *Only Yesterday: An Informal History of the 1920s* (New York: Harper and Brothers, 1931; Perennial Library edition, 1964), 23–24.

26. The notion in the 1920s that Wilson was credulous was given force by Keynes, who portrayed Wilson in *The Economic Consequences of the Peace* as a religious naïf who was tricked by cunning practitioners of *machtpolitik* into the illusion that the Treaty of Versailles was idealistic when in fact it was the reverse. Keynes wrote, for instance, that "the subtlest sophisters and most hypocritical draftsmen were set to work, and produced many ingenious exercises which might have deceived for more than an hour a cleverer man than the President. . . . It was a long theological struggle in which, after the rejection of many different arguments, the President finally capitulated before a masterpiece of the sophist's art" (*The Economic Consequences of the Peace* [New York: Harcourt, Brace and Howe, 1919], 39, 40). From this, it was a short step to the argument of certain isolationists in the 1930s that Wilson had been duped by financial interests that sought to get America into a war that could have been avoided in order to protect their loans and investments and establish economic hegemony.

Index